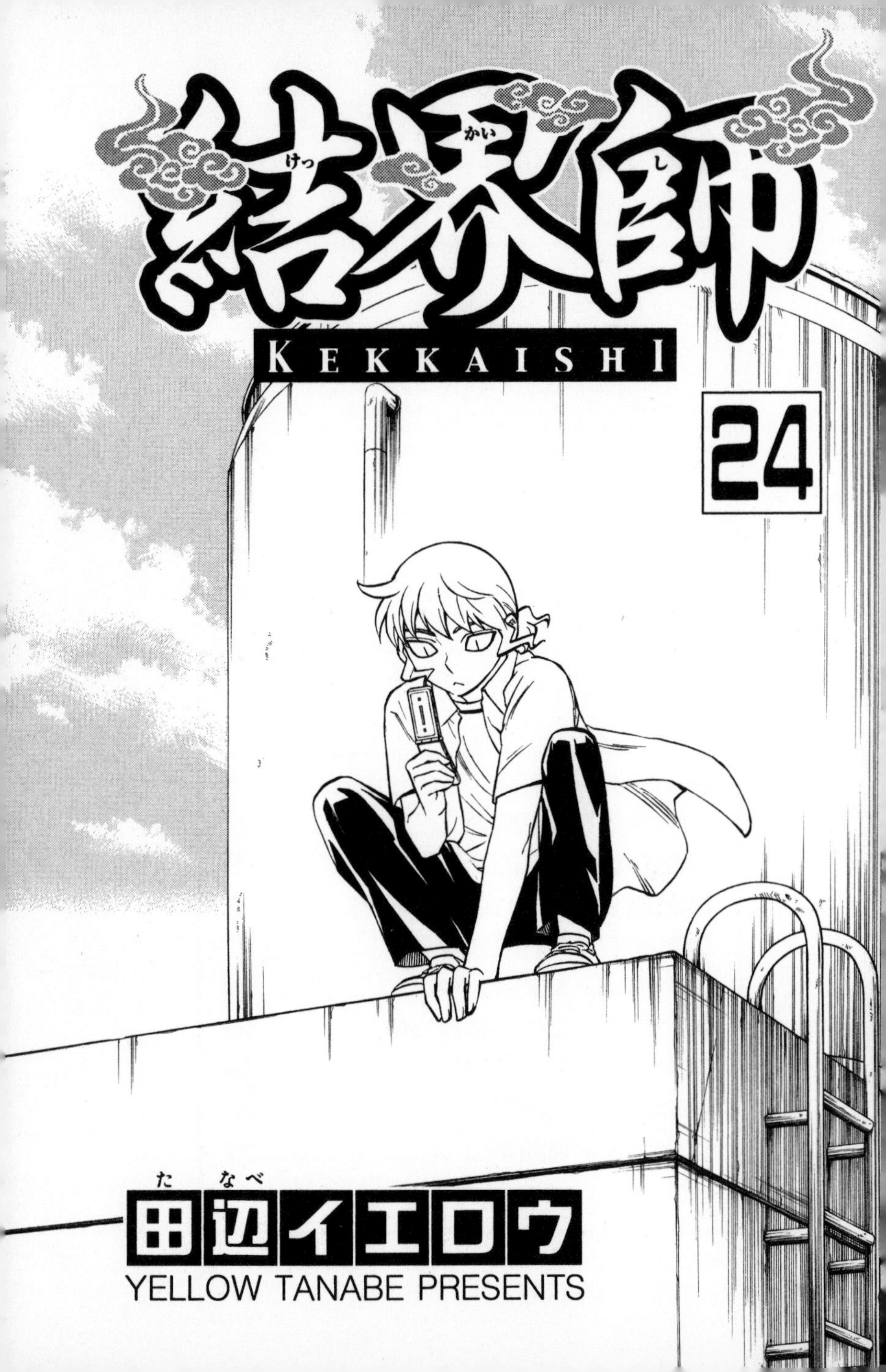

けっかいし
結界師
KEKKAISHI
24
たなべ
田辺イエロウ
YELLOW TANABE PRESENTS

The Story Thus Far

Yoshimori Sumimura and Tokine Yukimura have an ancestral duty to protect the Karasumori Forest from supernatural beings called *ayakashi*. People with their gift for terminating *ayakashi* are called *kekkaishi*, or "barrier masters."

Mt. Okubi, a prominent mystical site, is attacked and destroyed. A mysterious fissure cracks open the ground of the Karasumori Site. What is the connection between these two events...?

A crack team of three warriors from the Night Troops come to Karasumori. Then fifteen-year-old Soji arrives, claiming he was sent by the Shadow Organization. But Yoshimori thinks Soji is the masked attacker who assaulted him in Hida Village...

Now Karasumori is attacked by two huge ayakashi. To test Soji's loyalty and talents, Yoshimori sics him on one of the intruders. Will Soji prove to be an ally or an enemy...?!

KEKKAISHI VOL. 24
TABLE OF CONTENTS

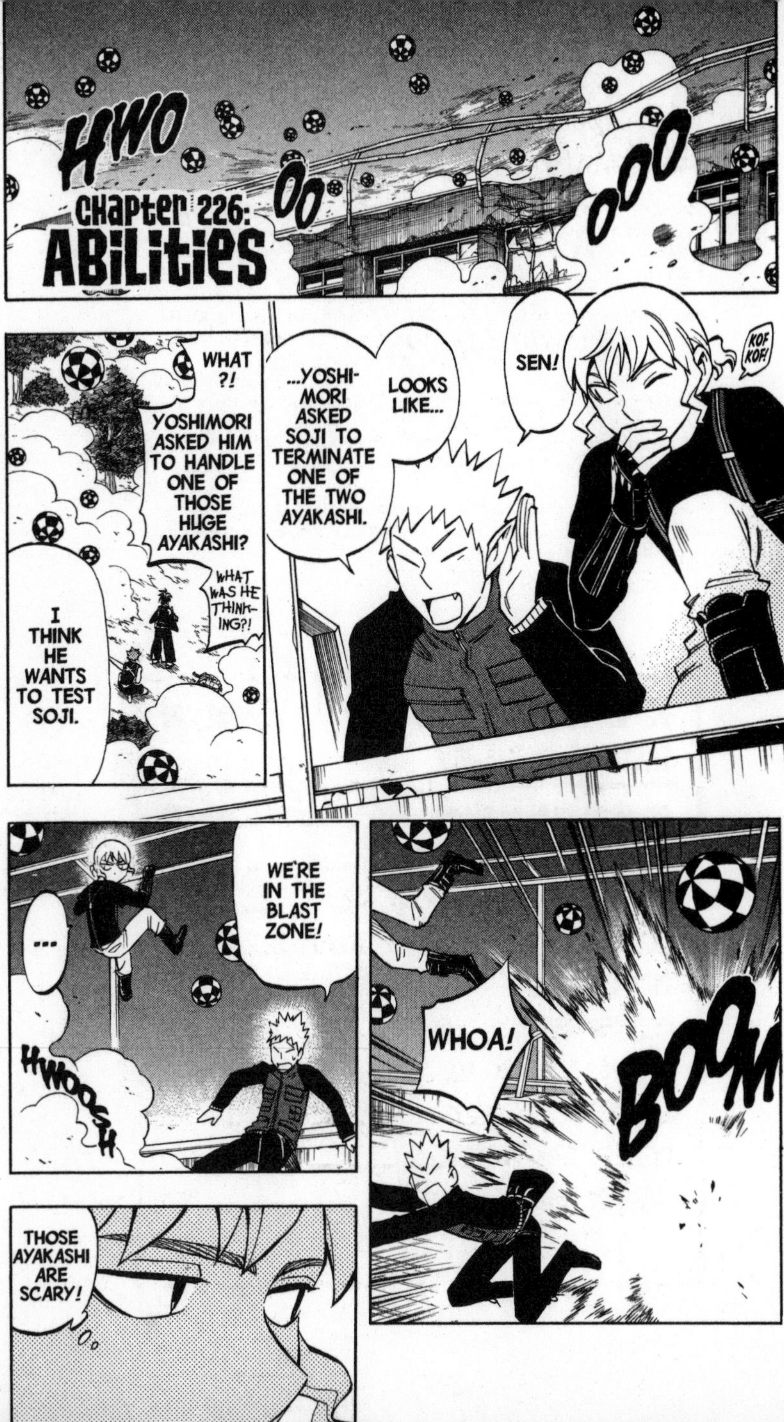
HWOOOOOO
Chapter 226: Abilities
SEN!
KOF KOF!
LOOKS LIKE...
...YOSHIMORI ASKED SOJI TO TERMINATE ONE OF THE TWO AYAKASHI.
WHAT?!
YOSHIMORI ASKED HIM TO HANDLE ONE OF THOSE HUGE AYAKASHI?
WHAT WAS HE THINKING?!
I THINK HE WANTS TO TEST SOJI.
WHOA!
BOOM
WE'RE IN THE BLAST ZONE!
...
HWOOSH
THOSE AYAKASHI ARE SCARY!

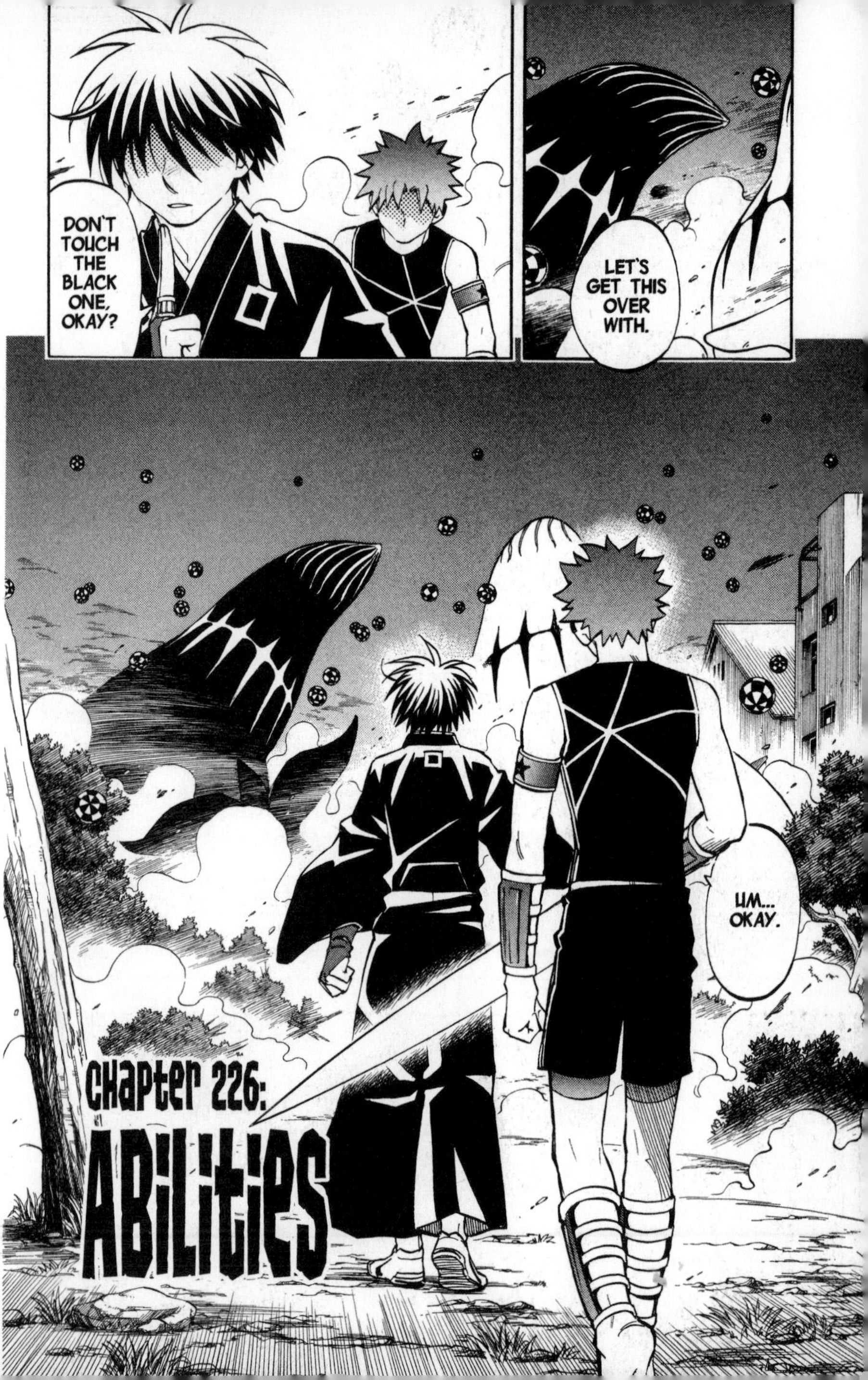
LET'S GET THIS OVER WITH.
DON'T TOUCH THE BLACK ONE, OKAY?
UM... OKAY.
Chapter 226:
Abilities

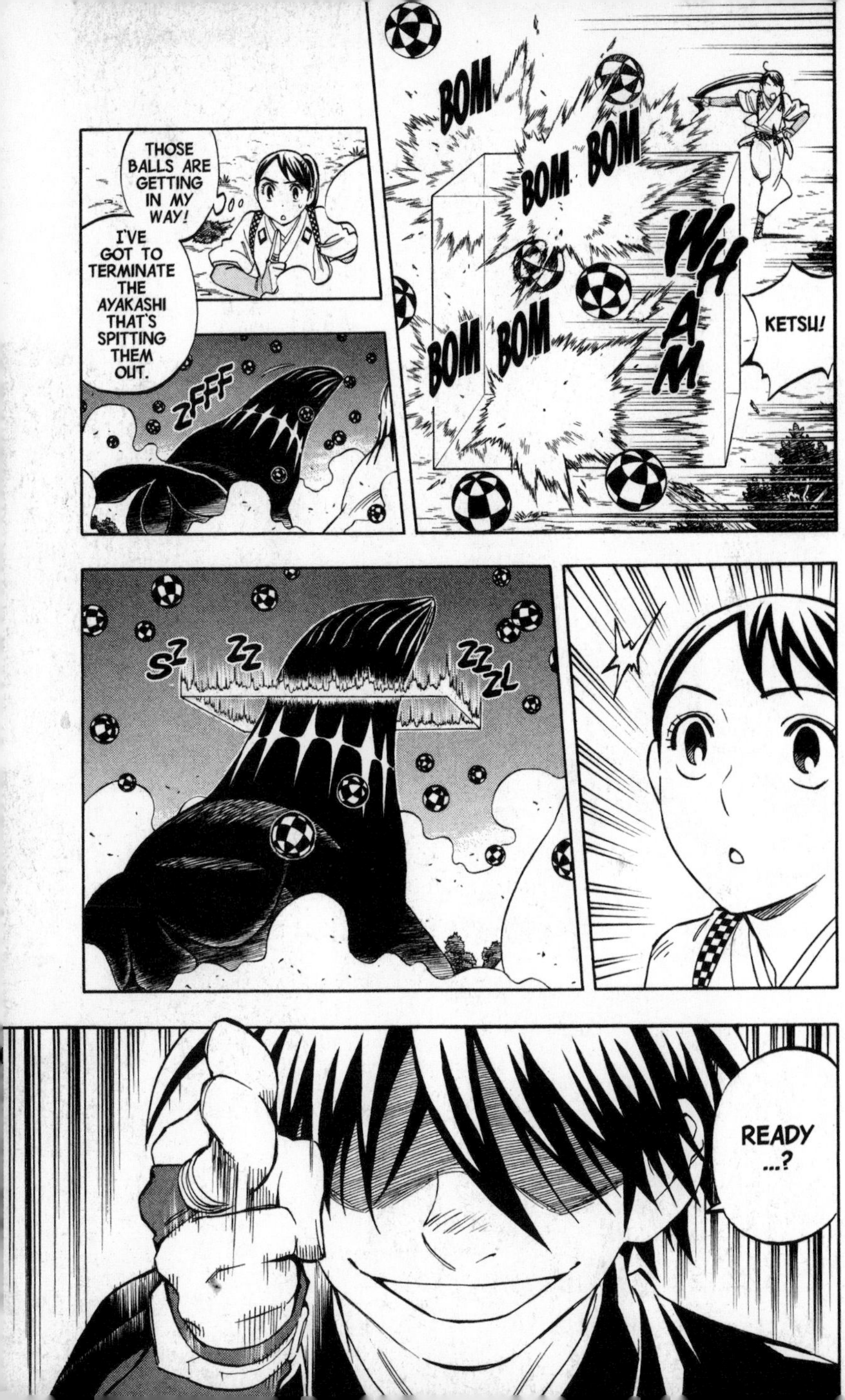
BOM
BOM BOM
BOM BOM
WHAM
KETSU!
THOSE BALLS ARE GETTING IN MY WAY!
I'VE GOT TO TERMINATE THE AYAKASHI THAT'S SPITTING THEM OUT.
ZFFF
SZ ZZ ZZZL
READY ...?

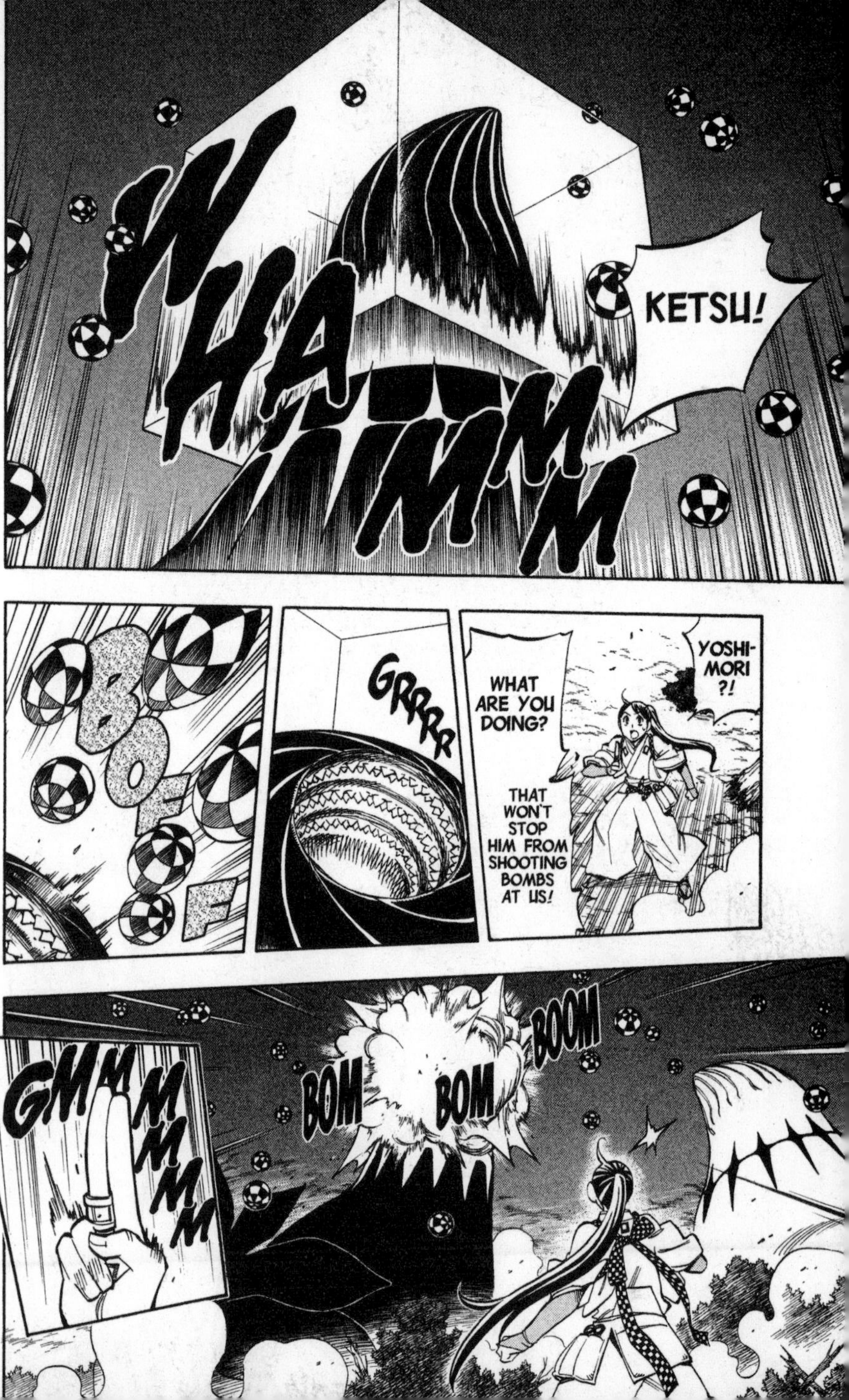
WHAMMMM
KETSU!
YOSHIMORI?!
WHAT ARE YOU DOING?
THAT WON'T STOP HIM FROM SHOOTING BOMBS AT US!
GRRRRR
BOOF
BOOM
BOM
BOM
GMMMMMMM

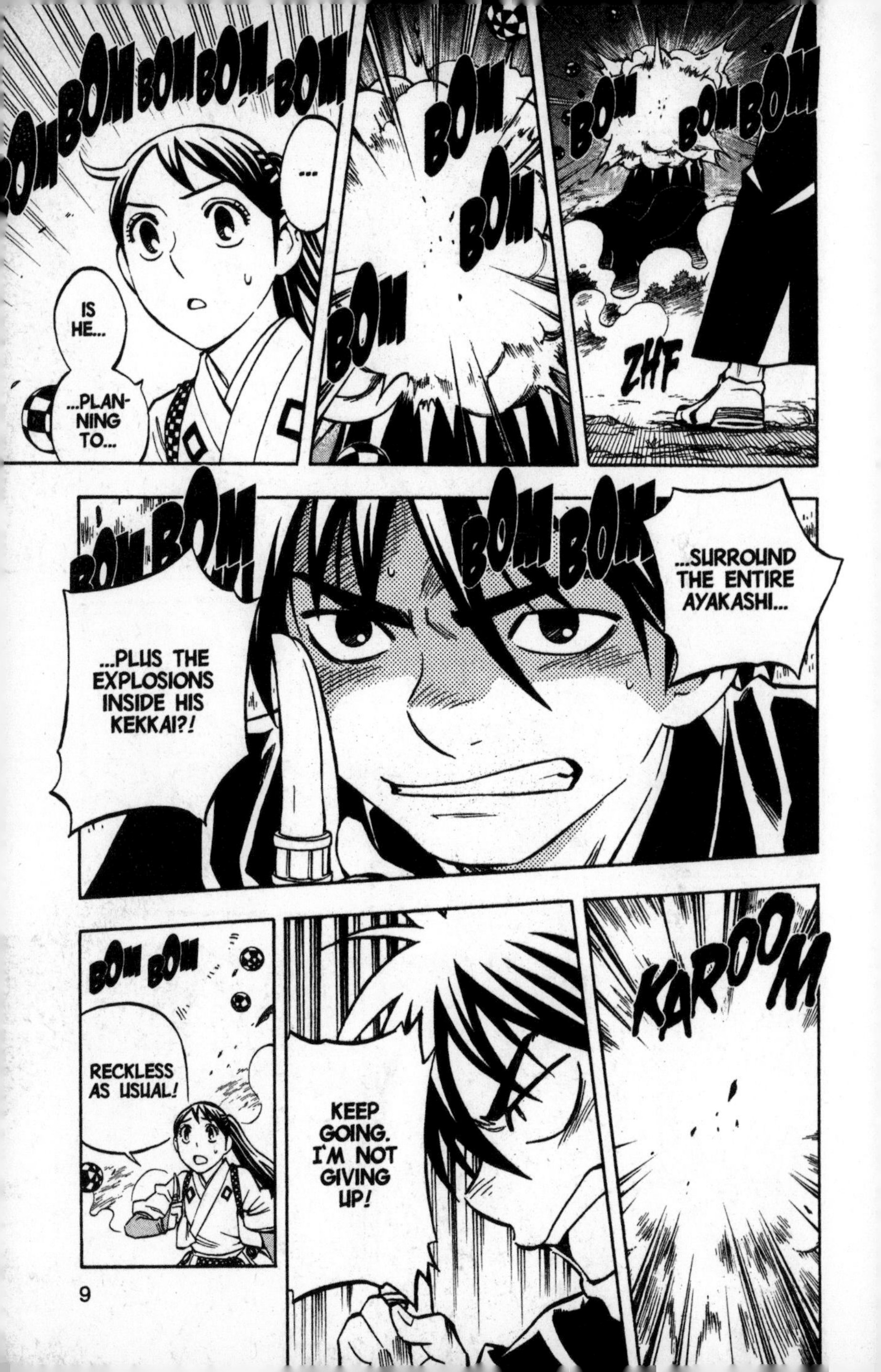
BOM BOMBOM
ZHF
BOM
BOM
BOM
BOMBOMBOMBOM-BOM
...
IS HE...
...PLANNING TO...
BOM BOM
...SURROUND THE ENTIRE AYAKASHI...
BOM BOM!
...PLUS THE EXPLOSIONS INSIDE HIS KEKKAI?!
KAROOM
KEEP GOING. I'M NOT GIVING UP!
BOM BOM
RECKLESS AS USUAL!

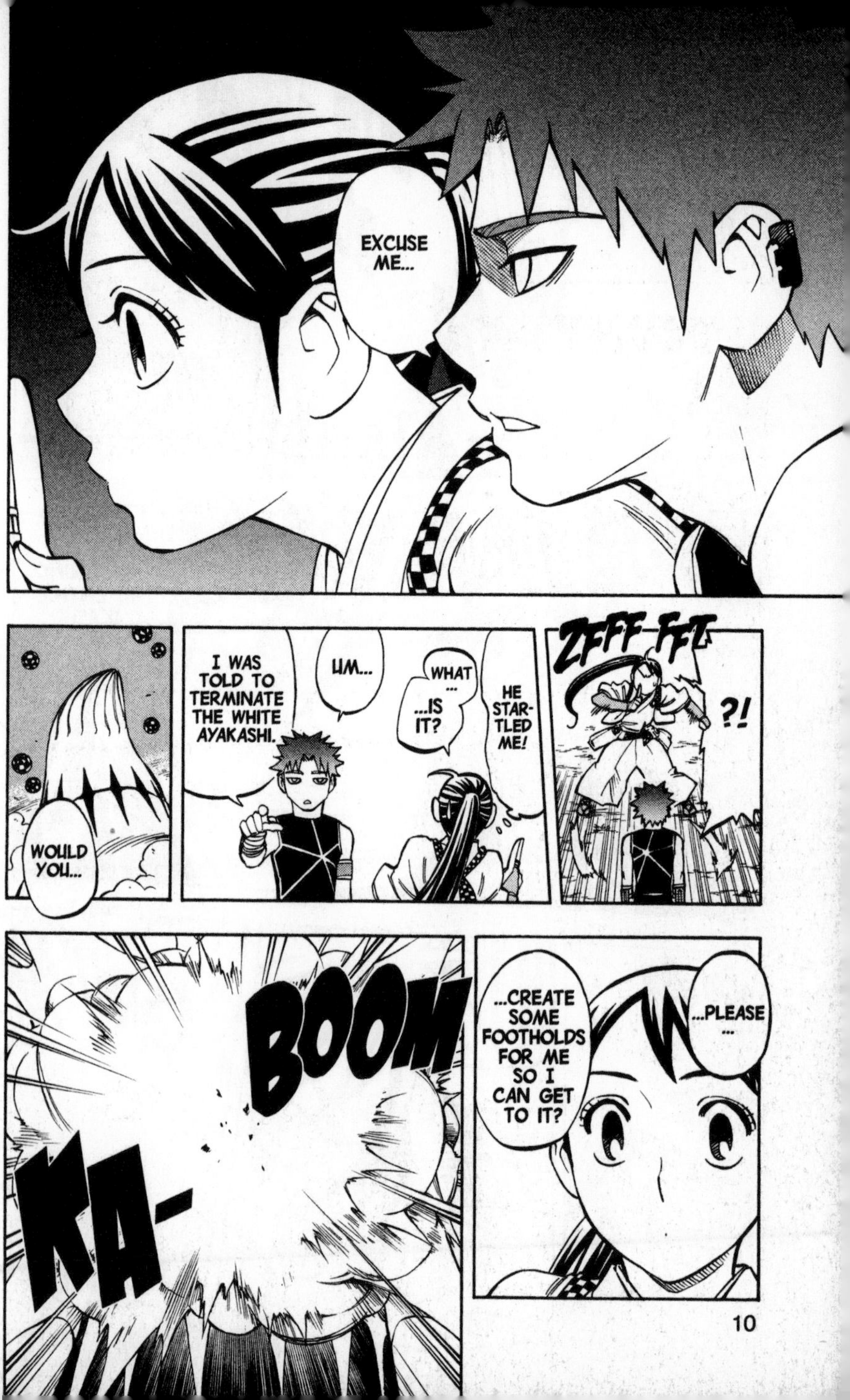
EXCUSE ME...
ZFFF-FFT
?!
HE STARTLED ME!
WHAT... ...IS IT?
UM...
I WAS TOLD TO TERMINATE THE WHITE AYAKASHI.
WOULD YOU...
...CREATE SOME FOOTHOLDS FOR ME SO I CAN GET TO IT?
...PLEASE...
KA-BOOM

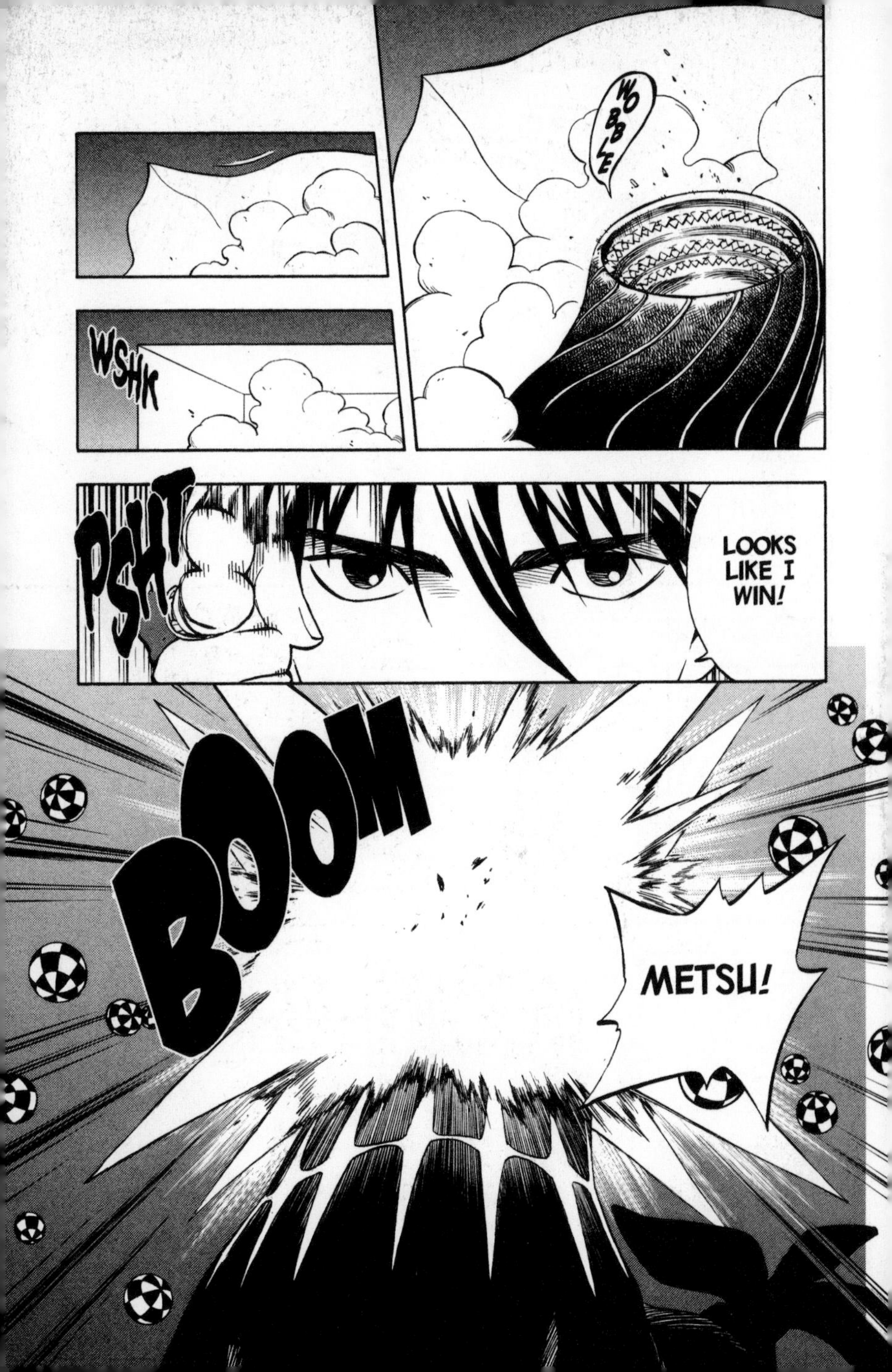
WOBBLE
WSHK
LOOKS LIKE I WIN!
PSHT
METSU!
BOOM

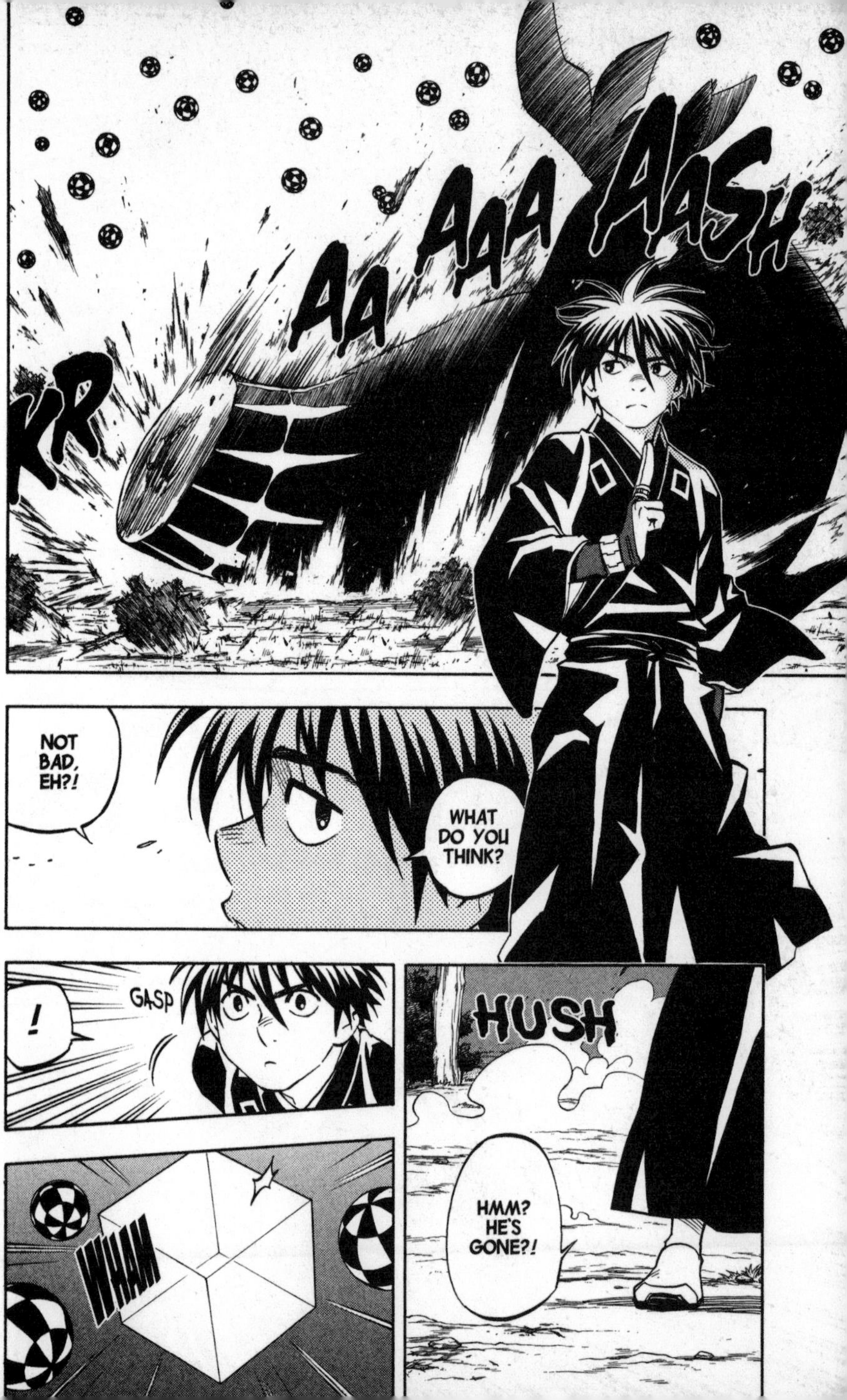
KR
Aa AAA AASH
WHAT DO YOU THINK?
NOT BAD, EH?!
HUSH
HMM? HE'S GONE?!
GASP
!
WHAM

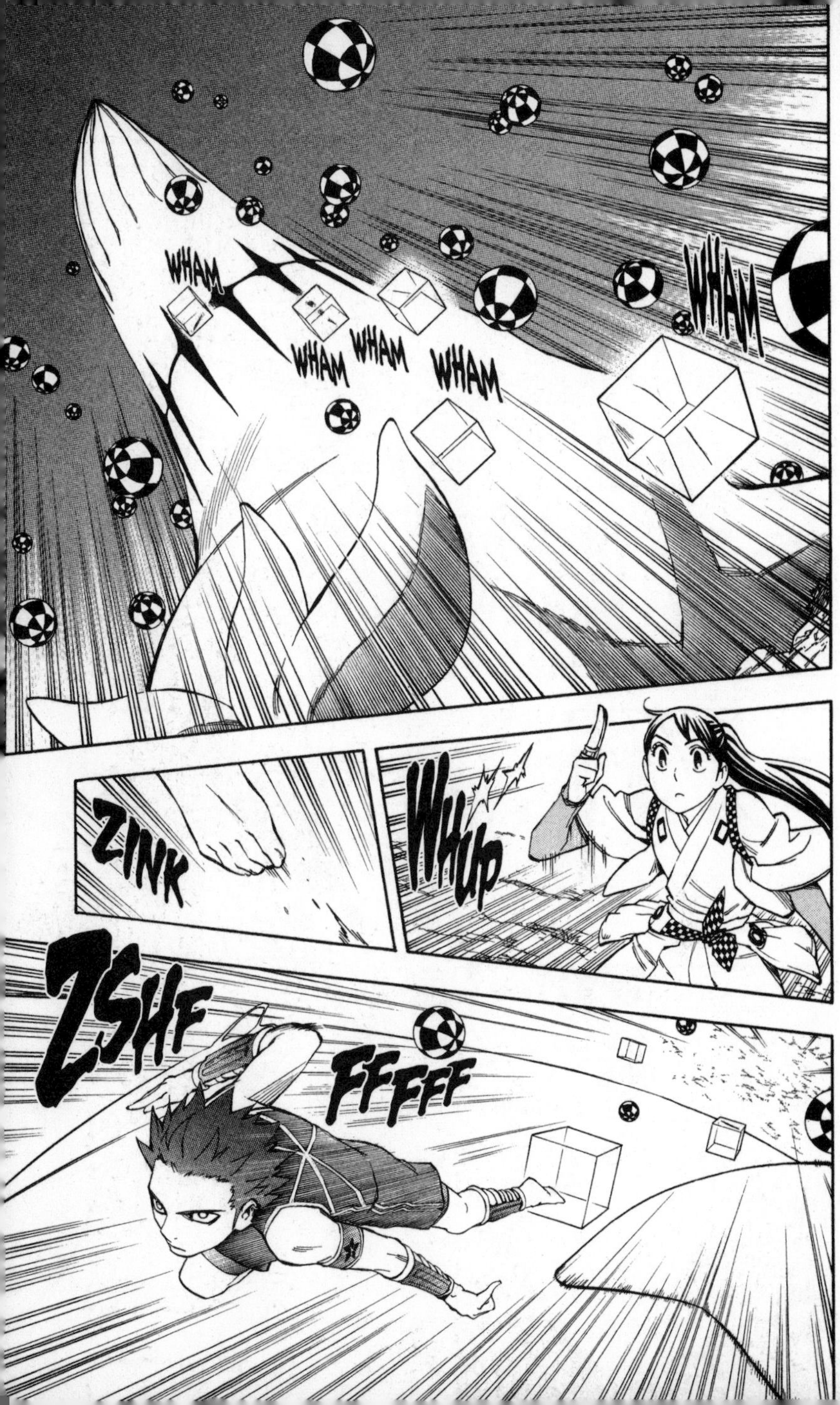
WHAM
WHAM
WHAM
WHAM
WHAM
WHUP
ZINK
ZSHF
FFFFF

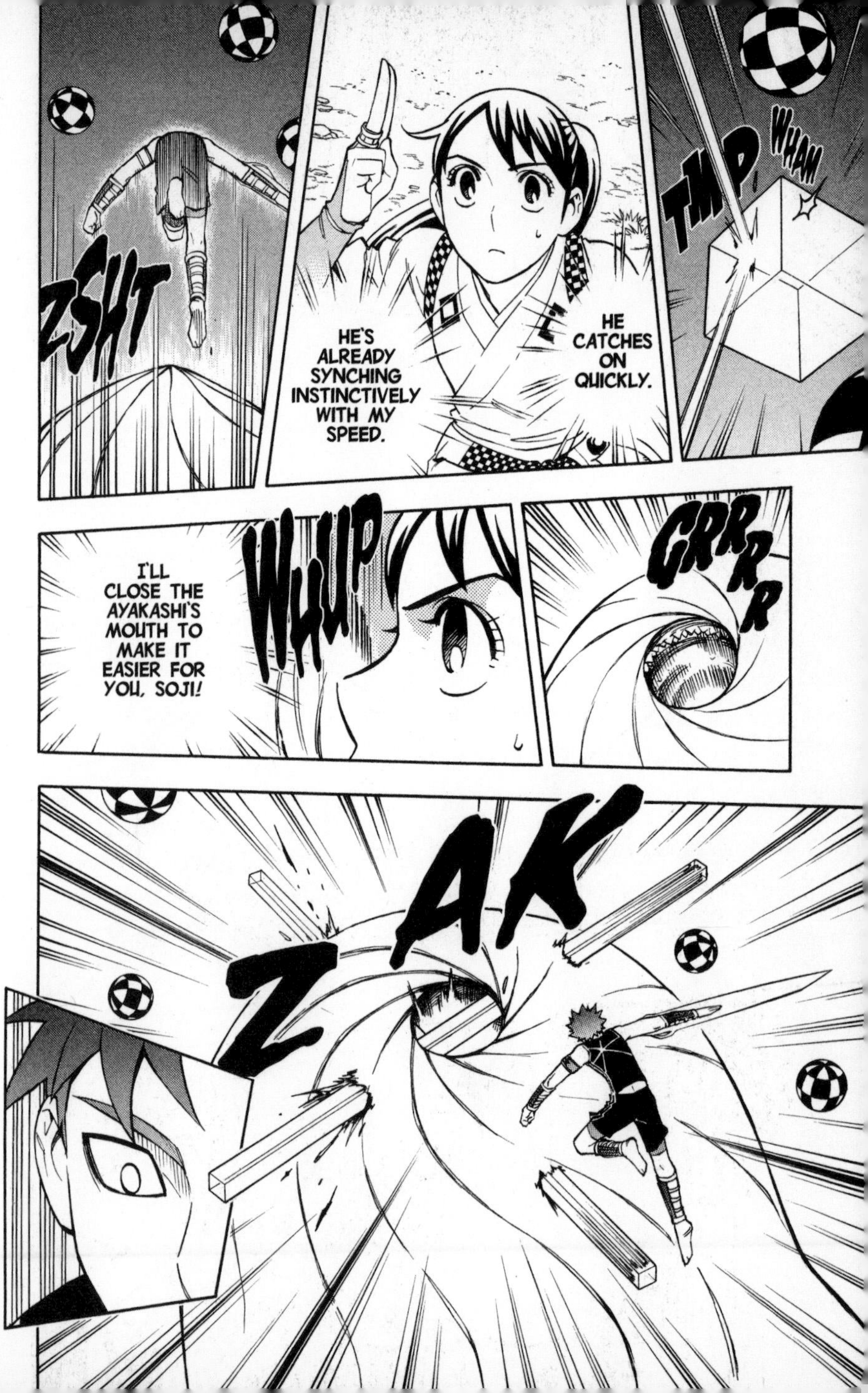
WHAM
TMP
HE CATCHES ON QUICKLY.
HE'S ALREADY SYNCHING INSTINCTIVELY WITH MY SPEED.
ZSHT
CRRRR
WHUP
I'LL CLOSE THE AYAKASHI'S MOUTH TO MAKE IT EASIER FOR YOU, SOJI!
ZAK

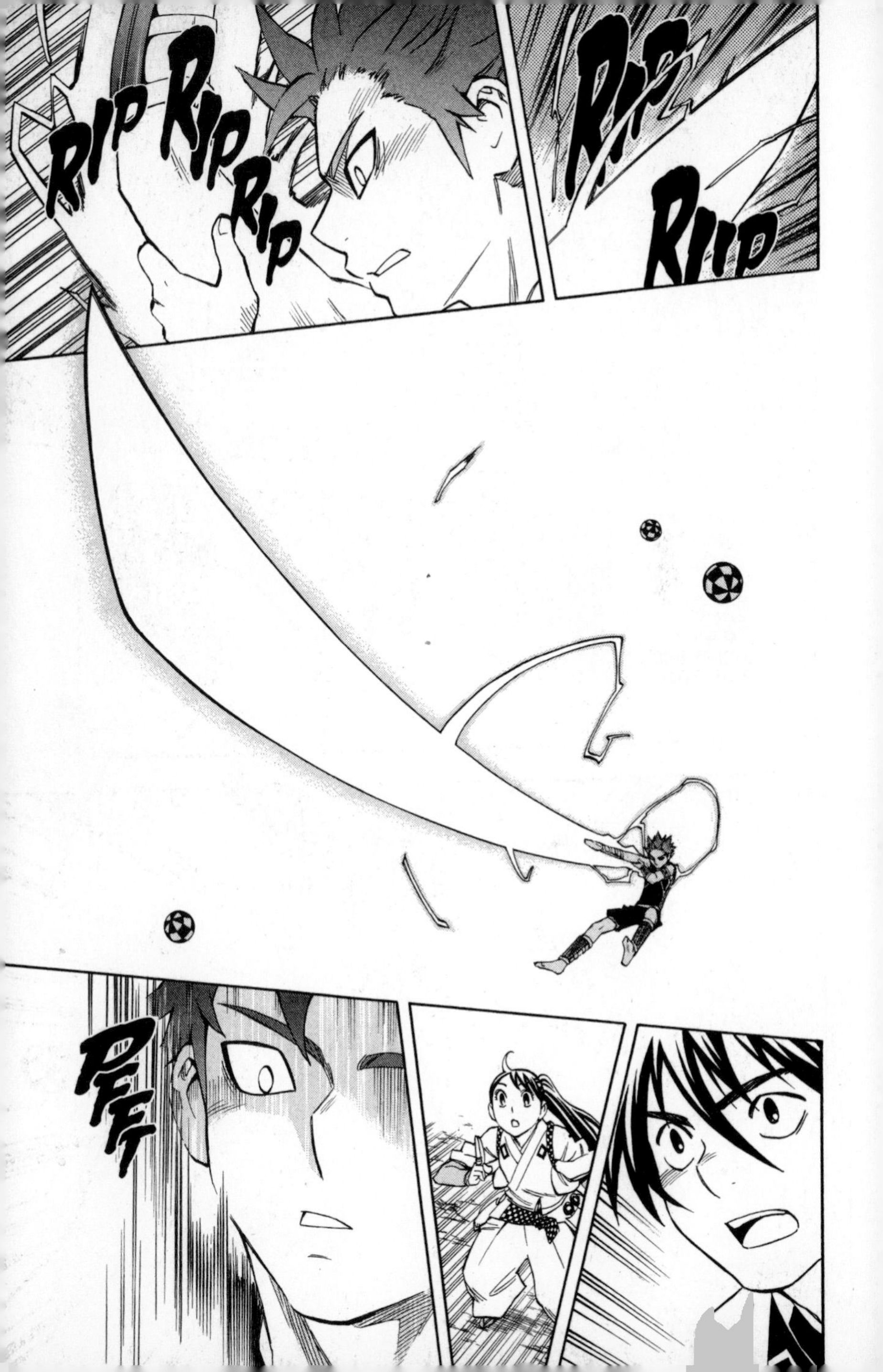
RIP
RIIP
RIP RIP RIP RIP
PFFT

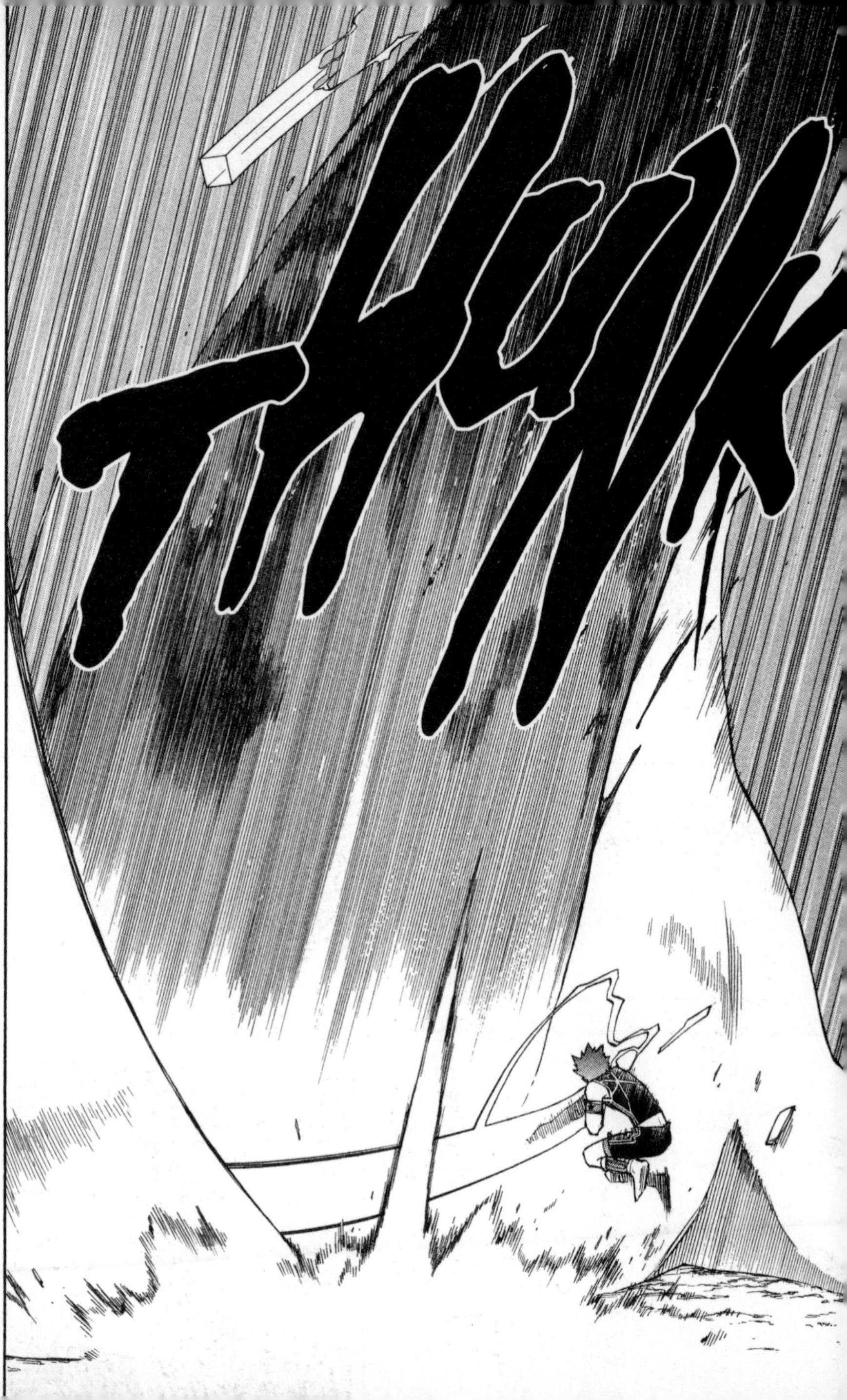
THUNK

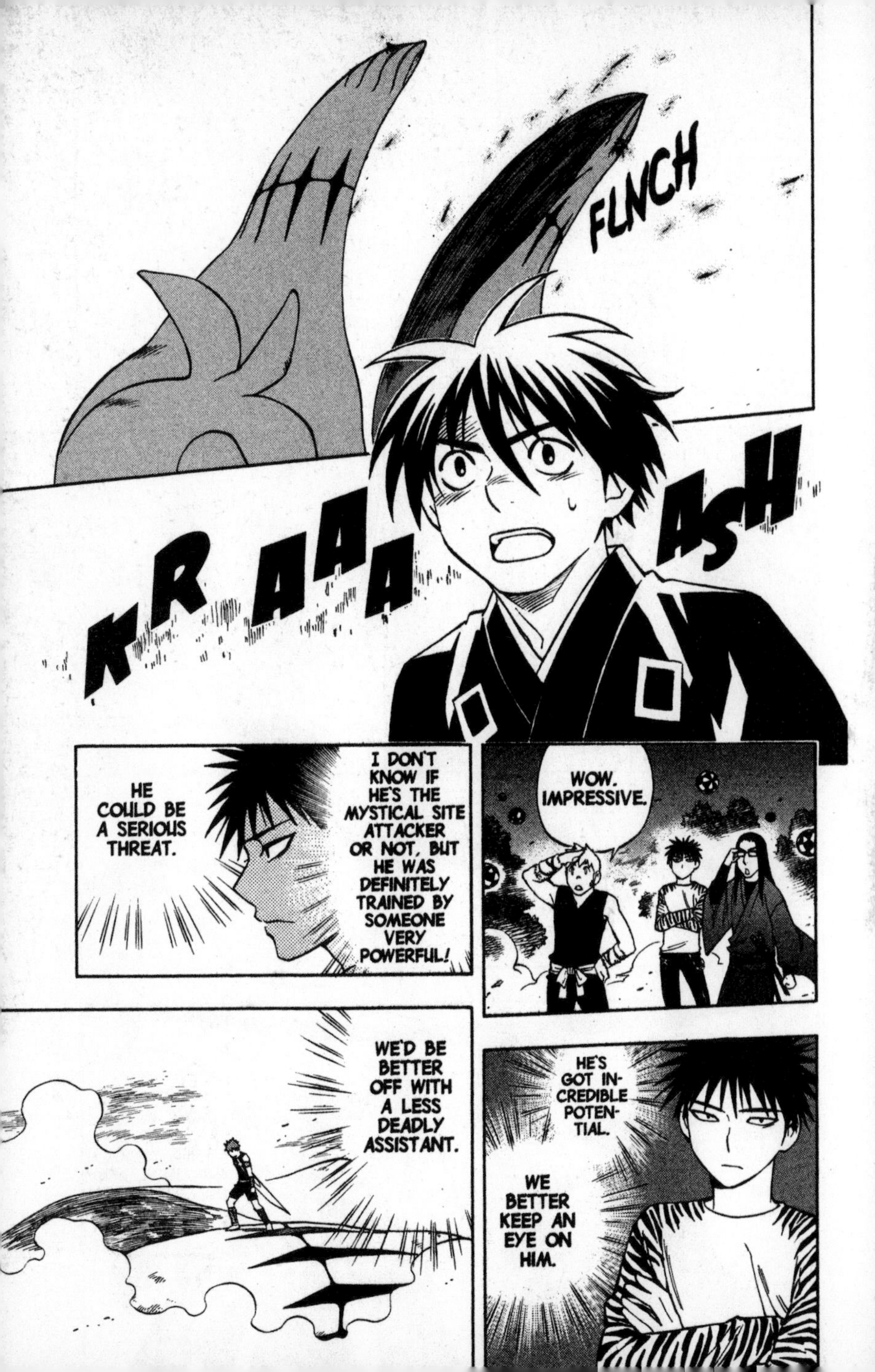
FLINCH
KRAAAAASH
WOW. IMPRESSIVE.
I DON'T KNOW IF HE'S THE MYSTICAL SITE ATTACKER OR NOT, BUT HE WAS DEFINITELY TRAINED BY SOMEONE VERY POWERFUL!
HE COULD BE A SERIOUS THREAT.
HE'S GOT IN-CREDIBLE POTEN-TIAL.
WE BETTER KEEP AN EYE ON HIM.
WE'D BE BETTER OFF WITH A LESS DEADLY ASSISTANT.

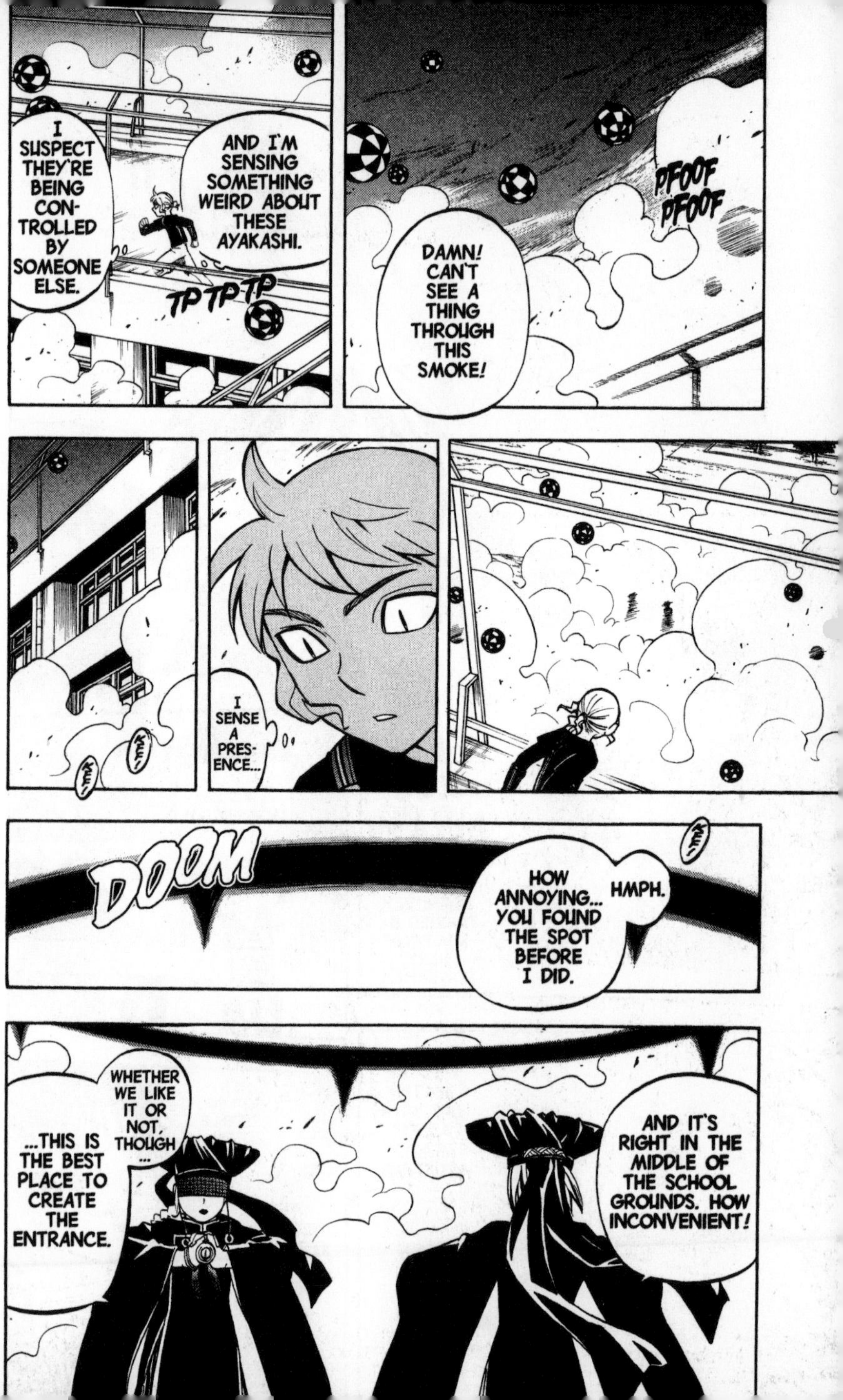
PFOOF PFOOF
DAMN! CAN'T SEE A THING THROUGH THIS SMOKE!
AND I'M SENSING SOMETHING WEIRD ABOUT THESE AYAKASHI.
I SUSPECT THEY'RE BEING CONTROLLED BY SOMEONE ELSE.
TP TP TP
I SENSE A PRESENCE...
KEE
KEE
KEE
HMPH.
HOW ANNOYING... YOU FOUND THE SPOT BEFORE I DID.
DOOM
AND IT'S RIGHT IN THE MIDDLE OF THE SCHOOL GROUNDS. HOW INCONVENIENT!
WHETHER WE LIKE IT OR NOT, THOUGH...
...THIS IS THE BEST PLACE TO CREATE THE ENTRANCE.

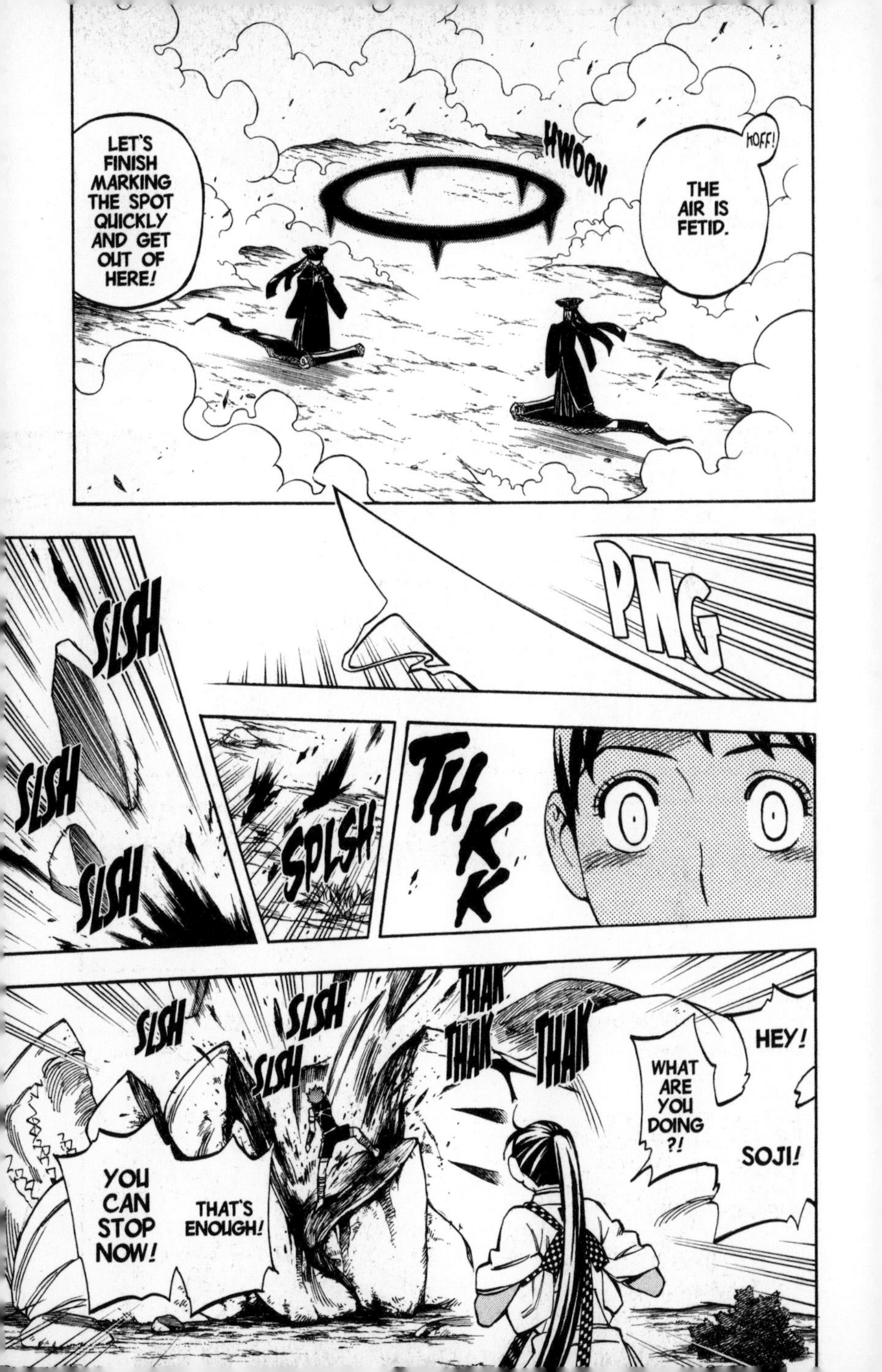
KOFF!
THE AIR IS FETID.
HWOON
LET'S FINISH MARKING THE SPOT QUICKLY AND GET OUT OF HERE!
PNG
THKK
SPLSH
SLSH
SLSH
SLSH
HEY!
SOJI!
WHAT ARE YOU DOING?!
THAK
THAK
THAK
SLSH
SLSH
SLSH
THAT'S ENOUGH!
YOU CAN STOP NOW!

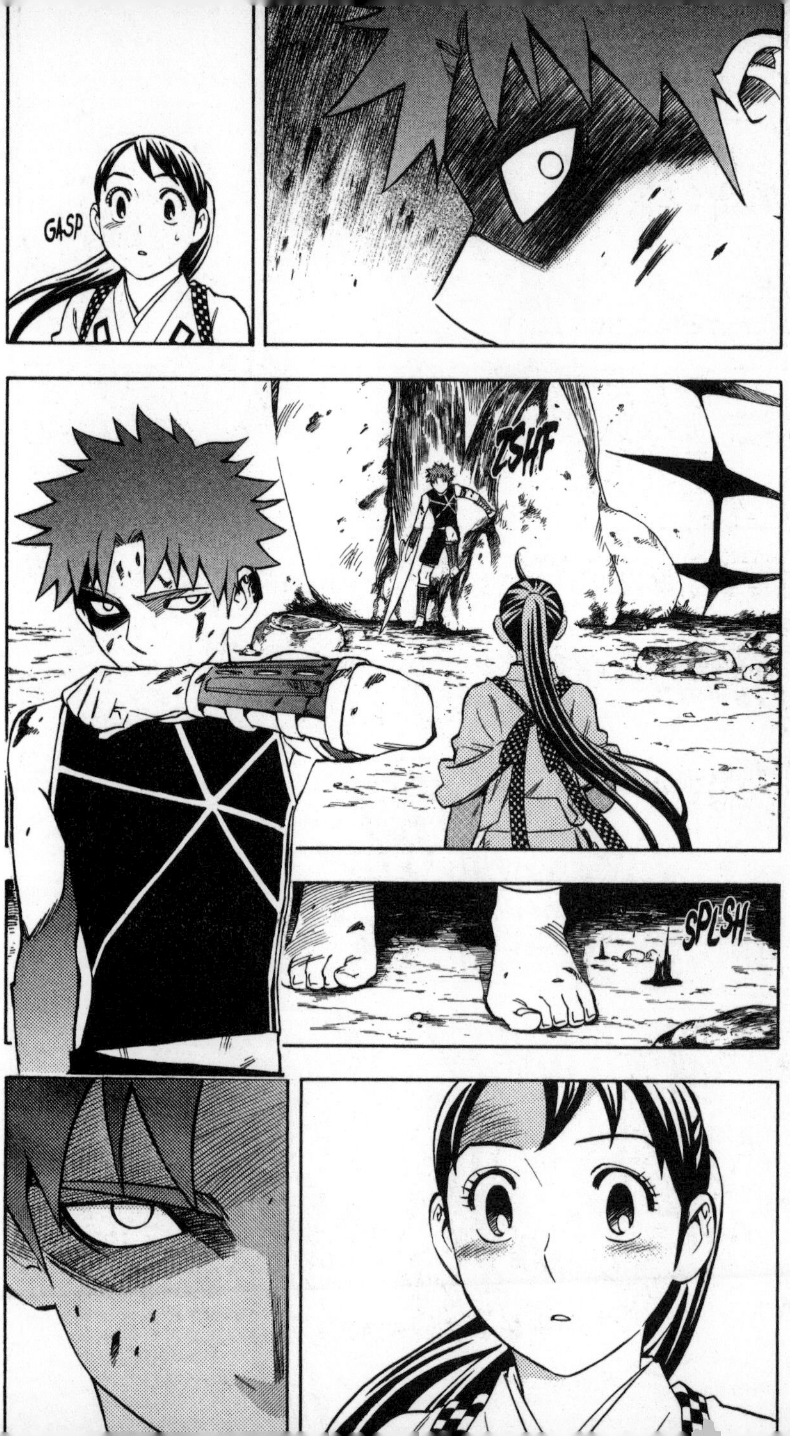
GASP
ZSHF
SPLSH

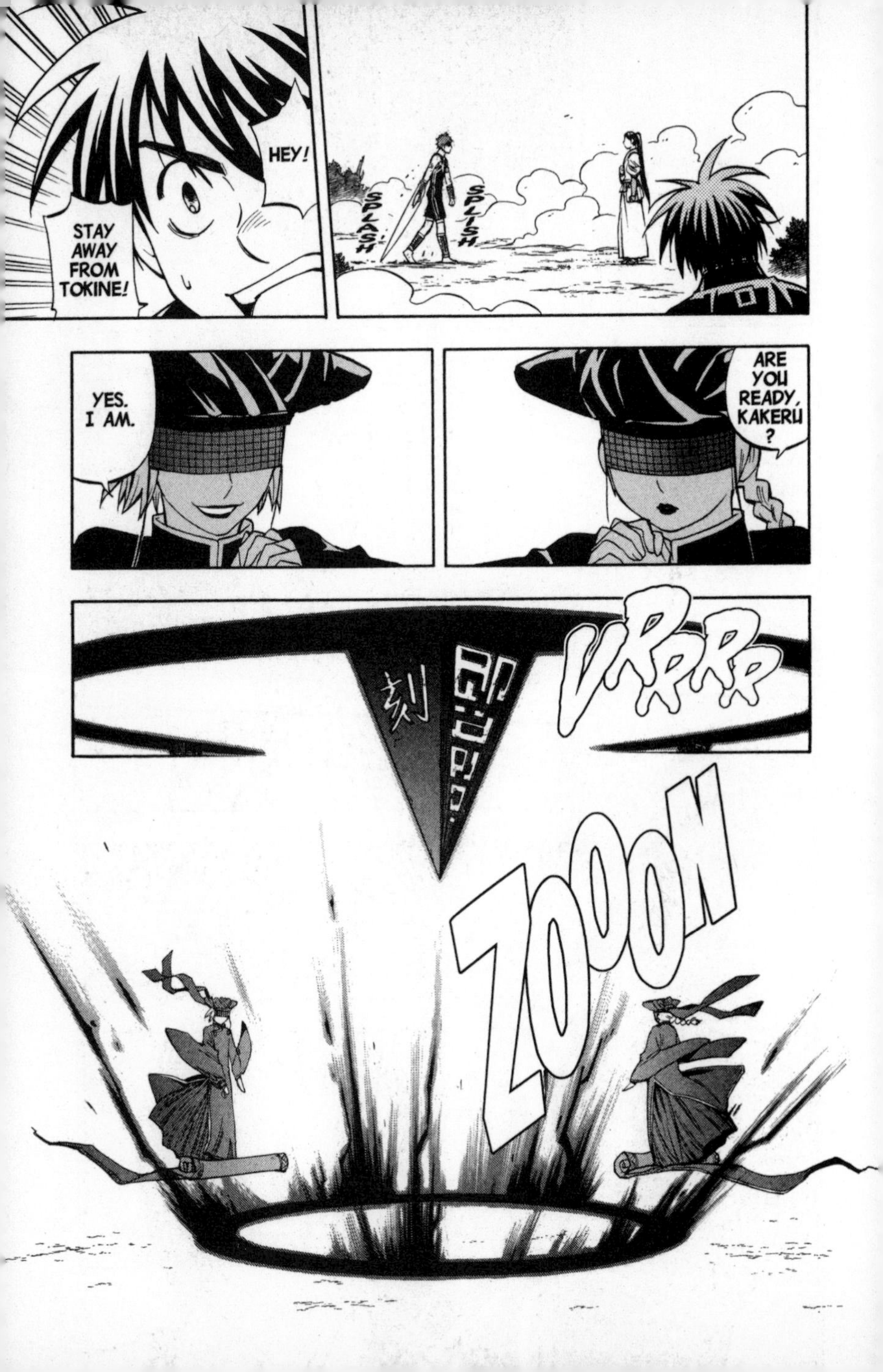
SPLISH
SPLASH
HEY!
STAY AWAY FROM TOKINE!
ARE YOU READY, KAKERU?
YES. I AM.
VRRRR
刻
ZOOOON

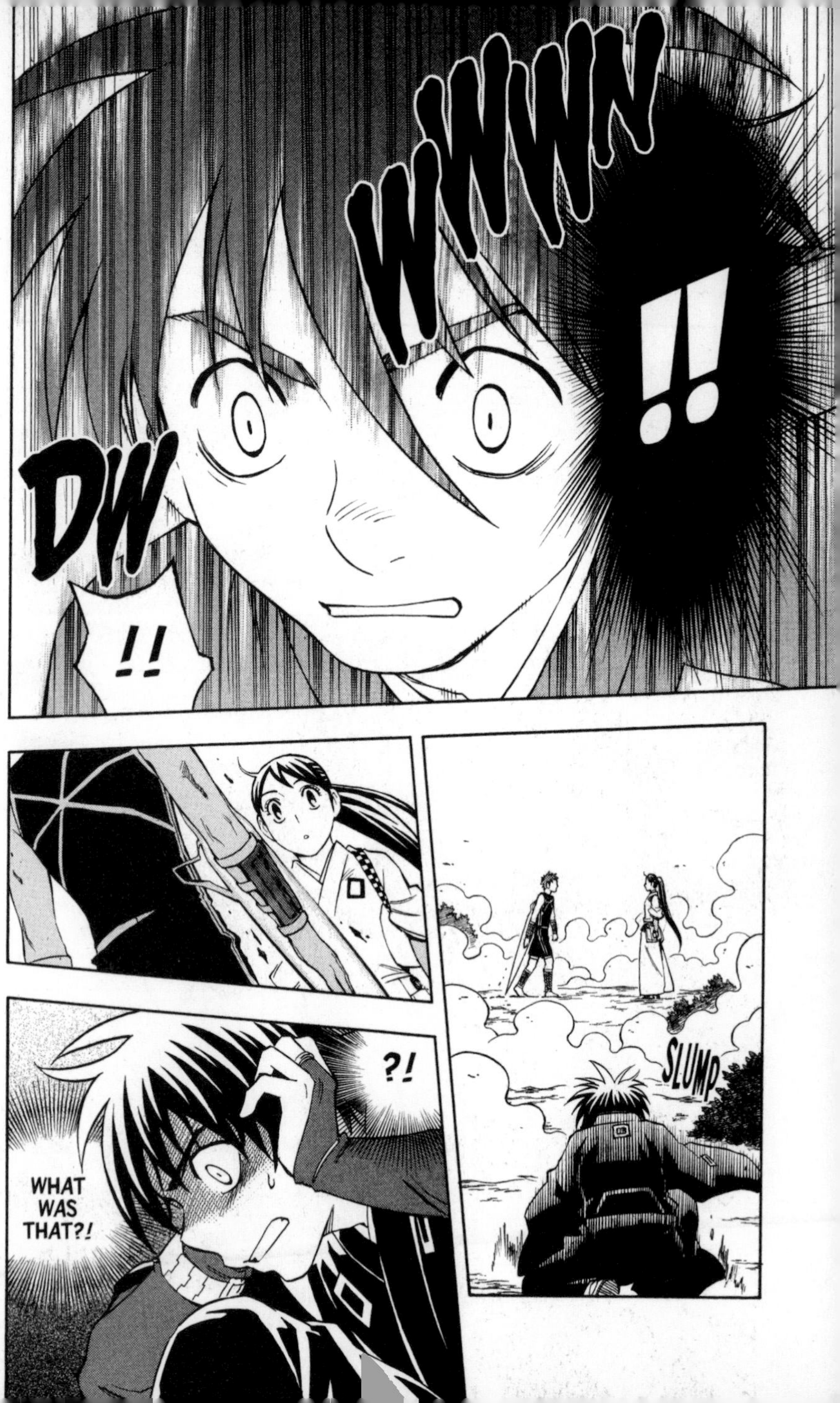
WNWN
!!
DW
!!
SLUMP
?!
WHAT WAS THAT?!

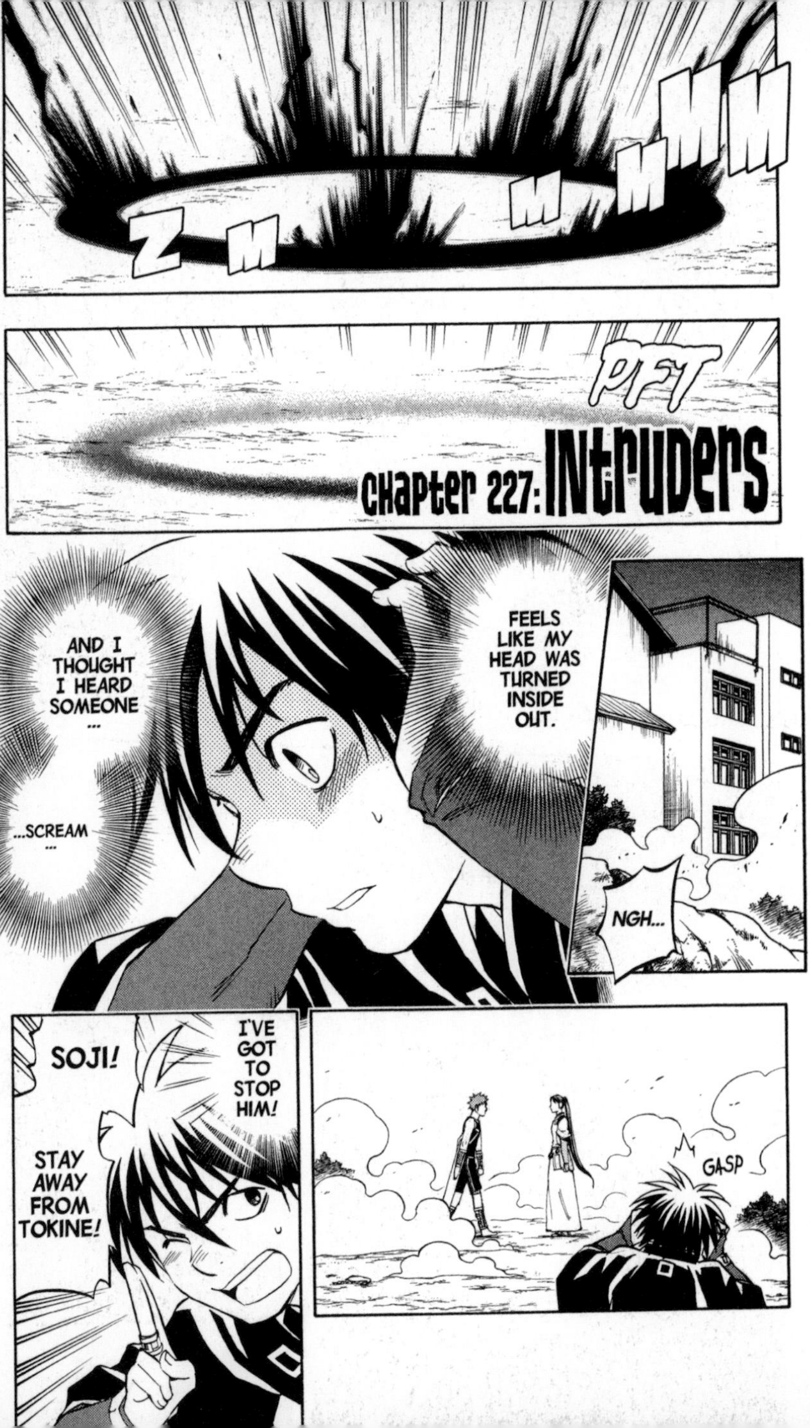
ZMMMMMMMM
PFT
Chapter 227: Intruders
NGH...
FEELS LIKE MY HEAD WAS TURNED INSIDE OUT.
AND I THOUGHT I HEARD SOMEONE...
...SCREAM...
GASP
I'VE GOT TO STOP HIM!
SOJI!
STAY AWAY FROM TOKINE!

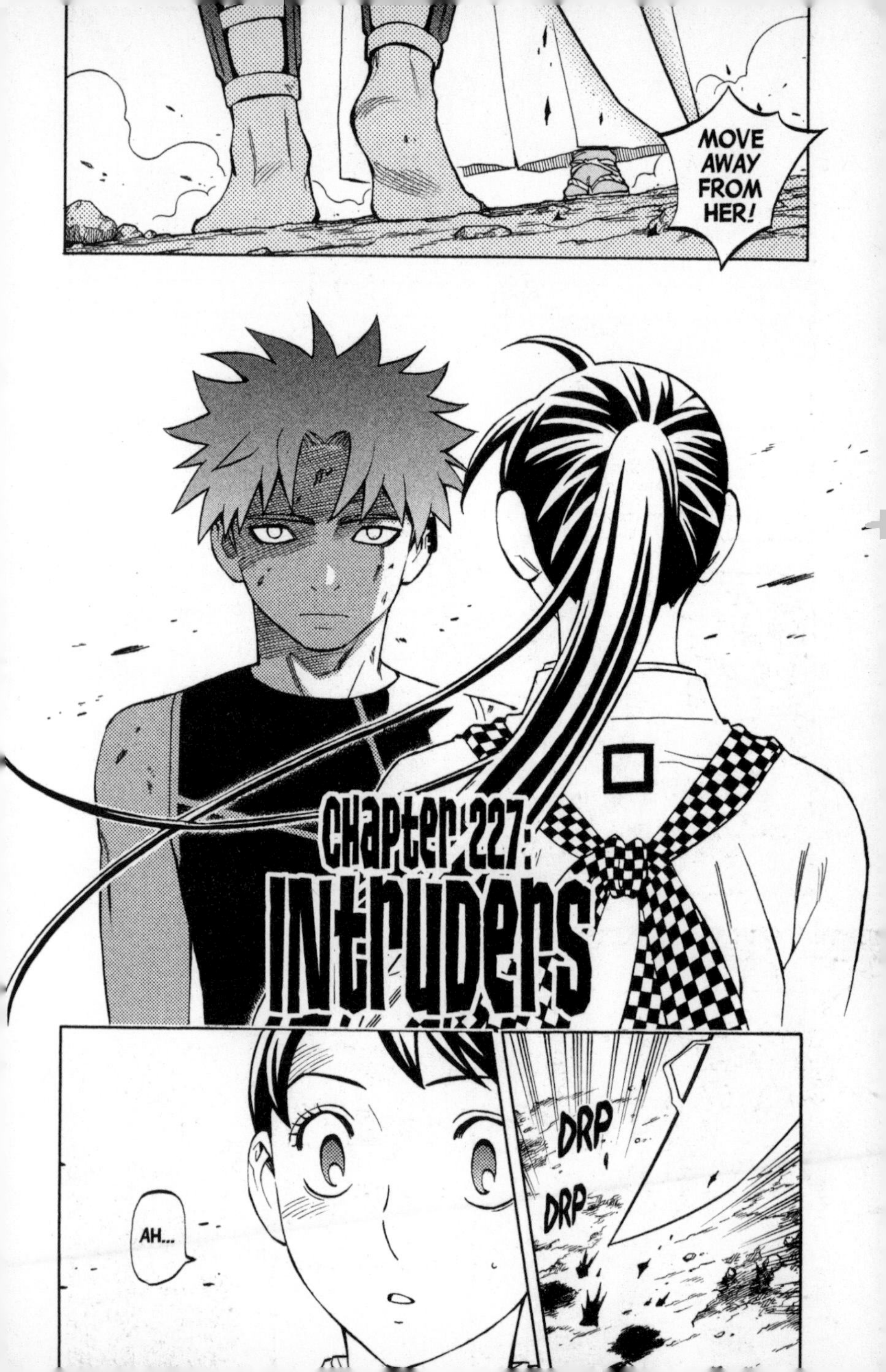
MOVE AWAY FROM HER!
CHAPTER 227: INTRUDERS
DRP
DRP
AH...

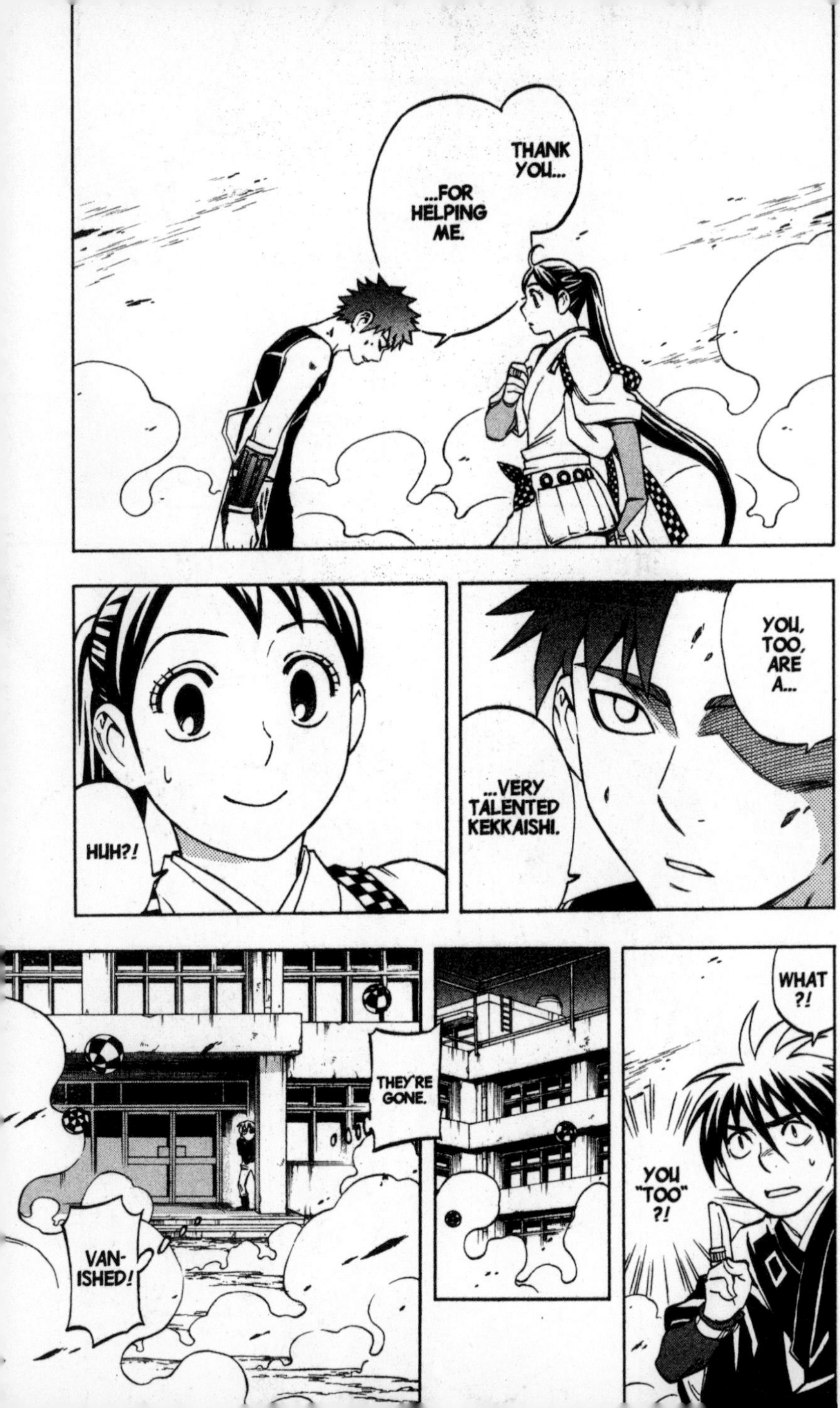
THANK YOU...
...FOR HELPING ME.
YOU, TOO, ARE A...
...VERY TALENTED KEKKAISHI.
HUH?!
WHAT?!
YOU "TOO"?!
THEY'RE GONE.
VAN-ISHED!

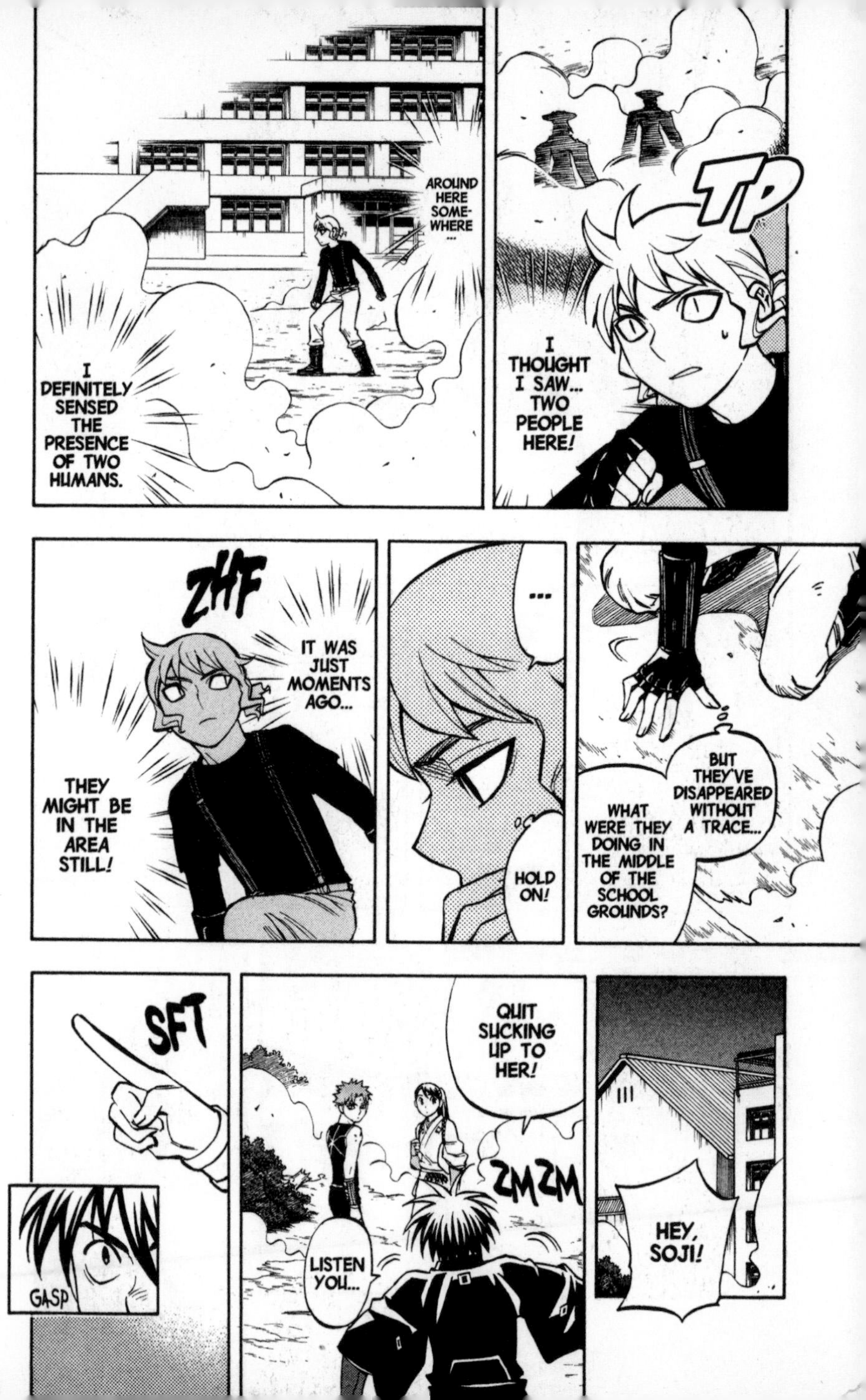
TP
I THOUGHT I SAW... TWO PEOPLE HERE!
AROUND HERE SOMEWHERE...
I DEFINITELY SENSED THE PRESENCE OF TWO HUMANS.
BUT THEY'VE DISAPPEARED WITHOUT A TRACE...
WHAT WERE THEY DOING IN THE MIDDLE OF THE SCHOOL GROUNDS?
...
HOLD ON!
ZHF
IT WAS JUST MOMENTS AGO...
THEY MIGHT BE IN THE AREA STILL!
HEY, SOJI!
QUIT SUCKING UP TO HER!
ZMZM
LISTEN YOU...
SFT
GASP

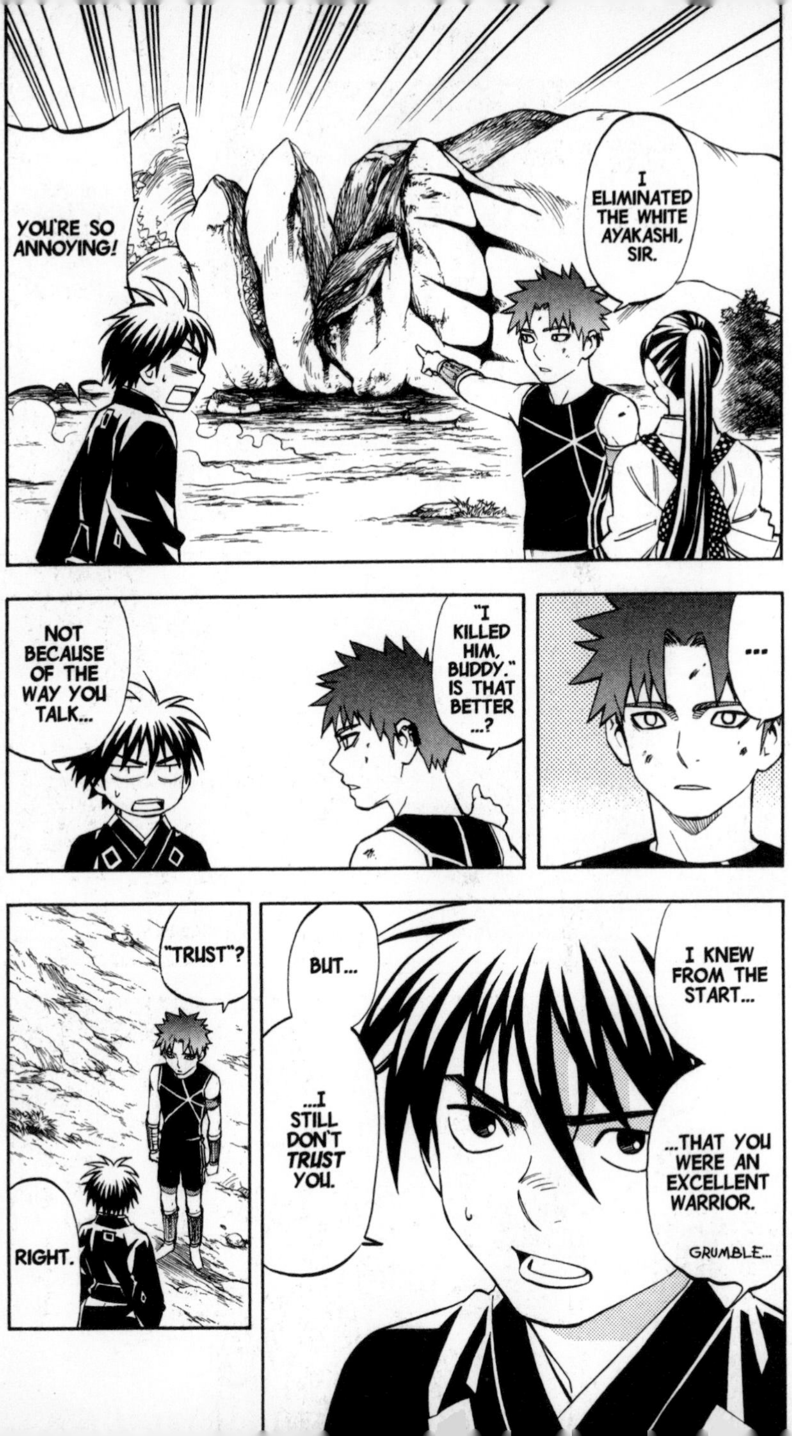
I ELIMINATED THE WHITE AYAKASHI, SIR.
YOU'RE SO ANNOYING!
...
"I KILLED HIM, BUDDY." IS THAT BETTER ...?
NOT BECAUSE OF THE WAY YOU TALK...
I KNEW FROM THE START...
...THAT YOU WERE AN EXCELLENT WARRIOR.
GRUMBLE...
BUT...
...I STILL DON'T *TRUST* YOU.
"TRUST"?
RIGHT.

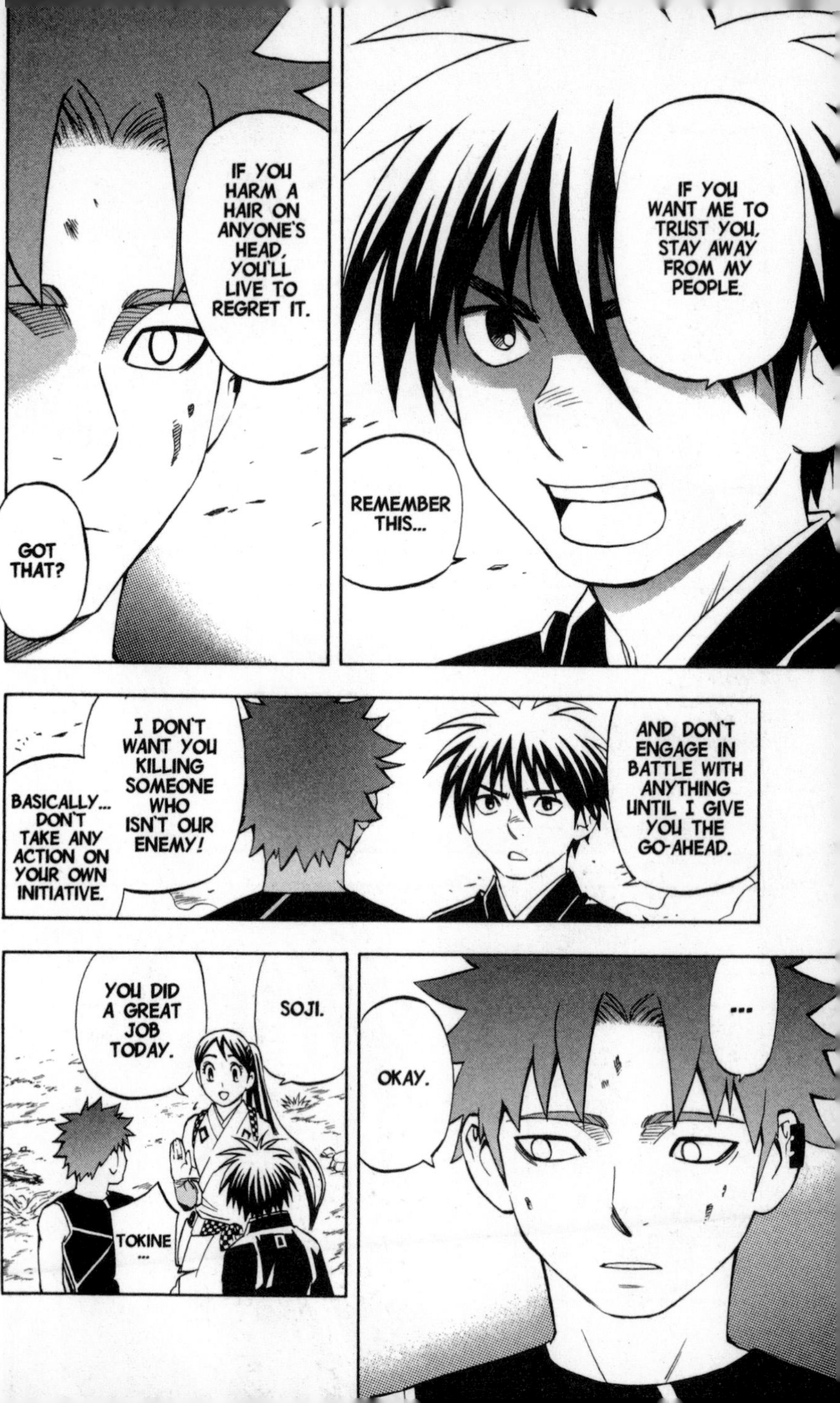
IF YOU WANT ME TO TRUST YOU, STAY AWAY FROM MY PEOPLE.
REMEMBER THIS...
IF YOU HARM A HAIR ON ANYONE'S HEAD, YOU'LL LIVE TO REGRET IT.
GOT THAT?
AND DON'T ENGAGE IN BATTLE WITH ANYTHING UNTIL I GIVE YOU THE GO-AHEAD.
I DON'T WANT YOU KILLING SOMEONE WHO ISN'T OUR ENEMY!
BASICALLY... DON'T TAKE ANY ACTION ON YOUR OWN INITIATIVE.
...
OKAY.
SOJI.
YOU DID A GREAT JOB TODAY.
TOKINE ...

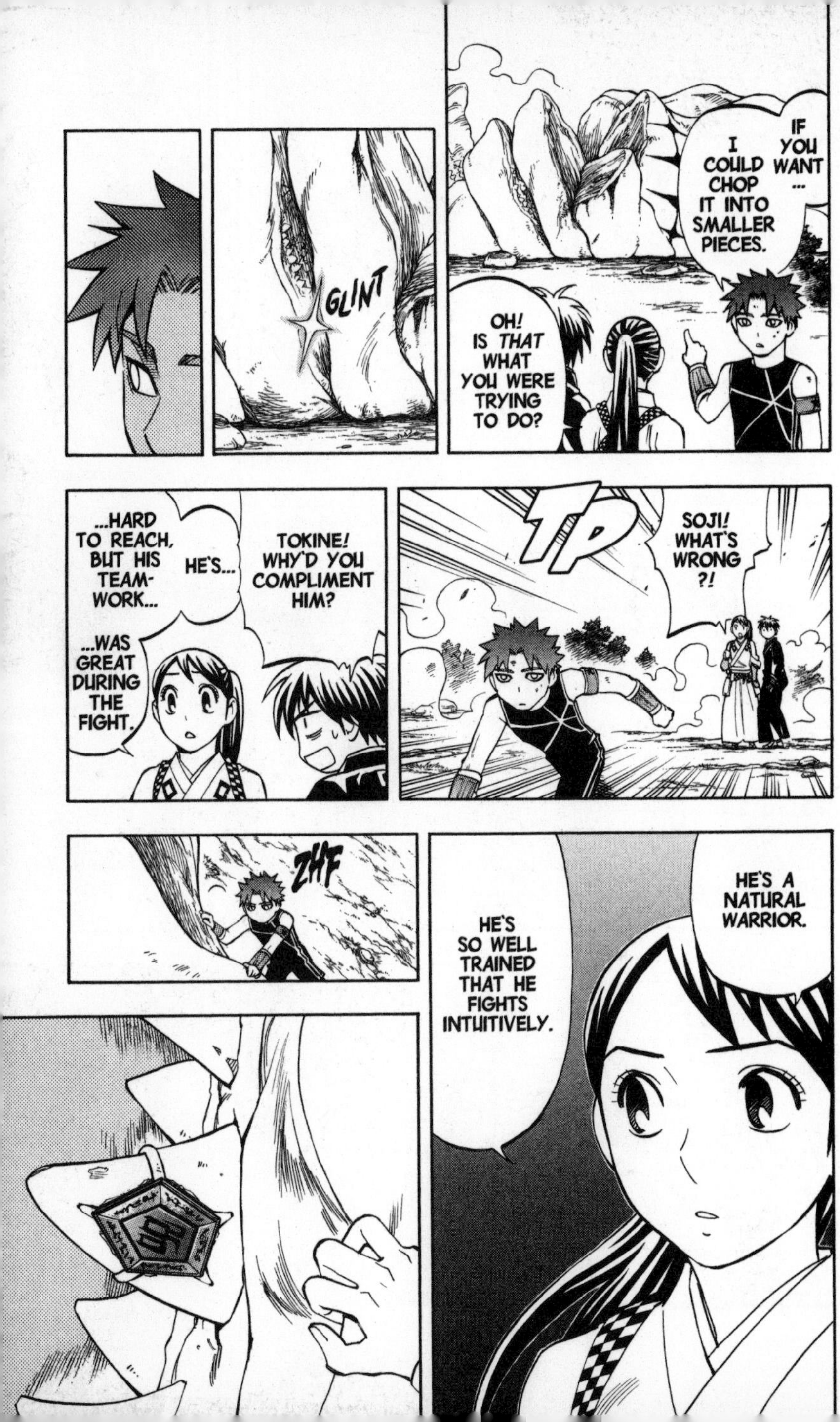
IF YOU WANT... I COULD CHOP IT INTO SMALLER PIECES.
OH! IS *THAT* WHAT YOU WERE TRYING TO DO?
GLINT
TP
SOJI! WHAT'S WRONG?!
TOKINE! WHY'D YOU COMPLIMENT HIM?
HE'S...
...HARD TO REACH, BUT HIS TEAM-WORK...
...WAS GREAT DURING THE FIGHT.
HE'S A NATURAL WARRIOR.
HE'S SO WELL TRAINED THAT HE FIGHTS INTUITIVELY.
ZHF

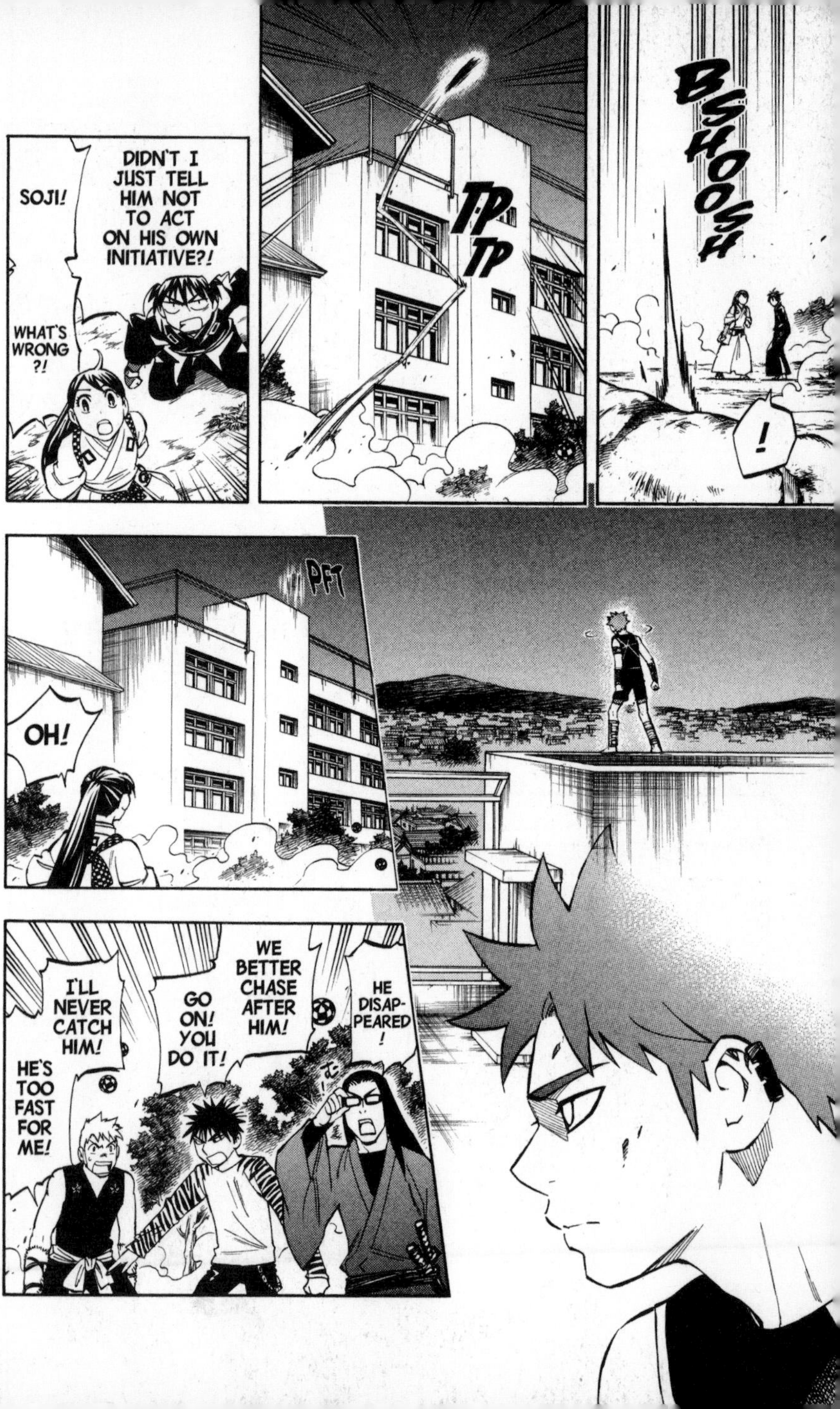
BSHOOSH
!
TP TP
DIDN'T I JUST TELL HIM NOT TO ACT ON HIS OWN INITIATIVE?!
SOJI!
WHAT'S WRONG?!
PFT
OH!
HE DISAPPEARED!
WE BETTER CHASE AFTER HIM!
GO ON! YOU DO IT!
I'LL NEVER CATCH HIM!
HE'S TOO FAST FOR ME!

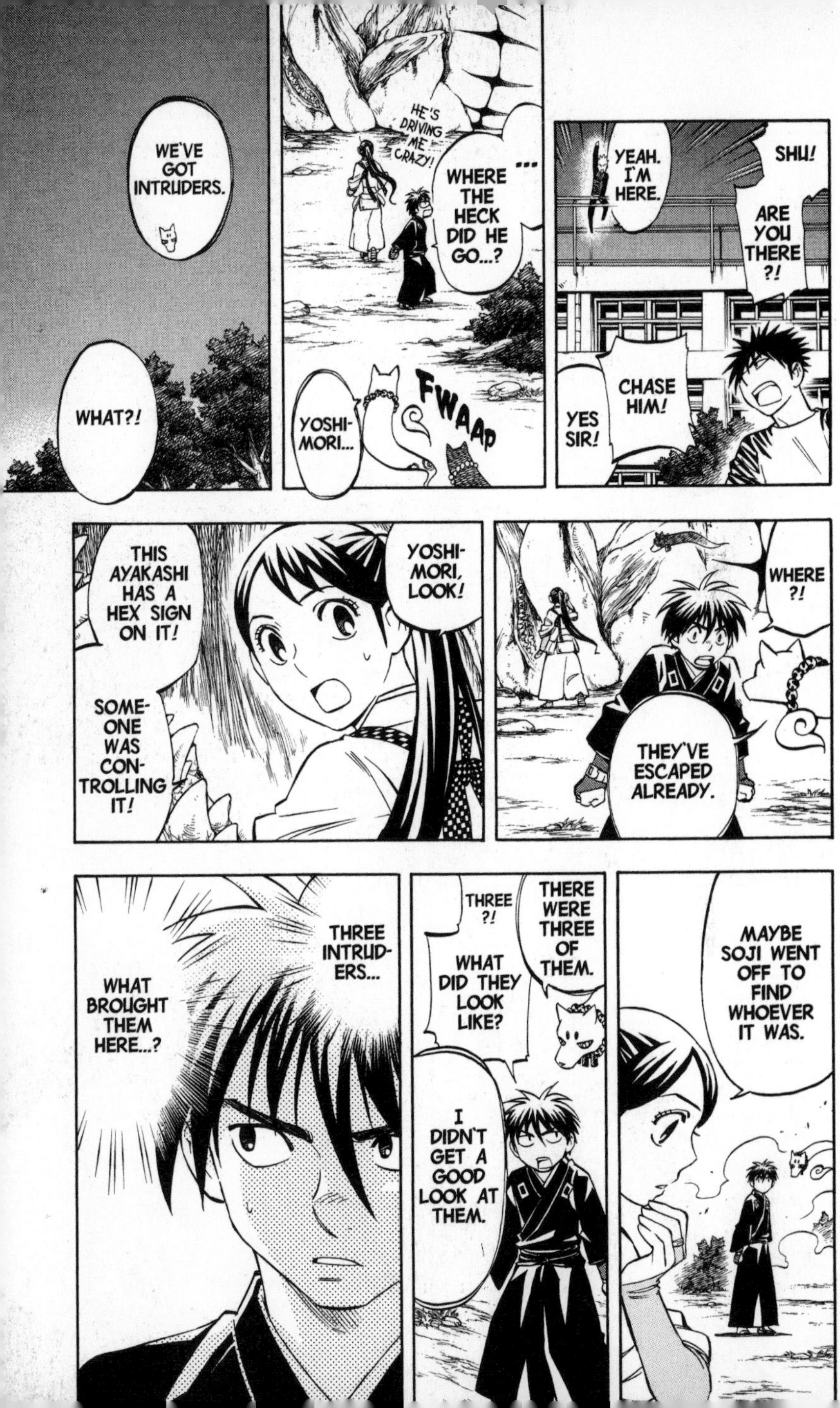
SHU!
ARE YOU THERE?!
YEAH. I'M HERE.
CHASE HIM!
YES SIR!
HE'S DRIVING ME CRAZY!
...
WHERE THE HECK DID HE GO...?
FWAAP
YOSHI-MORI...
WE'VE GOT INTRUDERS.
WHAT?!
WHERE?!
THEY'VE ESCAPED ALREADY.
YOSHI-MORI, LOOK!
THIS AYAKASHI HAS A HEX SIGN ON IT!
SOME-ONE WAS CON-TROLLING IT!
MAYBE SOJI WENT OFF TO FIND WHOEVER IT WAS.
THERE WERE THREE OF THEM.
THREE?!
WHAT DID THEY LOOK LIKE?
I DIDN'T GET A GOOD LOOK AT THEM.
THREE INTRUD-ERS...
WHAT BROUGHT THEM HERE...?

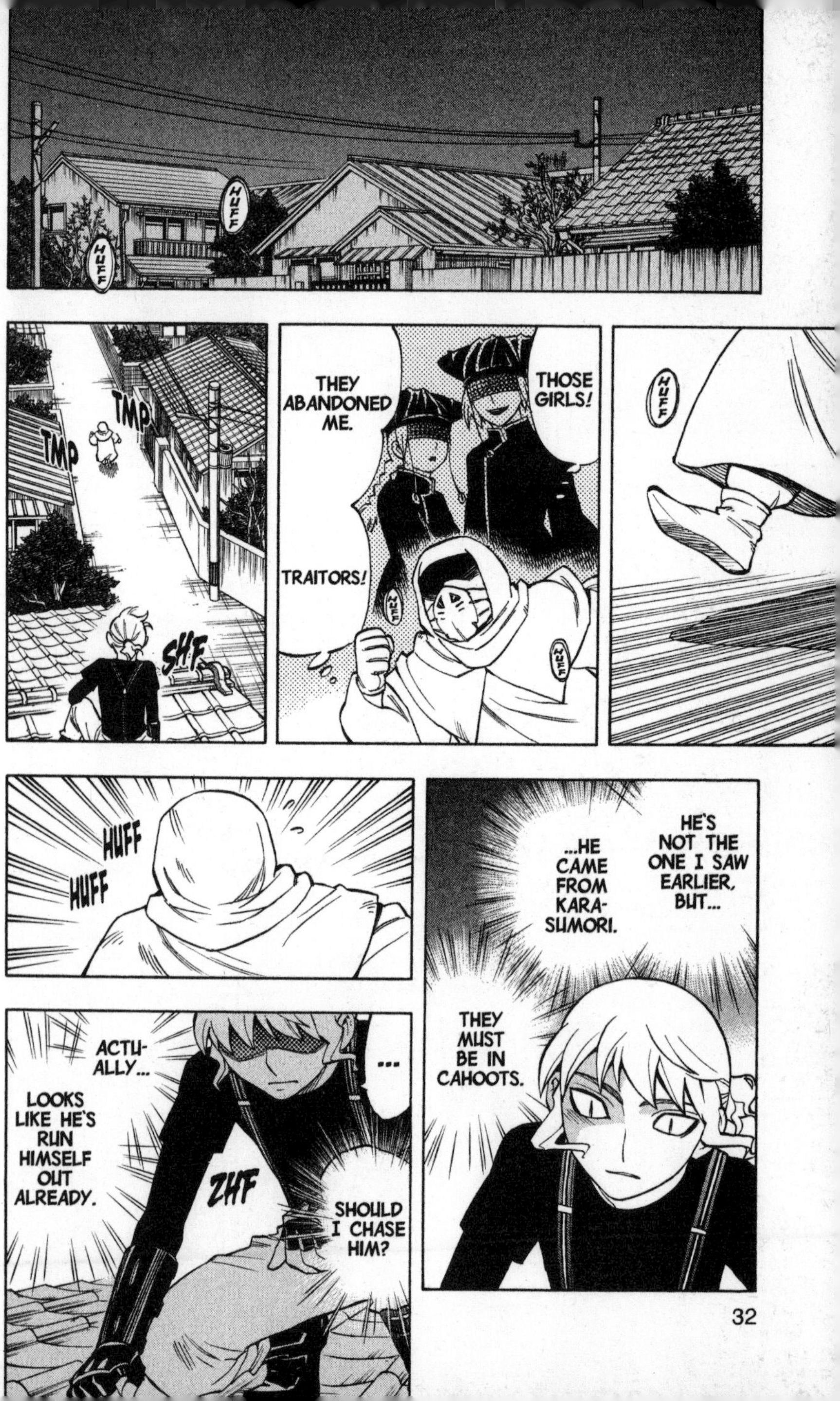
HUFF
HUFF
HUFF
THOSE GIRLS!
THEY ABANDONED ME.
TRAITORS!
HUFF
HUFF
TMP
TMP
SHF
HE'S NOT THE ONE I SAW EARLIER, BUT...
...HE CAME FROM KARA-SUMORI.
THEY MUST BE IN CAHOOTS.
HUFF
HUFF
...
ACTU-ALLY...
LOOKS LIKE HE'S RUN HIMSELF OUT ALREADY.
ZHF
SHOULD I CHASE HIM?

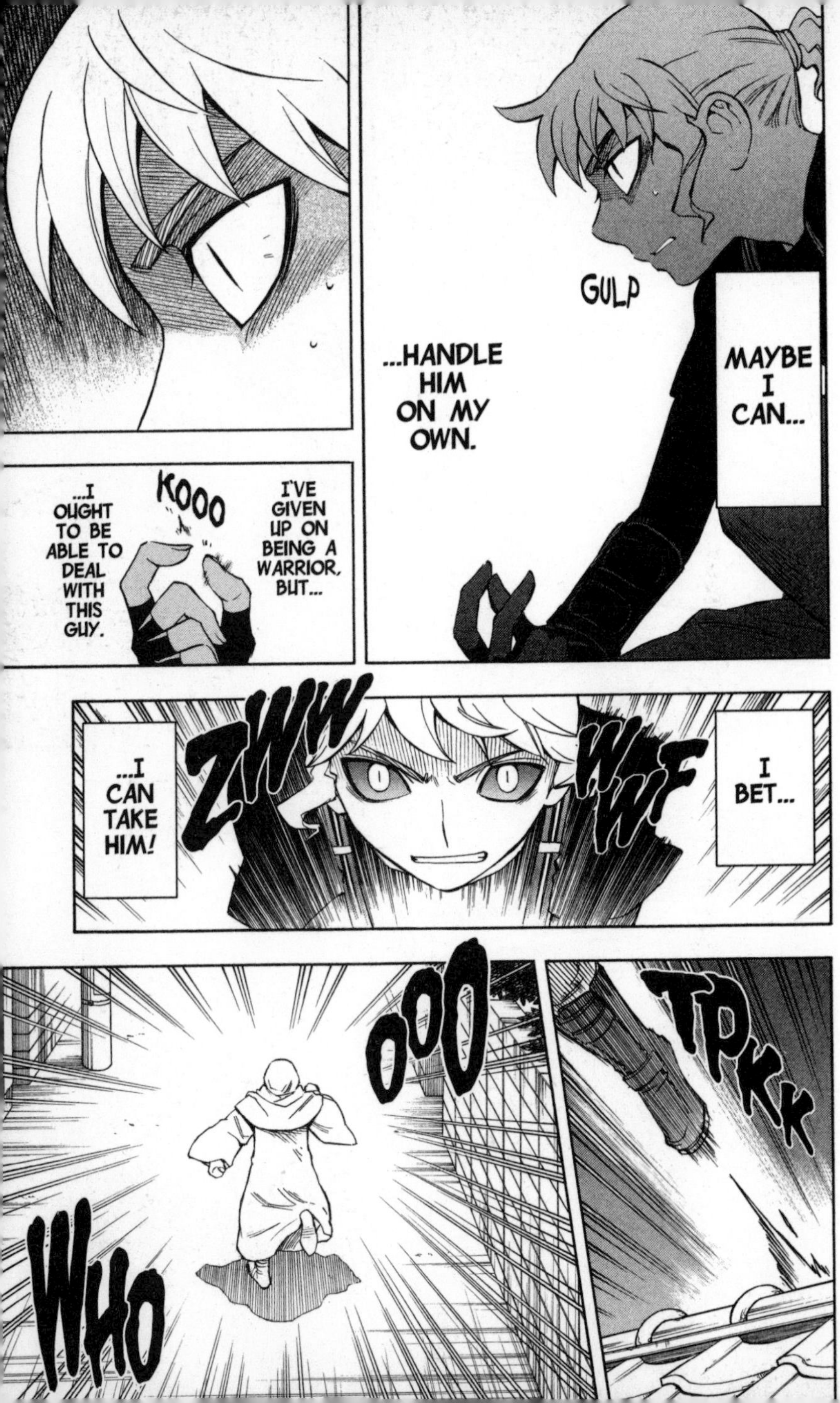
GULP
MAYBE I CAN...
...HANDLE HIM ON MY OWN.
I'VE GIVEN UP ON BEING A WARRIOR, BUT...
KOOO
...I OUGHT TO BE ABLE TO DEAL WITH THIS GUY.
I BET...
WHIF
ZWW
...I CAN TAKE HIM!
TPKK
OOO
WHO

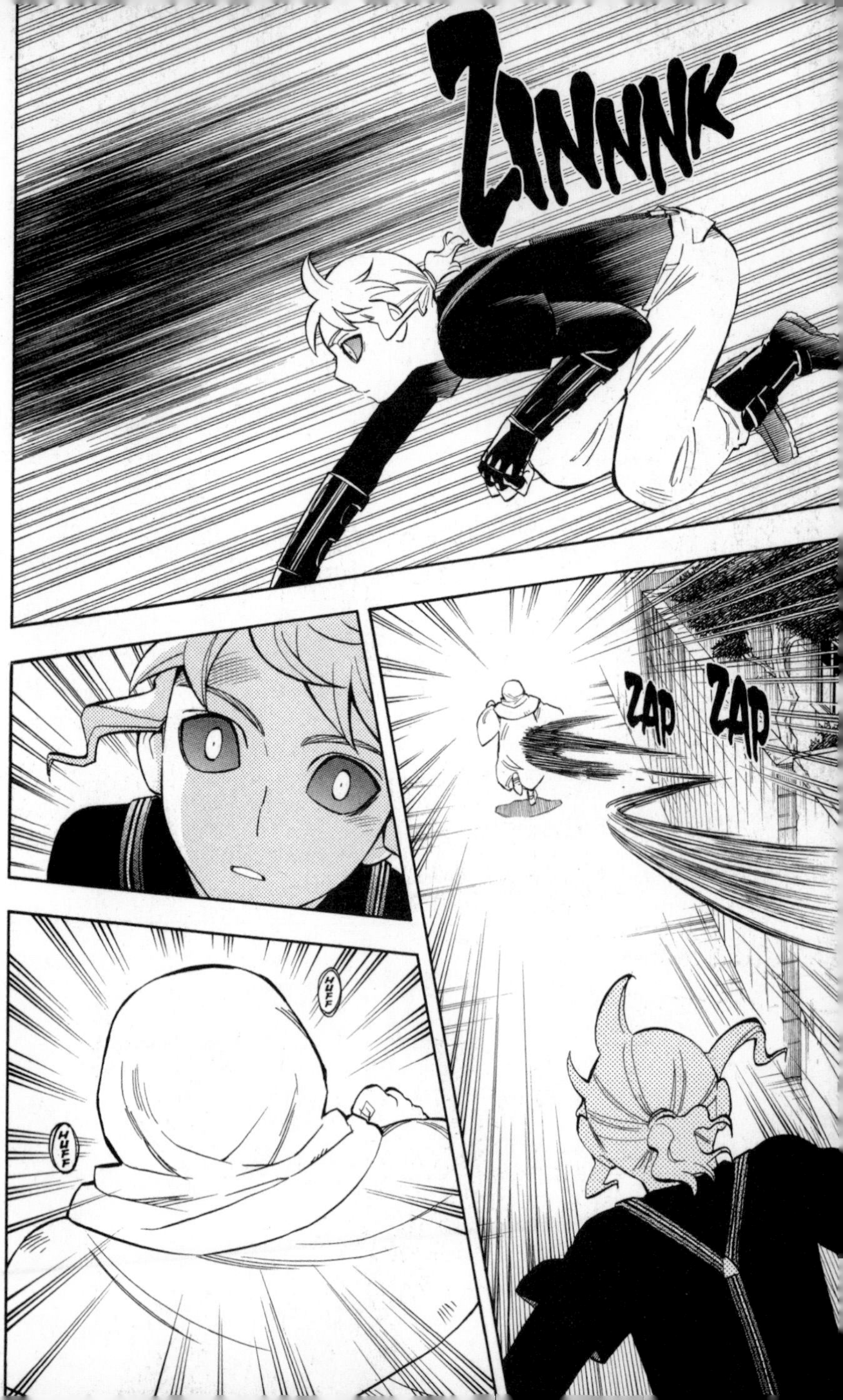
ZINNNK
ZAP ZAP
HUFF
HUFF

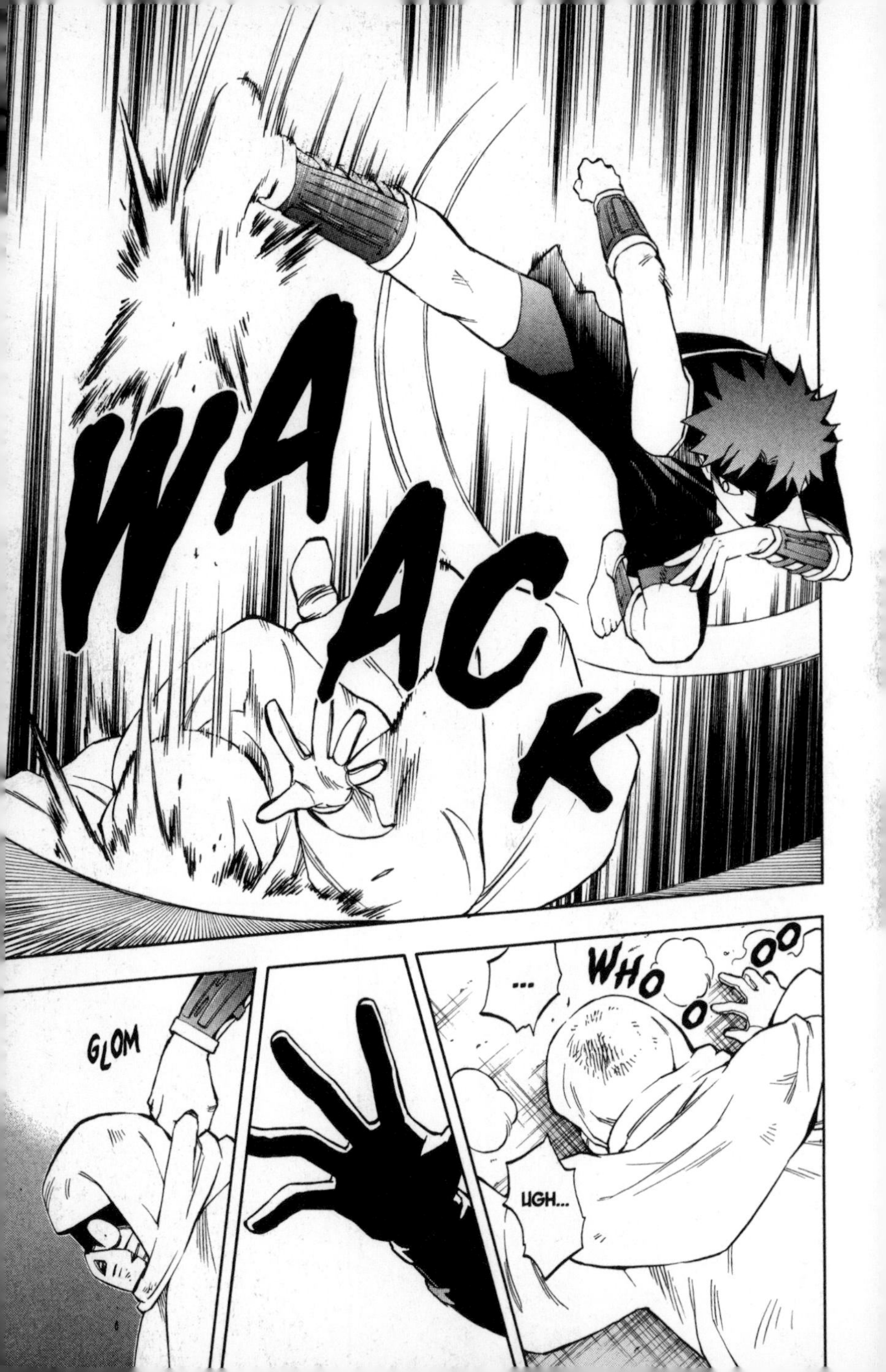
WAACK
...
WHOOOOO
UGH...
GLOM

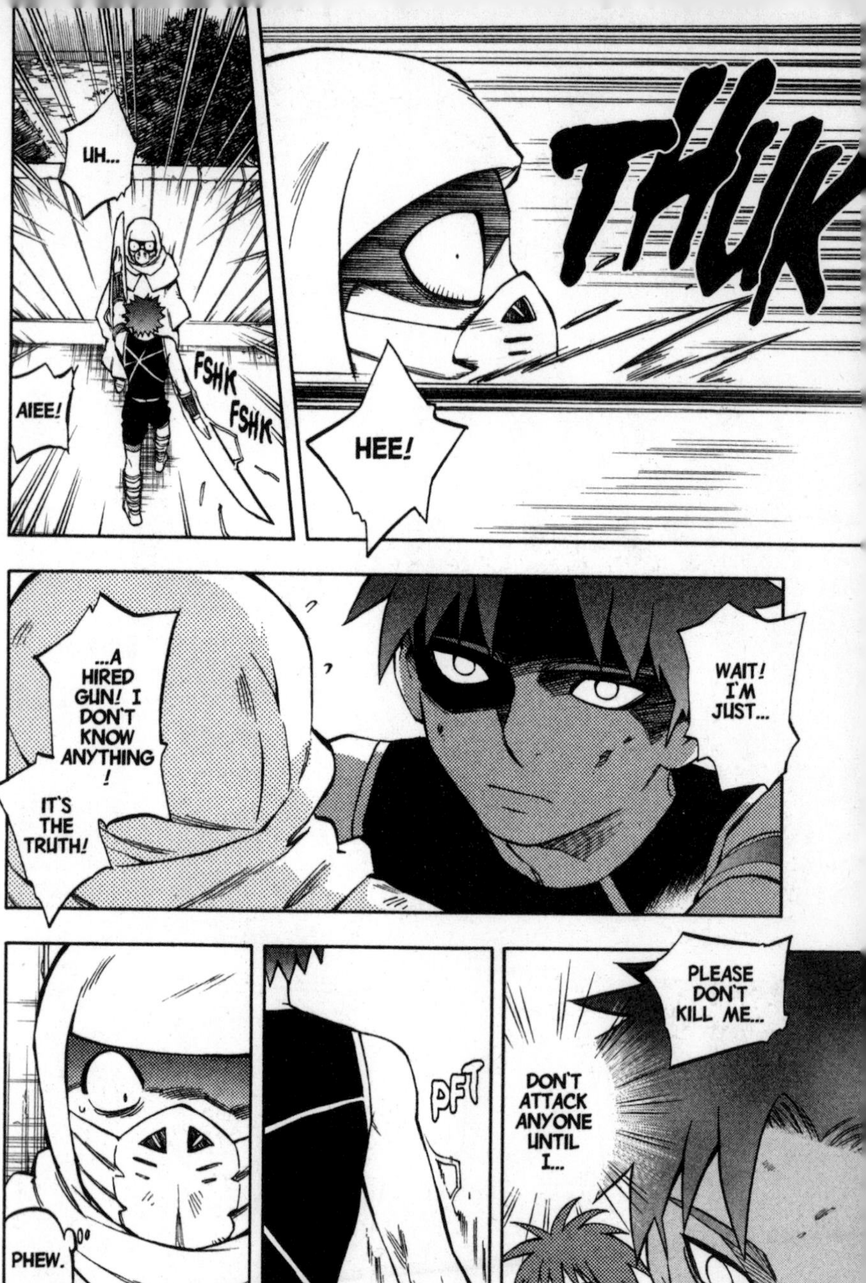
THUK
HEE!
UH...
FSHK
FSHK
AIEE!
WAIT! I'M JUST...
...A HIRED GUN! I DON'T KNOW ANYTHING!
IT'S THE TRUTH!
PLEASE DON'T KILL ME...
DON'T ATTACK ANYONE UNTIL I...
PFT
PHEW.

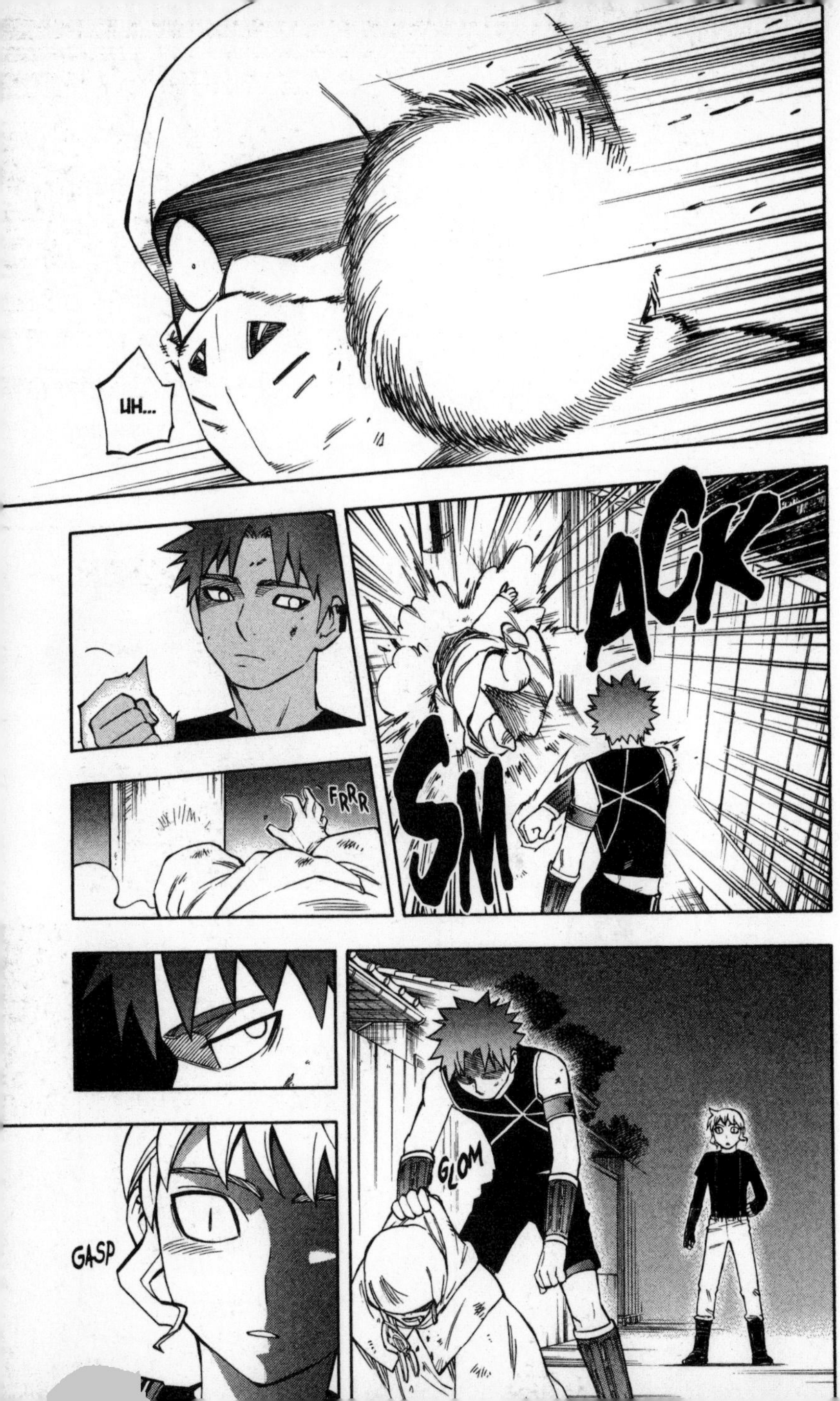

UH...
SMACK
FRRR
GLOM
GASP

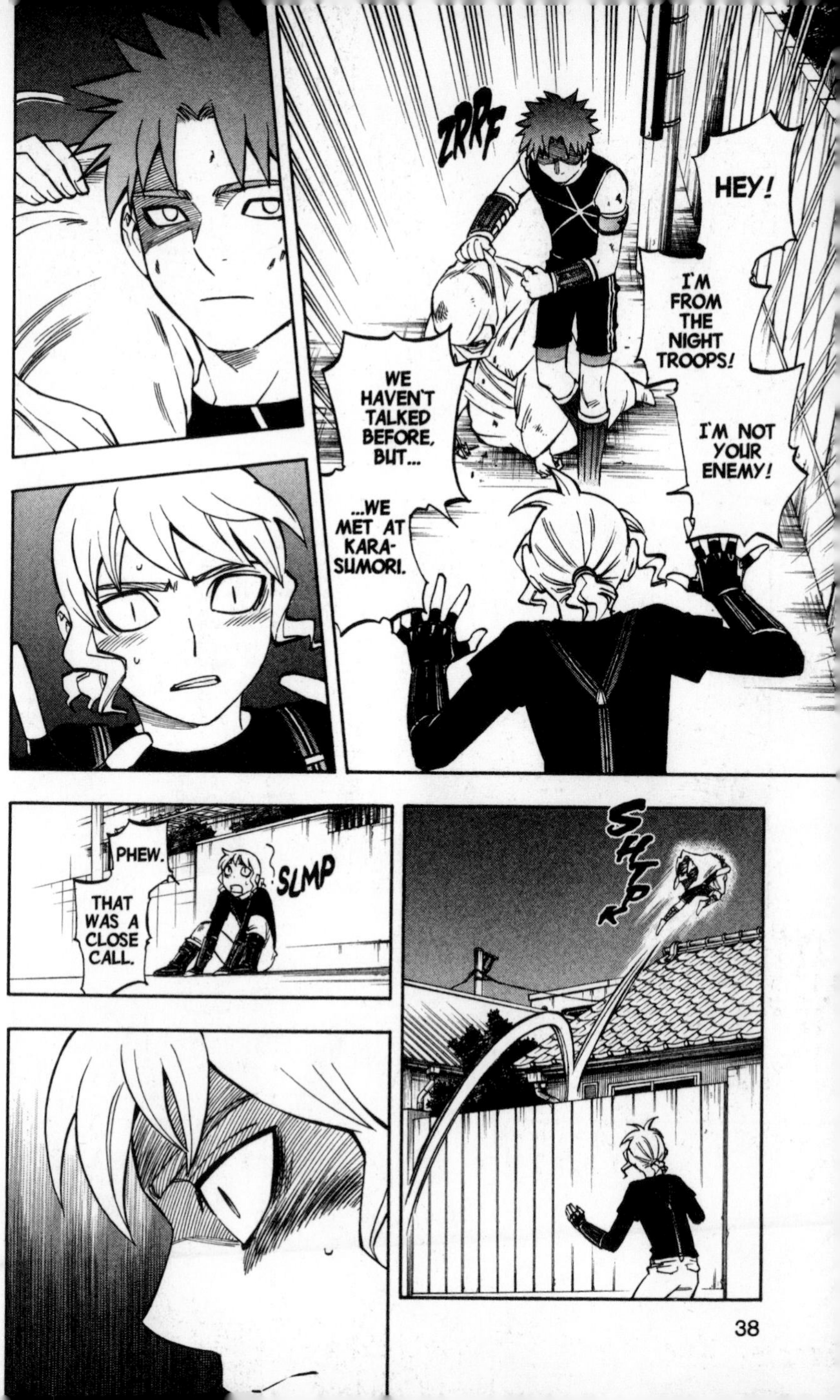
ZRRF
HEY!
I'M FROM THE NIGHT TROOPS!
I'M NOT YOUR ENEMY!
WE HAVEN'T TALKED BEFORE, BUT...
...WE MET AT KARA-SUMORI.
SHTOK
PHEW.
THAT WAS A CLOSE CALL.
SLMP

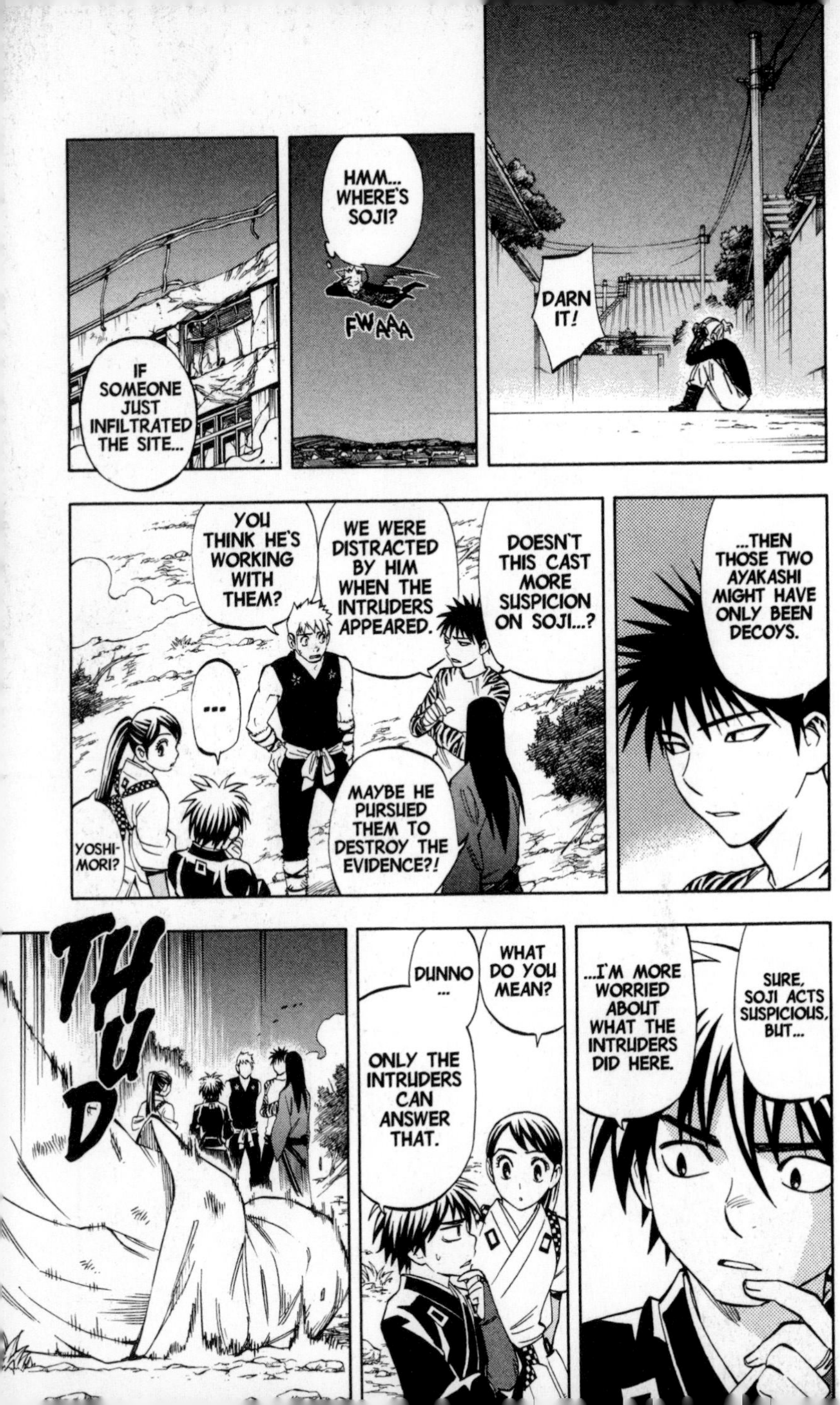
DARN IT!
HMM... WHERE'S SOJI?
FWAAA
IF SOMEONE JUST INFILTRATED THE SITE...
...THEN THOSE TWO AYAKASHI MIGHT HAVE ONLY BEEN DECOYS.
DOESN'T THIS CAST MORE SUSPICION ON SOJI...?
WE WERE DISTRACTED BY HIM WHEN THE INTRUDERS APPEARED.
YOU THINK HE'S WORKING WITH THEM?
MAYBE HE PURSUED THEM TO DESTROY THE EVIDENCE?!
...
YOSHI-MORI?
SURE, SOJI ACTS SUSPICIOUS, BUT...
...I'M MORE WORRIED ABOUT WHAT THE INTRUDERS DID HERE.
WHAT DO YOU MEAN?
DUNNO...
ONLY THE INTRUDERS CAN ANSWER THAT.
THUD

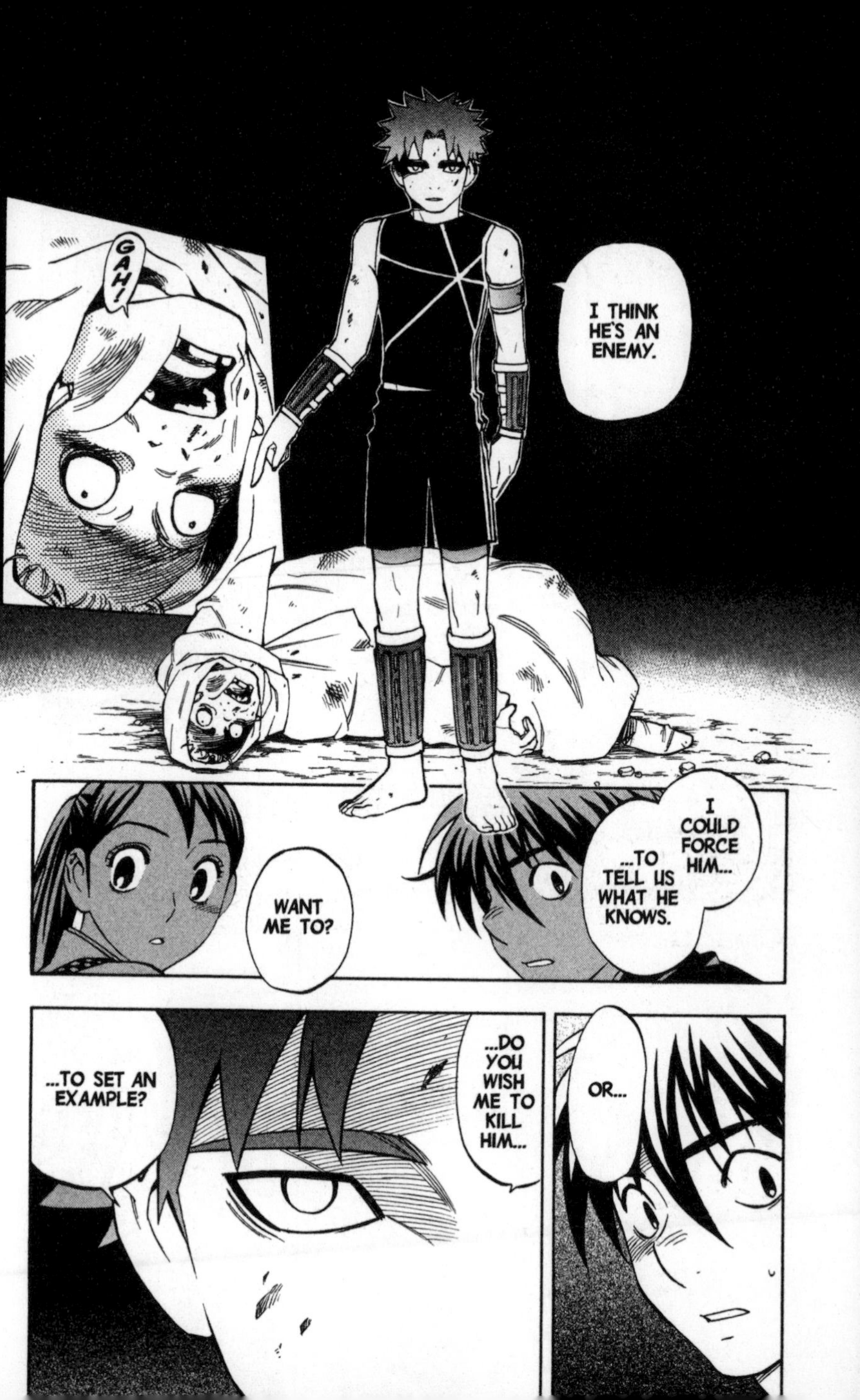
I THINK HE'S AN ENEMY.
GAH!
I COULD FORCE HIM...
...TO TELL US WHAT HE KNOWS.
WANT ME TO?
OR...
...DO YOU WISH ME TO KILL HIM...
...TO SET AN EXAMPLE?

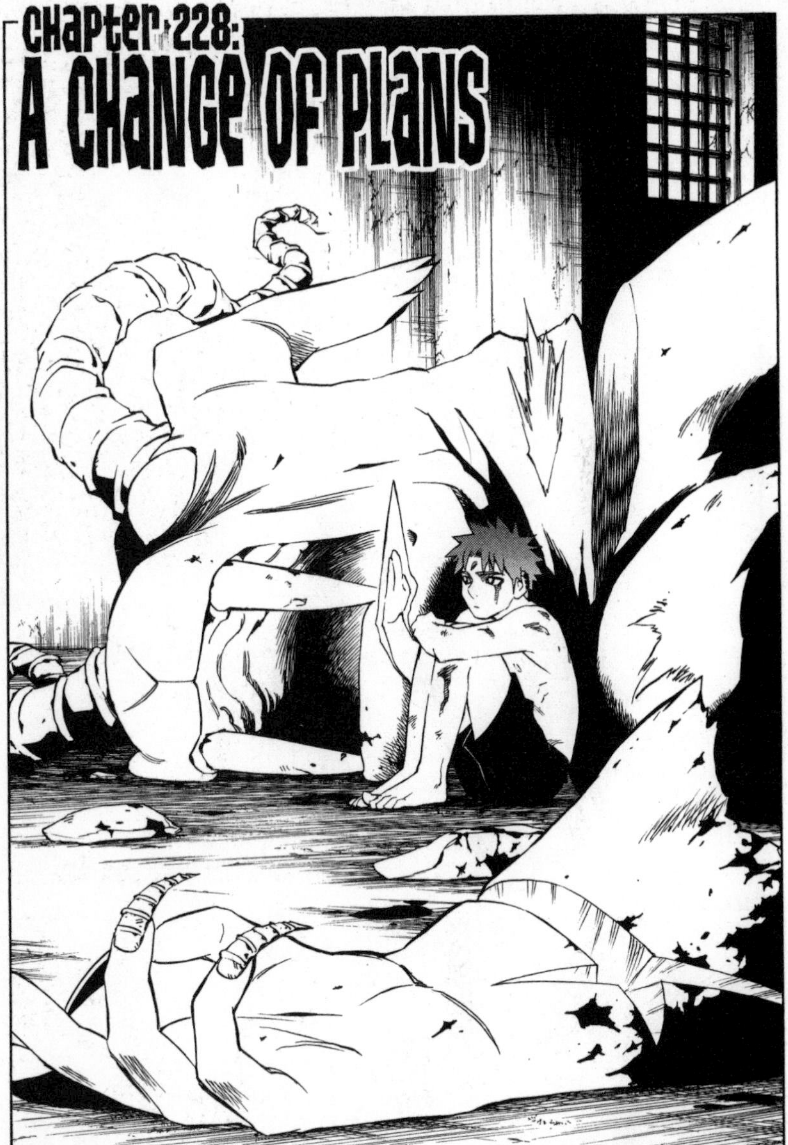
Chapter 228:
A Change of Plans

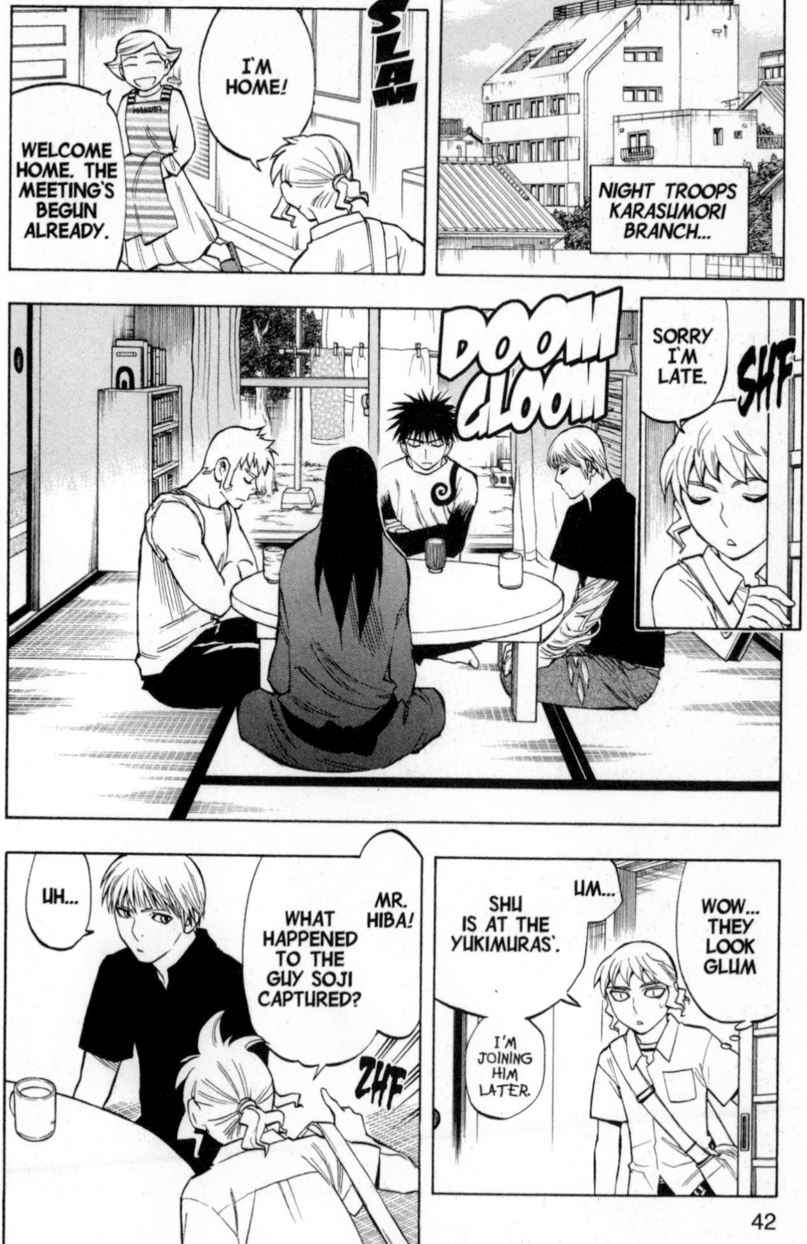
NIGHT TROOPS KARASUMORI BRANCH...
SLAM
I'M HOME!
WELCOME HOME. THE MEETING'S BEGUN ALREADY.
SORRY I'M LATE.
SHF
DOOM GLOOM
WOW... THEY LOOK GLUM
UM...
SHU IS AT THE YUKIMURAS'.
I'M JOINING HIM LATER.
MR. HIBA! WHAT HAPPENED TO THE GUY SOJI CAPTURED?
ZHF
UH...

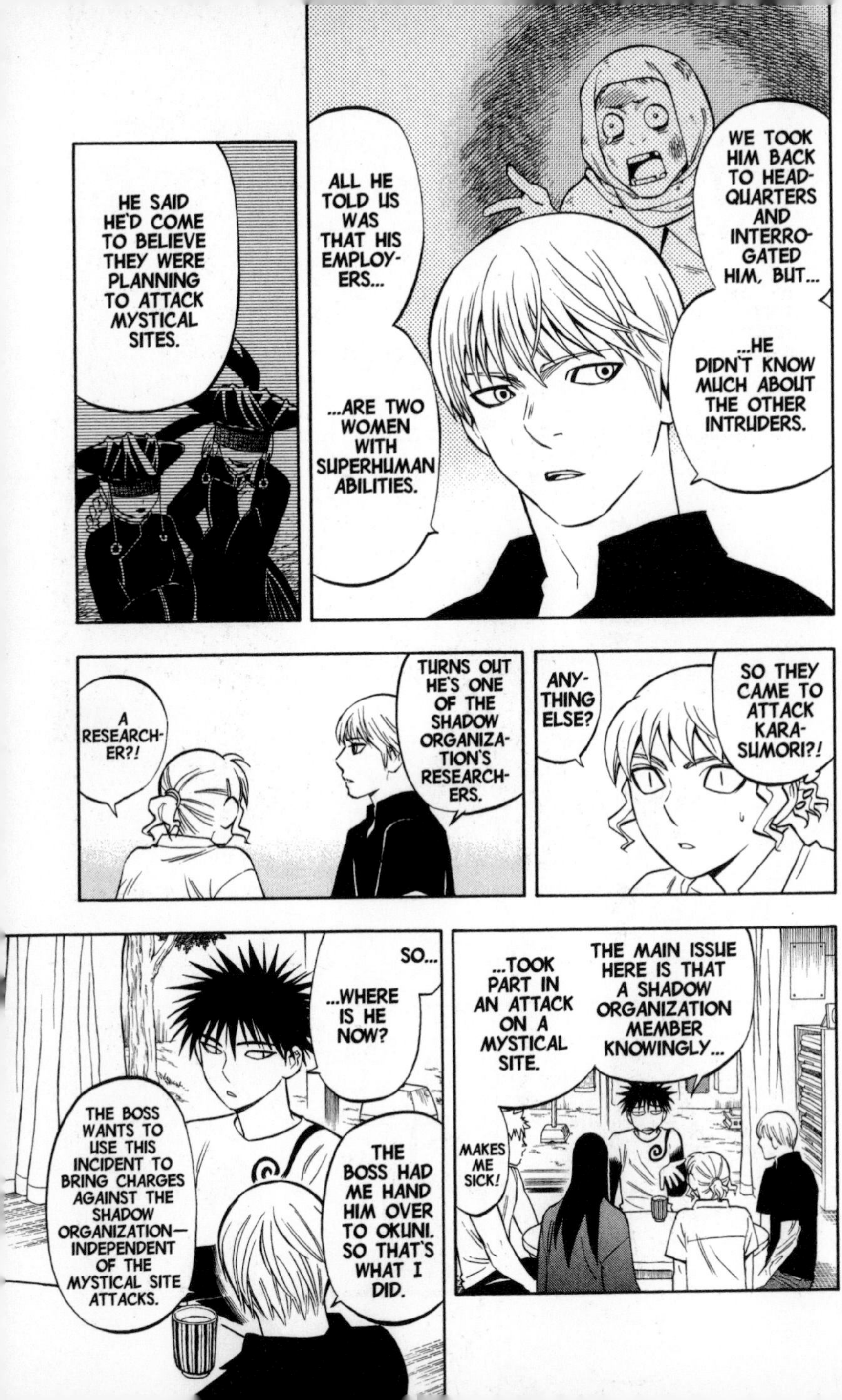
WE TOOK HIM BACK TO HEADQUARTERS AND INTERROGATED HIM, BUT...
...HE DIDN'T KNOW MUCH ABOUT THE OTHER INTRUDERS.
ALL HE TOLD US WAS THAT HIS EMPLOYERS...
...ARE TWO WOMEN WITH SUPERHUMAN ABILITIES.
HE SAID HE'D COME TO BELIEVE THEY WERE PLANNING TO ATTACK MYSTICAL SITES.
SO THEY CAME TO ATTACK KARASUMORI?!
ANYTHING ELSE?
TURNS OUT HE'S ONE OF THE SHADOW ORGANIZATION'S RESEARCHERS.
A RESEARCHER?!
THE MAIN ISSUE HERE IS THAT A SHADOW ORGANIZATION MEMBER KNOWINGLY...
...TOOK PART IN AN ATTACK ON A MYSTICAL SITE.
MAKES ME SICK!
SO...
...WHERE IS HE NOW?
THE BOSS HAD ME HAND HIM OVER TO OKUNI. SO THAT'S WHAT I DID.
THE BOSS WANTS TO USE THIS INCIDENT TO BRING CHARGES AGAINST THE SHADOW ORGANIZATION—INDEPENDENT OF THE MYSTICAL SITE ATTACKS.

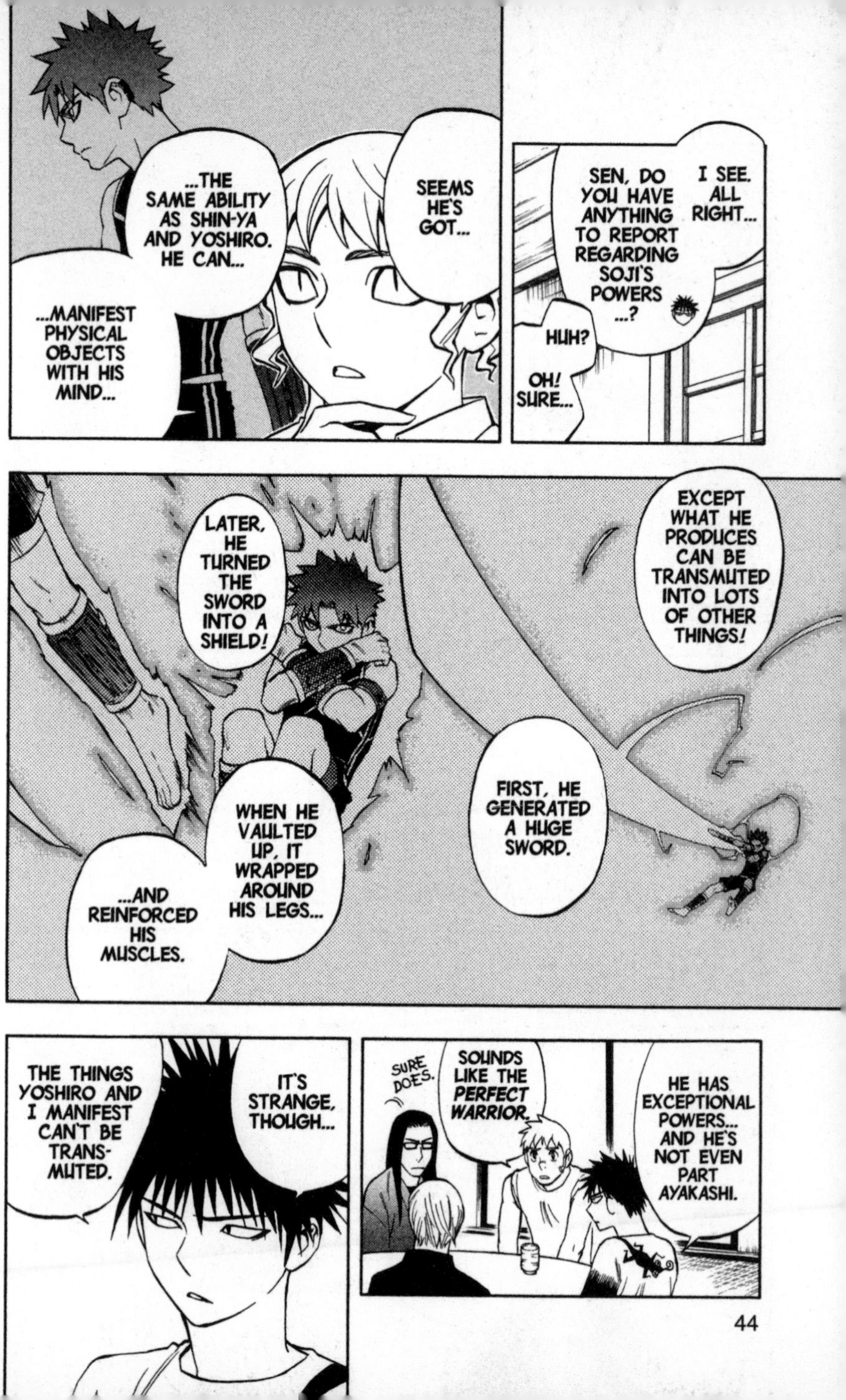
I SEE. ALL RIGHT...
SEN, DO YOU HAVE ANYTHING TO REPORT REGARDING SOJI'S POWERS ...?
HUH?
OH! SURE...
SEEMS HE'S GOT...
...THE SAME ABILITY AS SHIN-YA AND YOSHIRO. HE CAN...
...MANIFEST PHYSICAL OBJECTS WITH HIS MIND...
EXCEPT WHAT HE PRODUCES CAN BE TRANSMUTED INTO LOTS OF OTHER THINGS!
FIRST, HE GENERATED A HUGE SWORD.
LATER, HE TURNED THE SWORD INTO A SHIELD!
WHEN HE VAULTED UP, IT WRAPPED AROUND HIS LEGS...
...AND REINFORCED HIS MUSCLES.
HE HAS EXCEPTIONAL POWERS... AND HE'S NOT EVEN PART AYAKASHI.
SOUNDS LIKE THE *PERFECT WARRIOR*.
SURE DOES.
IT'S STRANGE, THOUGH...
THE THINGS YOSHIRO AND I MANIFEST CAN'T BE TRANS-MUTED.

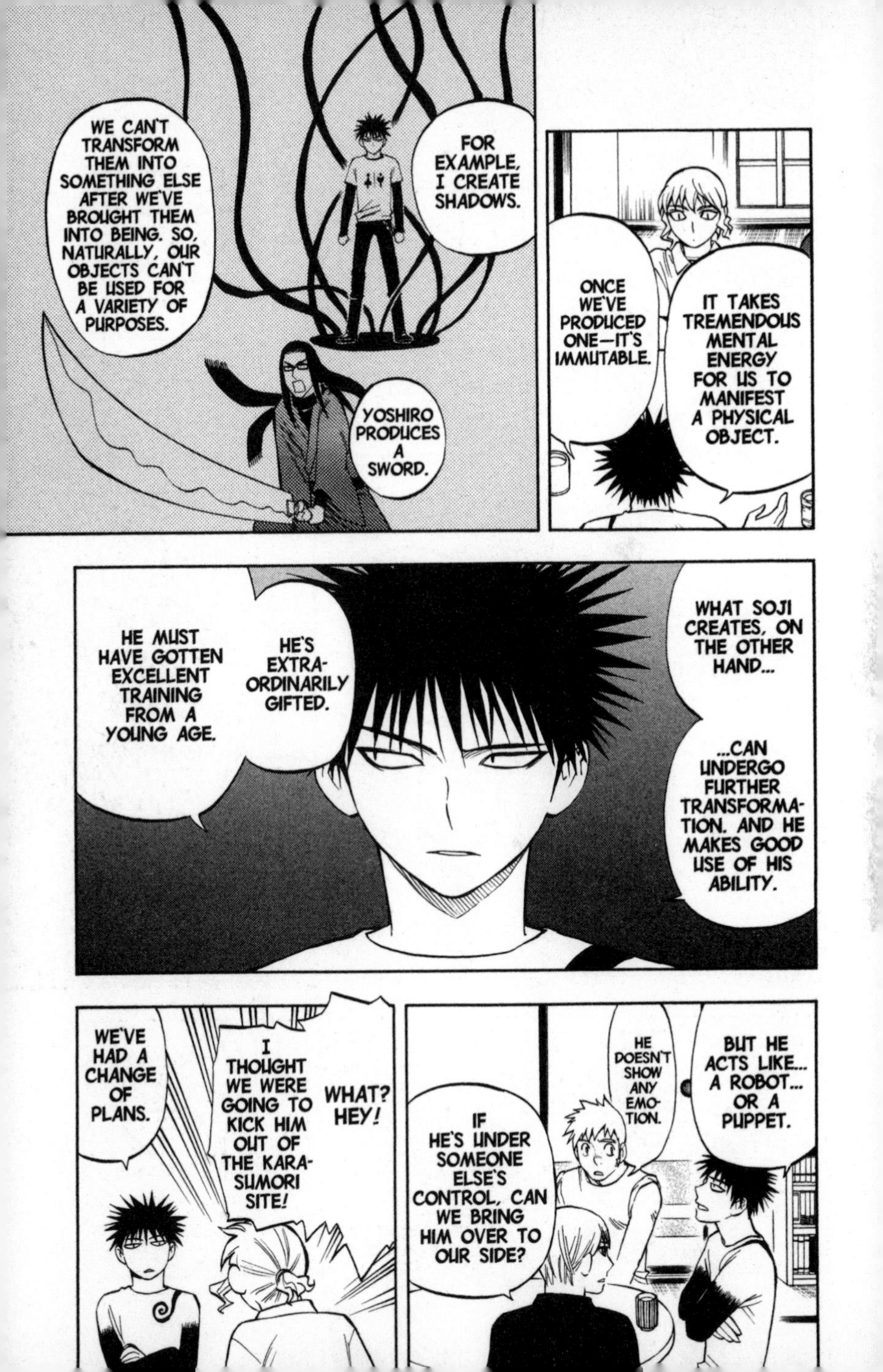
IT TAKES TREMENDOUS MENTAL ENERGY FOR US TO MANIFEST A PHYSICAL OBJECT.
ONCE WE'VE PRODUCED ONE—IT'S IMMUTABLE.
FOR EXAMPLE, I CREATE SHADOWS.
YOSHIRO PRODUCES A SWORD.
WE CAN'T TRANSFORM THEM INTO SOMETHING ELSE AFTER WE'VE BROUGHT THEM INTO BEING. SO, NATURALLY, OUR OBJECTS CAN'T BE USED FOR A VARIETY OF PURPOSES.
WHAT SOJI CREATES, ON THE OTHER HAND...
...CAN UNDERGO FURTHER TRANSFORMATION. AND HE MAKES GOOD USE OF HIS ABILITY.
HE'S EXTRAORDINARILY GIFTED.
HE MUST HAVE GOTTEN EXCELLENT TRAINING FROM A YOUNG AGE.
BUT HE ACTS LIKE... A ROBOT... OR A PUPPET.
HE DOESN'T SHOW ANY EMOTION.
IF HE'S UNDER SOMEONE ELSE'S CONTROL, CAN WE BRING HIM OVER TO OUR SIDE?
WHAT? HEY!
I THOUGHT WE WERE GOING TO KICK HIM OUT OF THE KARASUMORI SITE!
WE'VE HAD A CHANGE OF PLANS.

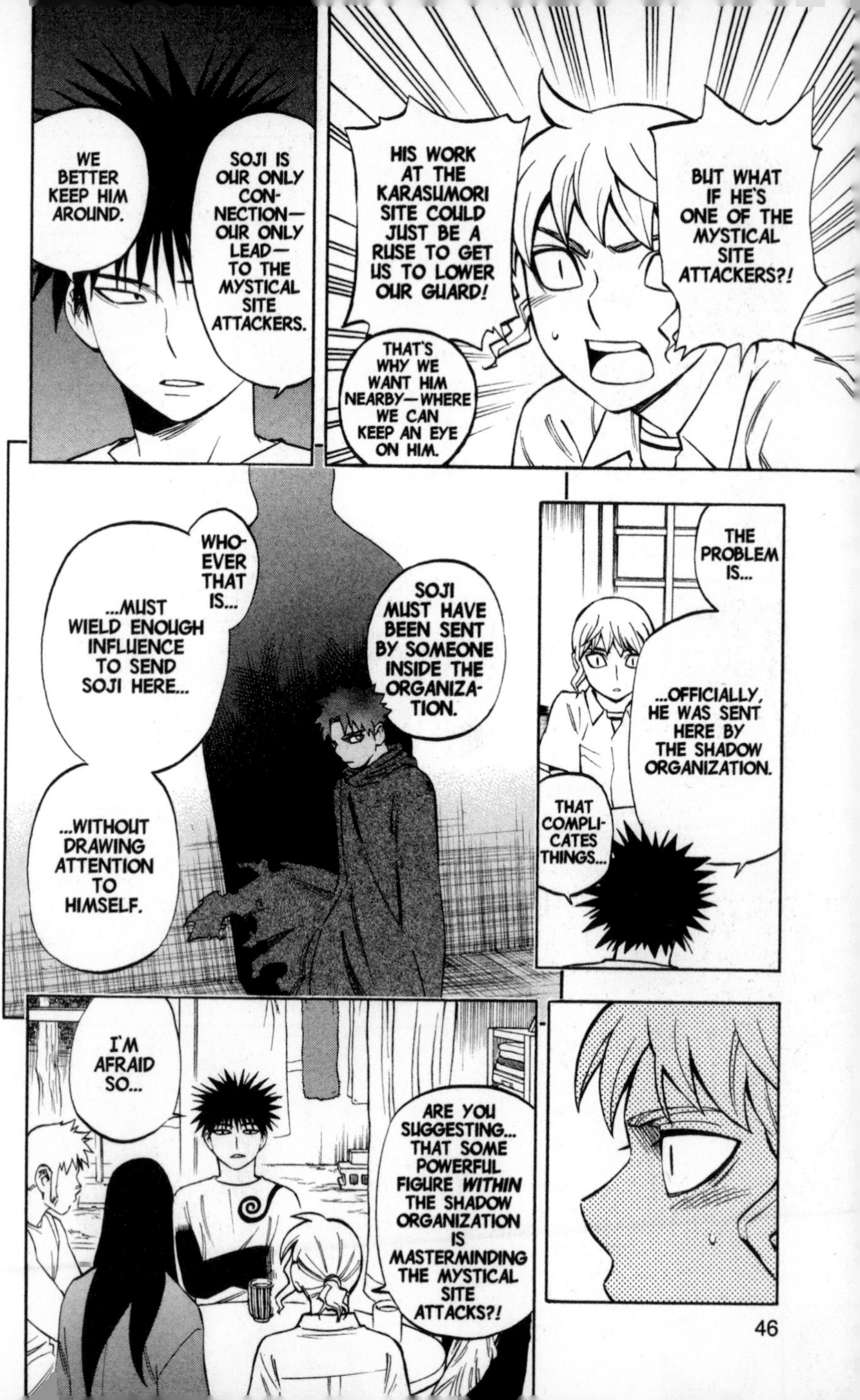
BUT WHAT IF HE'S ONE OF THE MYSTICAL SITE ATTACKERS?!
HIS WORK AT THE KARASUMORI SITE COULD JUST BE A RUSE TO GET US TO LOWER OUR GUARD!
THAT'S WHY WE WANT HIM NEARBY—WHERE WE CAN KEEP AN EYE ON HIM.
SOJI IS OUR ONLY CONNECTION—OUR ONLY LEAD—TO THE MYSTICAL SITE ATTACKERS.
WE BETTER KEEP HIM AROUND.
THE PROBLEM IS...
...OFFICIALLY, HE WAS SENT HERE BY THE SHADOW ORGANIZATION.
THAT COMPLICATES THINGS...
SOJI MUST HAVE BEEN SENT BY SOMEONE INSIDE THE ORGANIZATION.
WHOEVER THAT IS...
...MUST WIELD ENOUGH INFLUENCE TO SEND SOJI HERE...
...WITHOUT DRAWING ATTENTION TO HIMSELF.
ARE YOU SUGGESTING... THAT SOME POWERFUL FIGURE *WITHIN* THE SHADOW ORGANIZATION IS MASTERMINDING THE MYSTICAL SITE ATTACKS?!
I'M AFRAID SO...

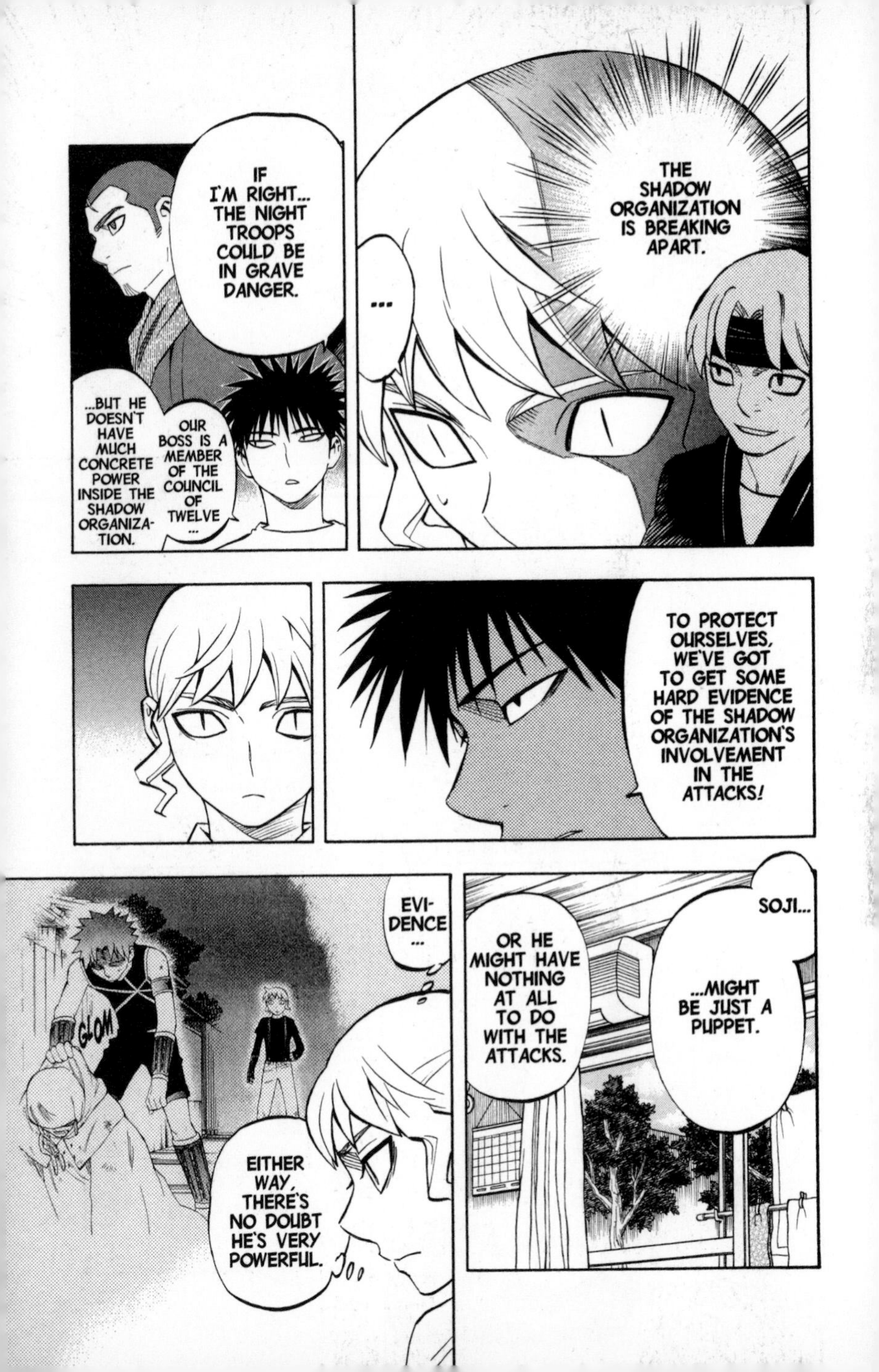
THE SHADOW ORGANIZATION IS BREAKING APART.
...
IF I'M RIGHT... THE NIGHT TROOPS COULD BE IN GRAVE DANGER.
OUR BOSS IS A MEMBER OF THE COUNCIL OF TWELVE...
...BUT HE DOESN'T HAVE MUCH CONCRETE POWER INSIDE THE SHADOW ORGANIZATION.
TO PROTECT OURSELVES, WE'VE GOT TO GET SOME HARD EVIDENCE OF THE SHADOW ORGANIZATION'S INVOLVEMENT IN THE ATTACKS!
SOJI...
...MIGHT BE JUST A PUPPET.
OR HE MIGHT HAVE NOTHING AT ALL TO DO WITH THE ATTACKS.
EVIDENCE...
GLOM
EITHER WAY, THERE'S NO DOUBT HE'S VERY POWERFUL.

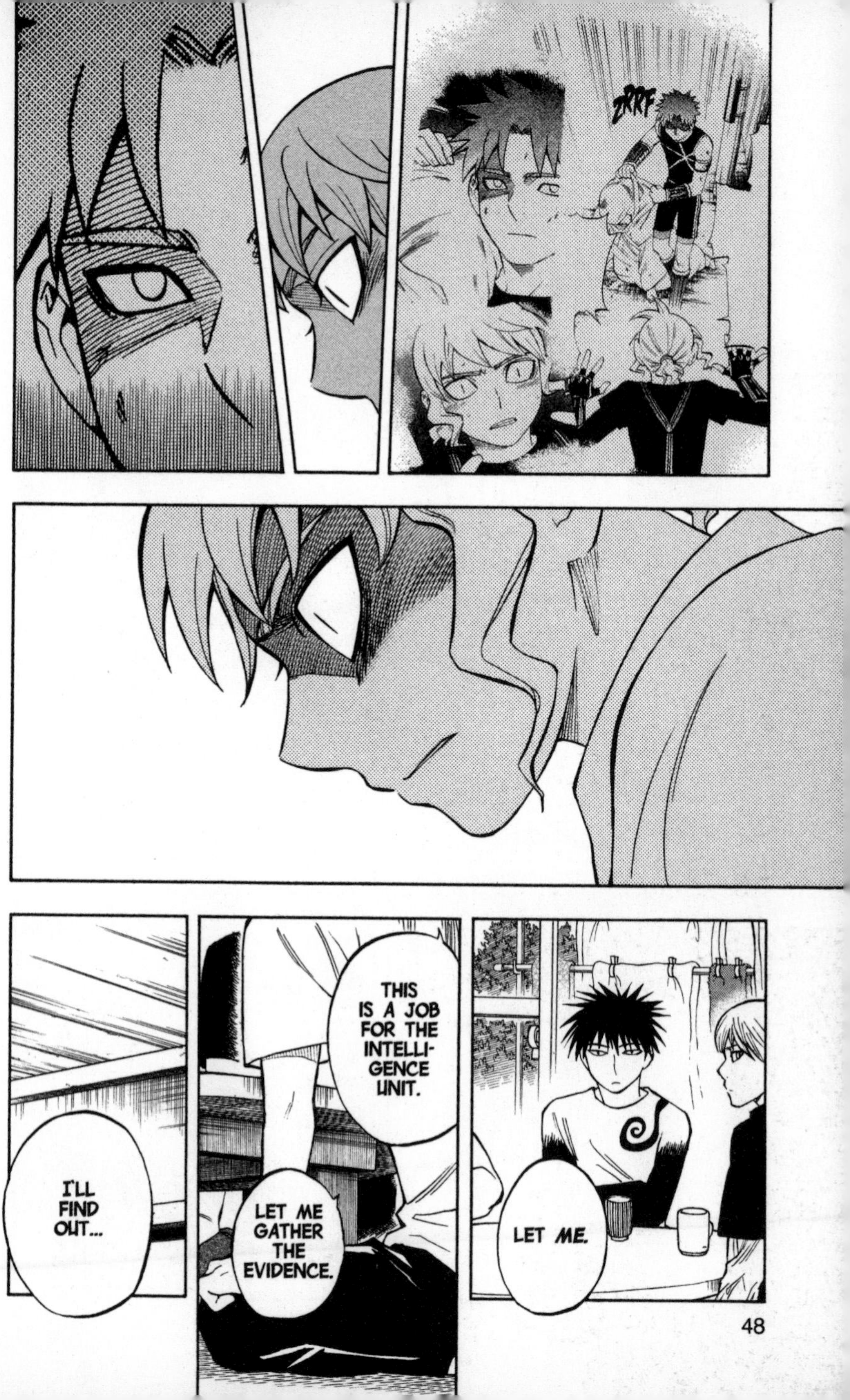
ZRRF
LET *ME.*
THIS IS A JOB FOR THE INTELLI-GENCE UNIT.
LET ME GATHER THE EVIDENCE.
I'LL FIND OUT...

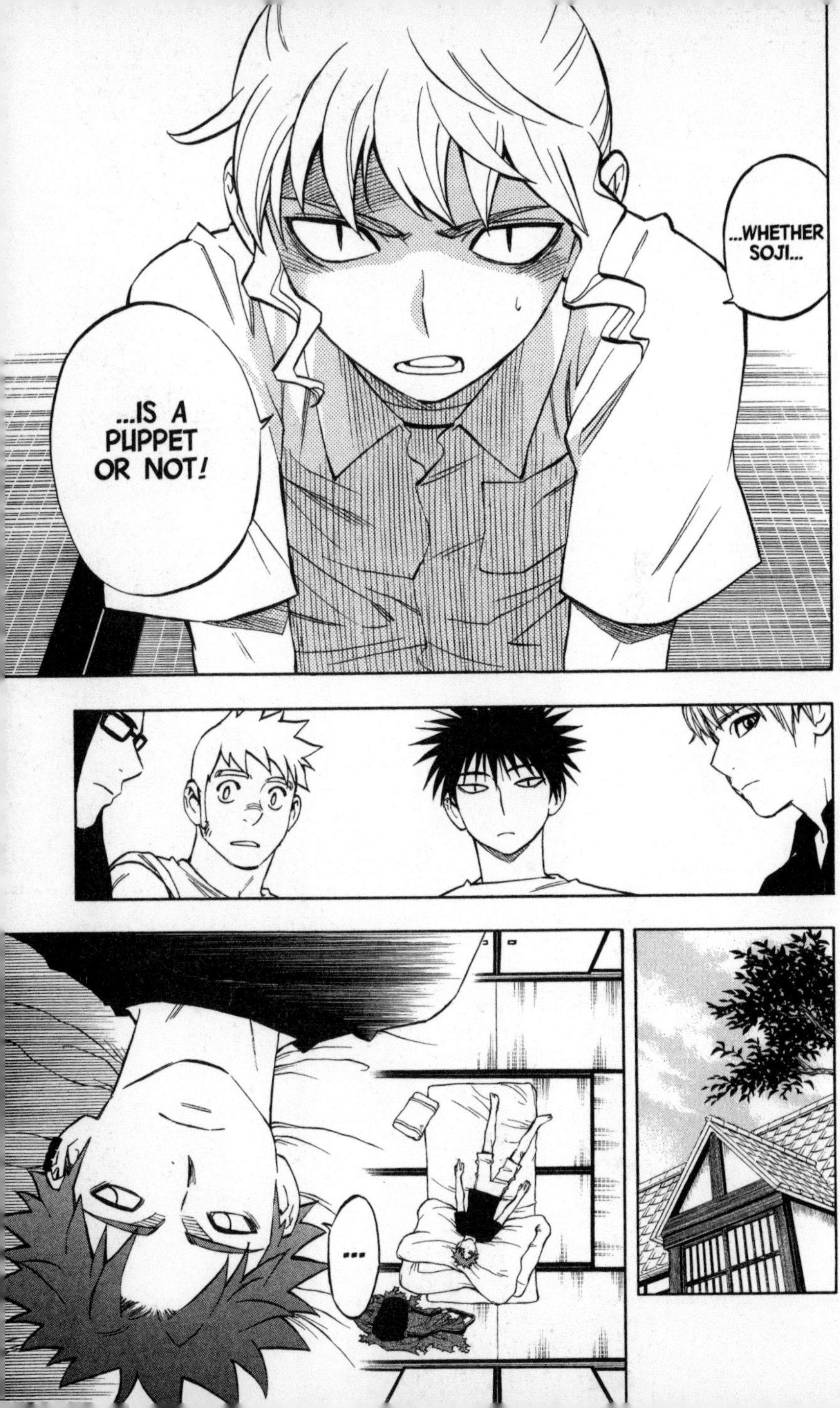
...WHETHER SOJI...
...IS A PUPPET OR NOT!
...

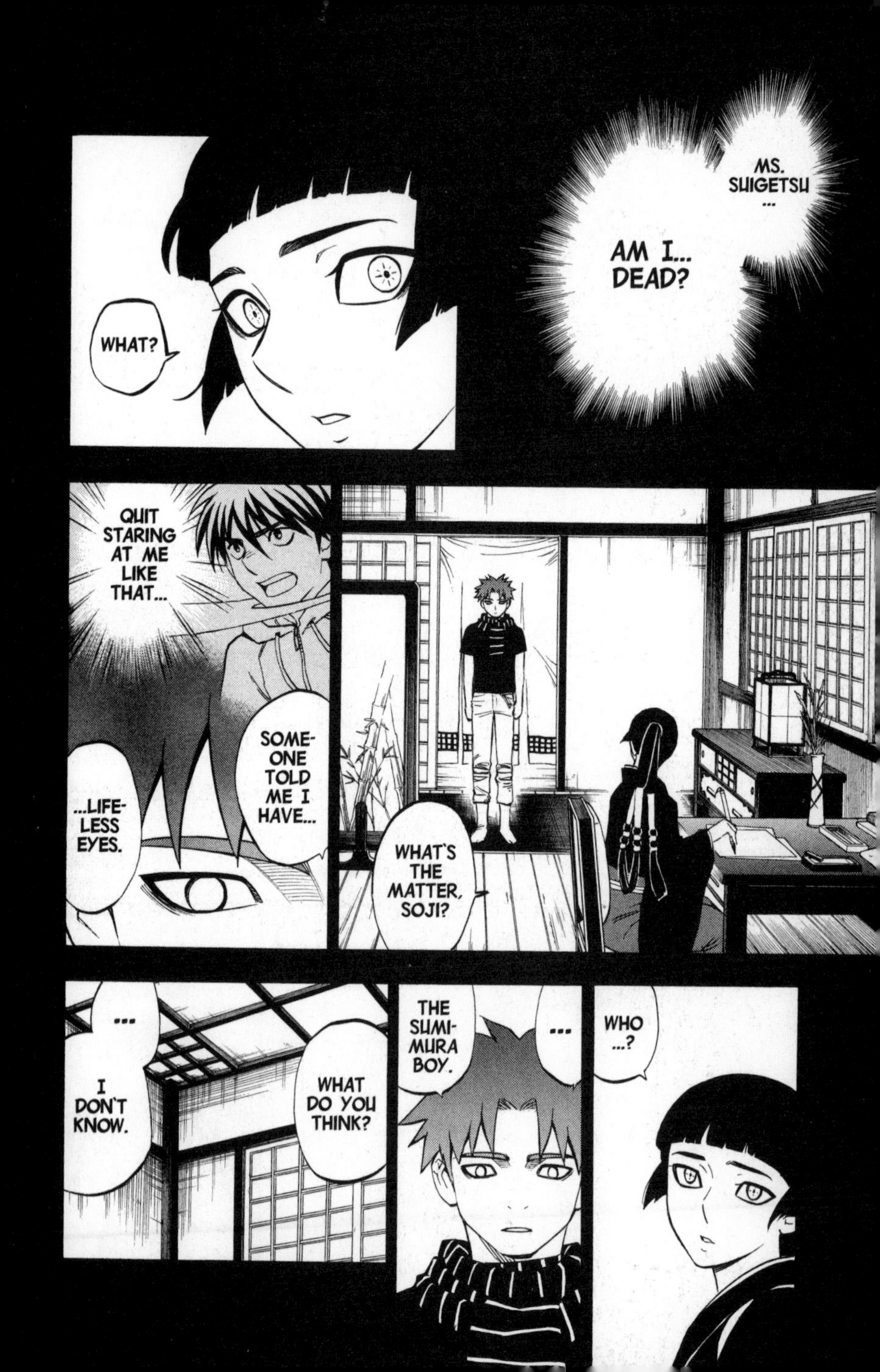

MS. SUIGETSU...
AM I... DEAD?
WHAT?
WHAT'S THE MATTER, SOJI?
QUIT STARING AT ME LIKE THAT...
SOME-ONE TOLD ME I HAVE...
...LIFE-LESS EYES.
WHO...?
...
THE SUMI-MURA BOY.
WHAT DO YOU THINK?
...
I DON'T KNOW.

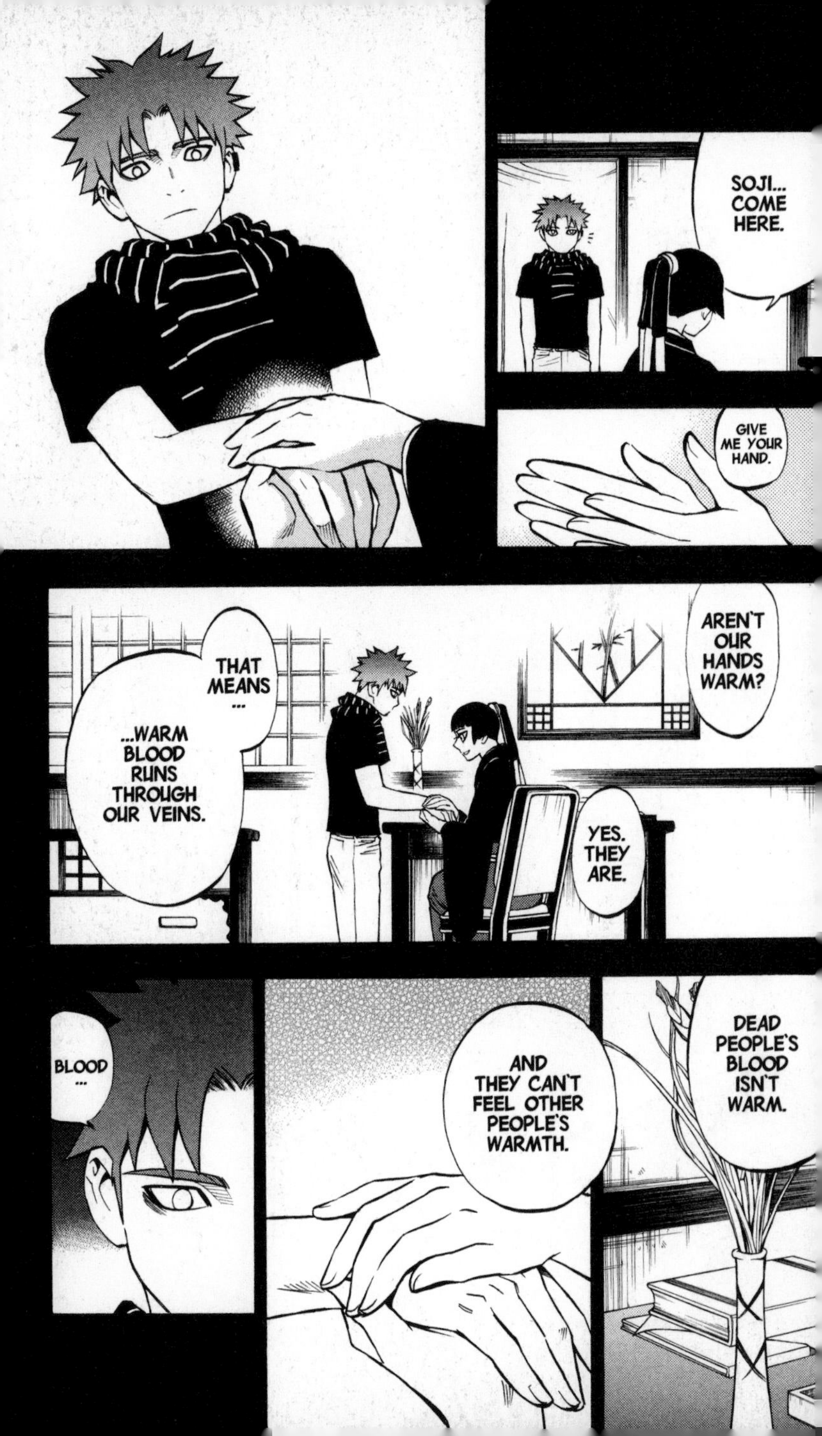
SOJI... COME HERE.
GIVE ME YOUR HAND.
AREN'T OUR HANDS WARM?
YES. THEY ARE.
THAT MEANS...
...WARM BLOOD RUNS THROUGH OUR VEINS.
DEAD PEOPLE'S BLOOD ISN'T WARM.
AND THEY CAN'T FEEL OTHER PEOPLE'S WARMTH.
BLOOD...

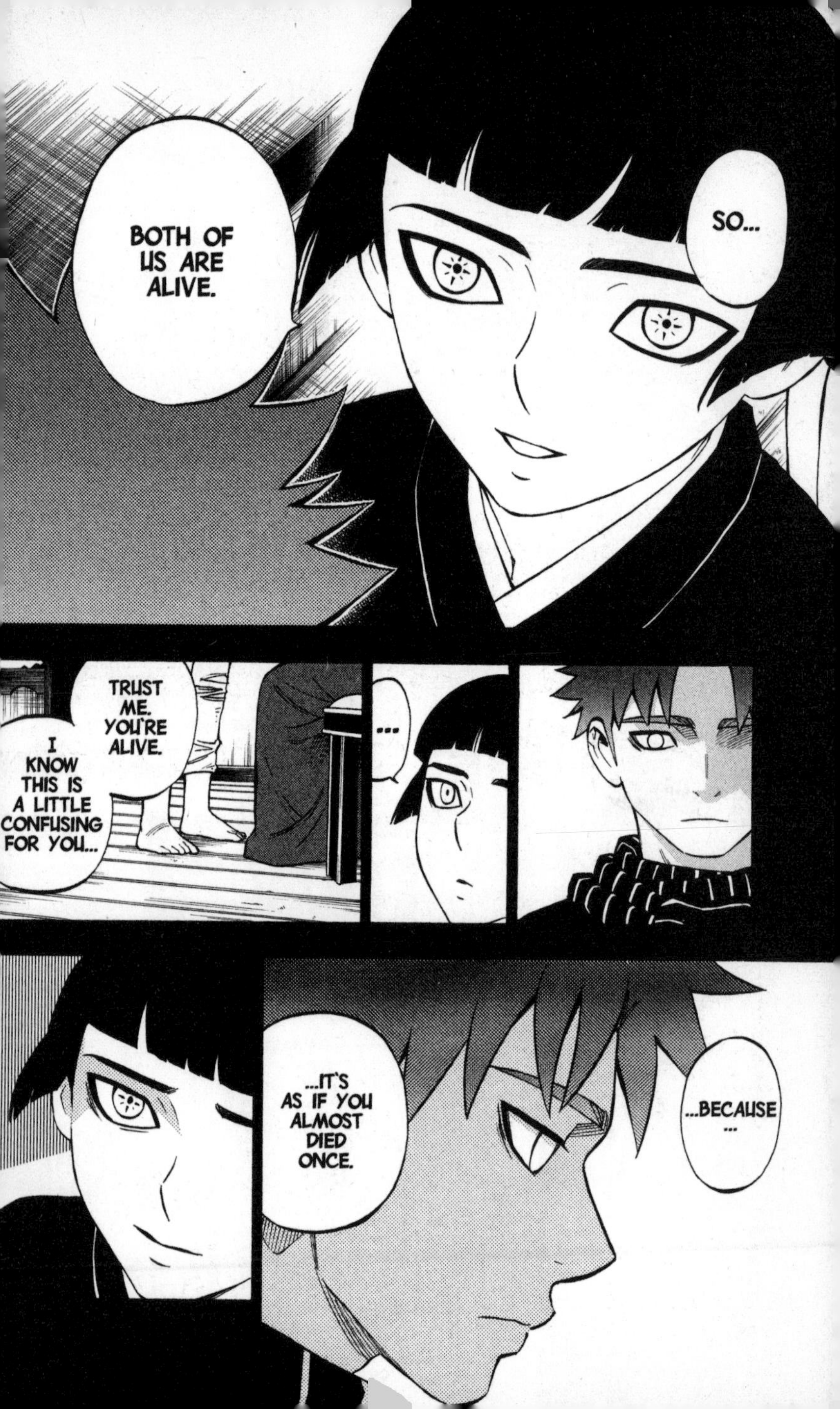
SO...
BOTH OF US ARE ALIVE.
...
TRUST ME. YOU'RE ALIVE.
I KNOW THIS IS A LITTLE CONFUSING FOR YOU...
...BECAUSE ...
...IT'S AS IF YOU ALMOST DIED ONCE.

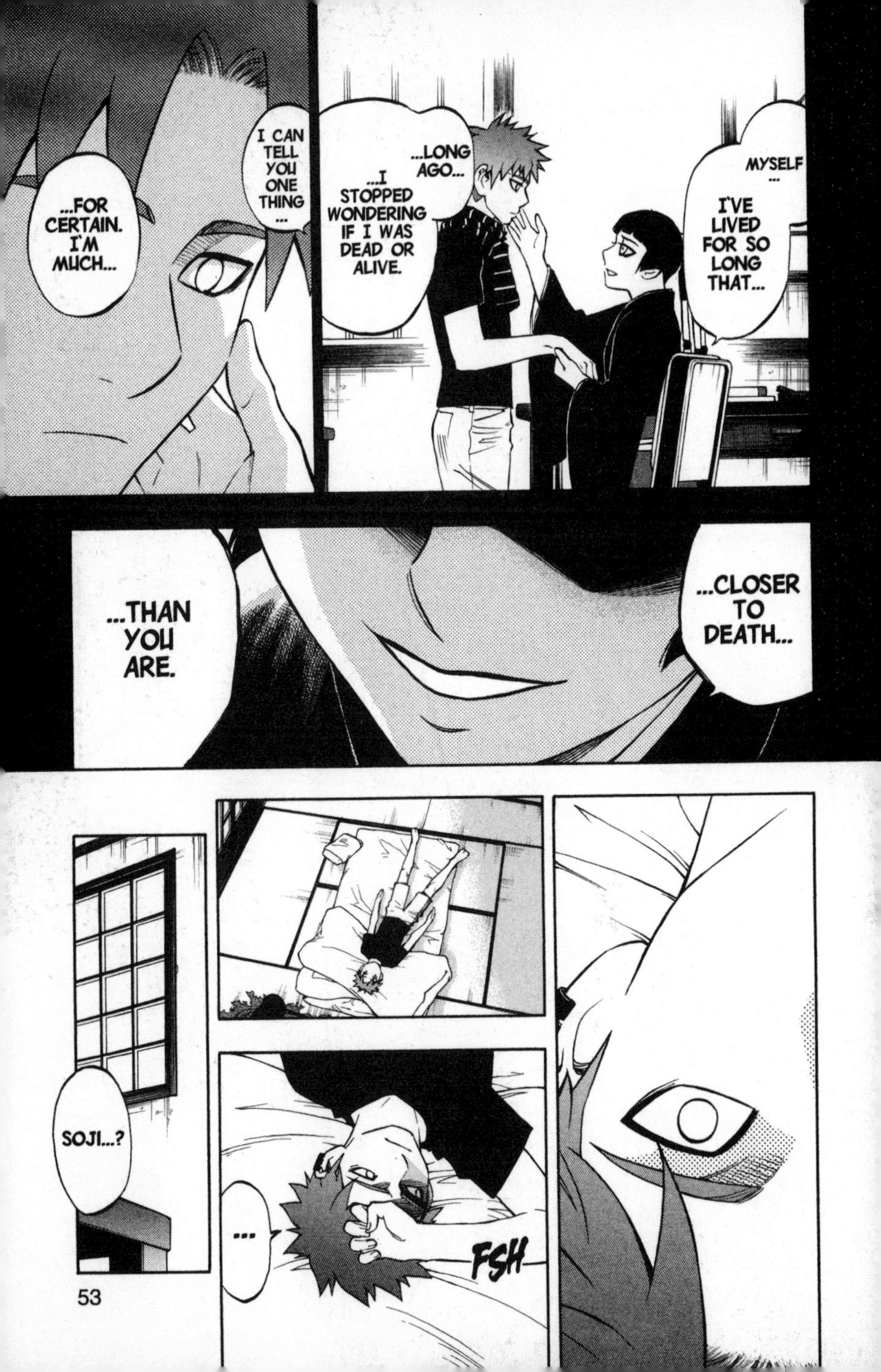
MYSELF...
I'VE LIVED FOR SO LONG THAT...
...LONG AGO...
...I STOPPED WONDERING IF I WAS DEAD OR ALIVE.
I CAN TELL YOU ONE THING...
...FOR CERTAIN. I'M MUCH...
...CLOSER TO DEATH...
...THAN YOU ARE.
FSH
...
SOJI...?

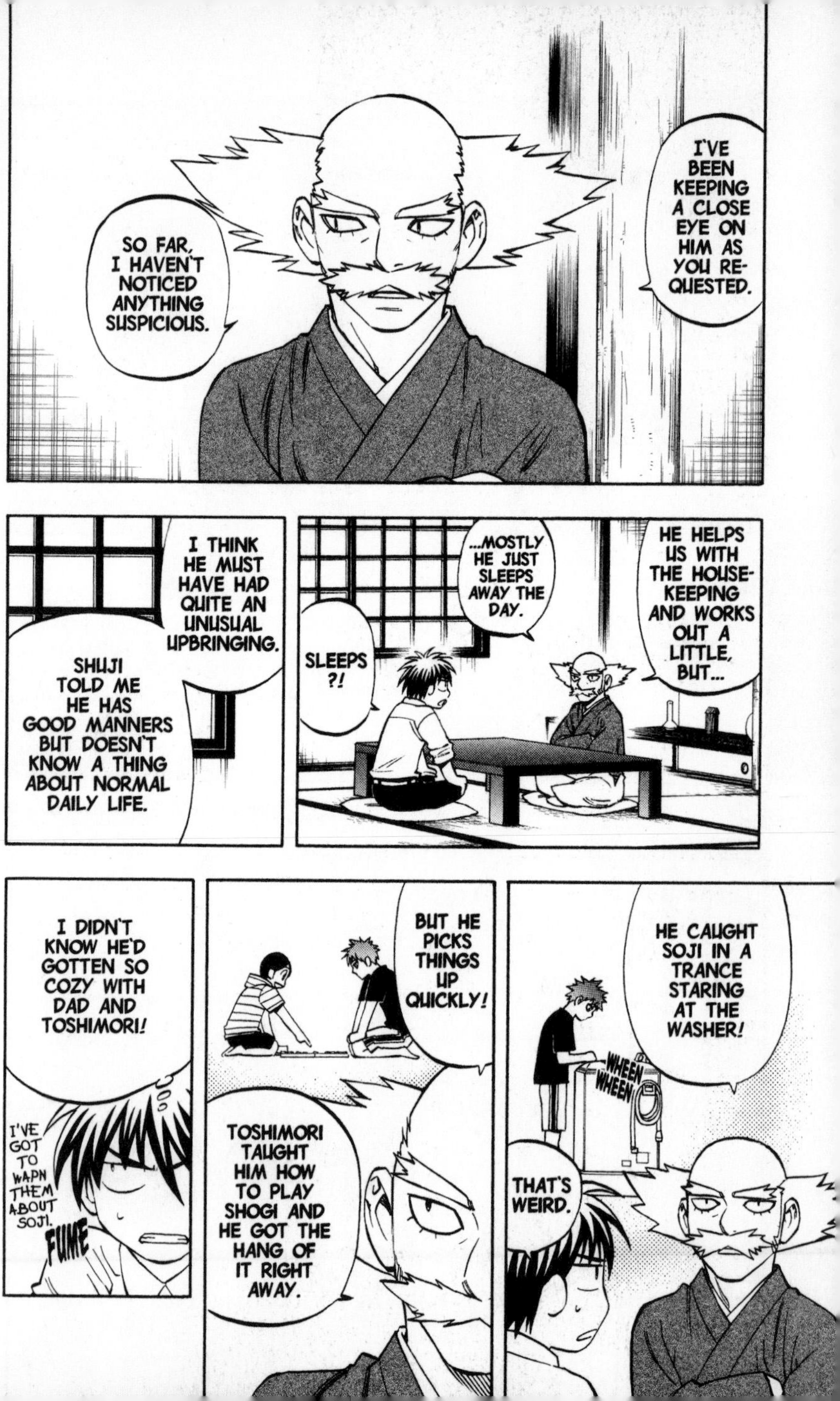
I'VE BEEN KEEPING A CLOSE EYE ON HIM AS YOU RE-QUESTED.
SO FAR, I HAVEN'T NOTICED ANYTHING SUSPICIOUS.
HE HELPS US WITH THE HOUSE-KEEPING AND WORKS OUT A LITTLE, BUT...
...MOSTLY HE JUST SLEEPS AWAY THE DAY.
SLEEPS ?!
I THINK HE MUST HAVE HAD QUITE AN UNUSUAL UPBRINGING.
SHUJI TOLD ME HE HAS GOOD MANNERS BUT DOESN'T KNOW A THING ABOUT NORMAL DAILY LIFE.
HE CAUGHT SOJI IN A TRANCE STARING AT THE WASHER!
WHEEN WHEEN
THAT'S WEIRD.
BUT HE PICKS THINGS UP QUICKLY!
TOSHIMORI TAUGHT HIM HOW TO PLAY SHOGI AND HE GOT THE HANG OF IT RIGHT AWAY.
I DIDN'T KNOW HE'D GOTTEN SO COZY WITH DAD AND TOSHIMORI!
I'VE GOT TO WARN THEM ABOUT SOJI.
FUME

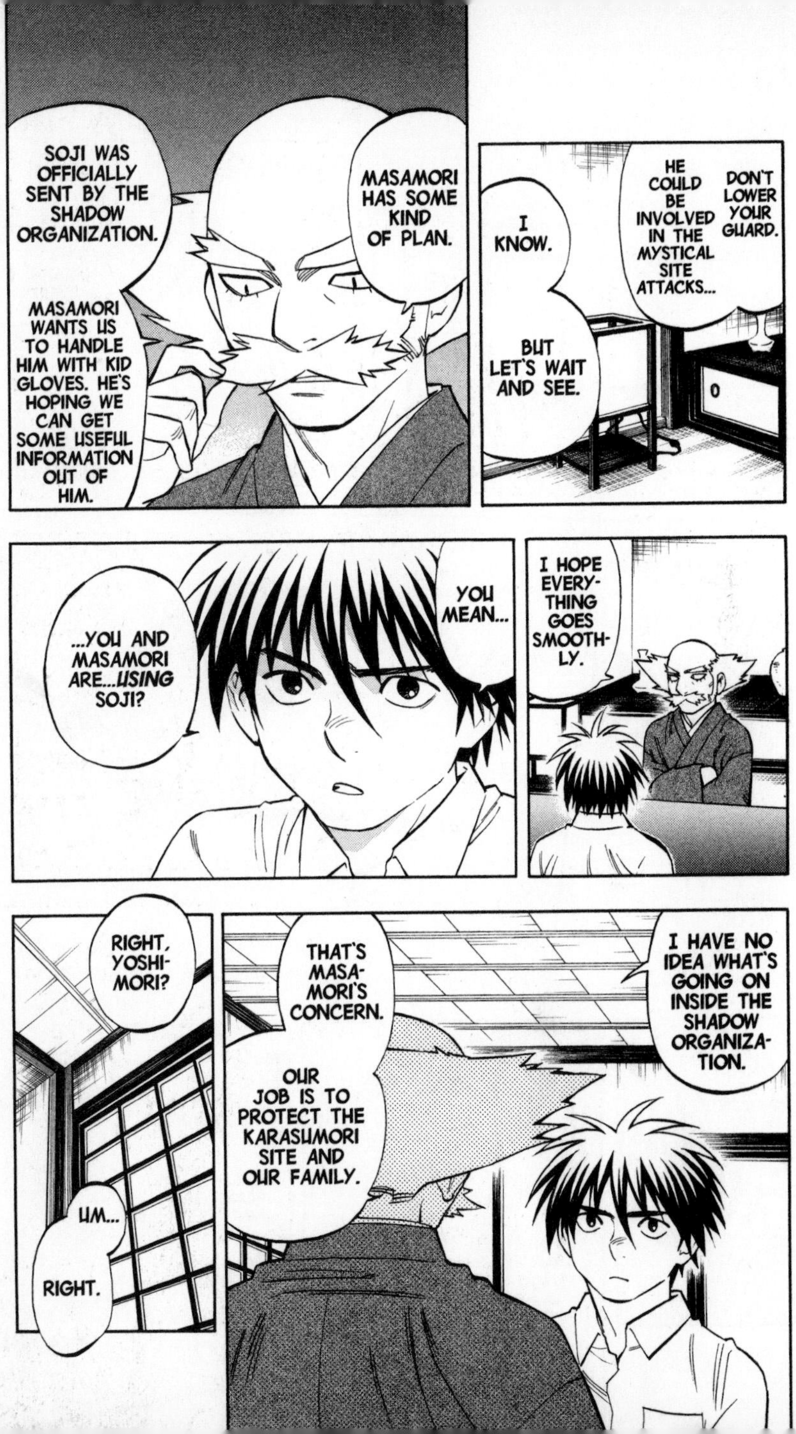
DON'T LOWER YOUR GUARD.
HE COULD BE INVOLVED IN THE MYSTICAL SITE ATTACKS...
I KNOW.
BUT LET'S WAIT AND SEE.
MASAMORI HAS SOME KIND OF PLAN.
SOJI WAS OFFICIALLY SENT BY THE SHADOW ORGANIZATION.
MASAMORI WANTS US TO HANDLE HIM WITH KID GLOVES. HE'S HOPING WE CAN GET SOME USEFUL INFORMATION OUT OF HIM.
I HOPE EVERYTHING GOES SMOOTHLY.
YOU MEAN...
...YOU AND MASAMORI ARE...*USING* SOJI?
I HAVE NO IDEA WHAT'S GOING ON INSIDE THE SHADOW ORGANIZATION.
THAT'S MASAMORI'S CONCERN.
OUR JOB IS TO PROTECT THE KARASUMORI SITE AND OUR FAMILY.
RIGHT, YOSHIMORI?
UM...
RIGHT.

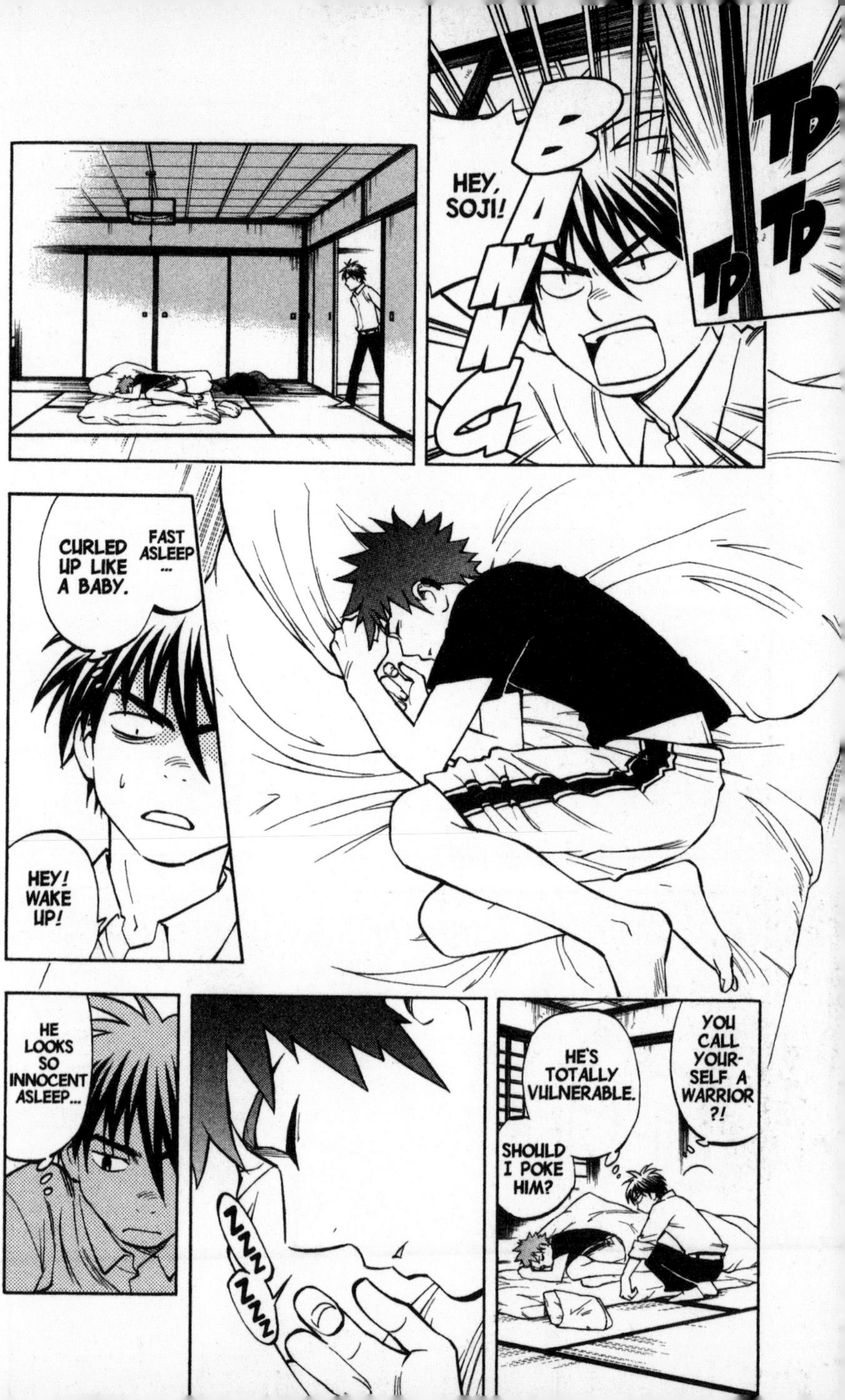
TP TP TP TP
HEY, SOJI!
BANNNG
FAST ASLEEP...
CURLED UP LIKE A BABY.
HEY! WAKE UP!
YOU CALL YOURSELF A WARRIOR?!
HE'S TOTALLY VULNERABLE.
SHOULD I POKE HIM?
ZZZ ZZZ
HE LOOKS SO INNOCENT ASLEEP...

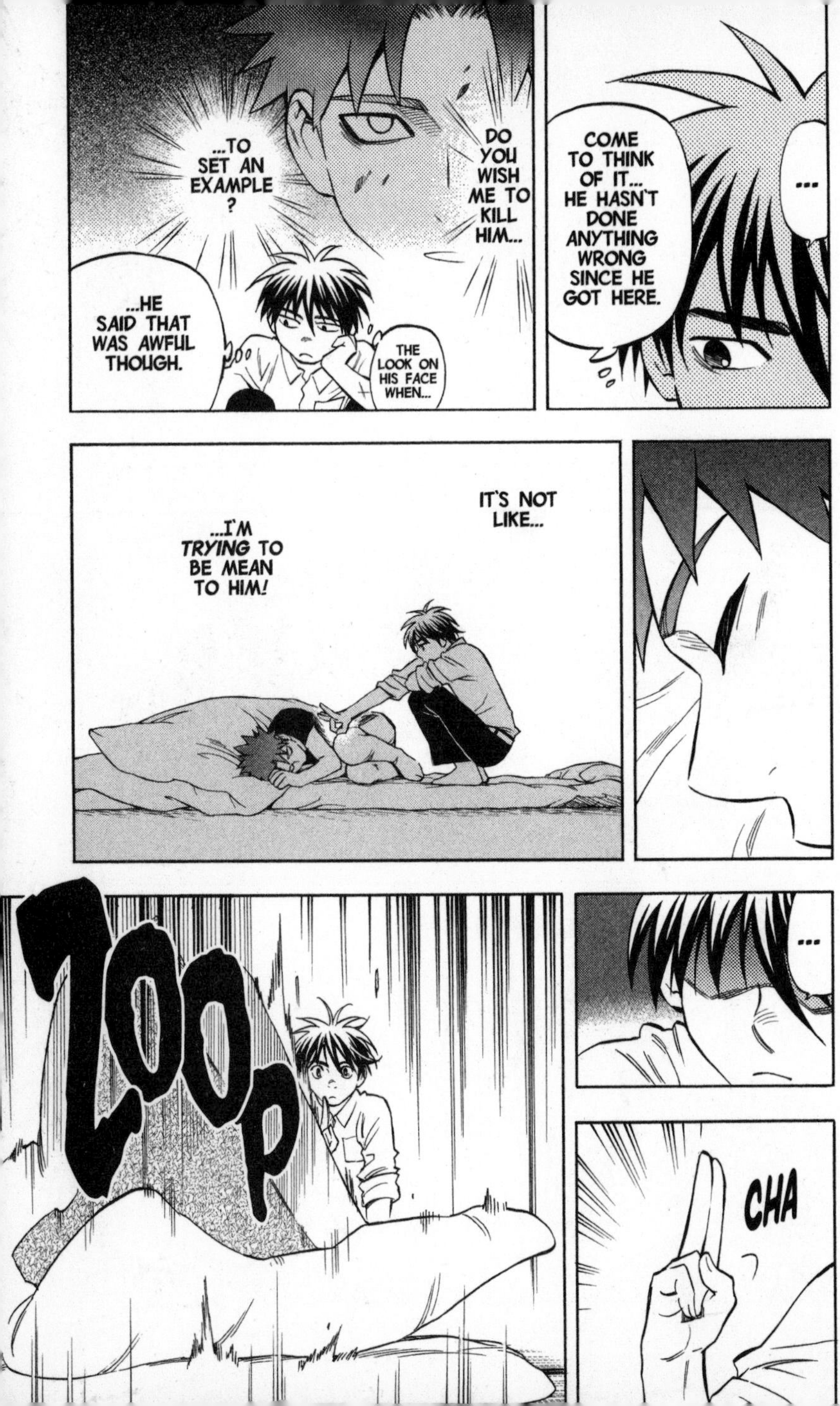
...
COME TO THINK OF IT... HE HASN'T DONE ANYTHING WRONG SINCE HE GOT HERE.
DO YOU WISH ME TO KILL HIM...
...TO SET AN EXAMPLE ?
THE LOOK ON HIS FACE WHEN...
...HE SAID THAT WAS AWFUL THOUGH.
IT'S NOT LIKE...
...I'M *TRYING* TO BE MEAN TO HIM!
...
CHA
ZOOP

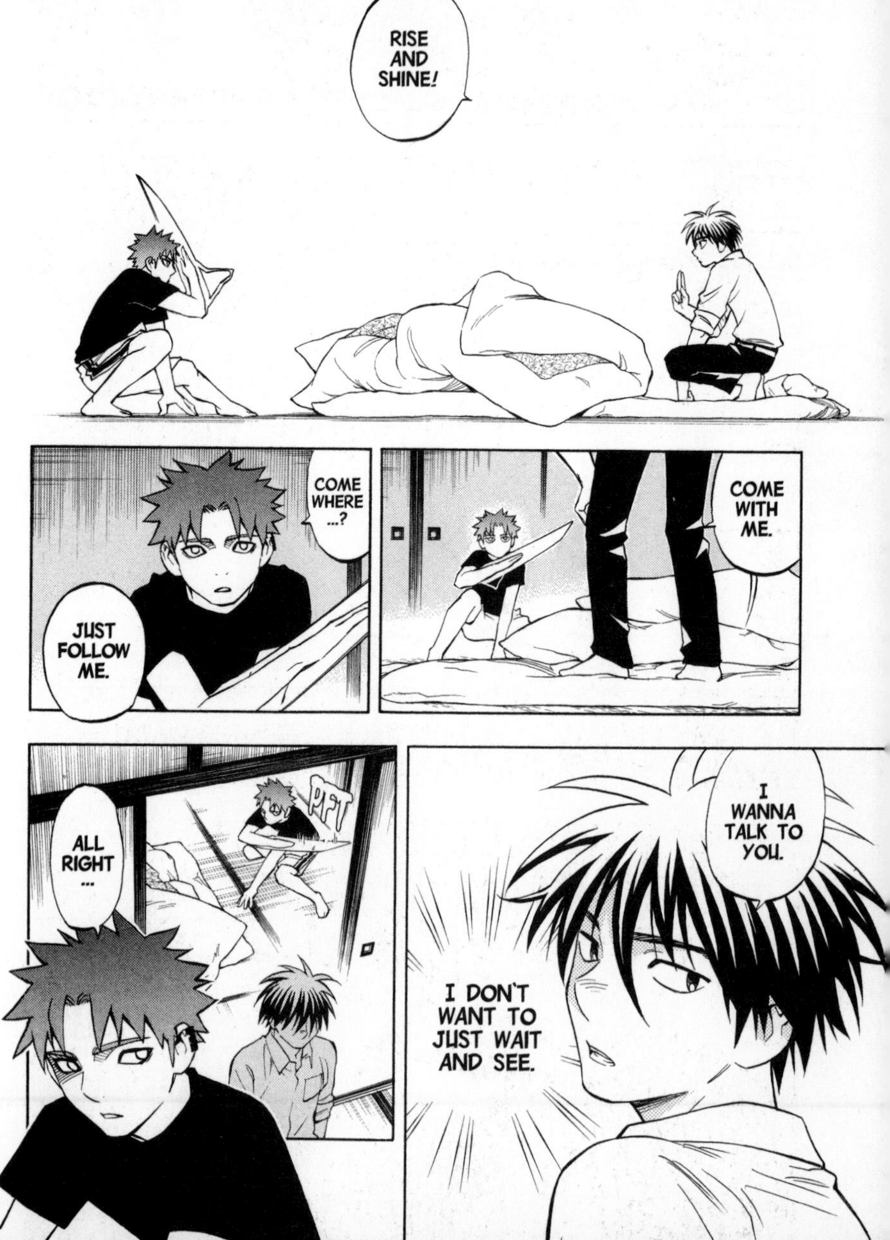
RISE AND SHINE!
COME WITH ME.
COME WHERE ...?
JUST FOLLOW ME.
I WANNA TALK TO YOU.
I DON'T WANT TO JUST WAIT AND SEE.
PFT
ALL RIGHT ...

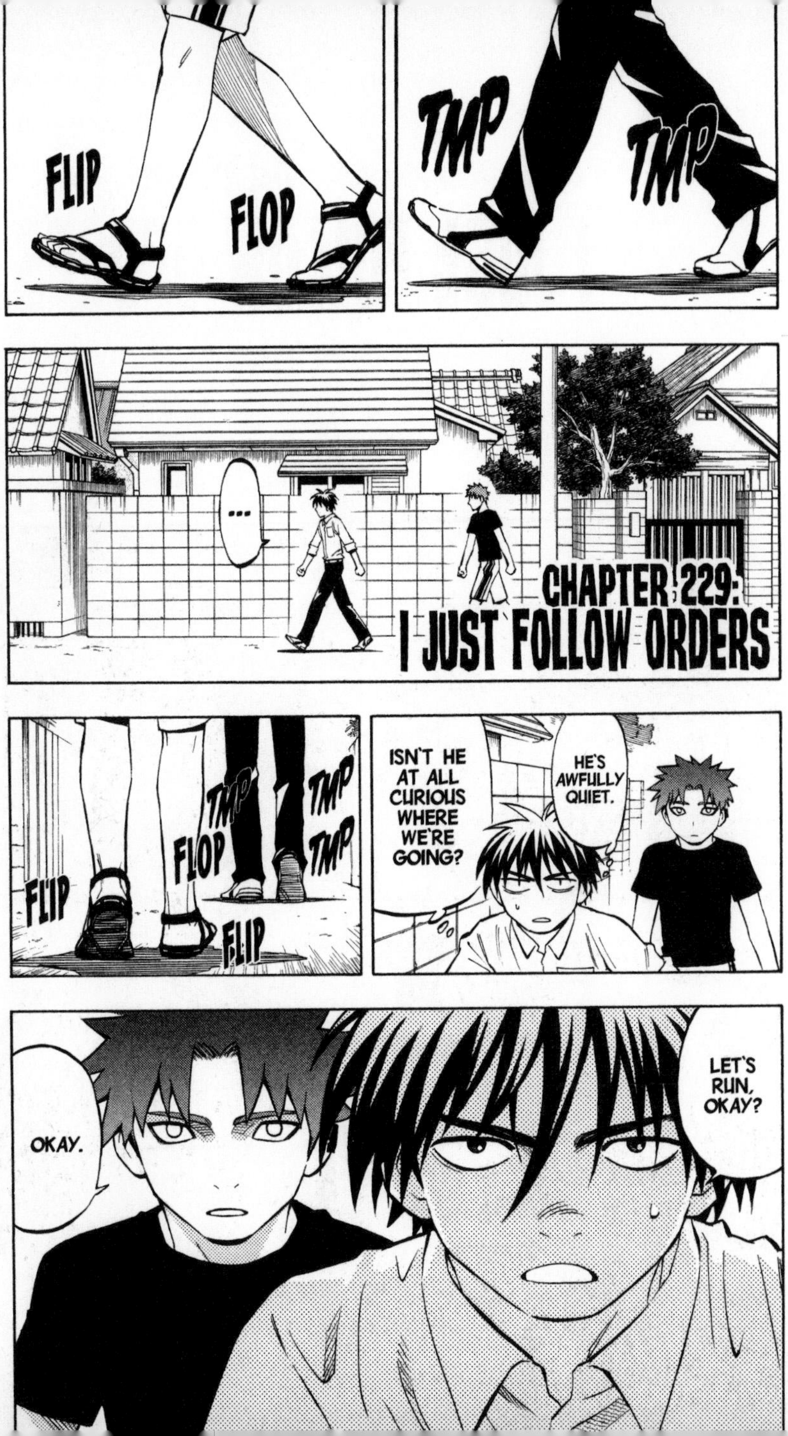
TMP
TMP
FLIP
FLOP
...
CHAPTER 229:
I JUST FOLLOW ORDERS
HE'S AWFULLY QUIET.
ISN'T HE AT ALL CURIOUS WHERE WE'RE GOING?
TMP
TMP
TMP
FLOP
FLIP
FLIP
LET'S RUN, OKAY?
OKAY.

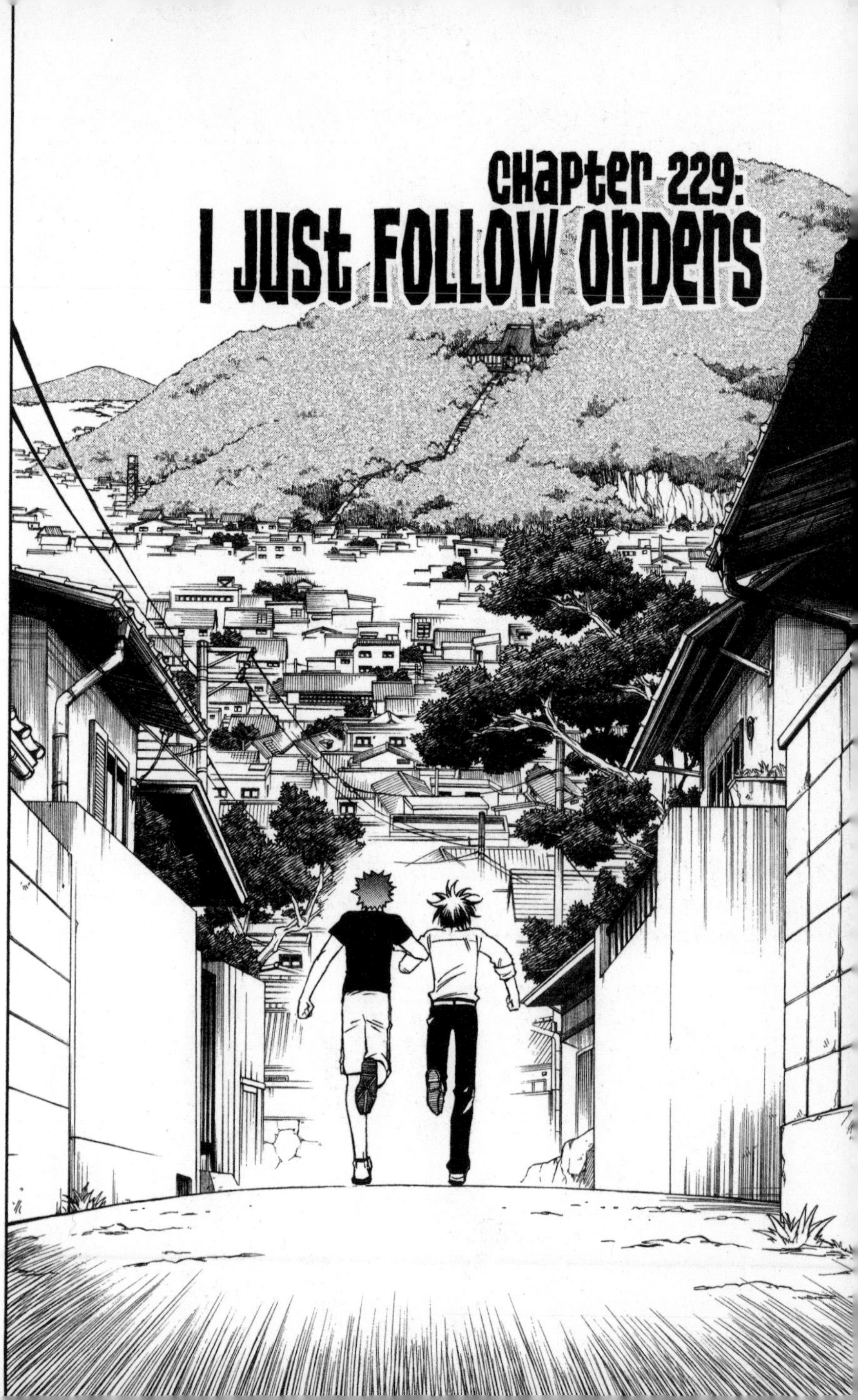
Chapter 229:
I Just Follow Orders

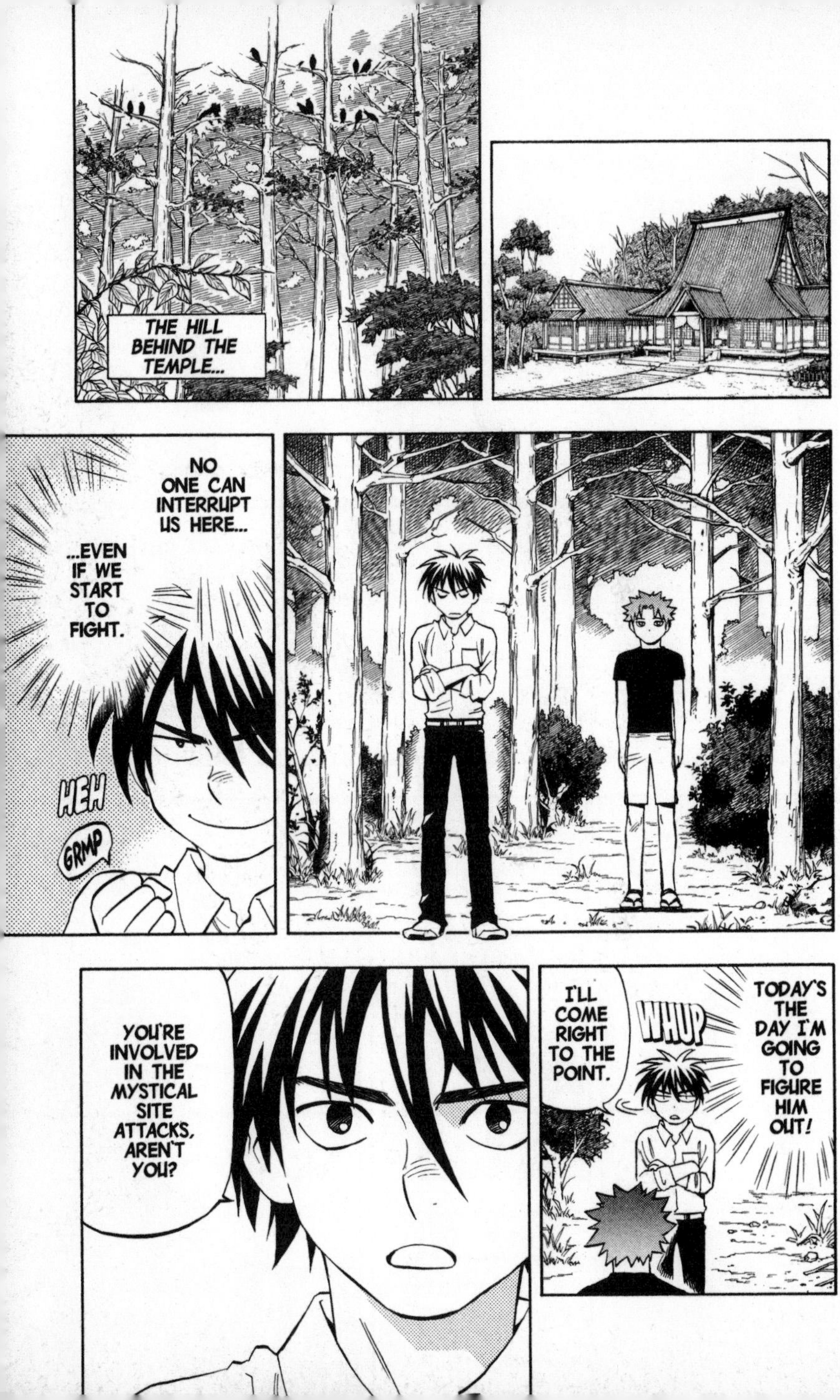
THE HILL BEHIND THE TEMPLE...
NO ONE CAN INTERRUPT US HERE...
...EVEN IF WE START TO FIGHT.
HEH
GRMP
TODAY'S THE DAY I'M GOING TO FIGURE HIM OUT!
WHUP
I'LL COME RIGHT TO THE POINT.
YOU'RE INVOLVED IN THE MYSTICAL SITE ATTACKS, AREN'T YOU?

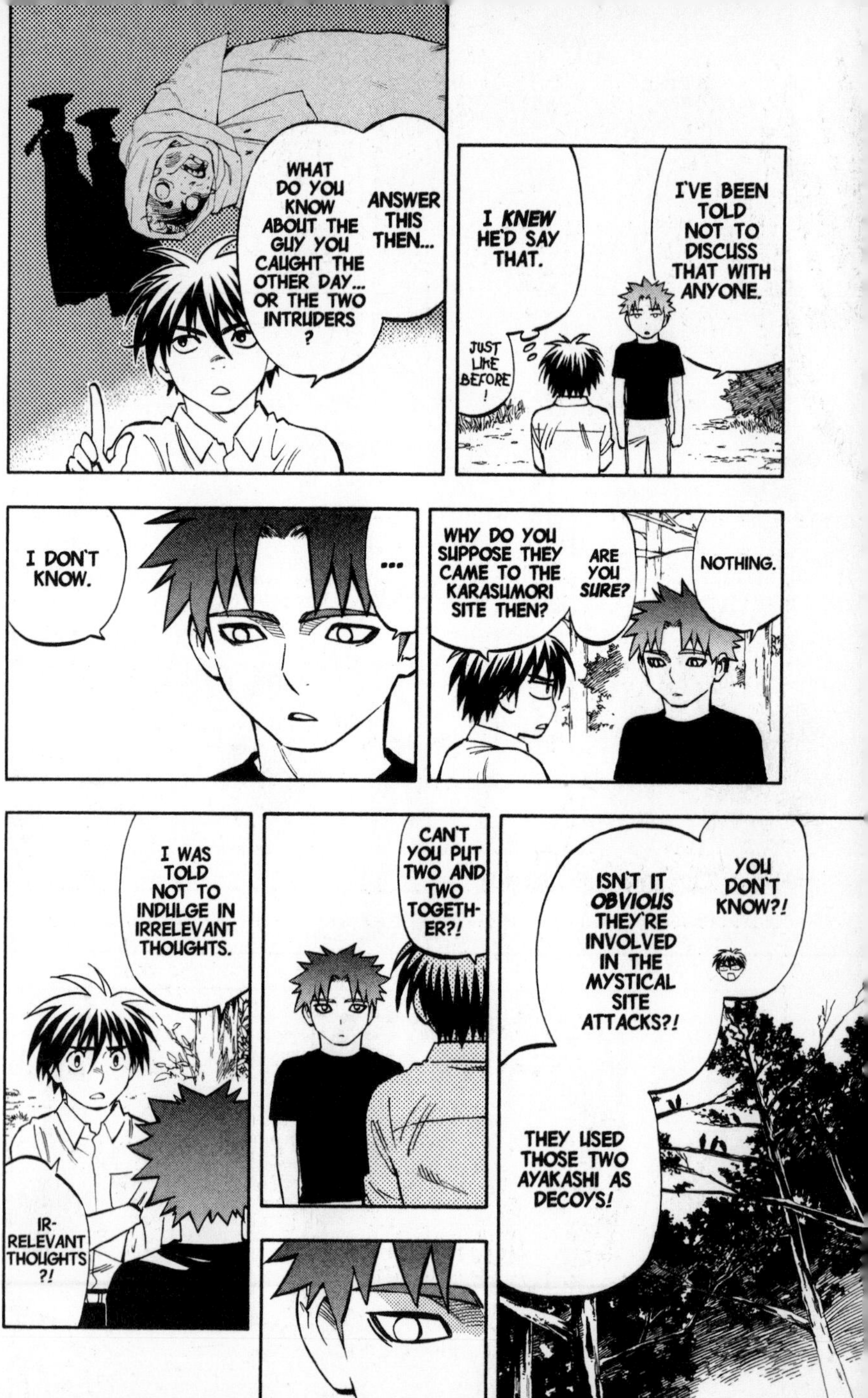
I'VE BEEN TOLD NOT TO DISCUSS THAT WITH ANYONE.
I *KNEW* HE'D SAY THAT.
JUST LIKE BEFORE!
ANSWER THIS THEN...
WHAT DO YOU KNOW ABOUT THE GUY YOU CAUGHT THE OTHER DAY... OR THE TWO INTRUDERS?
NOTHING.
ARE YOU *SURE?*
WHY DO YOU SUPPOSE THEY CAME TO THE KARASUMORI SITE THEN?
...
I DON'T KNOW.
YOU DON'T KNOW?!
ISN'T IT *OBVIOUS* THEY'RE INVOLVED IN THE MYSTICAL SITE ATTACKS?!
THEY USED THOSE TWO AYAKASHI AS DECOYS!
CAN'T YOU PUT TWO AND TWO TOGETHER?!
I WAS TOLD NOT TO INDULGE IN IRRELEVANT THOUGHTS.
IRRELEVANT THOUGHTS?!

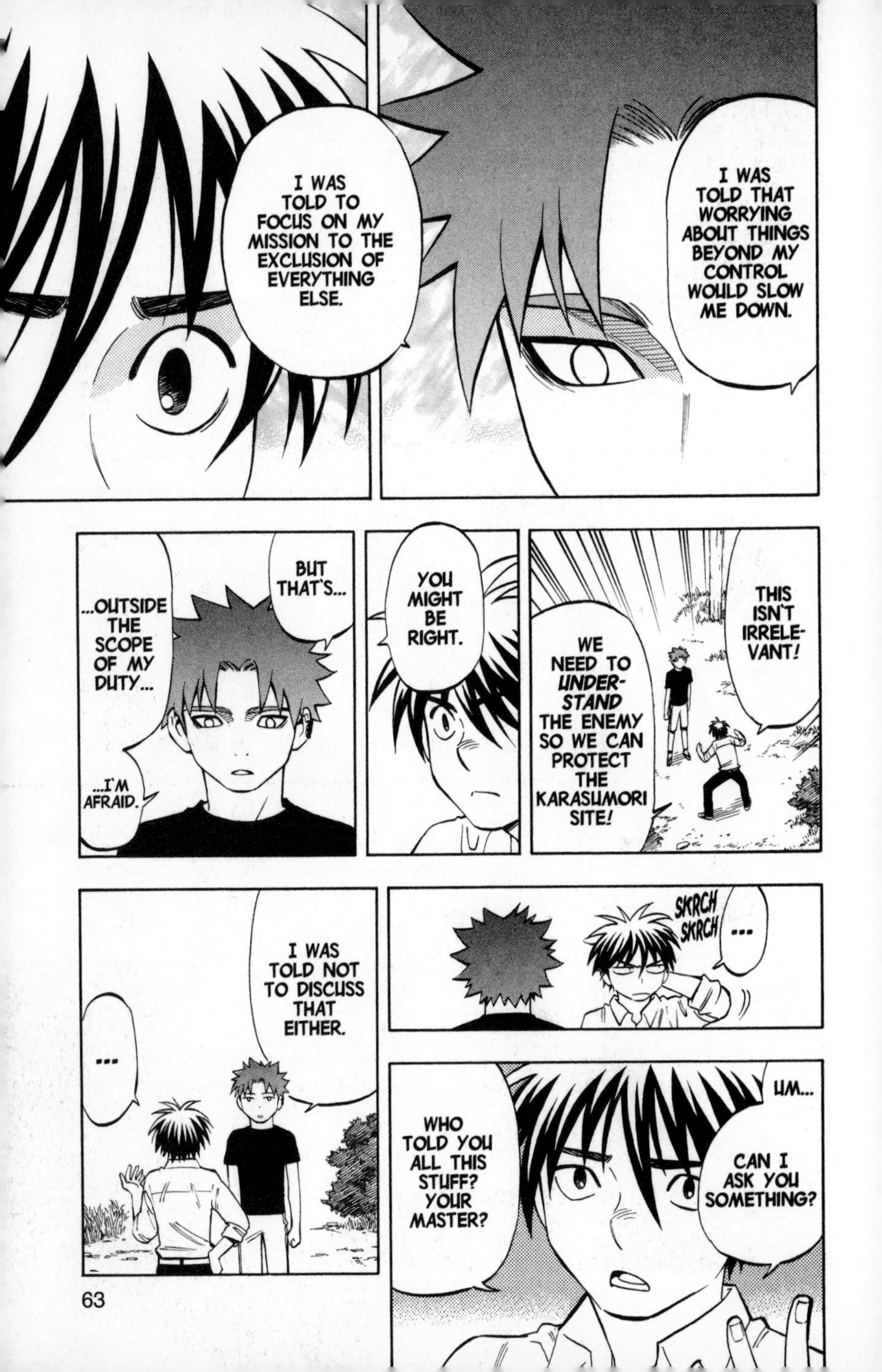
I WAS TOLD THAT WORRYING ABOUT THINGS BEYOND MY CONTROL WOULD SLOW ME DOWN.
I WAS TOLD TO FOCUS ON MY MISSION TO THE EXCLUSION OF EVERYTHING ELSE.
THIS ISN'T IRRELEVANT!
WE NEED TO *UNDERSTAND* THE ENEMY SO WE CAN PROTECT THE KARASUMORI SITE!
YOU MIGHT BE RIGHT.
BUT THAT'S...
...OUTSIDE THE SCOPE OF MY DUTY...
...I'M AFRAID.
SKRCH SKRCH
...
UM...
CAN I ASK YOU SOMETHING?
WHO TOLD YOU ALL THIS STUFF? YOUR MASTER?
I WAS TOLD NOT TO DISCUSS THAT EITHER.
...

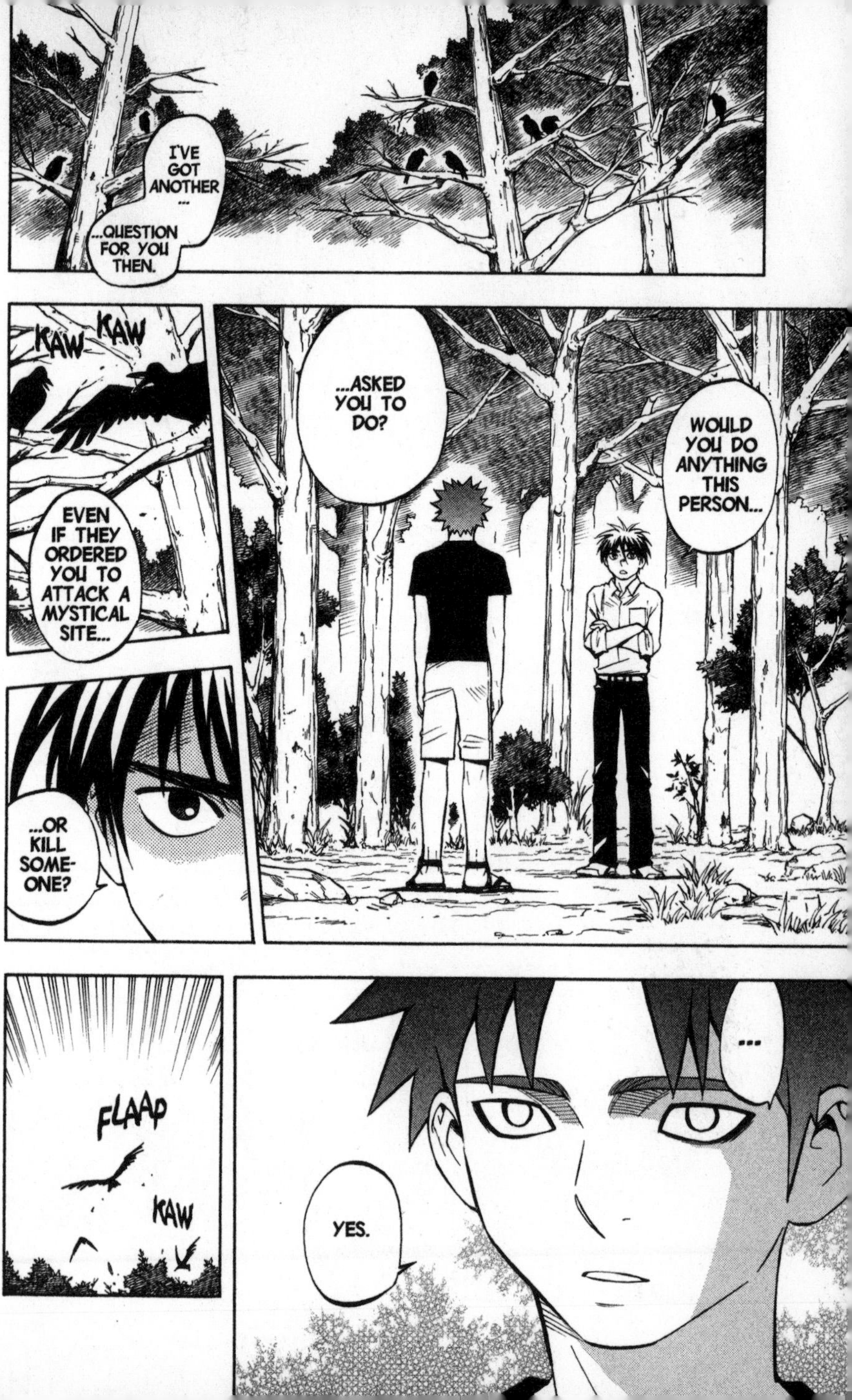
I'VE GOT ANOTHER ...
...QUESTION FOR YOU THEN.
WOULD YOU DO ANYTHING THIS PERSON...
...ASKED YOU TO DO?
KAW KAW
EVEN IF THEY ORDERED YOU TO ATTACK A MYSTICAL SITE...
...OR KILL SOME-ONE?
...
YES.
FLAAP
KAW

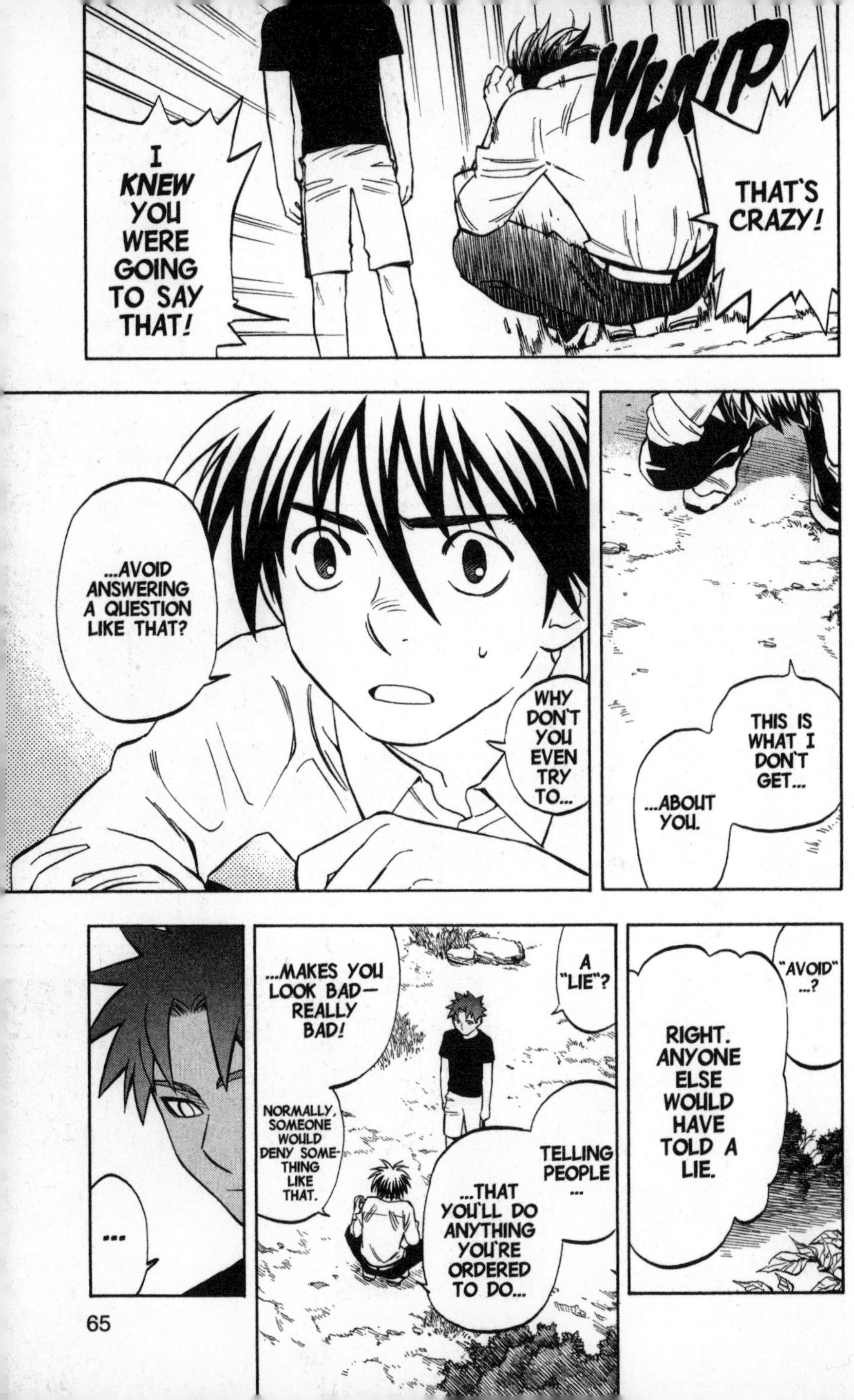
WHAP
THAT'S CRAZY!
I KNEW YOU WERE GOING TO SAY THAT!
THIS IS WHAT I DON'T GET...
...ABOUT YOU.
WHY DON'T YOU EVEN TRY TO...
...AVOID ANSWERING A QUESTION LIKE THAT?
"AVOID"...?
RIGHT. ANYONE ELSE WOULD HAVE TOLD A LIE.
A "LIE"?
TELLING PEOPLE...
...THAT YOU'LL DO ANYTHING YOU'RE ORDERED TO DO...
...MAKES YOU LOOK BAD—REALLY BAD!
NORMALLY, SOMEONE WOULD DENY SOME-THING LIKE THAT.
...

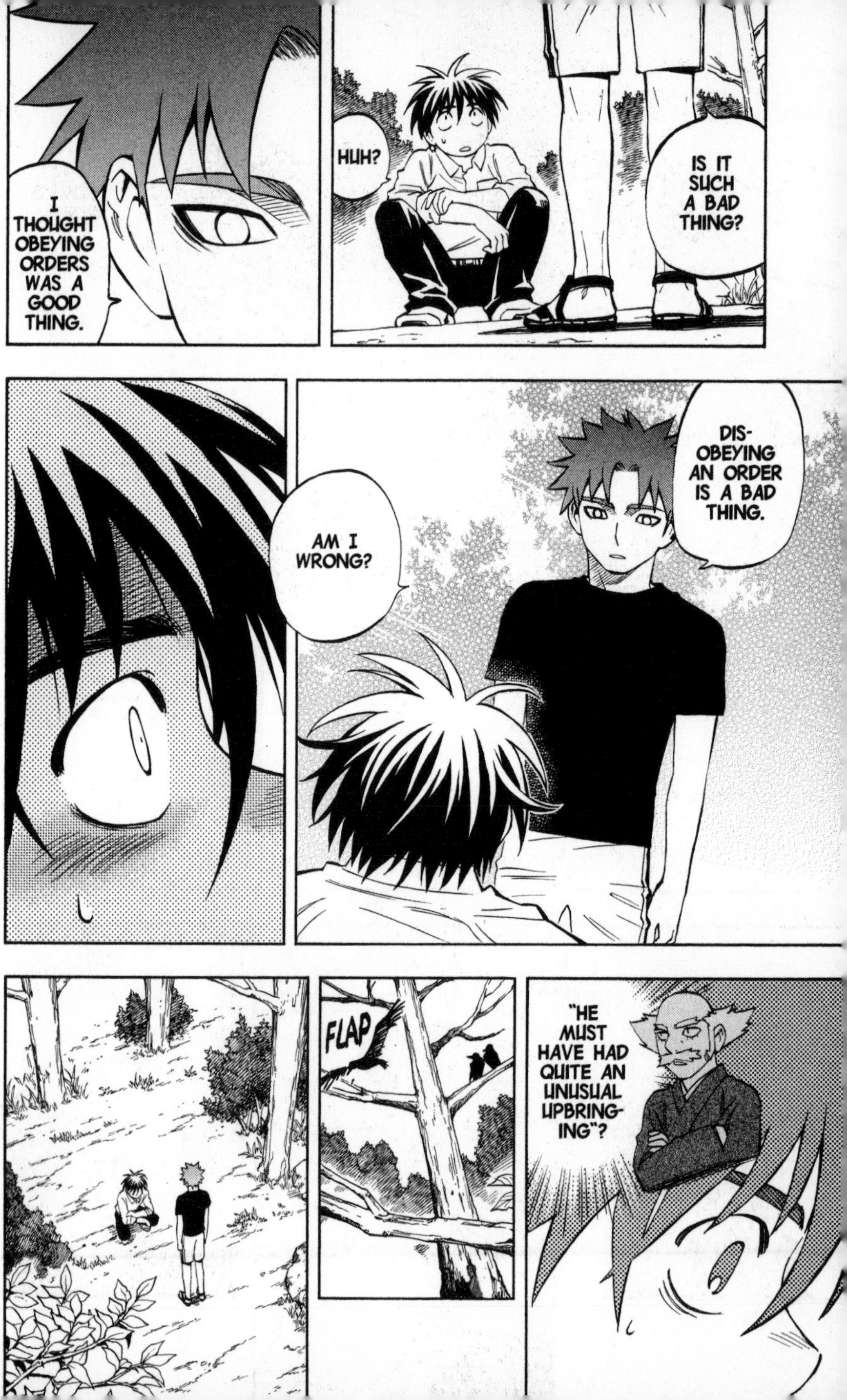
IS IT SUCH A BAD THING?
HUH?
I THOUGHT OBEYING ORDERS WAS A GOOD THING.
DIS-OBEYING AN ORDER IS A BAD THING.
AM I WRONG?
"HE MUST HAVE HAD QUITE AN UNUSUAL UPBRING-ING"?
FLAP

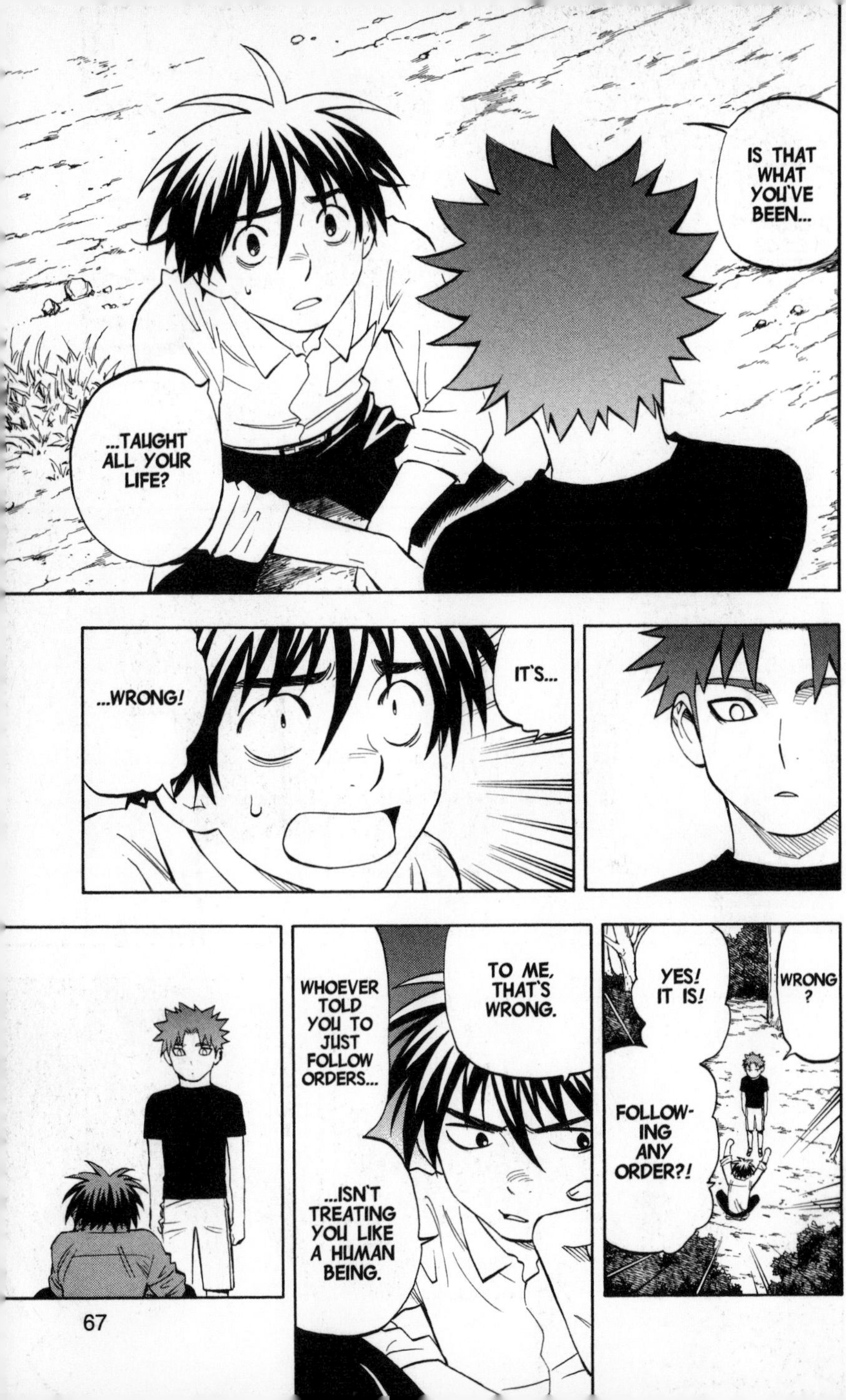
IS THAT WHAT YOU'VE BEEN...
...TAUGHT ALL YOUR LIFE?
IT'S...
...WRONG!
WRONG?
YES! IT IS!
FOLLOW-ING ANY ORDER?!
TO ME, THAT'S WRONG.
WHOEVER TOLD YOU TO JUST FOLLOW ORDERS...
...ISN'T TREATING YOU LIKE A HUMAN BEING.

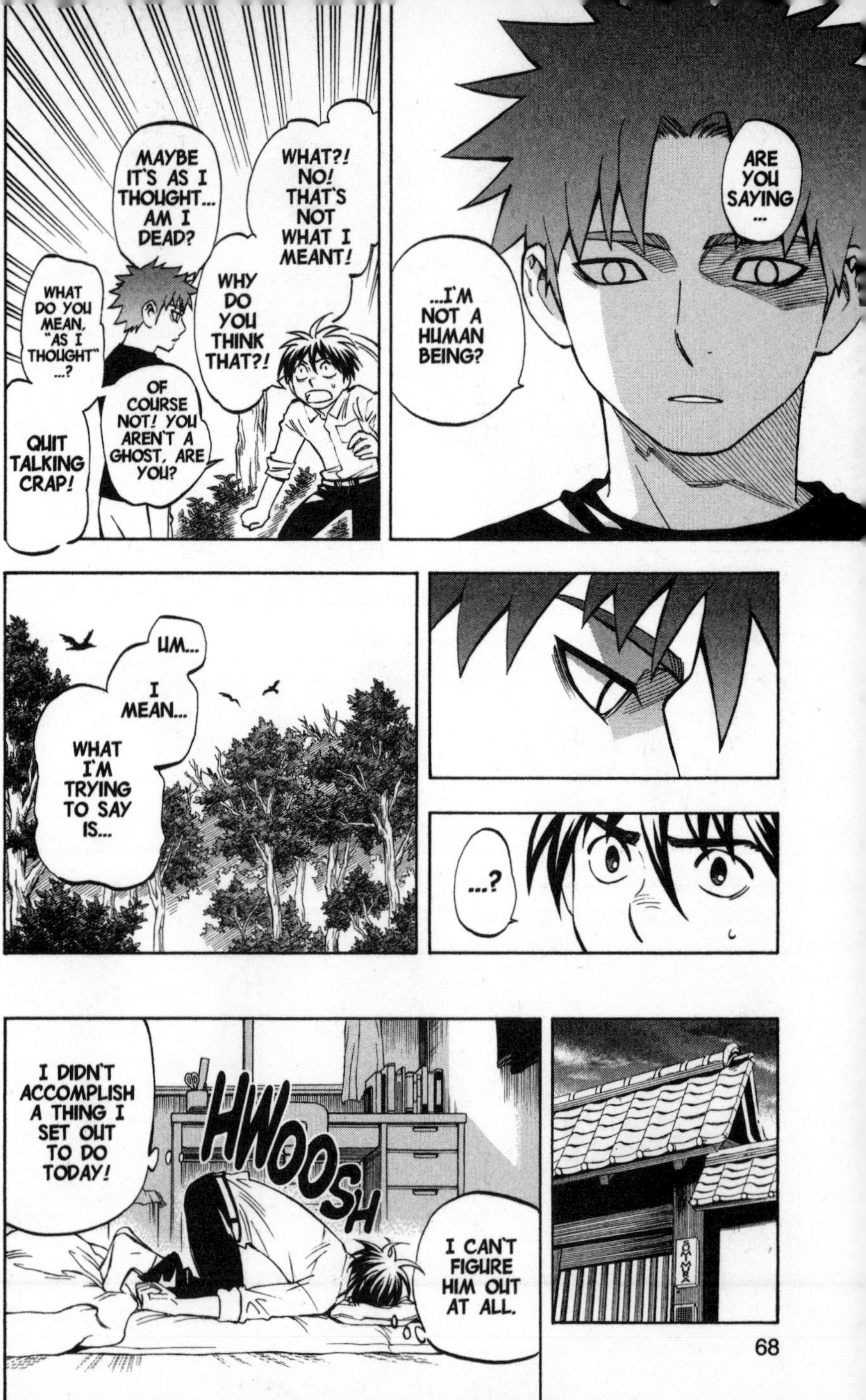
ARE YOU SAYING ...
...I'M NOT A HUMAN BEING?
WHAT?! NO! THAT'S NOT WHAT I MEANT!
MAYBE IT'S AS I THOUGHT... AM I DEAD?
WHY DO YOU THINK THAT?!
WHAT DO YOU MEAN, "AS I THOUGHT" ...?
OF COURSE NOT! YOU AREN'T A GHOST, ARE YOU?
QUIT TALKING CRAP!
...?
UM...
I MEAN...
WHAT I'M TRYING TO SAY IS...
I DIDN'T ACCOMPLISH A THING I SET OUT TO DO TODAY!
HWOOSH
I CAN'T FIGURE HIM OUT AT ALL.

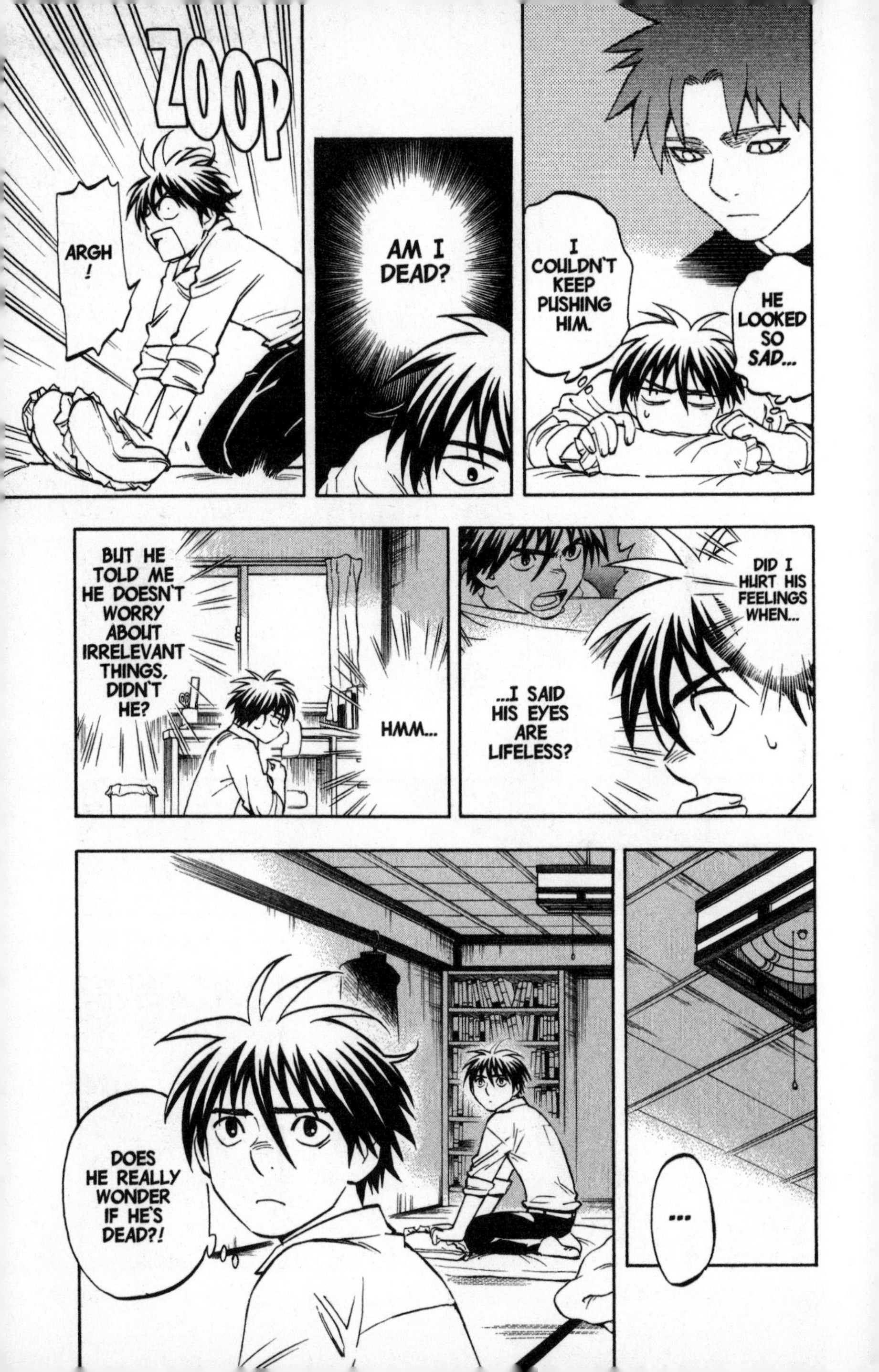
HE LOOKED SO SAD...
I COULDN'T KEEP PUSHING HIM.
AM I DEAD?
ZOOP
ARGH!
DID I HURT HIS FEELINGS WHEN...
...I SAID HIS EYES ARE LIFELESS?
HMM...
BUT HE TOLD ME HE DOESN'T WORRY ABOUT IRRELEVANT THINGS, DIDN'T HE?
...
DOES HE REALLY WONDER IF HE'S DEAD?!

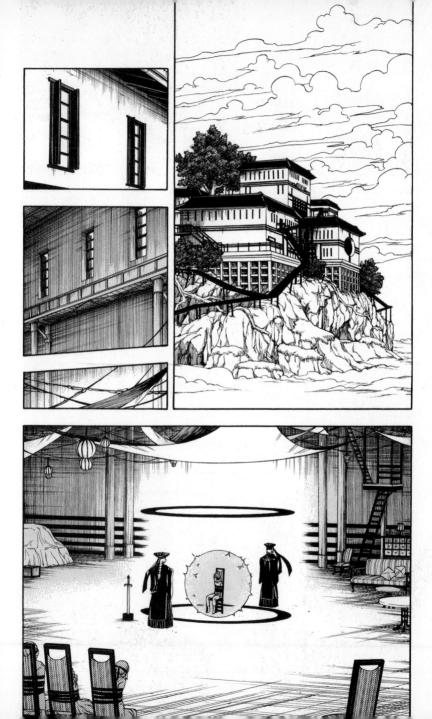

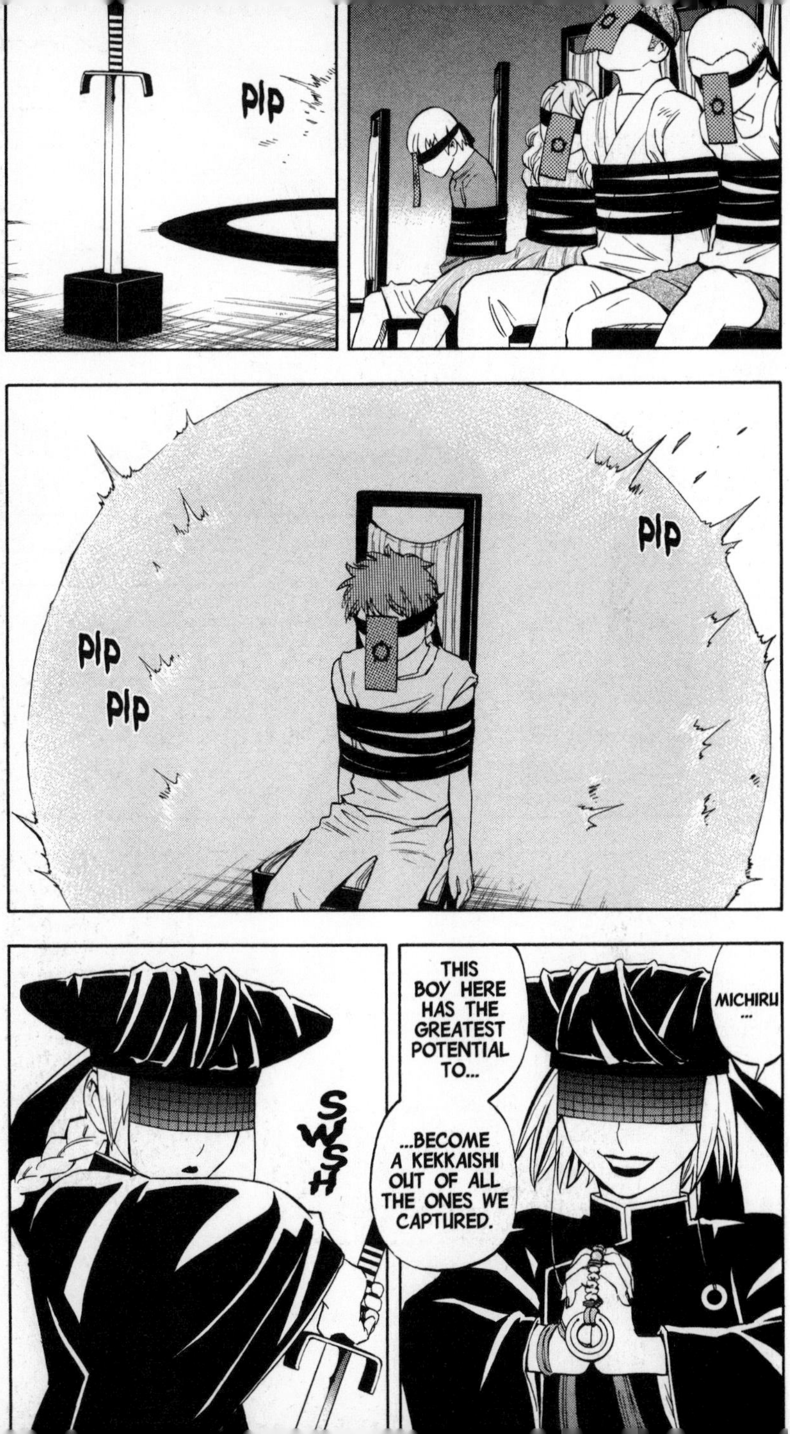
PIP
PIP
PIP
PIP
MICHIRU ...
THIS BOY HERE HAS THE GREATEST POTENTIAL TO...
...BECOME A KEKKAISHI OUT OF ALL THE ONES WE CAPTURED.
SWSH

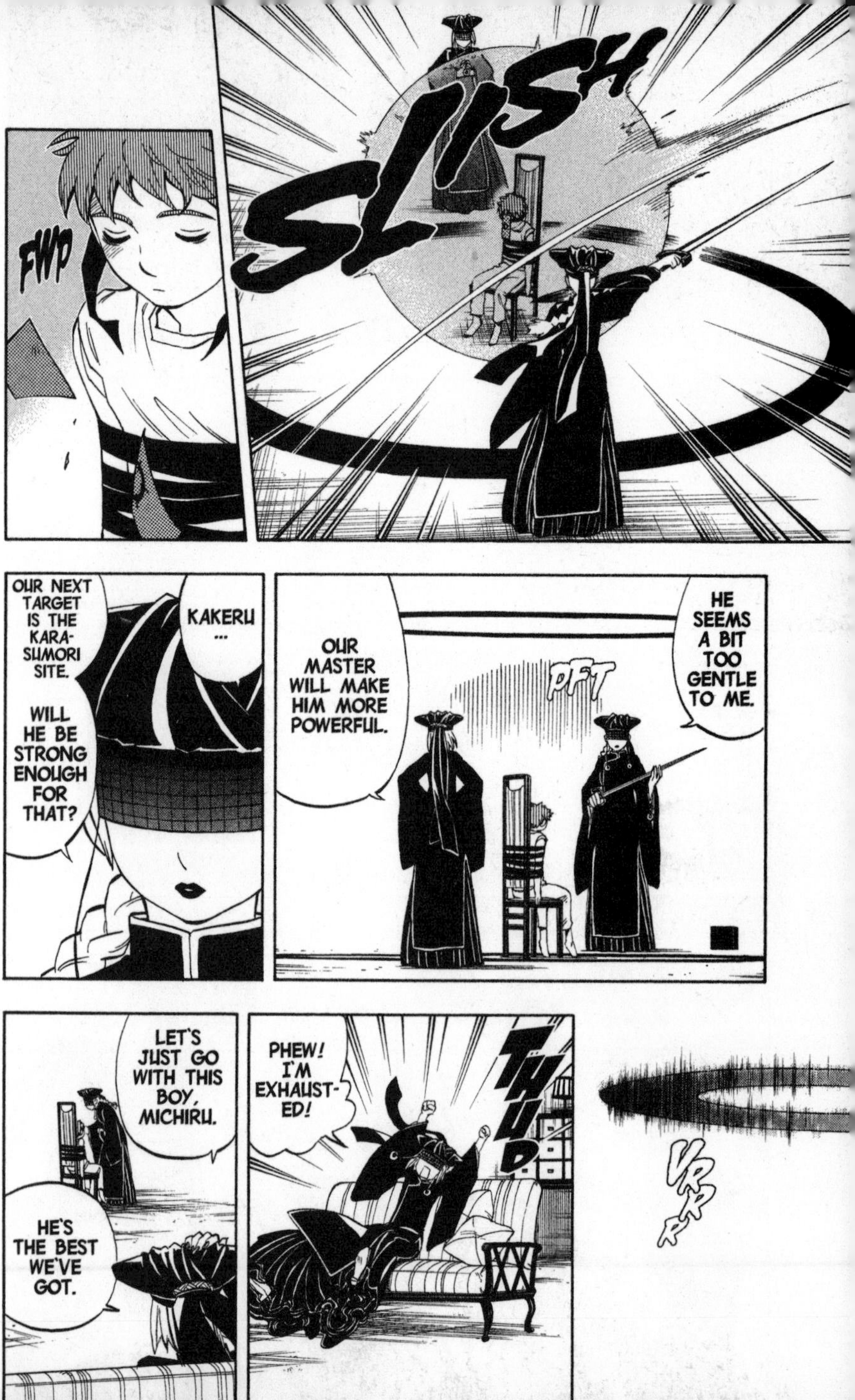
SLISH
FWP
HE SEEMS A BIT TOO GENTLE TO ME.
PFT
OUR MASTER WILL MAKE HIM MORE POWERFUL.
KAKERU ...
OUR NEXT TARGET IS THE KARA-SUMORI SITE.
WILL HE BE STRONG ENOUGH FOR THAT?
VRRR
THUD
PHEW! I'M EXHAUST-ED!
LET'S JUST GO WITH THIS BOY, MICHIRU.
HE'S THE BEST WE'VE GOT.

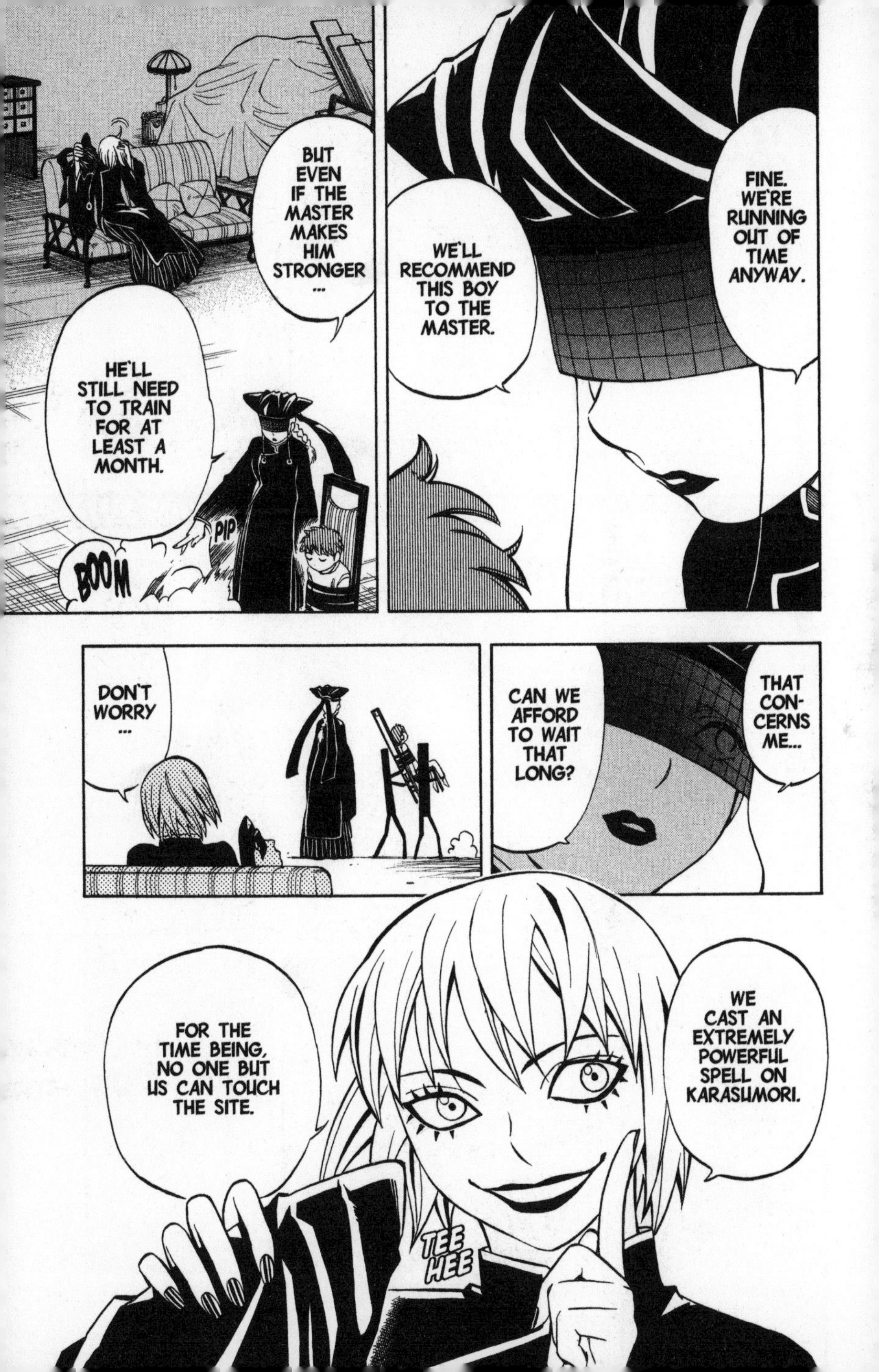
FINE. WE'RE RUNNING OUT OF TIME ANYWAY.
WE'LL RECOMMEND THIS BOY TO THE MASTER.
BUT EVEN IF THE MASTER MAKES HIM STRONGER...
HE'LL STILL NEED TO TRAIN FOR AT LEAST A MONTH.
PIP
BOOM
THAT CONCERNS ME...
CAN WE AFFORD TO WAIT THAT LONG?
DON'T WORRY...
WE CAST AN EXTREMELY POWERFUL SPELL ON KARASUMORI.
FOR THE TIME BEING, NO ONE BUT US CAN TOUCH THE SITE.
TEE HEE

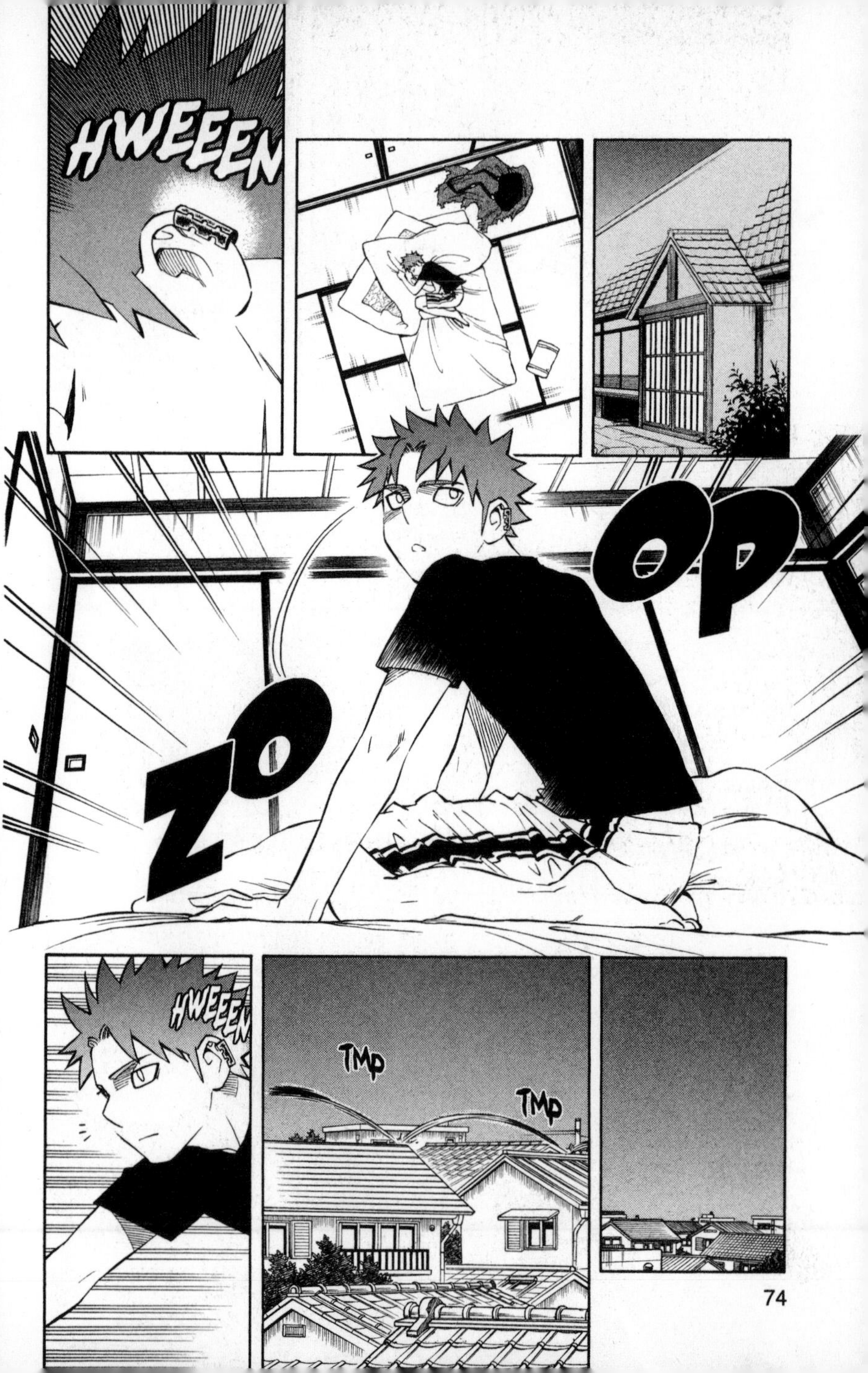
HWEEEN
ZOOP
TMP
TMP
HWEEEN

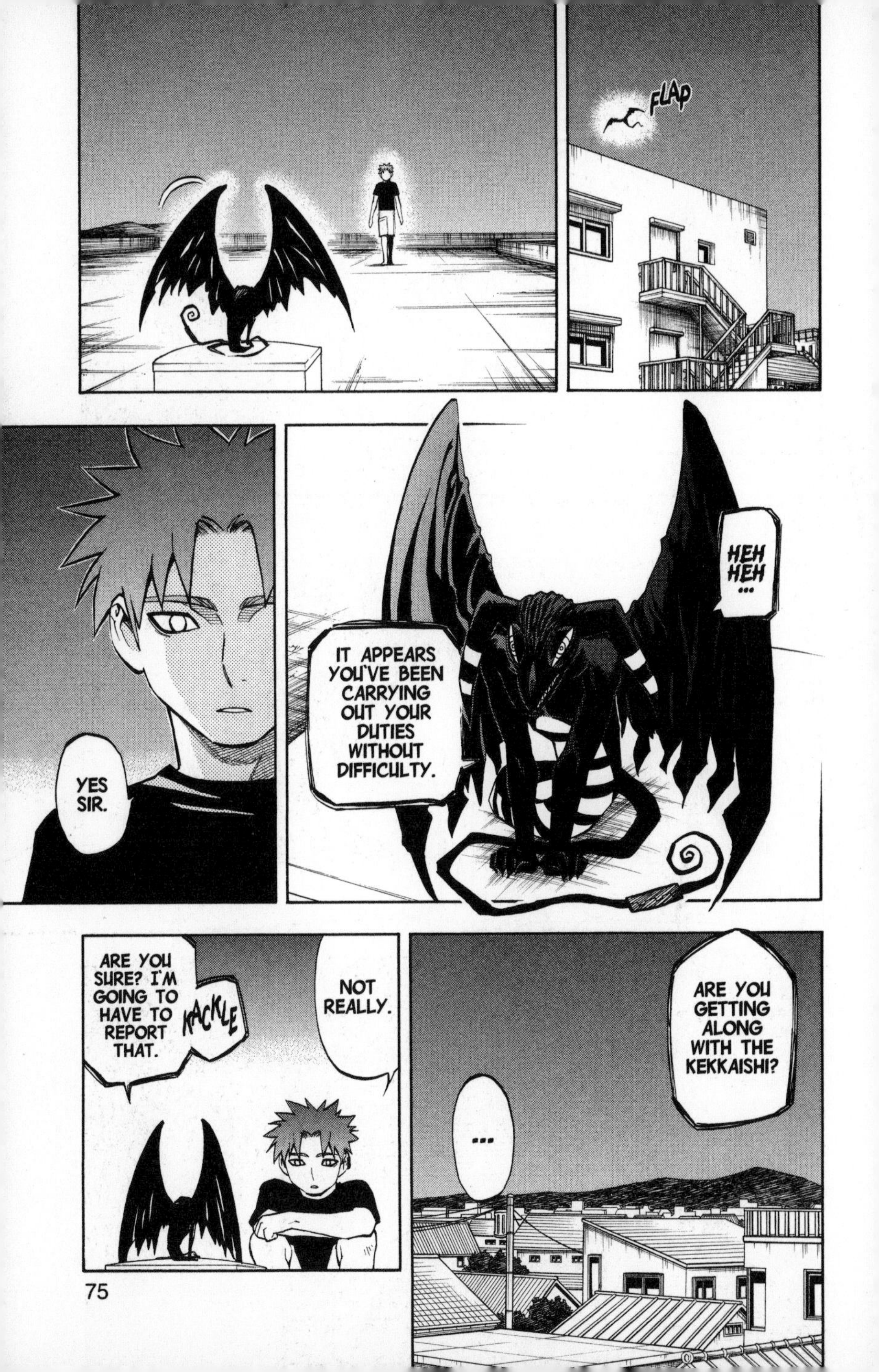
FLAP
HEH HEH...
IT APPEARS YOU'VE BEEN CARRYING OUT YOUR DUTIES WITHOUT DIFFICULTY.
YES SIR.
ARE YOU GETTING ALONG WITH THE KEKKAISHI?
...
NOT REALLY.
KACKLE
ARE YOU SURE? I'M GOING TO HAVE TO REPORT THAT.

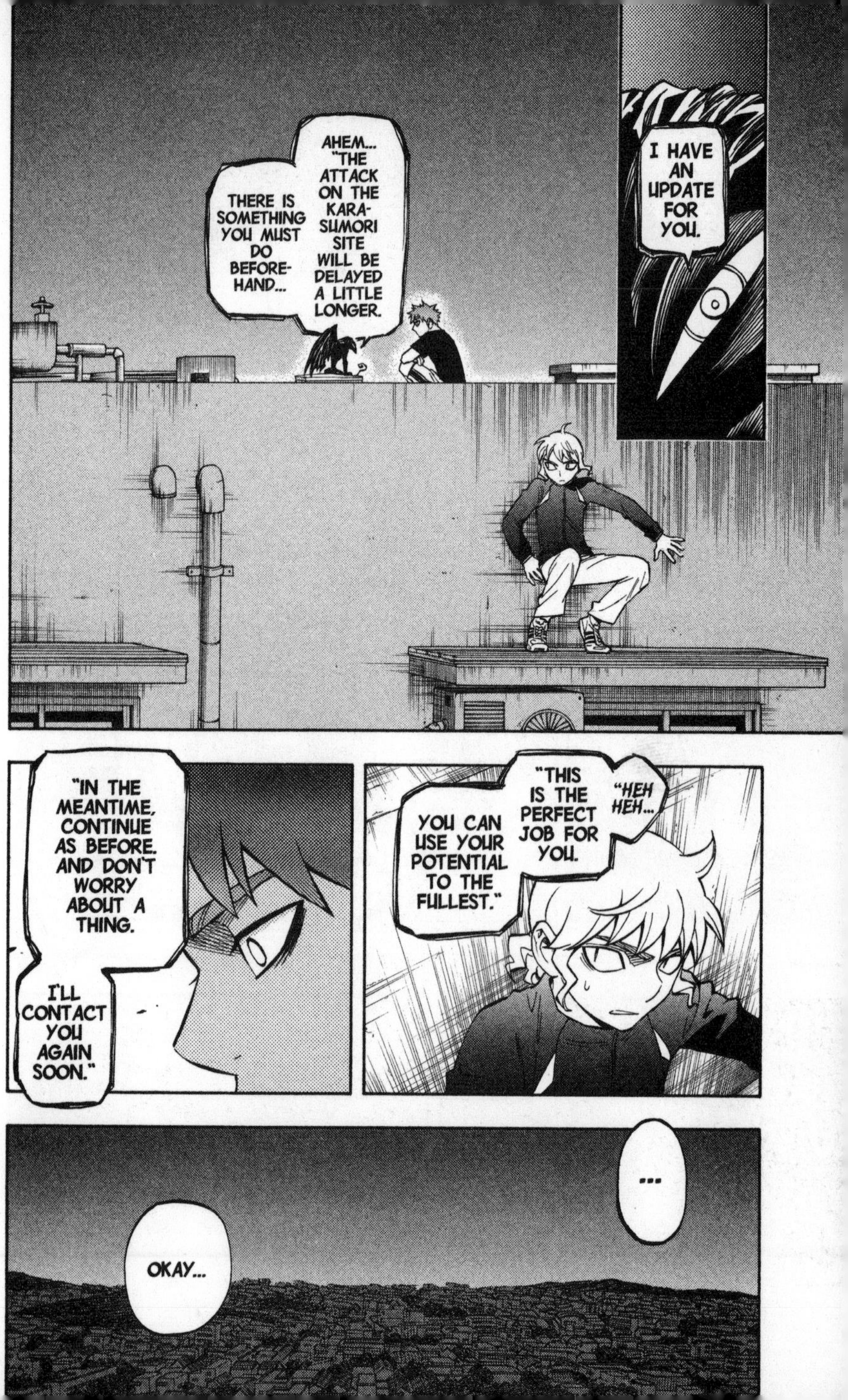
I HAVE AN UPDATE FOR YOU.
AHEM... "THE ATTACK ON THE KARA-SUMORI SITE WILL BE DELAYED A LITTLE LONGER.
THERE IS SOMETHING YOU MUST DO BEFORE-HAND...
"HEH HEH...
"THIS IS THE PERFECT JOB FOR YOU.
YOU CAN USE YOUR POTENTIAL TO THE FULLEST."
"IN THE MEANTIME, CONTINUE AS BEFORE. AND DON'T WORRY ABOUT A THING.
I'LL CONTACT YOU AGAIN SOON."
...
OKAY...

Chapter 230: The Unlucky One

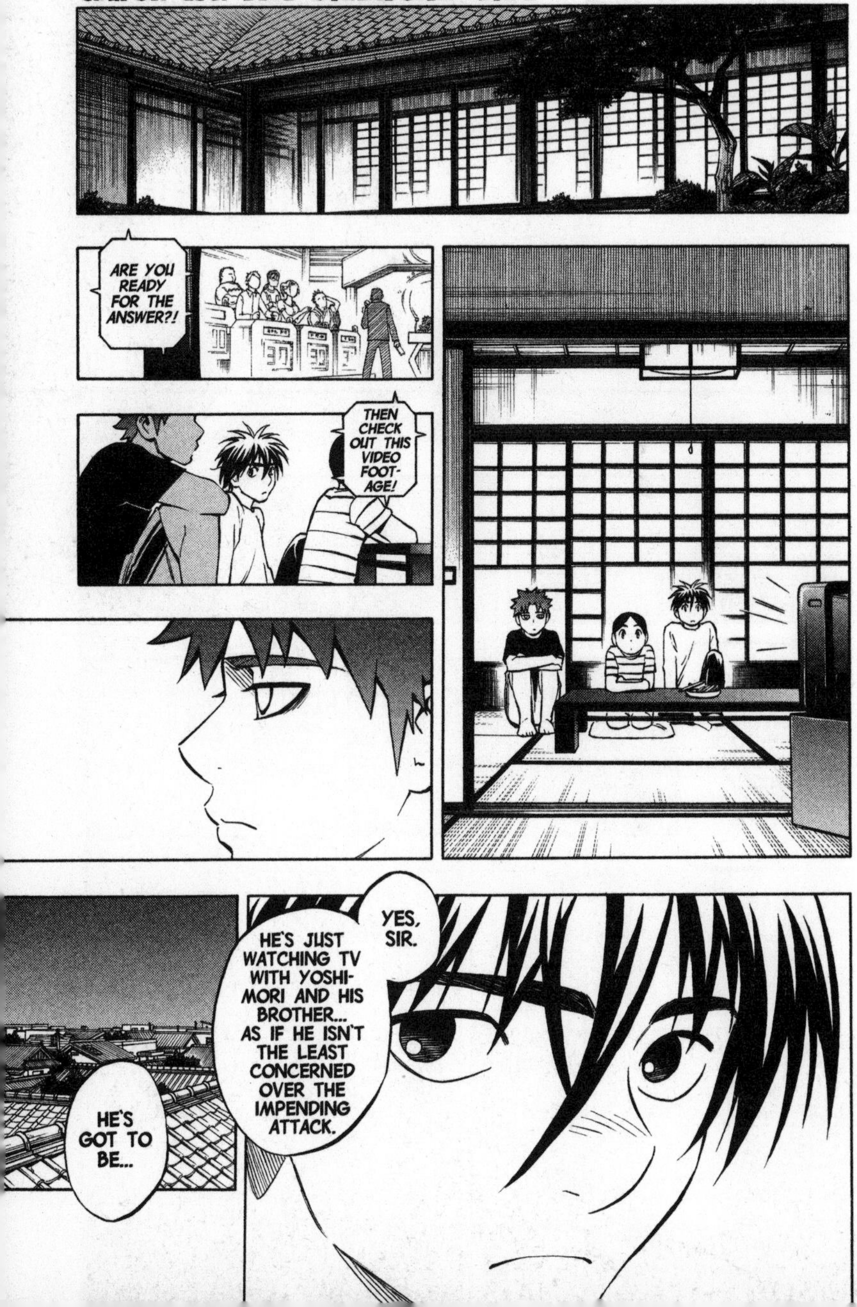
ARE YOU READY FOR THE ANSWER?!
THEN CHECK OUT THIS VIDEO FOOTAGE!
YES, SIR.
HE'S JUST WATCHING TV WITH YOSHIMORI AND HIS BROTHER... AS IF HE ISN'T THE LEAST CONCERNED OVER THE IMPENDING ATTACK.
HE'S GOT TO BE...

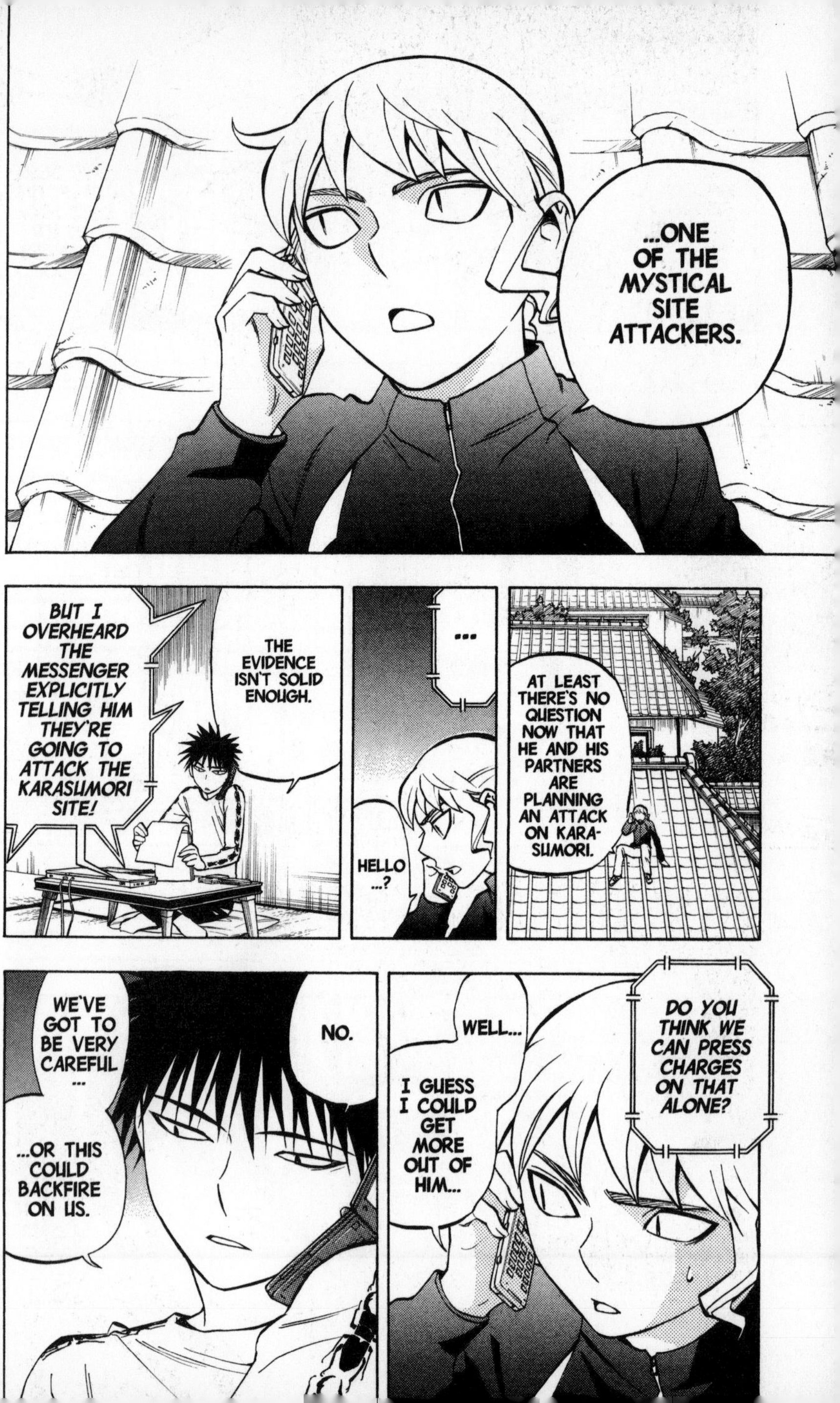
...ONE OF THE MYSTICAL SITE ATTACKERS.
AT LEAST THERE'S NO QUESTION NOW THAT HE AND HIS PARTNERS ARE PLANNING AN ATTACK ON KARA-SUMORI.
...
HELLO ...?
THE EVIDENCE ISN'T SOLID ENOUGH.
BUT I OVERHEARD THE MESSENGER EXPLICITLY TELLING HIM THEY'RE GOING TO ATTACK THE KARASUMORI SITE!
DO YOU THINK WE CAN PRESS CHARGES ON THAT ALONE?
WELL...
I GUESS I COULD GET MORE OUT OF HIM...
NO.
WE'VE GOT TO BE VERY CAREFUL ...
...OR THIS COULD BACKFIRE ON US.

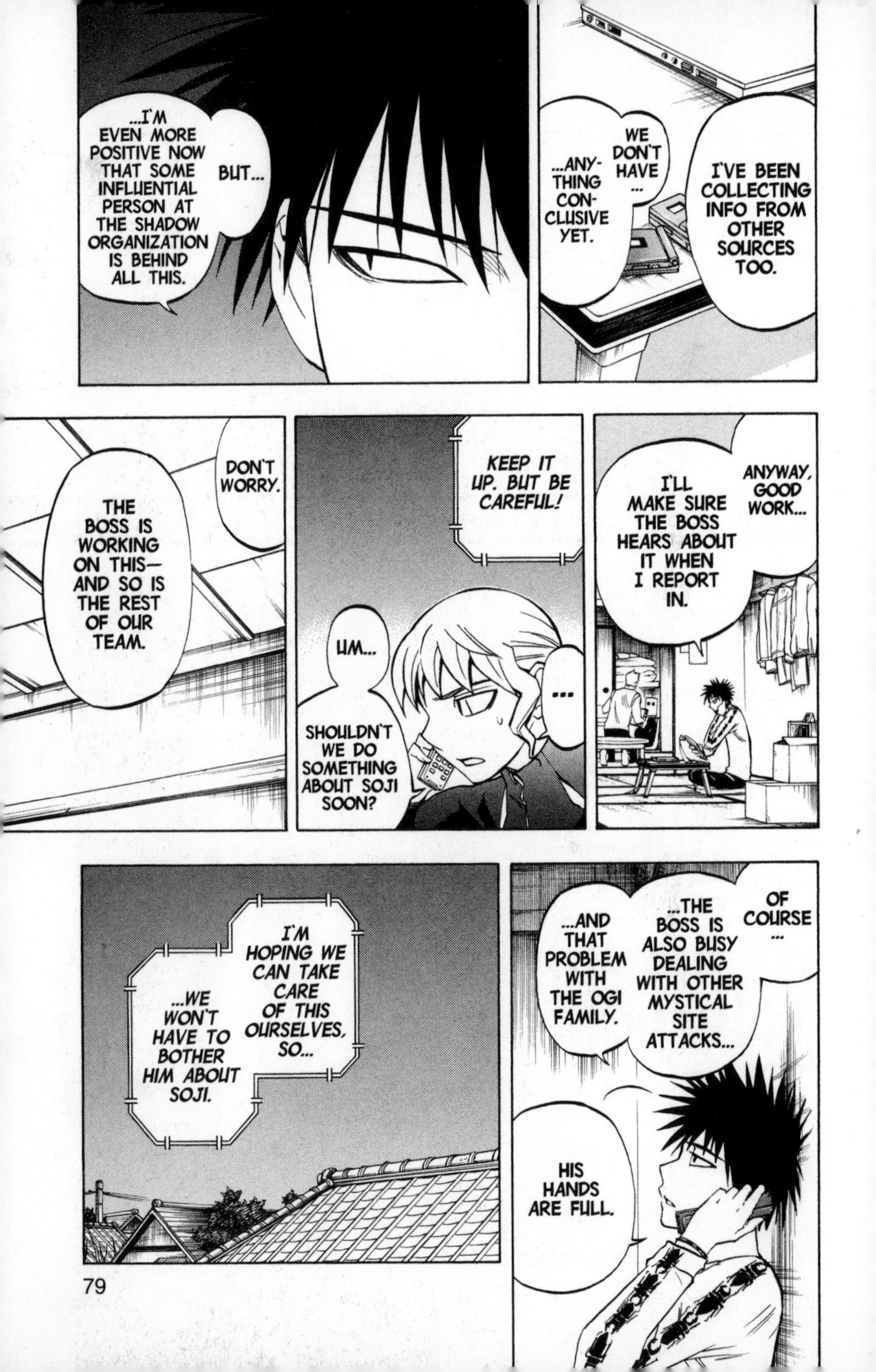
I'VE BEEN COLLECTING INFO FROM OTHER SOURCES TOO.
WE DON'T HAVE ...
...ANYTHING CONCLUSIVE YET.
BUT...
...I'M EVEN MORE POSITIVE NOW THAT SOME INFLUENTIAL PERSON AT THE SHADOW ORGANIZATION IS BEHIND ALL THIS.
ANYWAY, GOOD WORK...
I'LL MAKE SURE THE BOSS HEARS ABOUT IT WHEN I REPORT IN.
KEEP IT UP. BUT BE CAREFUL!
...
UM...
SHOULDN'T WE DO SOMETHING ABOUT SOJI SOON?
DON'T WORRY.
THE BOSS IS WORKING ON THIS—AND SO IS THE REST OF OUR TEAM.
OF COURSE ...
...THE BOSS IS ALSO BUSY DEALING WITH OTHER MYSTICAL SITE ATTACKS...
...AND THAT PROBLEM WITH THE OGI FAMILY.
HIS HANDS ARE FULL.
I'M HOPING WE CAN TAKE CARE OF THIS OURSELVES, SO...
...WE WON'T HAVE TO BOTHER HIM ABOUT SOJI.

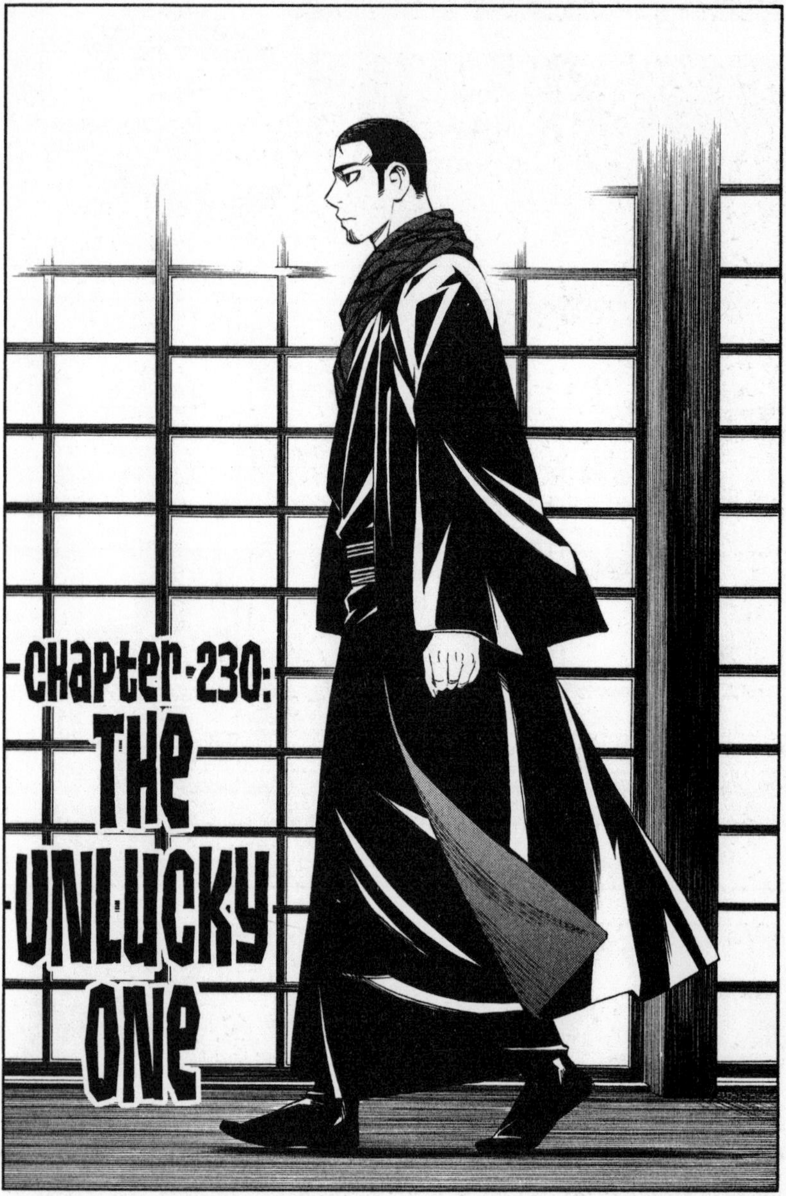
Chapter 230:
THE UNLUCKY ONE

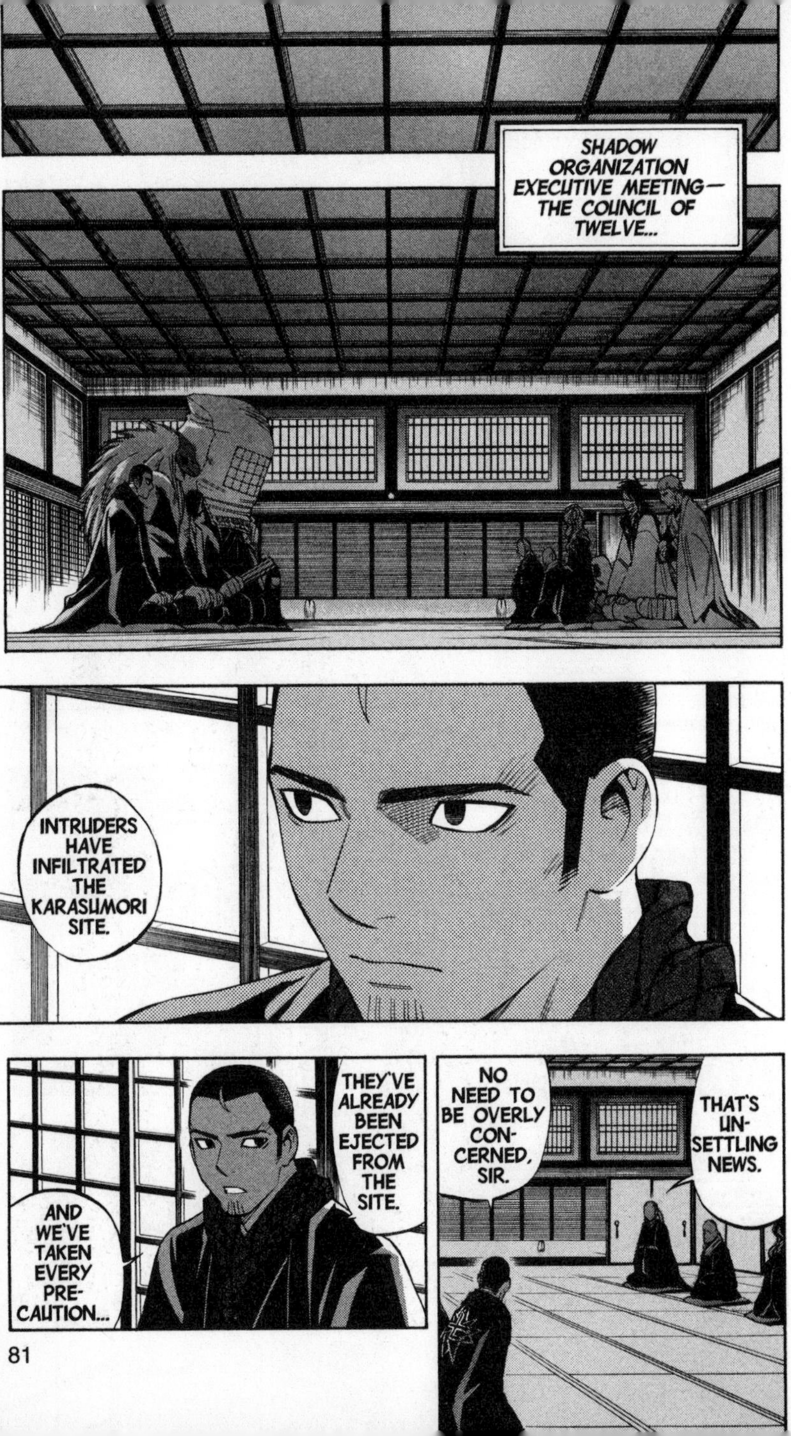
SHADOW ORGANIZATION EXECUTIVE MEETING— THE COUNCIL OF TWELVE...
INTRUDERS HAVE INFILTRATED THE KARASUMORI SITE.
THAT'S UN-SETTLING NEWS.
NO NEED TO BE OVERLY CON-CERNED, SIR.
THEY'VE ALREADY BEEN EJECTED FROM THE SITE.
AND WE'VE TAKEN EVERY PRE-CAUTION...

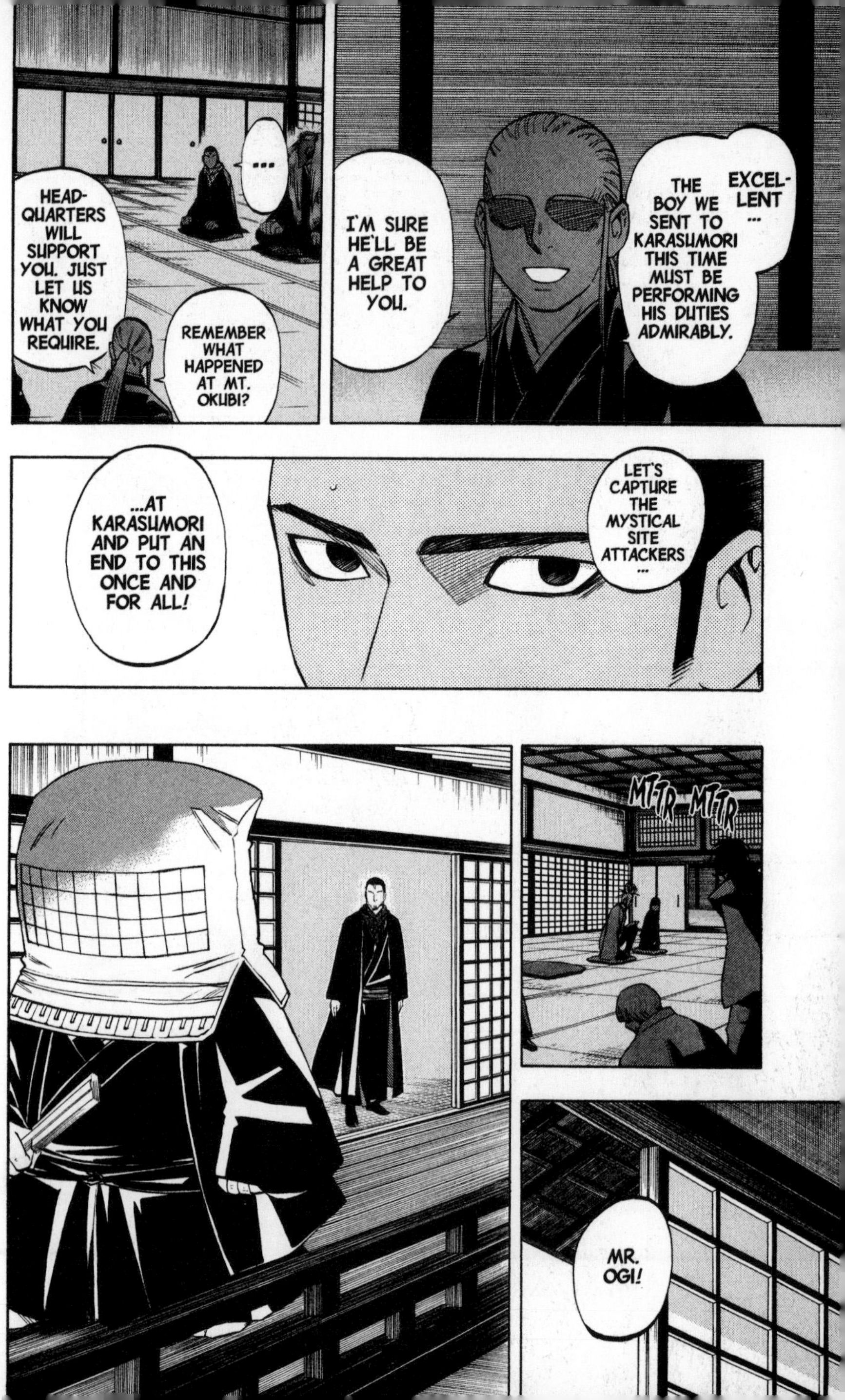
EXCEL-LENT...
THE BOY WE SENT TO KARASUMORI THIS TIME MUST BE PERFORMING HIS DUTIES ADMIRABLY.
I'M SURE HE'LL BE A GREAT HELP TO YOU.
...
HEAD-QUARTERS WILL SUPPORT YOU. JUST LET US KNOW WHAT YOU REQUIRE.
REMEMBER WHAT HAPPENED AT MT. OKUBI?
LET'S CAPTURE THE MYSTICAL SITE ATTACKERS...
...AT KARASUMORI AND PUT AN END TO THIS ONCE AND FOR ALL!
MTTR MTTR
MR. OGI!

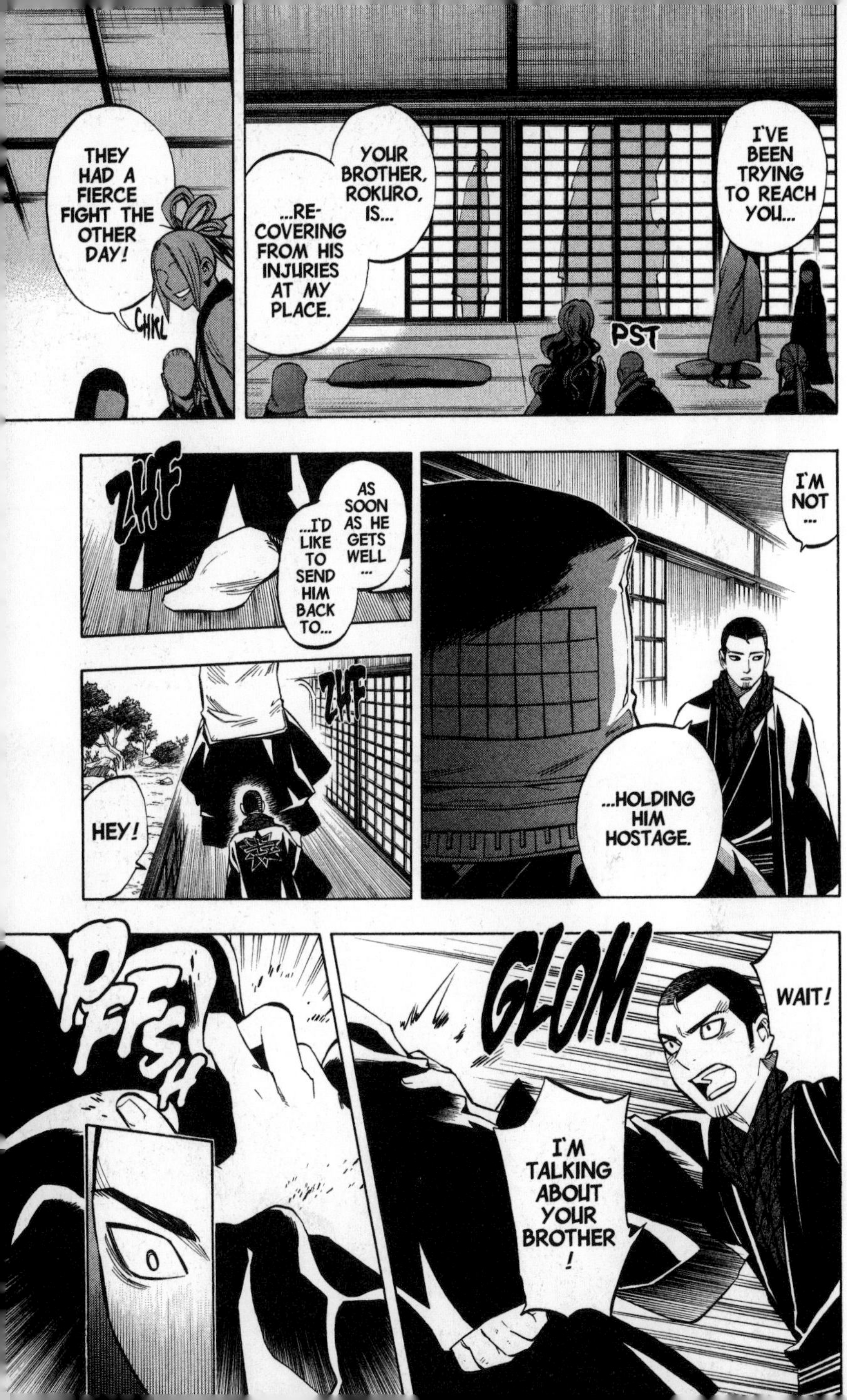
I'VE BEEN TRYING TO REACH YOU...
YOUR BROTHER, ROKURO, IS...
...RE-COVERING FROM HIS INJURIES AT MY PLACE.
PST
THEY HAD A FIERCE FIGHT THE OTHER DAY!
CHKL
I'M NOT ...
...HOLDING HIM HOSTAGE.
ZHF
AS SOON AS HE GETS WELL ...
...I'D LIKE TO SEND HIM BACK TO...
ZHF
HEY!
GLOM
WAIT!
I'M TALKING ABOUT YOUR BROTHER!
PFFSH

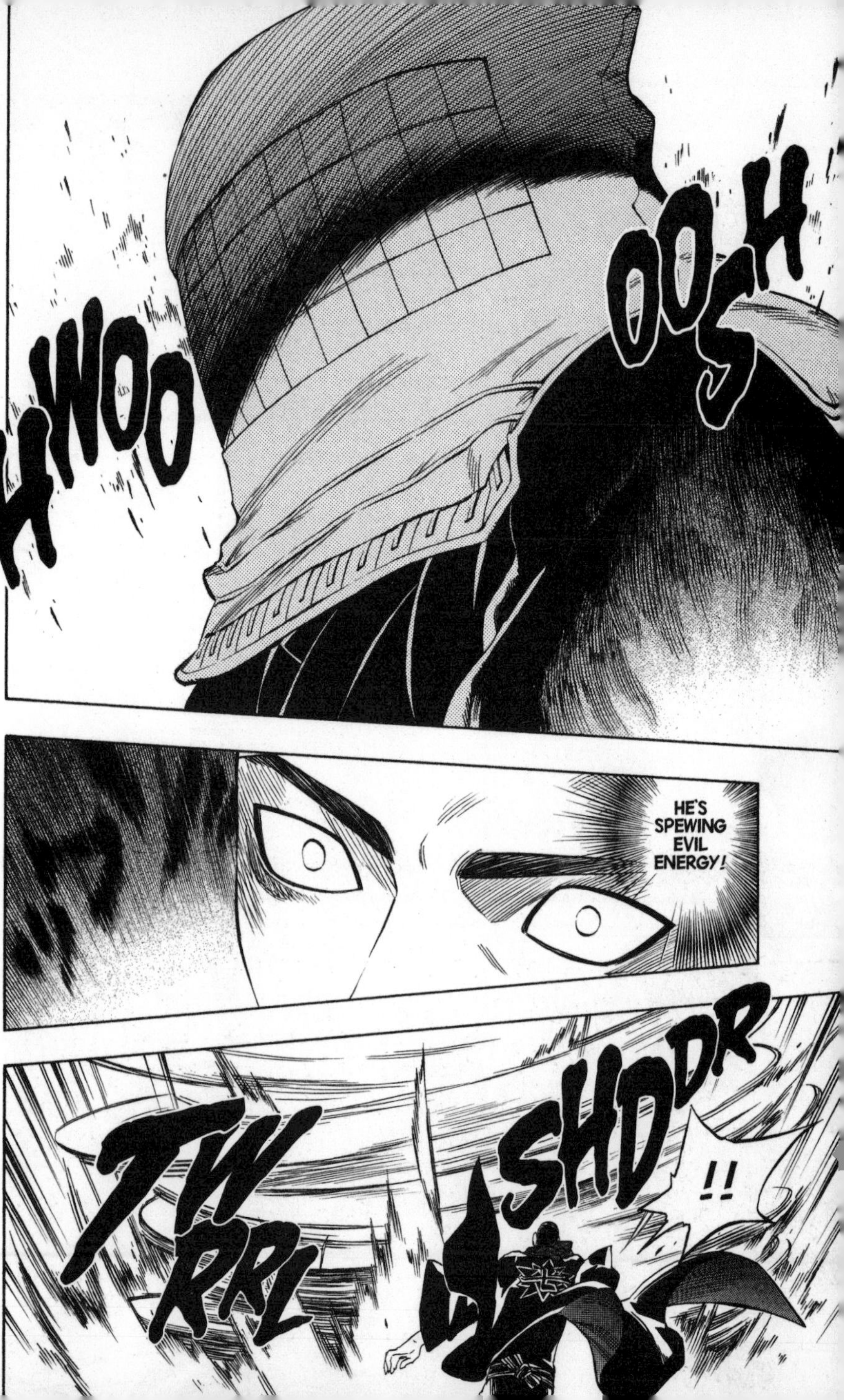
HWOO
OOSH
HE'S SPEWING EVIL ENERGY!
SHDDR
!!
TWRRL

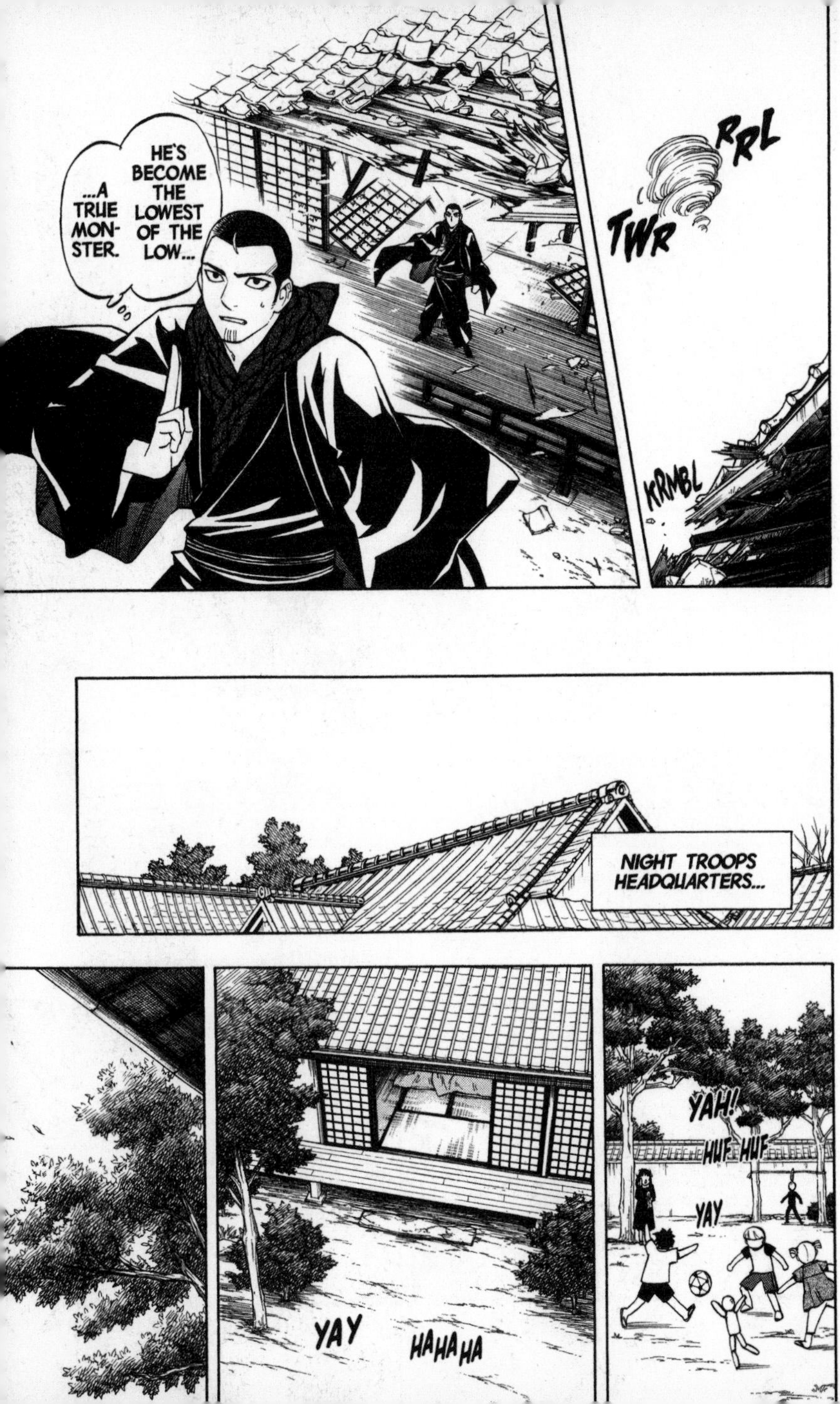
TWR RRL
KRMBL
HE'S BECOME THE LOWEST OF THE LOW...
...A TRUE MON-STER.
NIGHT TROOPS HEADQUARTERS...
YAH!
HUF HUF
YAY
YAY
HAHAHA

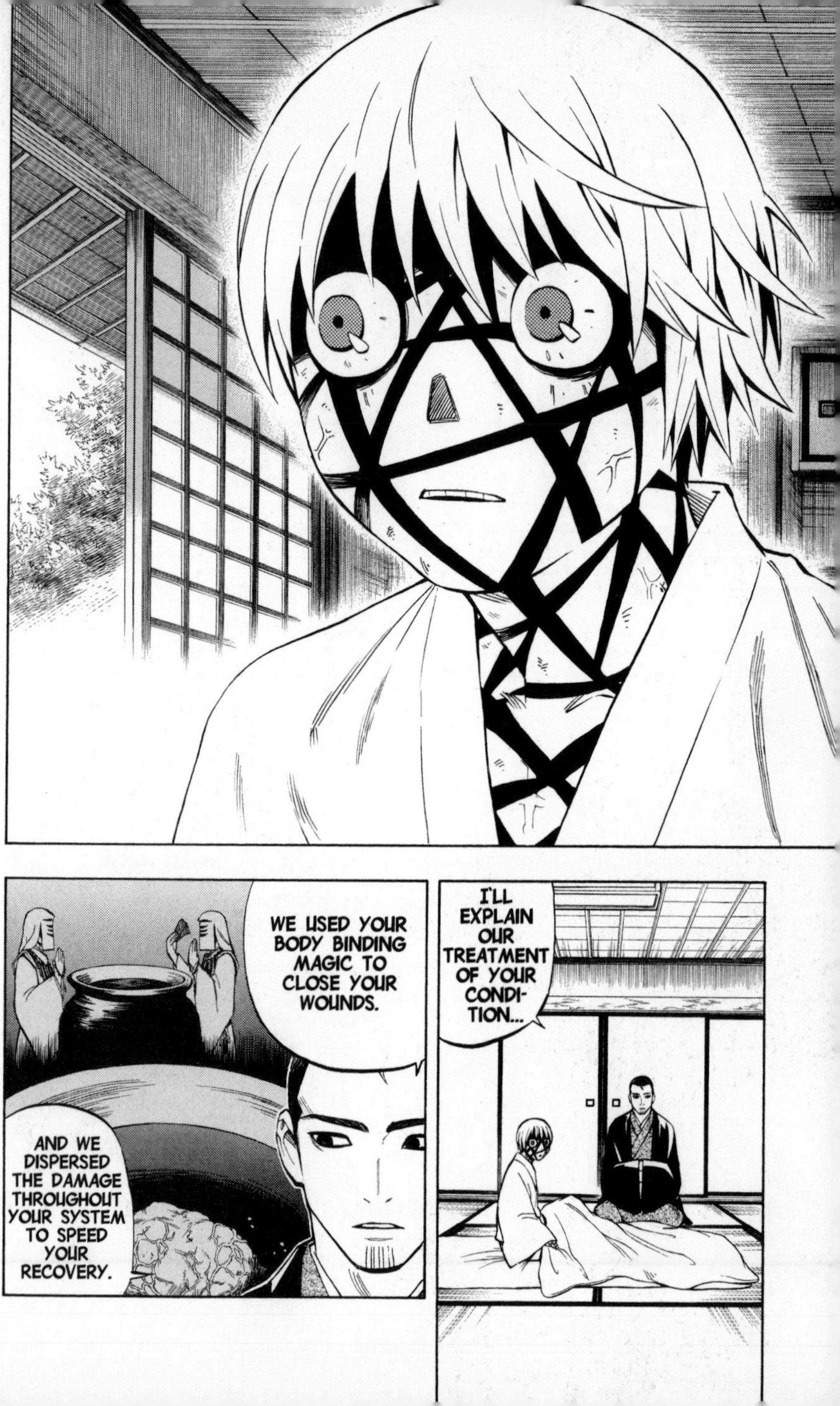
I'LL EXPLAIN OUR TREATMENT OF YOUR CONDITION...
WE USED YOUR BODY BINDING MAGIC TO CLOSE YOUR WOUNDS.
AND WE DISPERSED THE DAMAGE THROUGHOUT YOUR SYSTEM TO SPEED YOUR RECOVERY.

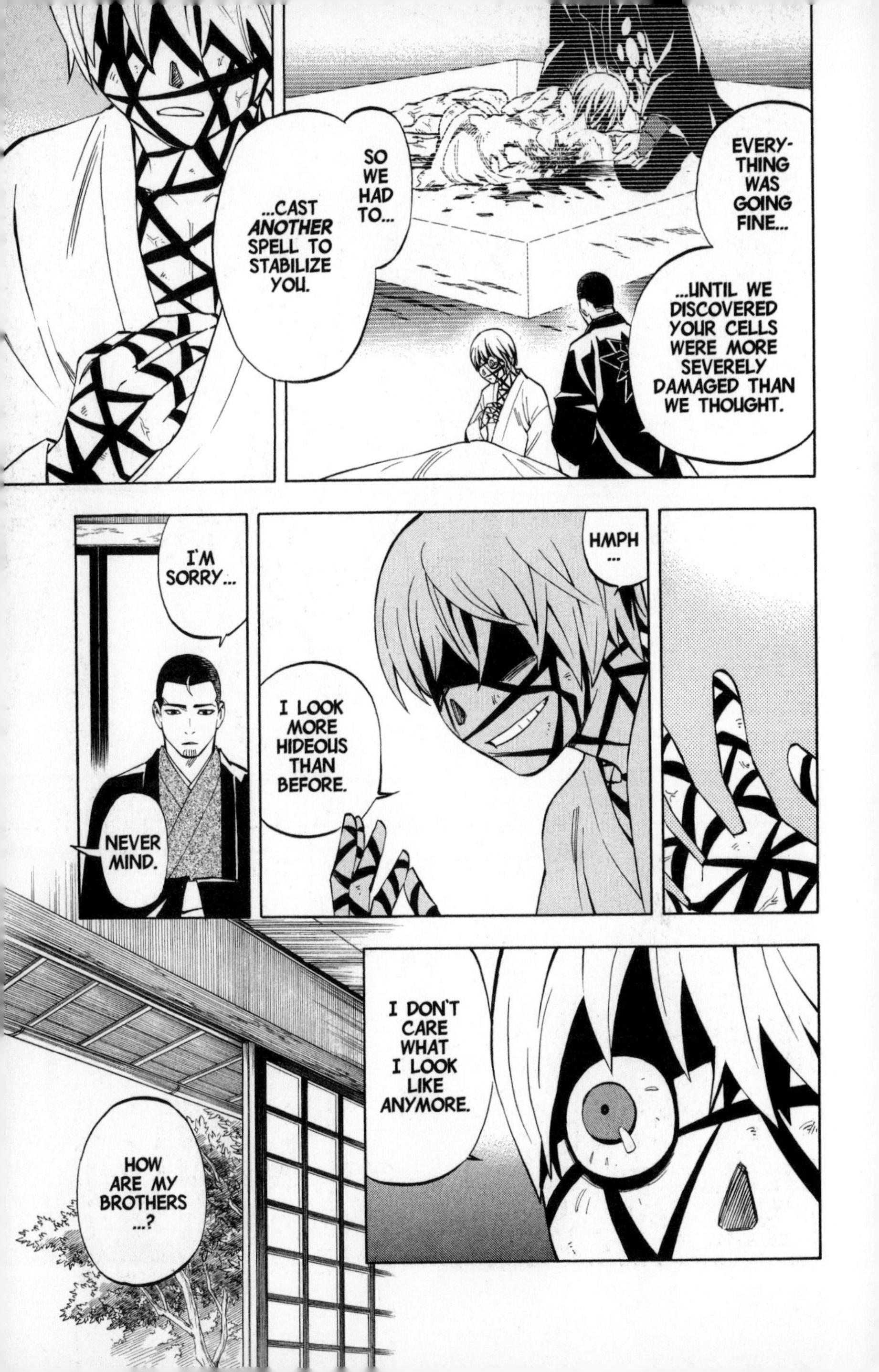
EVERYTHING WAS GOING FINE...
...UNTIL WE DISCOVERED YOUR CELLS WERE MORE SEVERELY DAMAGED THAN WE THOUGHT.
SO WE HAD TO...
...CAST ANOTHER SPELL TO STABILIZE YOU.
HMPH...
I LOOK MORE HIDEOUS THAN BEFORE.
I'M SORRY...
NEVER MIND.
I DON'T CARE WHAT I LOOK LIKE ANYMORE.
HOW ARE MY BROTHERS...?

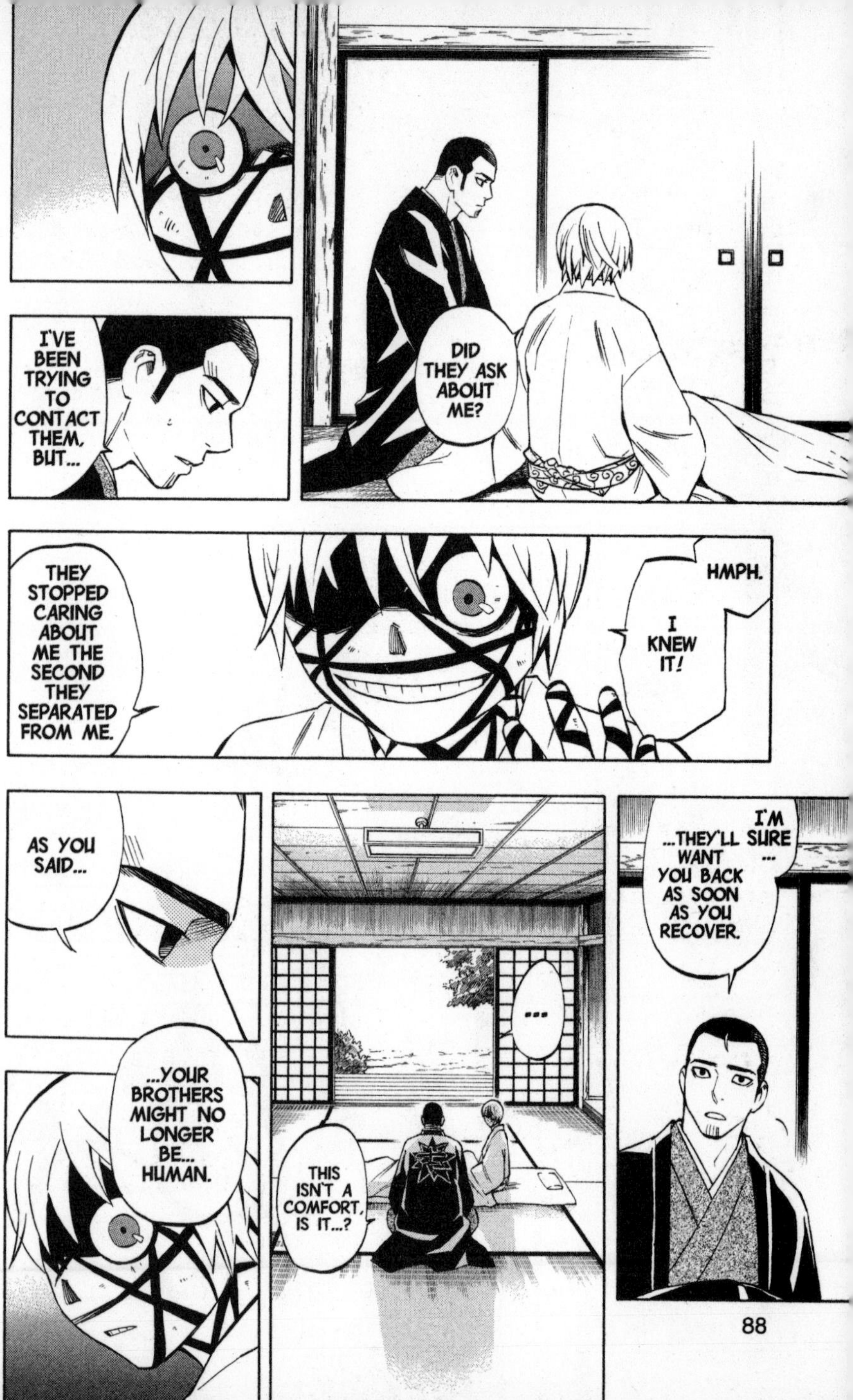
DID THEY ASK ABOUT ME?
I'VE BEEN TRYING TO CONTACT THEM, BUT...
HMPH.
I KNEW IT!
THEY STOPPED CARING ABOUT ME THE SECOND THEY SEPARATED FROM ME.
I'M SURE...
...THEY'LL WANT YOU BACK AS SOON AS YOU RECOVER.
...
THIS ISN'T A COMFORT, IS IT...?
AS YOU SAID...
...YOUR BROTHERS MIGHT NO LONGER BE... HUMAN.

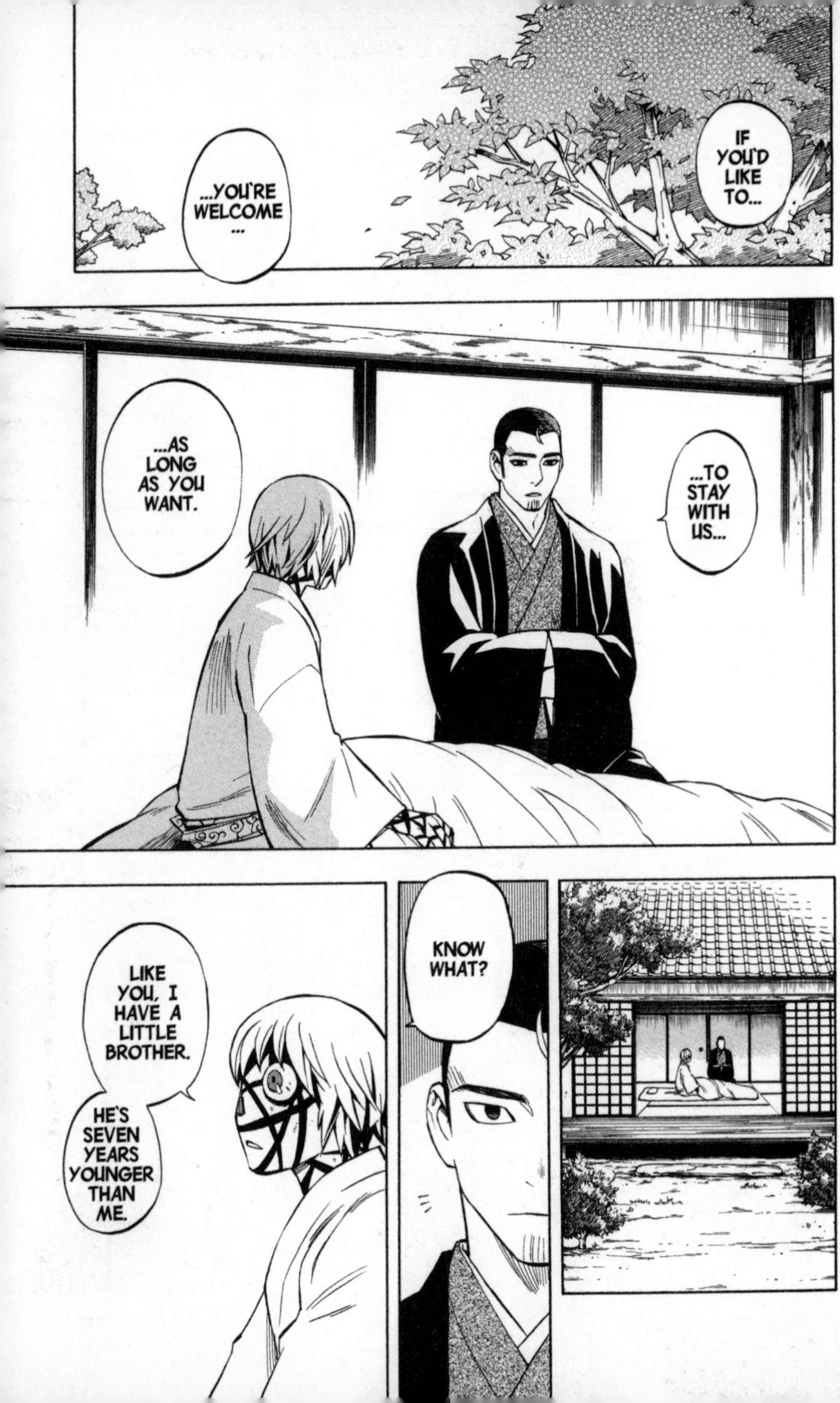
IF YOU'D LIKE TO...
...YOU'RE WELCOME ...
...TO STAY WITH US...
...AS LONG AS YOU WANT.
KNOW WHAT?
LIKE YOU, I HAVE A LITTLE BROTHER.
HE'S SEVEN YEARS YOUNGER THAN ME.

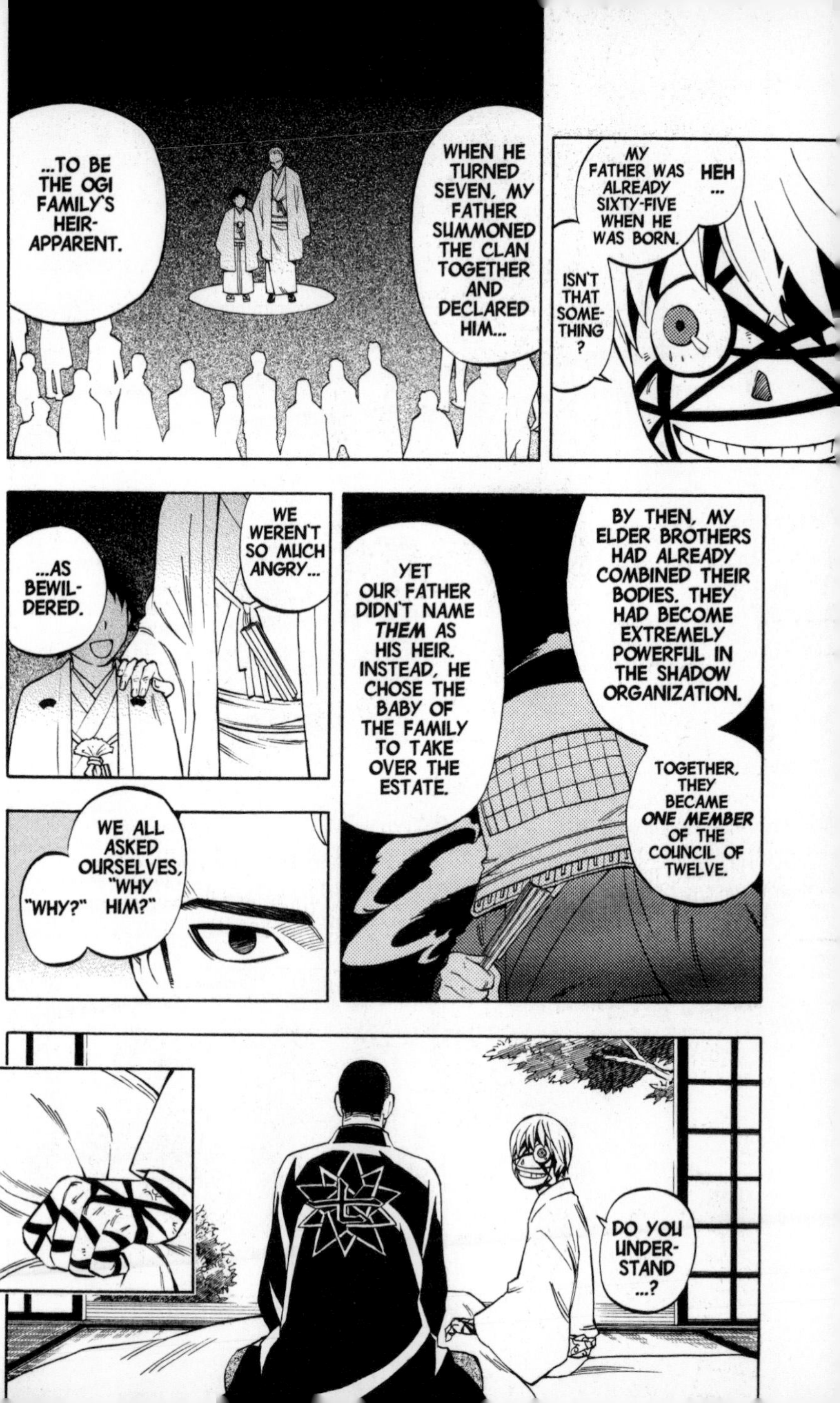
HEH...
MY FATHER WAS ALREADY SIXTY-FIVE WHEN HE WAS BORN.
ISN'T THAT SOMETHING?
WHEN HE TURNED SEVEN, MY FATHER SUMMONED THE CLAN TOGETHER AND DECLARED HIM...
...TO BE THE OGI FAMILY'S HEIR-APPARENT.
BY THEN, MY ELDER BROTHERS HAD ALREADY COMBINED THEIR BODIES. THEY HAD BECOME EXTREMELY POWERFUL IN THE SHADOW ORGANIZATION.
TOGETHER, THEY BECAME *ONE MEMBER* OF THE COUNCIL OF TWELVE.
YET OUR FATHER DIDN'T NAME *THEM* AS HIS HEIR. INSTEAD, HE CHOSE THE BABY OF THE FAMILY TO TAKE OVER THE ESTATE.
WE WEREN'T SO MUCH ANGRY...
...AS BEWILDERED.
WE ALL ASKED OURSELVES, "WHY HIM?"
"WHY?"
DO YOU UNDERSTAND...?

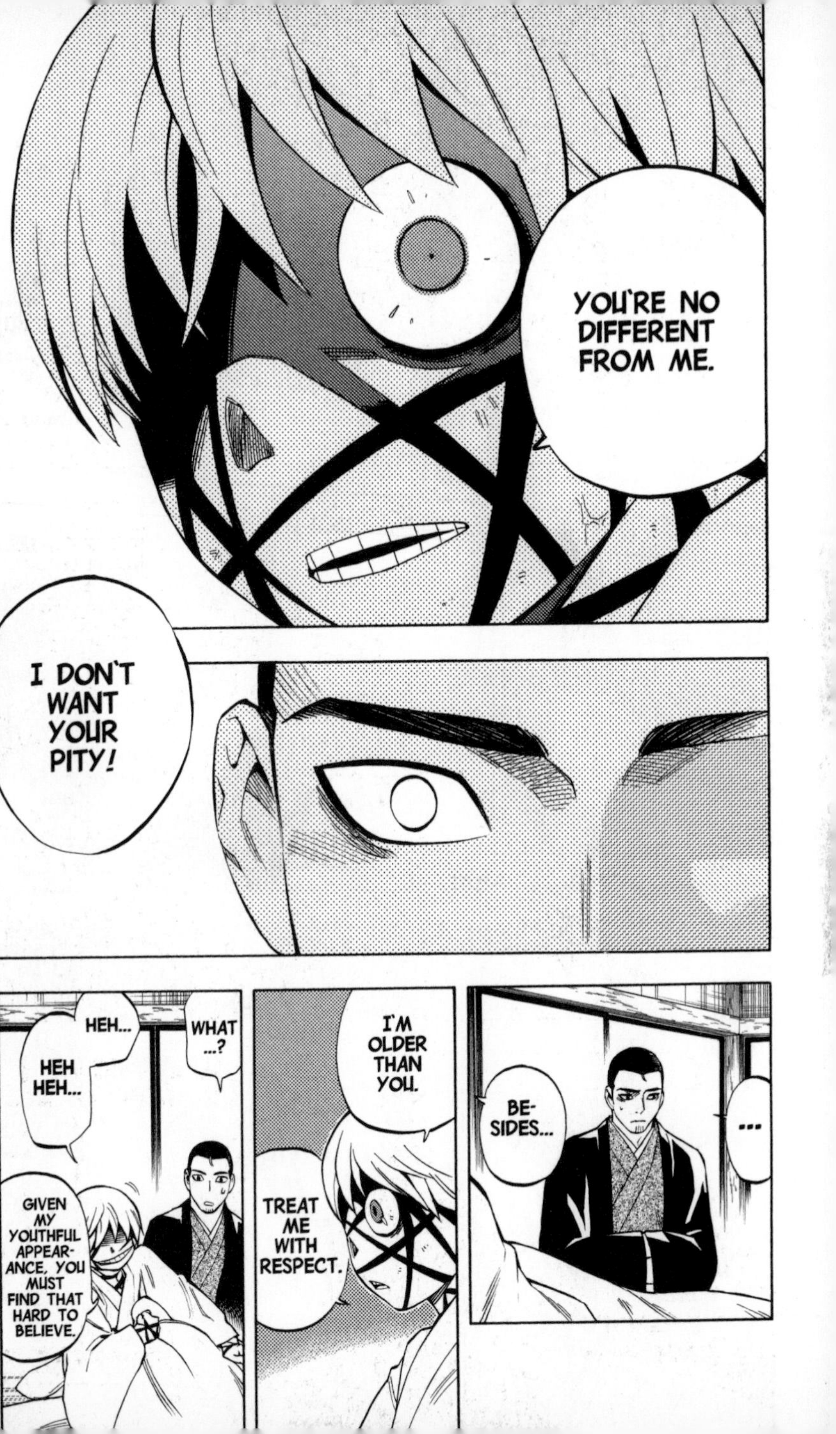
YOU'RE NO DIFFERENT FROM ME.
I DON'T WANT YOUR PITY!
...
BE-SIDES...
I'M OLDER THAN YOU.
TREAT ME WITH RESPECT.
WHAT ...?
HEH...
HEH HEH...
GIVEN MY YOUTHFUL APPEAR-ANCE, YOU MUST FIND THAT HARD TO BELIEVE.

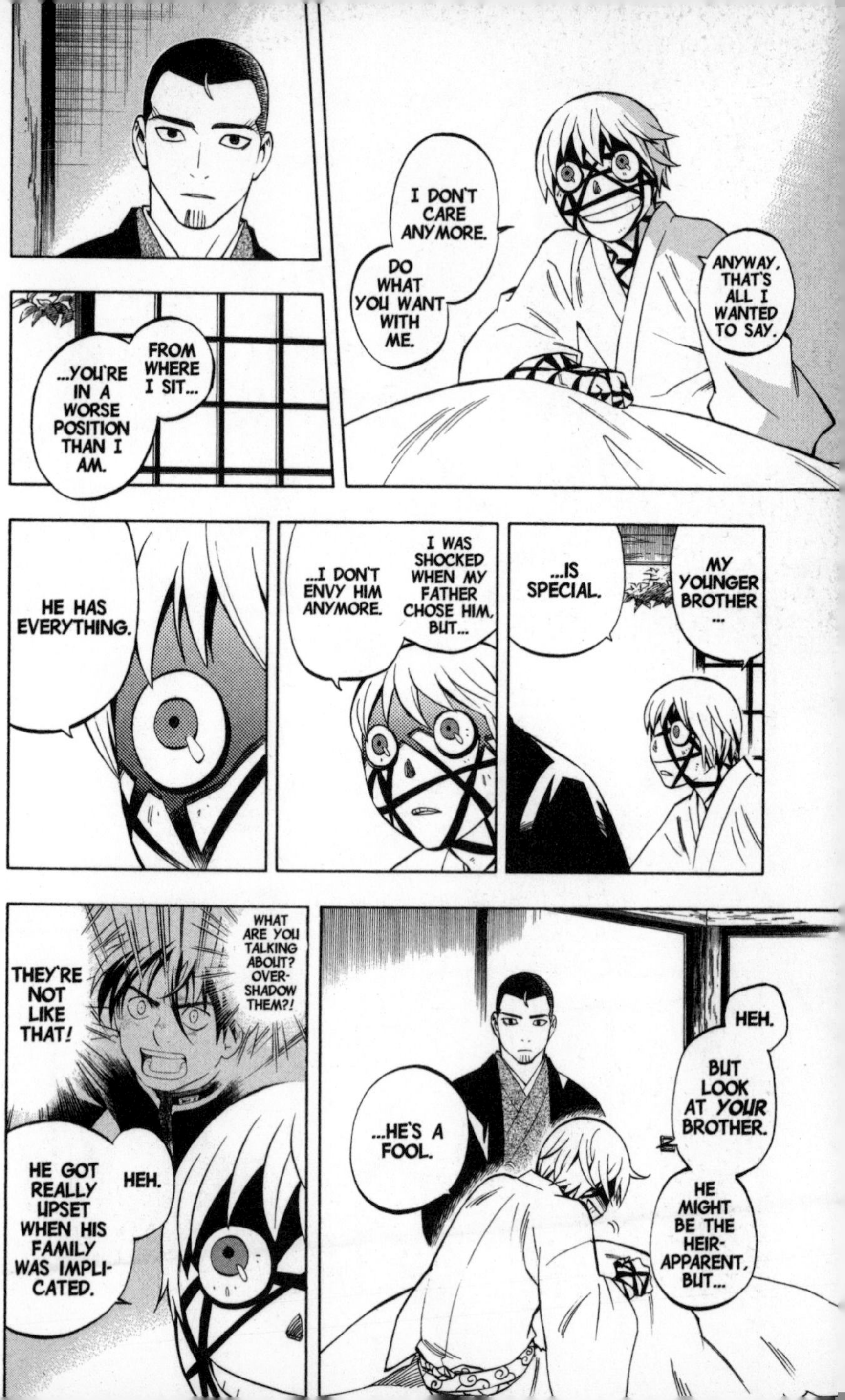
ANYWAY, THAT'S ALL I WANTED TO SAY.
I DON'T CARE ANYMORE.
DO WHAT YOU WANT WITH ME.
FROM WHERE I SIT...
...YOU'RE IN A WORSE POSITION THAN I AM.
MY YOUNGER BROTHER...
...IS SPECIAL.
I WAS SHOCKED WHEN MY FATHER CHOSE HIM, BUT...
...I DON'T ENVY HIM ANYMORE.
HE HAS EVERYTHING.
HEH.
BUT LOOK AT *YOUR* BROTHER.
HE MIGHT BE THE HEIR-APPARENT, BUT...
...HE'S A FOOL.
WHAT ARE YOU TALKING ABOUT? OVER-SHADOW THEM?!
THEY'RE NOT LIKE THAT!
HEH.
HE GOT REALLY UPSET WHEN HIS FAMILY WAS IMPLICATED.

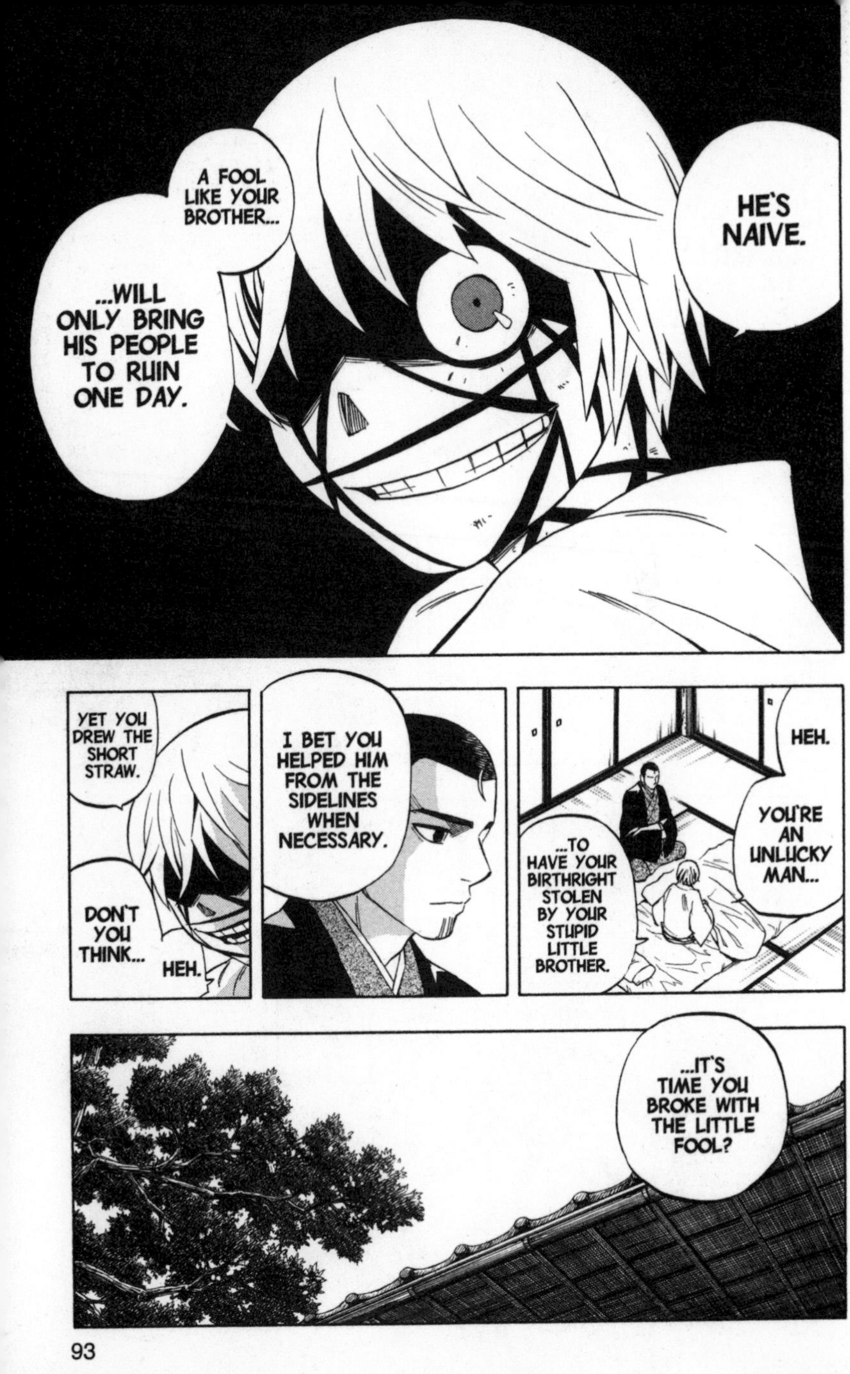
HE'S NAIVE.
A FOOL LIKE YOUR BROTHER...
...WILL ONLY BRING HIS PEOPLE TO RUIN ONE DAY.
HEH.
YOU'RE AN UNLUCKY MAN...
...TO HAVE YOUR BIRTHRIGHT STOLEN BY YOUR STUPID LITTLE BROTHER.
I BET YOU HELPED HIM FROM THE SIDELINES WHEN NECESSARY.
YET YOU DREW THE SHORT STRAW.
DON'T YOU THINK...
HEH.
...IT'S TIME YOU BROKE WITH THE LITTLE FOOL?

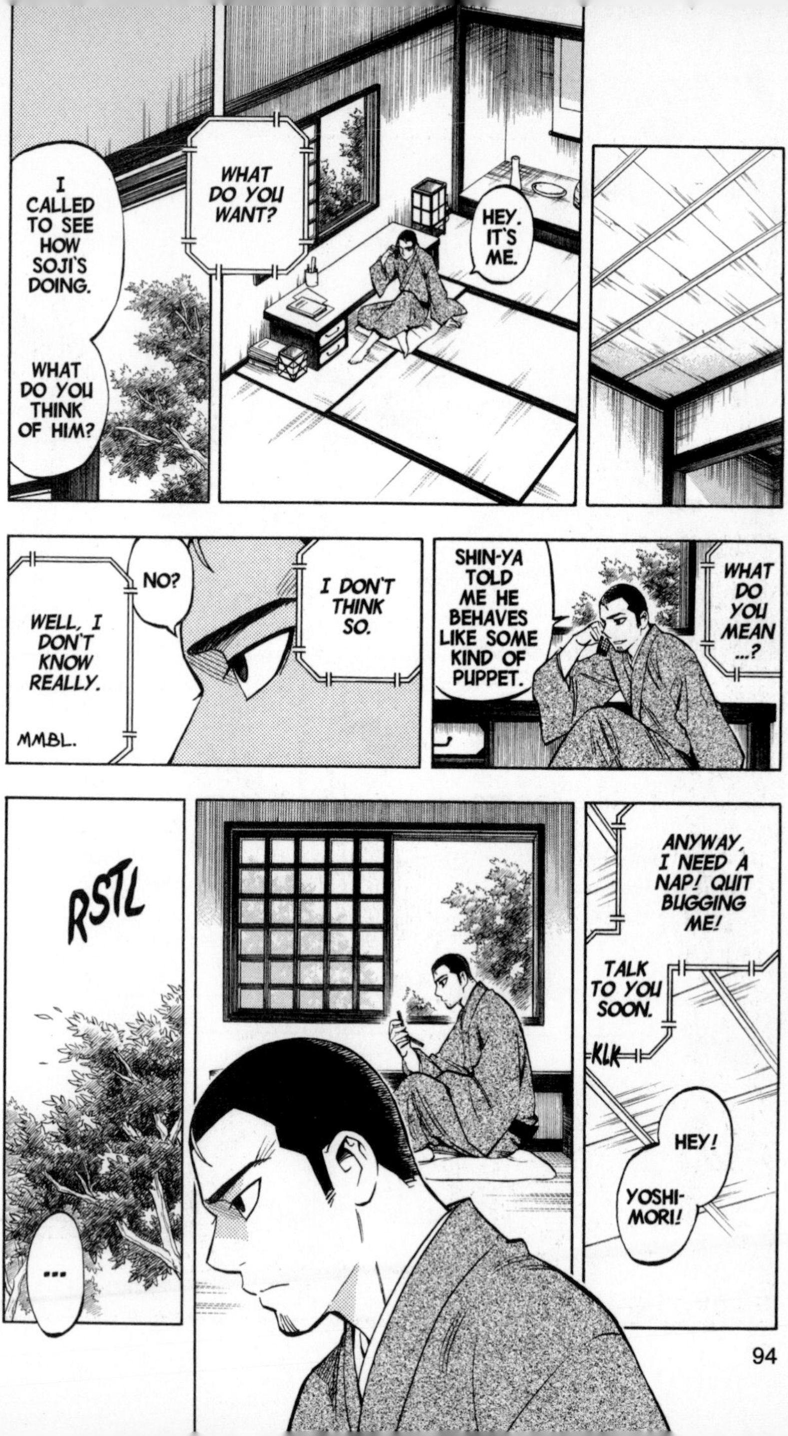
HEY. IT'S ME.
WHAT DO YOU WANT?
I CALLED TO SEE HOW SOJI'S DOING.
WHAT DO YOU THINK OF HIM?
WHAT DO YOU MEAN ...?
SHIN-YA TOLD ME HE BEHAVES LIKE SOME KIND OF PUPPET.
I DON'T THINK SO.
NO?
WELL, I DON'T KNOW REALLY.
MMBL.
ANYWAY, I NEED A NAP! QUIT BUGGING ME!
TALK TO YOU SOON.
KLK
HEY!
YOSHI-MORI!
RSTL
...

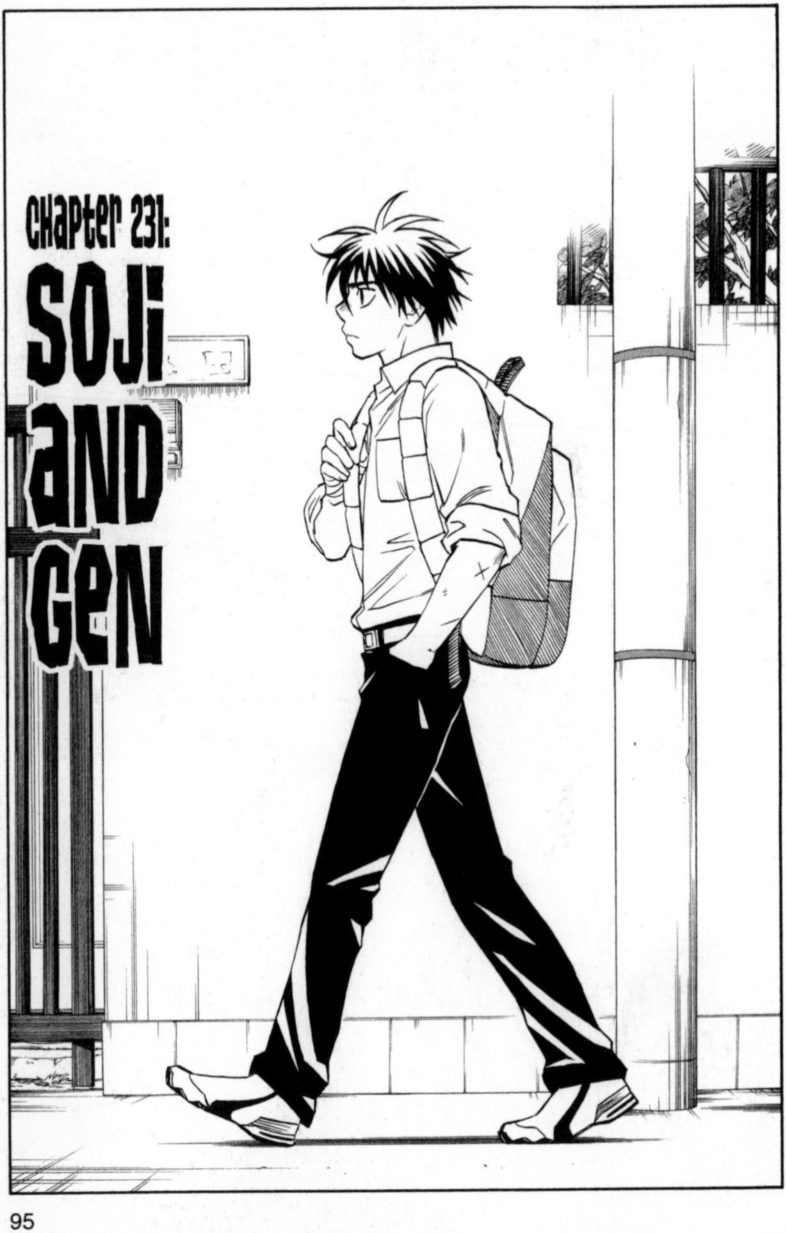
Chapter 231:
SOJi AND GEN

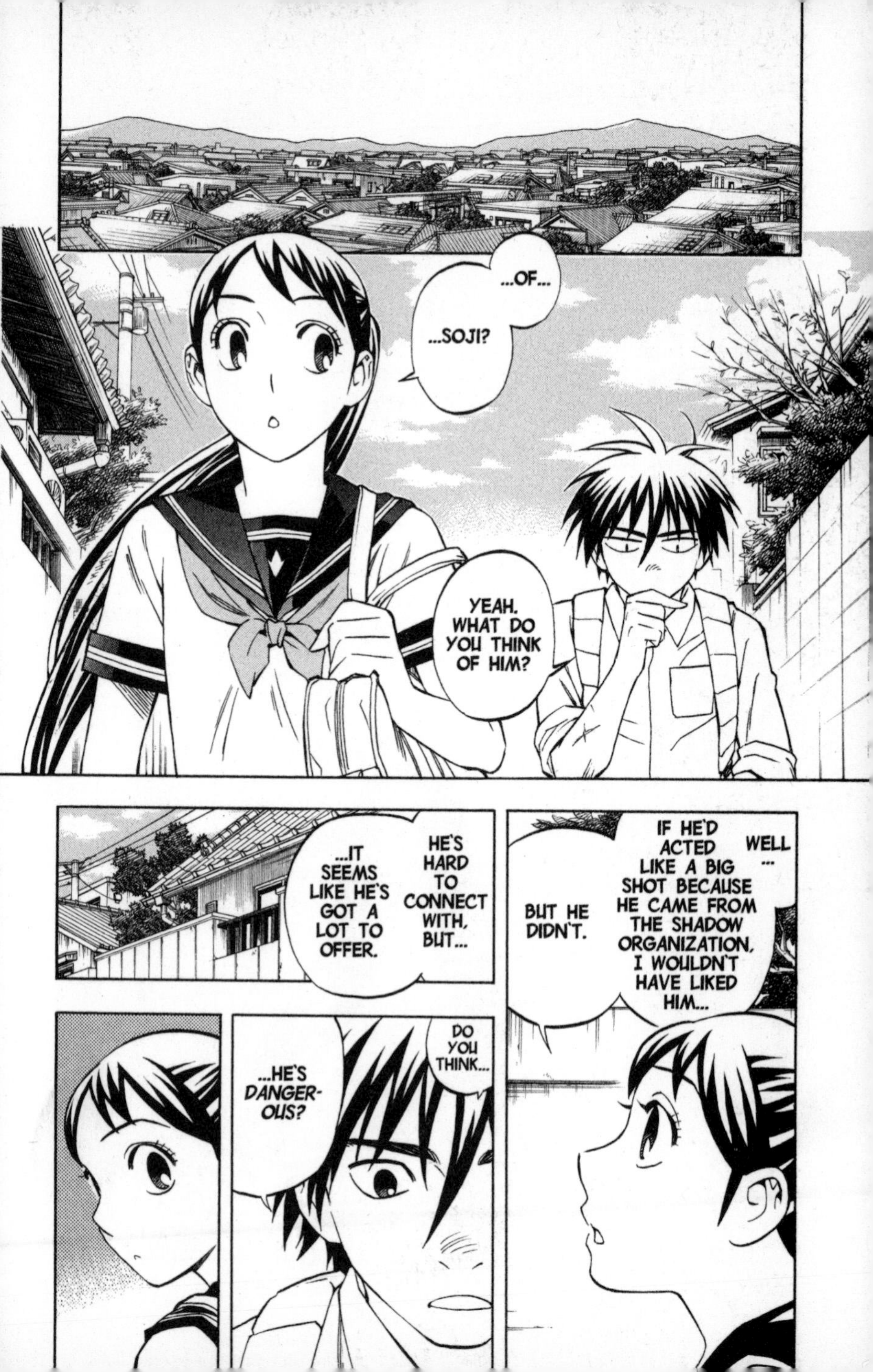
...OF...
...SOJI?
YEAH. WHAT DO YOU THINK OF HIM?
WELL...
IF HE'D ACTED LIKE A BIG SHOT BECAUSE HE CAME FROM THE SHADOW ORGANIZATION, I WOULDN'T HAVE LIKED HIM...
BUT HE DIDN'T.
HE'S HARD TO CONNECT WITH, BUT...
...IT SEEMS LIKE HE'S GOT A LOT TO OFFER.
DO YOU THINK...
...HE'S *DANGEROUS*?

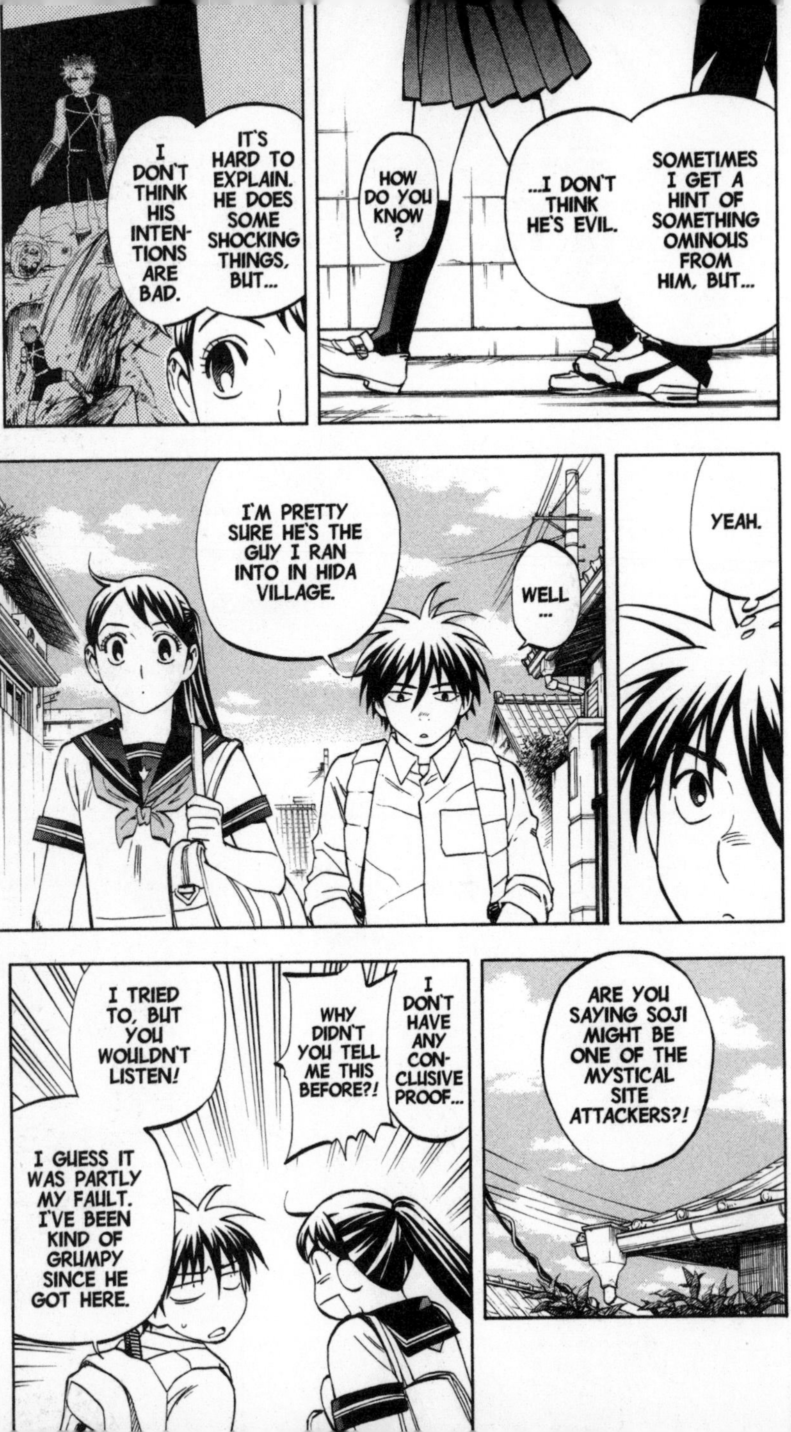
SOMETIMES I GET A HINT OF SOMETHING OMINOUS FROM HIM, BUT...
...I DON'T THINK HE'S EVIL.
HOW DO YOU KNOW?
IT'S HARD TO EXPLAIN. HE DOES SOME SHOCKING THINGS, BUT...
I DON'T THINK HIS INTEN-TIONS ARE BAD.
YEAH.
WELL...
I'M PRETTY SURE HE'S THE GUY I RAN INTO IN HIDA VILLAGE.
ARE YOU SAYING SOJI MIGHT BE ONE OF THE MYSTICAL SITE ATTACKERS?!
I DON'T HAVE ANY CON-CLUSIVE PROOF...
WHY DIDN'T YOU TELL ME THIS BEFORE?!
I TRIED TO, BUT YOU WOULDN'T LISTEN!
I GUESS IT WAS PARTLY MY FAULT. I'VE BEEN KIND OF GRUMPY SINCE HE GOT HERE.

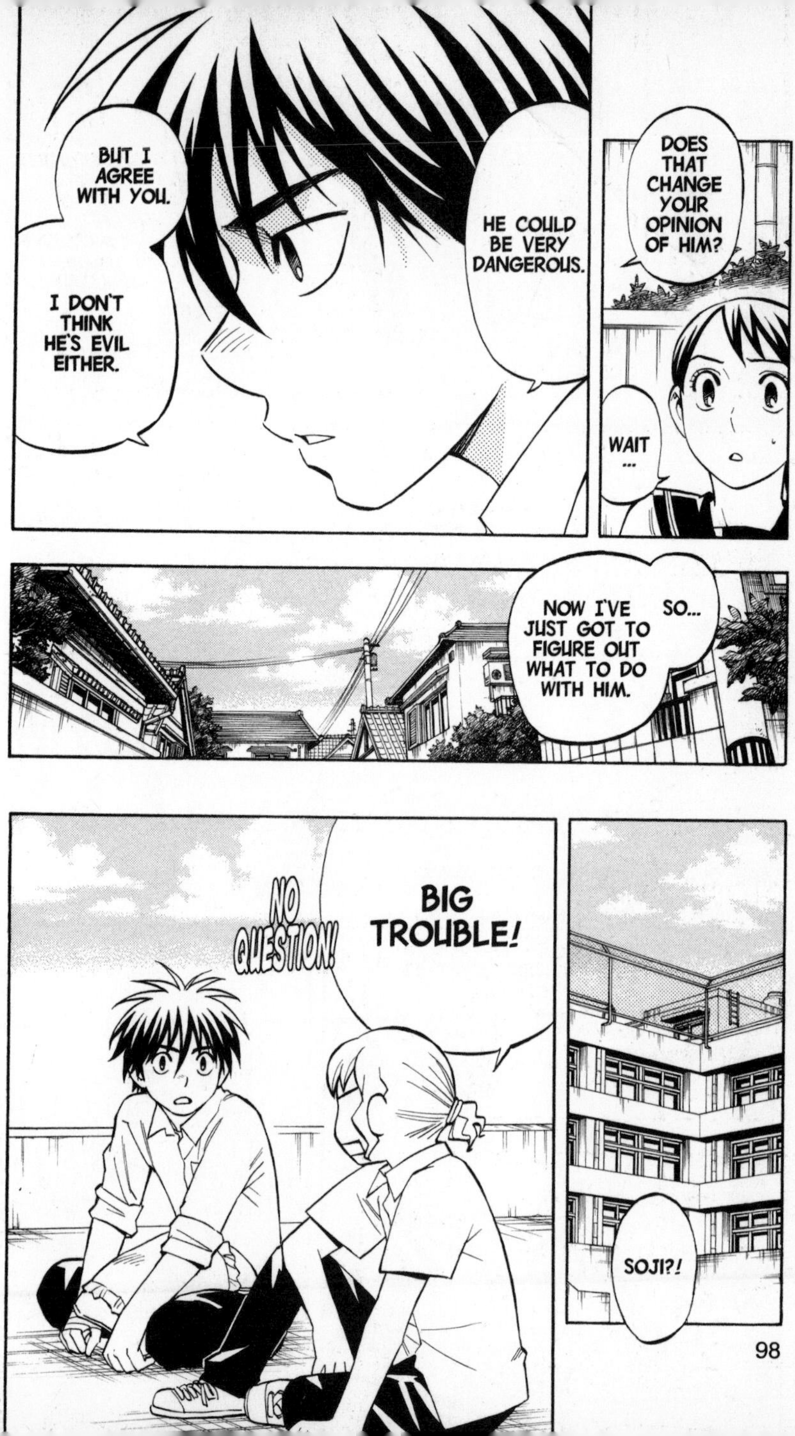
DOES THAT CHANGE YOUR OPINION OF HIM?
WAIT ...
HE COULD BE VERY DANGEROUS.
BUT I AGREE WITH YOU.
I DON'T THINK HE'S EVIL EITHER.
SO...
NOW I'VE JUST GOT TO FIGURE OUT WHAT TO DO WITH HIM.
SOJI?!
BIG TROUBLE!
NO QUESTION!

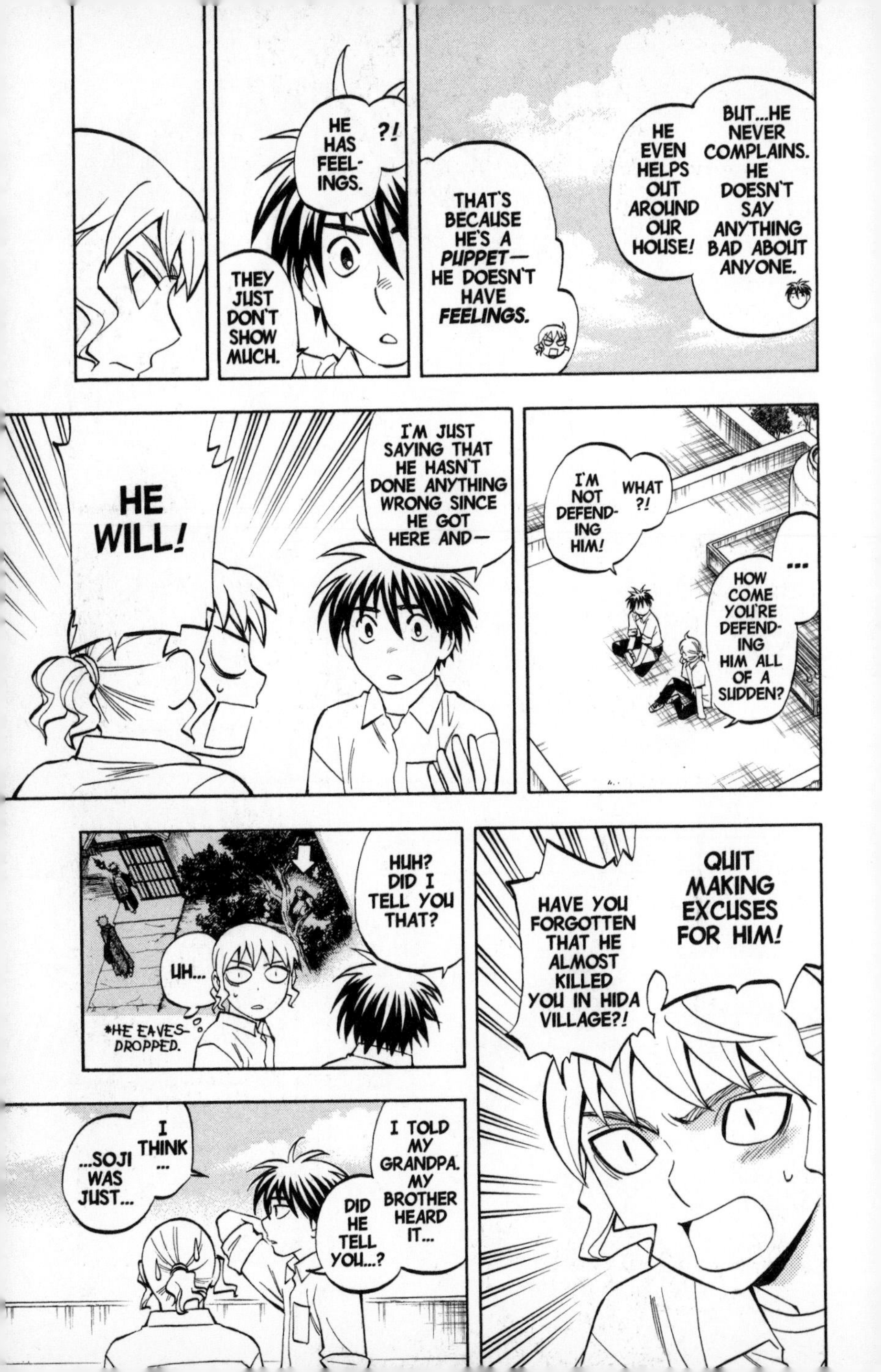
BUT...HE NEVER COMPLAINS. HE DOESN'T SAY ANYTHING BAD ABOUT ANYONE.
HE EVEN HELPS OUT AROUND OUR HOUSE!
THAT'S BECAUSE HE'S A *PUPPET*— HE DOESN'T HAVE *FEELINGS*.
?!
HE HAS FEEL-INGS.
THEY JUST DON'T SHOW MUCH.
...
HOW COME YOU'RE DEFENDING HIM ALL OF A SUDDEN?
WHAT?!
I'M NOT DEFENDING HIM!
I'M JUST SAYING THAT HE HASN'T DONE ANYTHING WRONG SINCE HE GOT HERE AND—
HE WILL!
QUIT MAKING EXCUSES FOR HIM!
HAVE YOU FORGOTTEN THAT HE ALMOST KILLED YOU IN HIDA VILLAGE?!
HUH? DID I TELL YOU THAT?
UH...
*HE EAVES-DROPPED.
I TOLD MY GRANDPA. MY BROTHER HEARD IT...
DID HE TELL YOU...?
I THINK...
...SOJI WAS JUST...

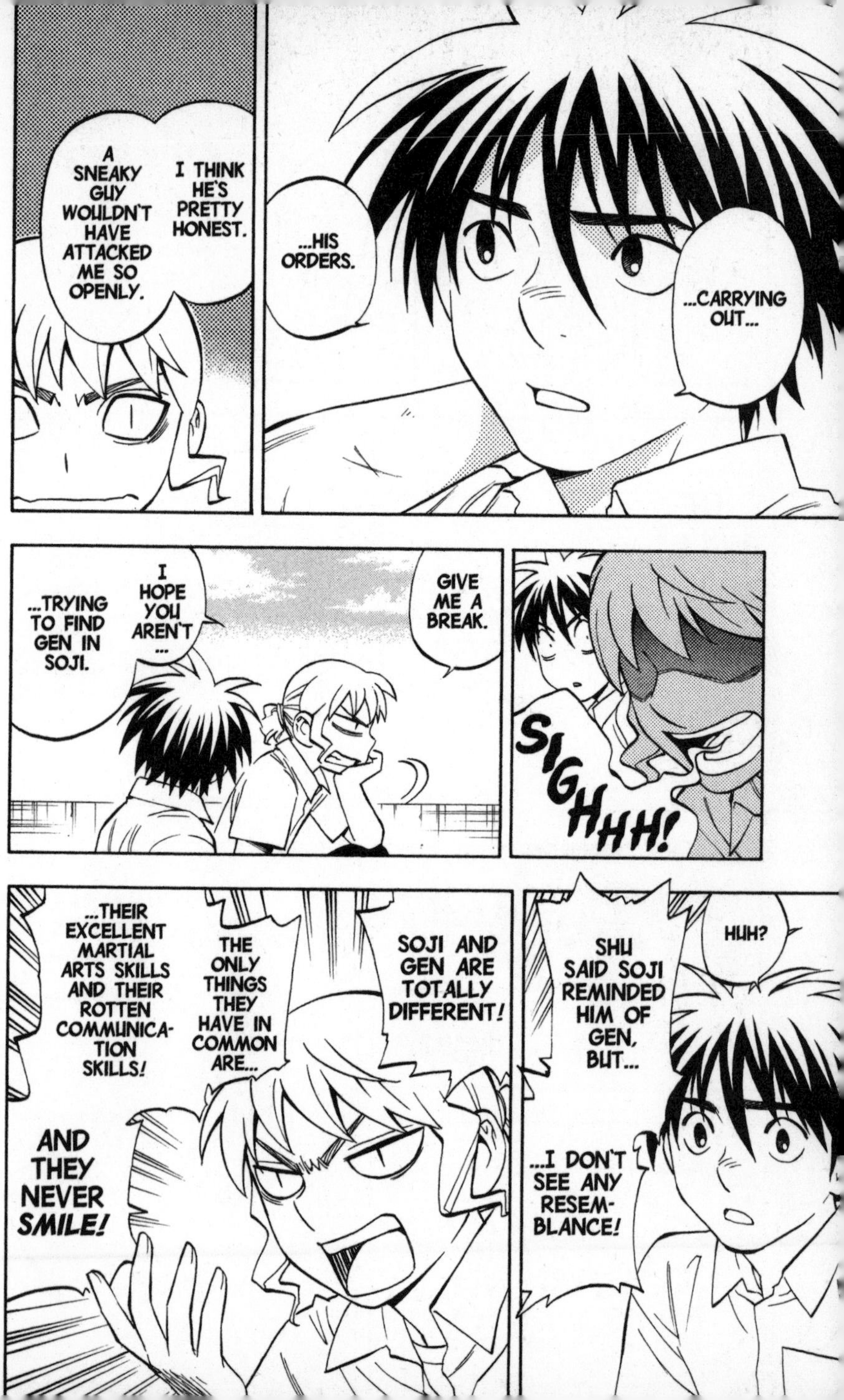
...CARRYING OUT...
...HIS ORDERS.
I THINK HE'S PRETTY HONEST.
A SNEAKY GUY WOULDN'T HAVE ATTACKED ME SO OPENLY.
SIGHHHH!
GIVE ME A BREAK.
I HOPE YOU AREN'T ...
...TRYING TO FIND GEN IN SOJI.
HUH?
SHU SAID SOJI REMINDED HIM OF GEN, BUT...
...I DON'T SEE ANY RESEMBLANCE!
SOJI AND GEN ARE TOTALLY DIFFERENT!
THE ONLY THINGS THEY HAVE IN COMMON ARE...
...THEIR EXCELLENT MARTIAL ARTS SKILLS AND THEIR ROTTEN COMMUNICATION SKILLS!
AND THEY NEVER SMILE!

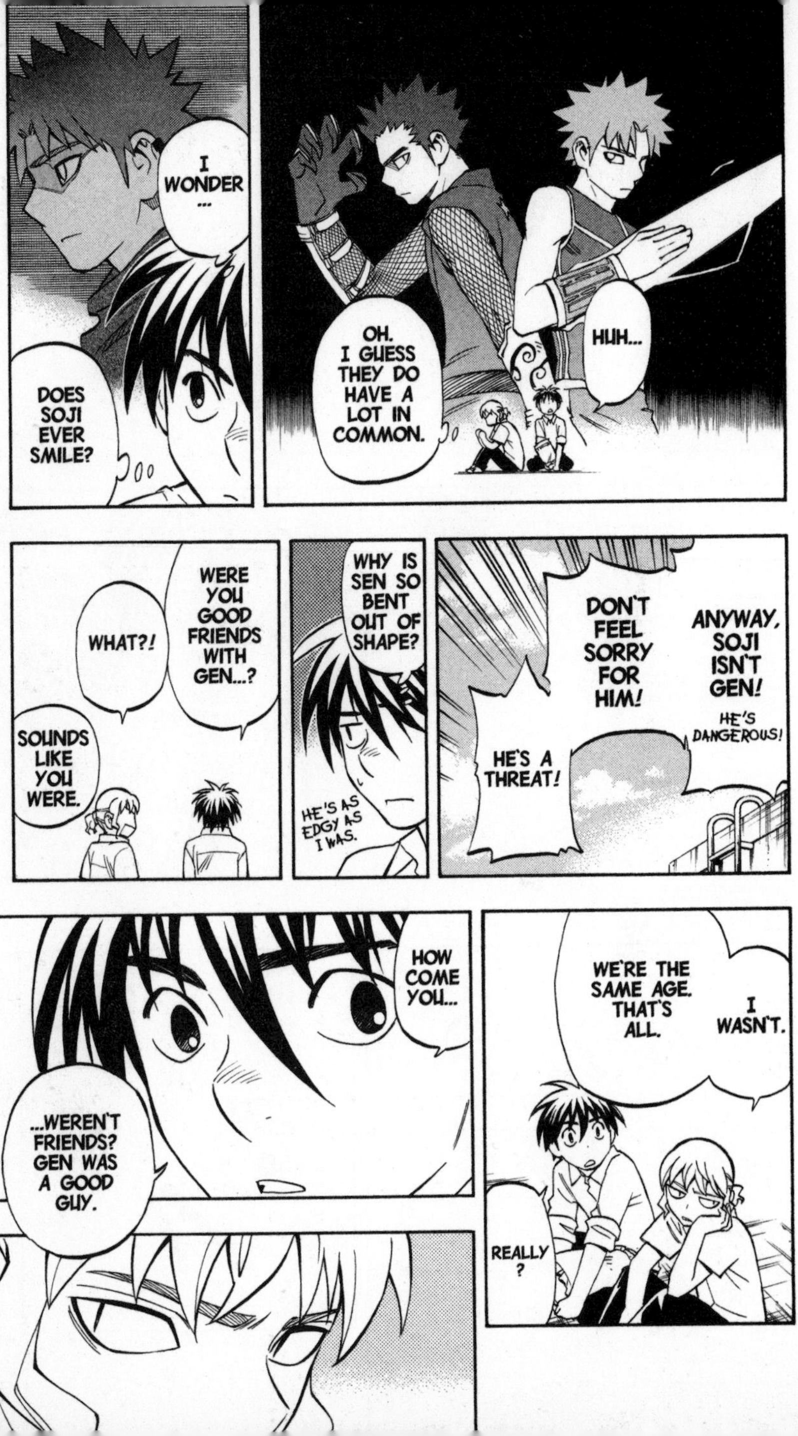
HUH...
OH. I GUESS THEY DO HAVE A LOT IN COMMON.
I WONDER ...
DOES SOJI EVER SMILE?
ANYWAY, SOJI ISN'T GEN!
HE'S DANGEROUS!
DON'T FEEL SORRY FOR HIM!
HE'S A THREAT!
WHY IS SEN SO BENT OUT OF SHAPE?
HE'S AS EDGY AS I WAS.
WERE YOU GOOD FRIENDS WITH GEN...?
WHAT?!
SOUNDS LIKE YOU WERE.
I WASN'T.
WE'RE THE SAME AGE. THAT'S ALL.
REALLY?
HOW COME YOU...
...WEREN'T FRIENDS? GEN WAS A GOOD GUY.

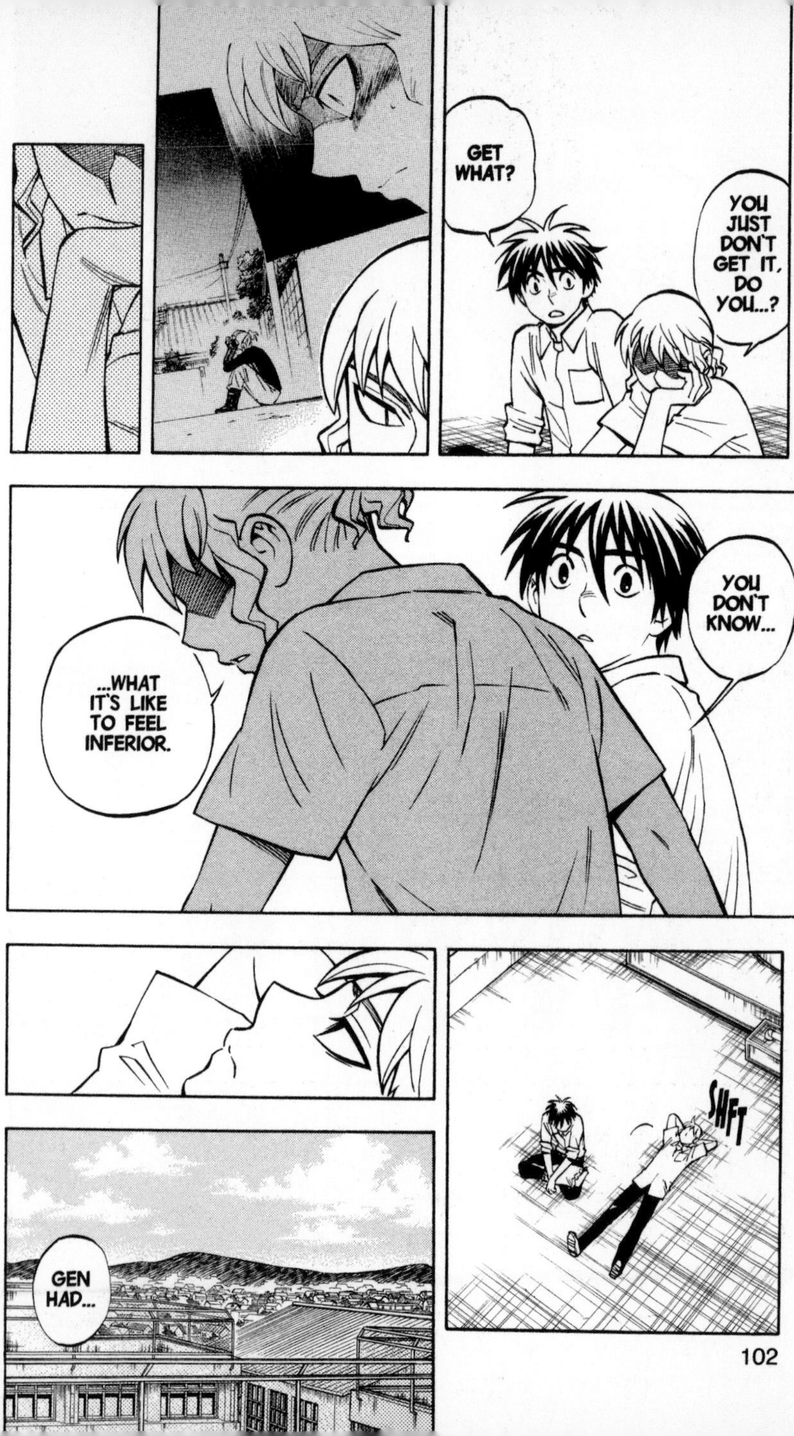
YOU JUST DON'T GET IT, DO YOU...?
GET WHAT?
YOU DON'T KNOW...
...WHAT IT'S LIKE TO FEEL INFERIOR.
SHFT
GEN HAD...

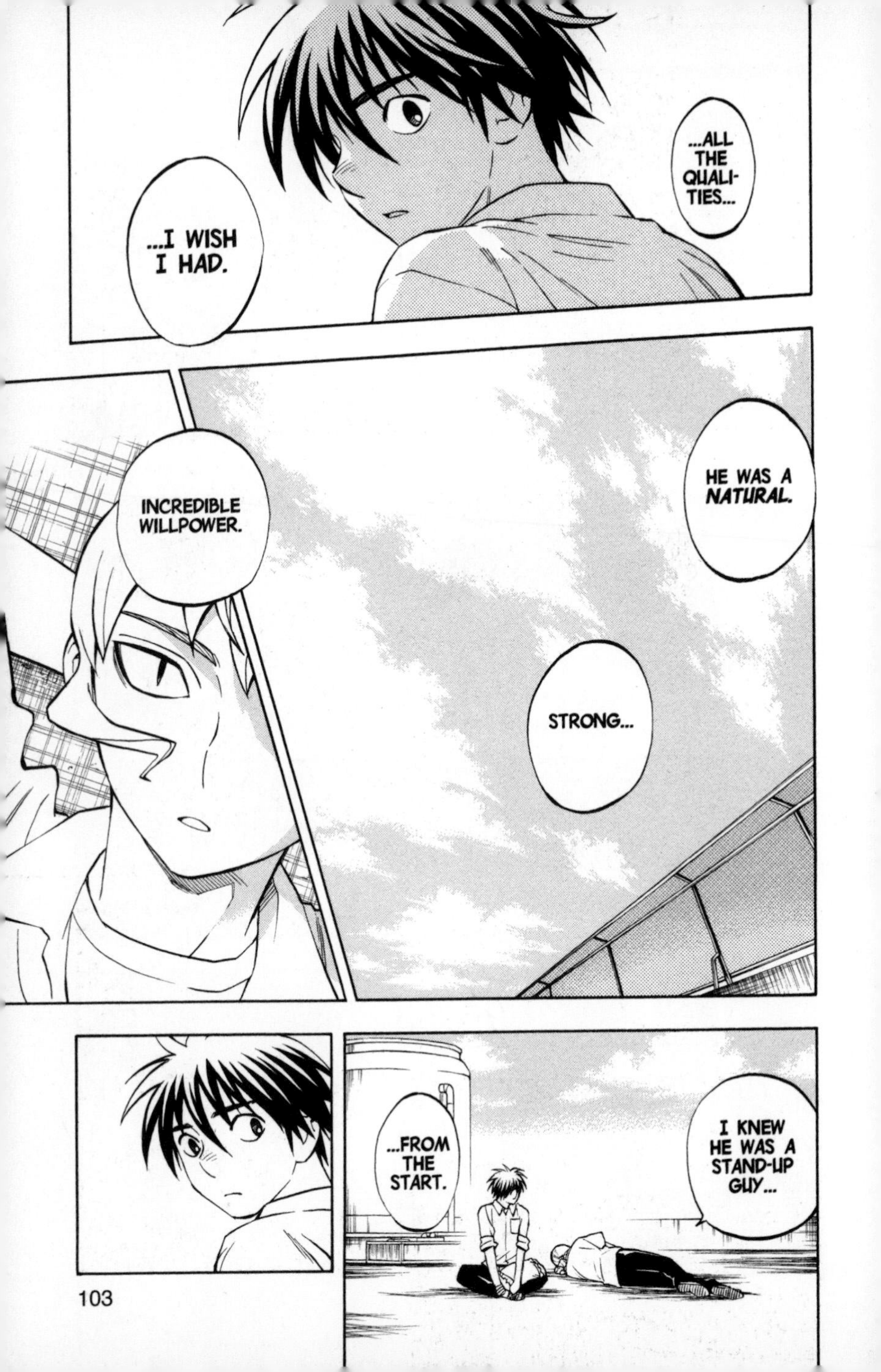
...ALL THE QUALITIES...
...I WISH I HAD.
HE WAS A *NATURAL.*
STRONG...
INCREDIBLE WILLPOWER.
I KNEW HE WAS A STAND-UP GUY...
...FROM THE START.

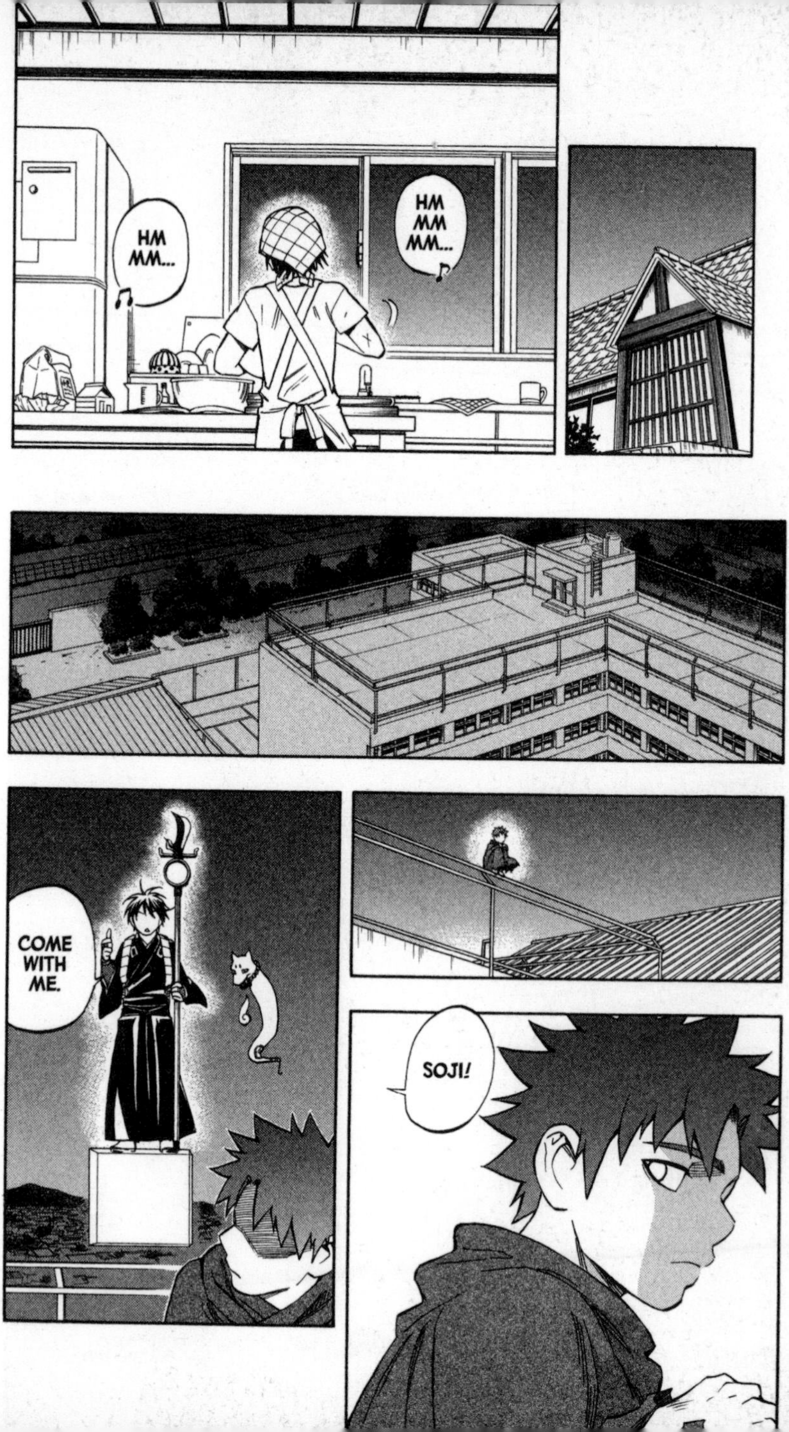
HM MM MM...
HM MM...
SOJI!
COME WITH ME.

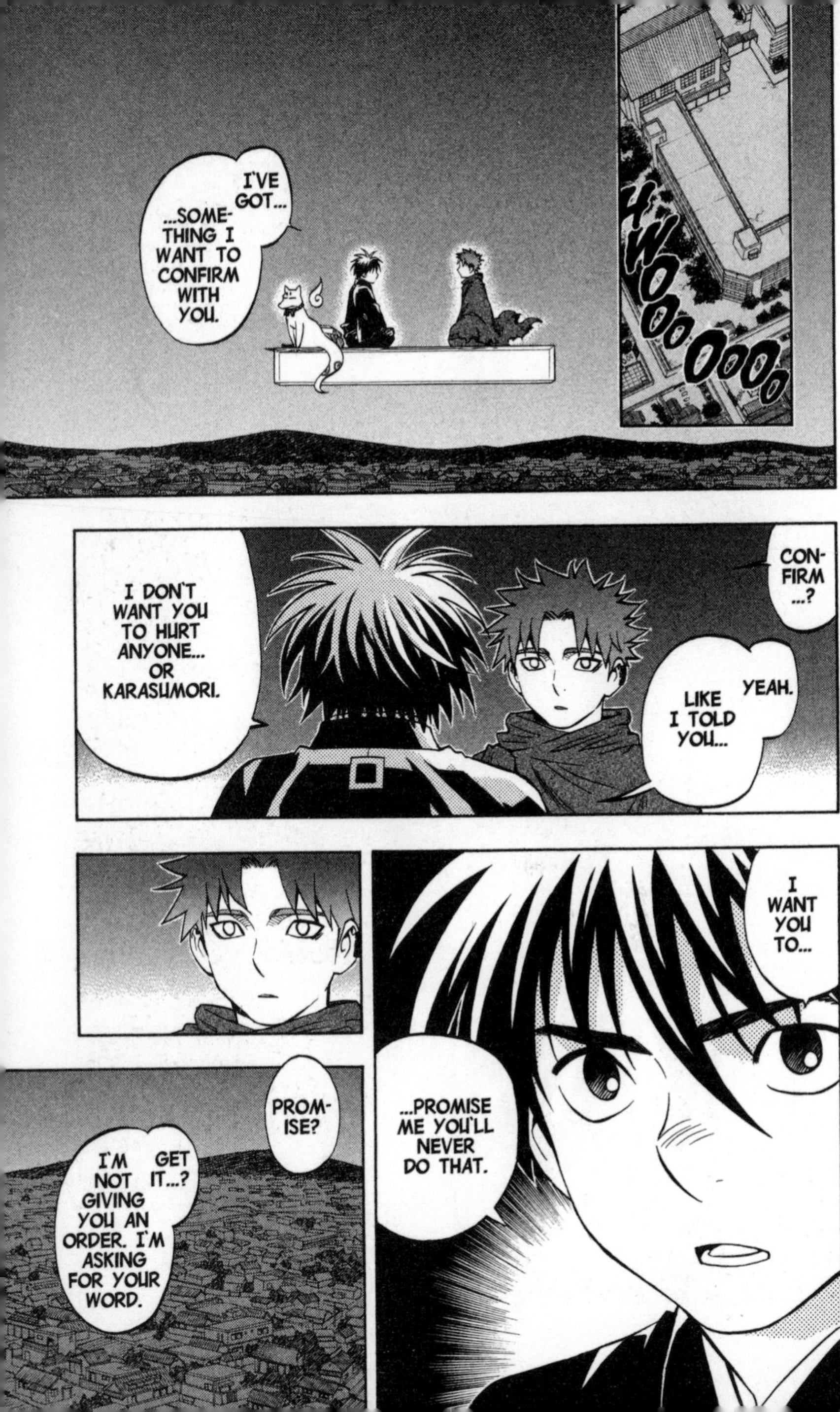
HWOOOOOOO
I'VE GOT... ...SOMETHING I WANT TO CONFIRM WITH YOU.
CONFIRM...?
YEAH. LIKE I TOLD YOU...
I DON'T WANT YOU TO HURT ANYONE... OR KARASUMORI.
I WANT YOU TO...
...PROMISE ME YOU'LL NEVER DO THAT.
PROMISE?
GET IT...? I'M NOT GIVING YOU AN ORDER. I'M ASKING FOR YOUR WORD.

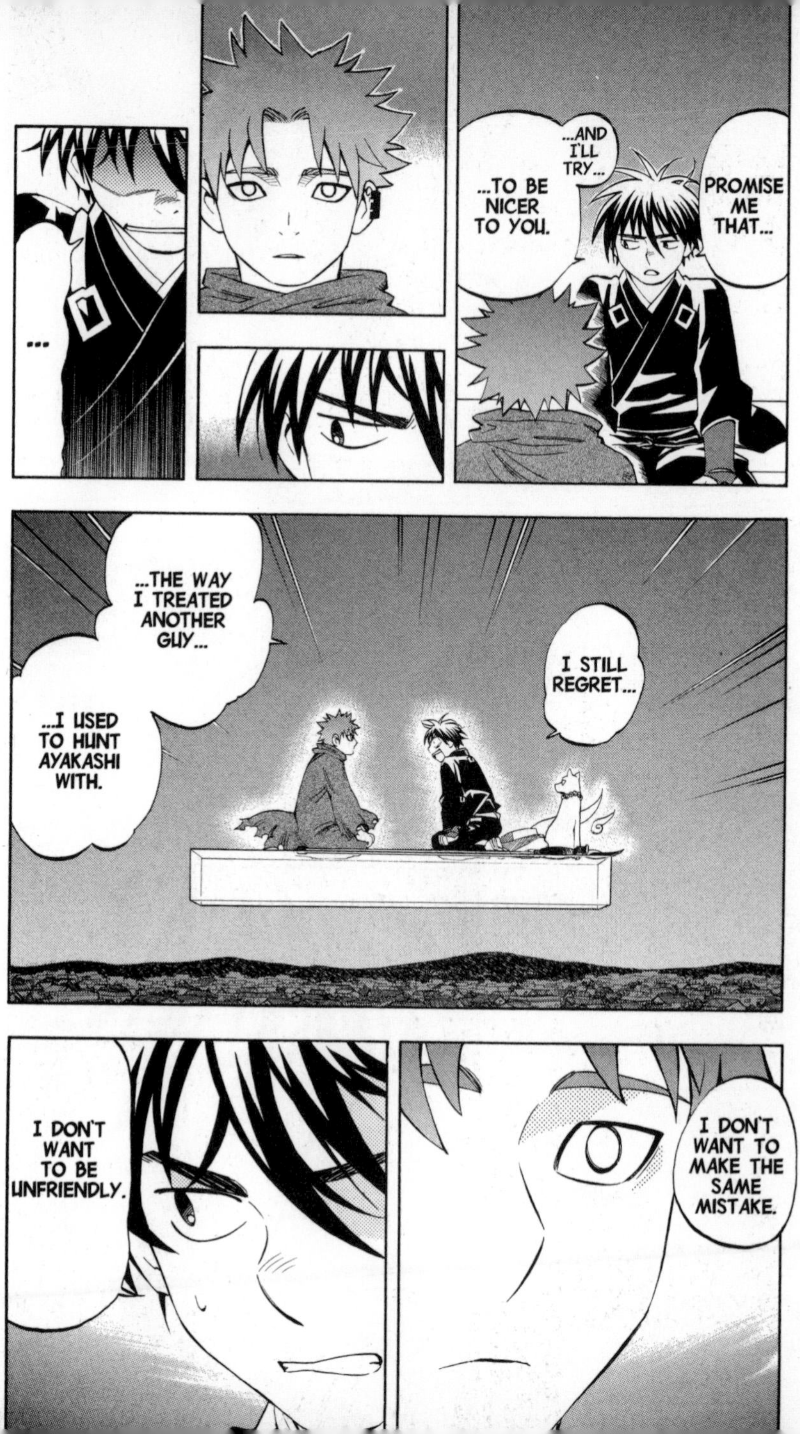
PROMISE ME THAT...
...AND I'LL TRY...
...TO BE NICER TO YOU.
...
I STILL REGRET...
...THE WAY I TREATED ANOTHER GUY...
...I USED TO HUNT AYAKASHI WITH.
I DON'T WANT TO MAKE THE SAME MISTAKE.
I DON'T WANT TO BE UNFRIENDLY.

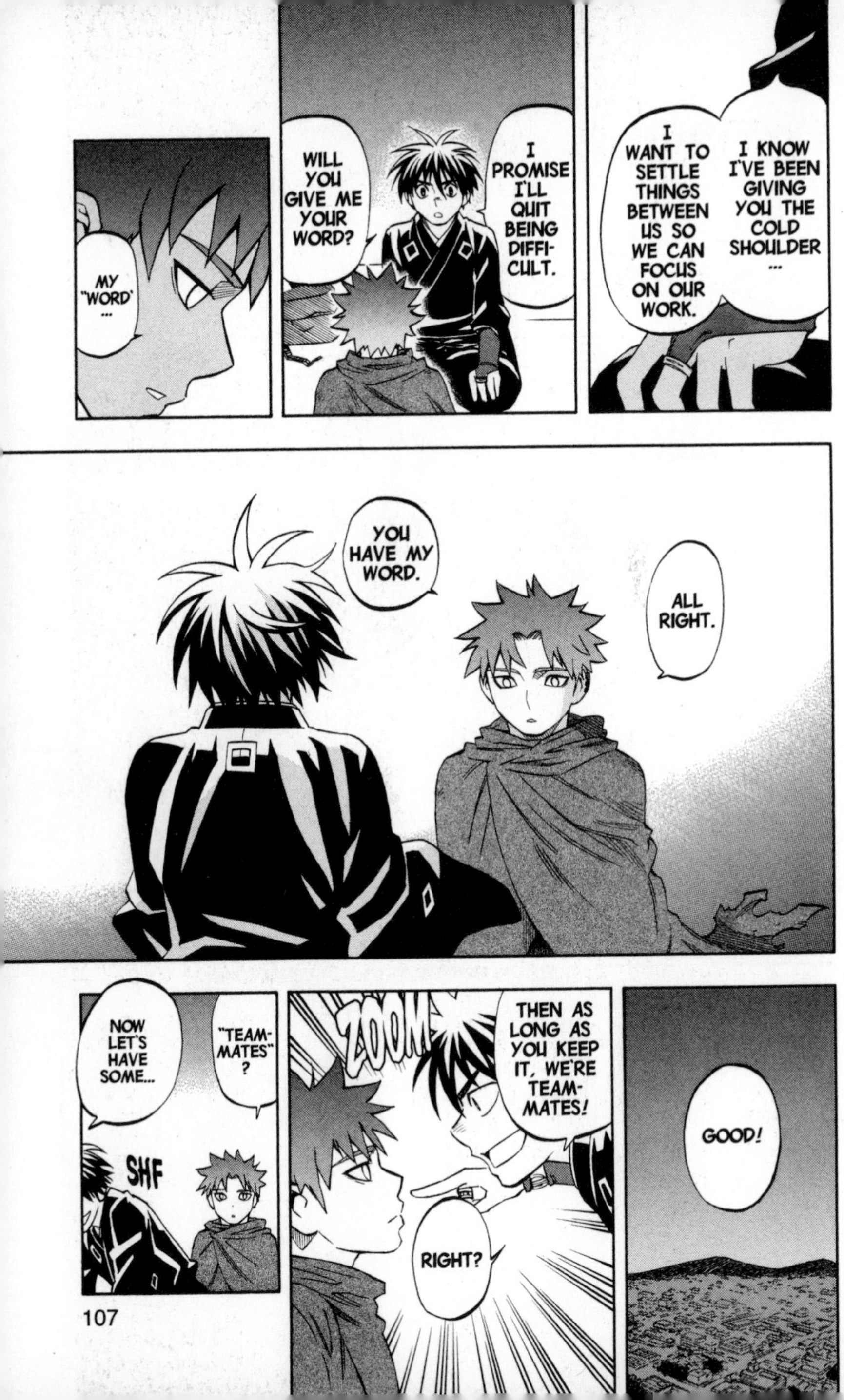
I KNOW I'VE BEEN GIVING YOU THE COLD SHOULDER...
I WANT TO SETTLE THINGS BETWEEN US SO WE CAN FOCUS ON OUR WORK.
I PROMISE I'LL QUIT BEING DIFFI-CULT.
WILL YOU GIVE ME YOUR WORD?
MY "WORD"...
ALL RIGHT.
YOU HAVE MY WORD.
GOOD!
ZOOM
THEN AS LONG AS YOU KEEP IT, WE'RE TEAM-MATES!
RIGHT?
"TEAM-MATES"?
NOW LET'S HAVE SOME...
SHF

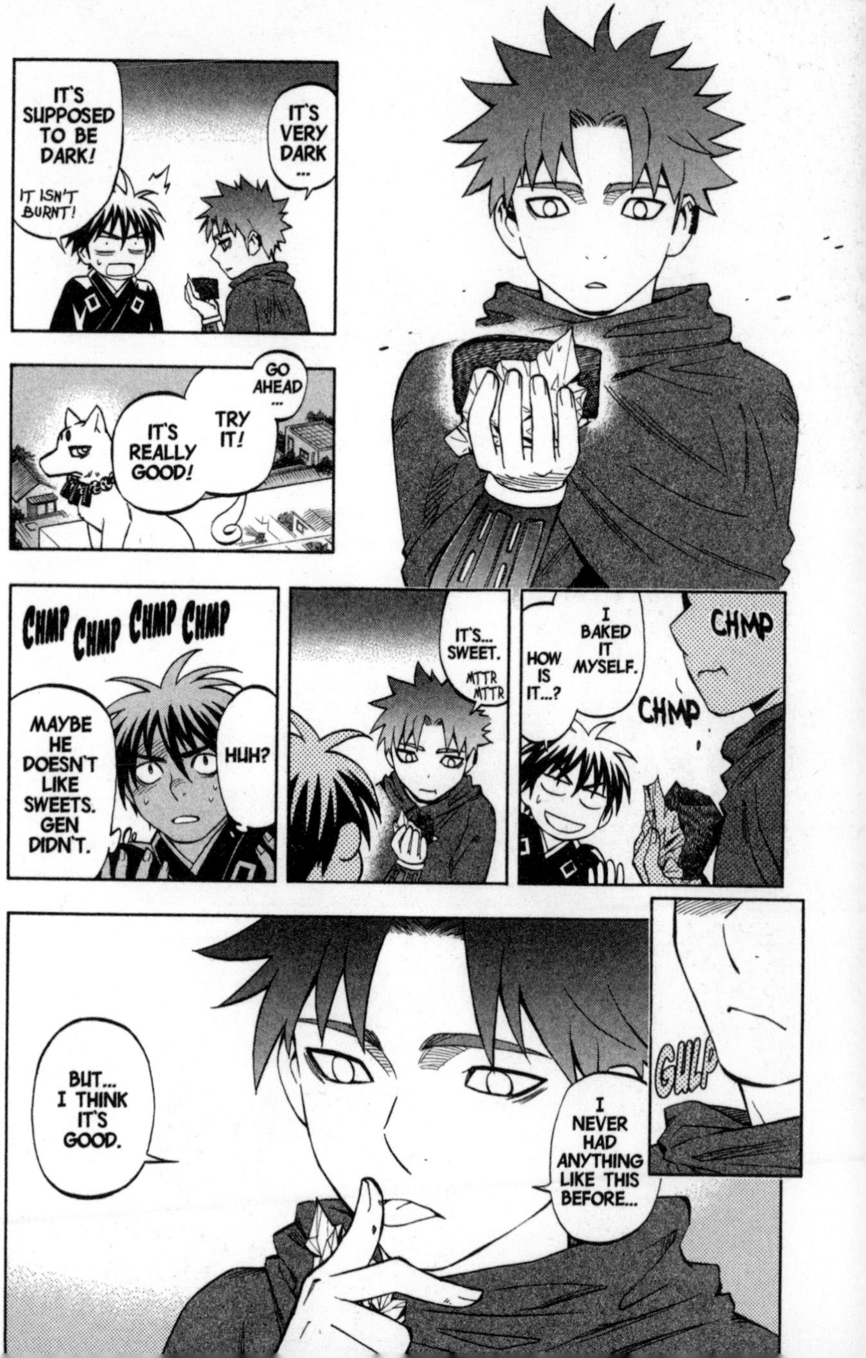
IT'S VERY DARK ...
IT'S SUPPOSED TO BE DARK!
IT ISN'T BURNT!
GO AHEAD ...
TRY IT!
IT'S REALLY GOOD!
CHMP
I BAKED IT MYSELF.
HOW IS IT...?
CHMP
IT'S... SWEET.
MTTR MTTR
CHMP CHMP CHMP CHMP
HUH?
MAYBE HE DOESN'T LIKE SWEETS. GEN DIDN'T.
GULP
I NEVER HAD ANYTHING LIKE THIS BEFORE...
BUT... I THINK IT'S GOOD.

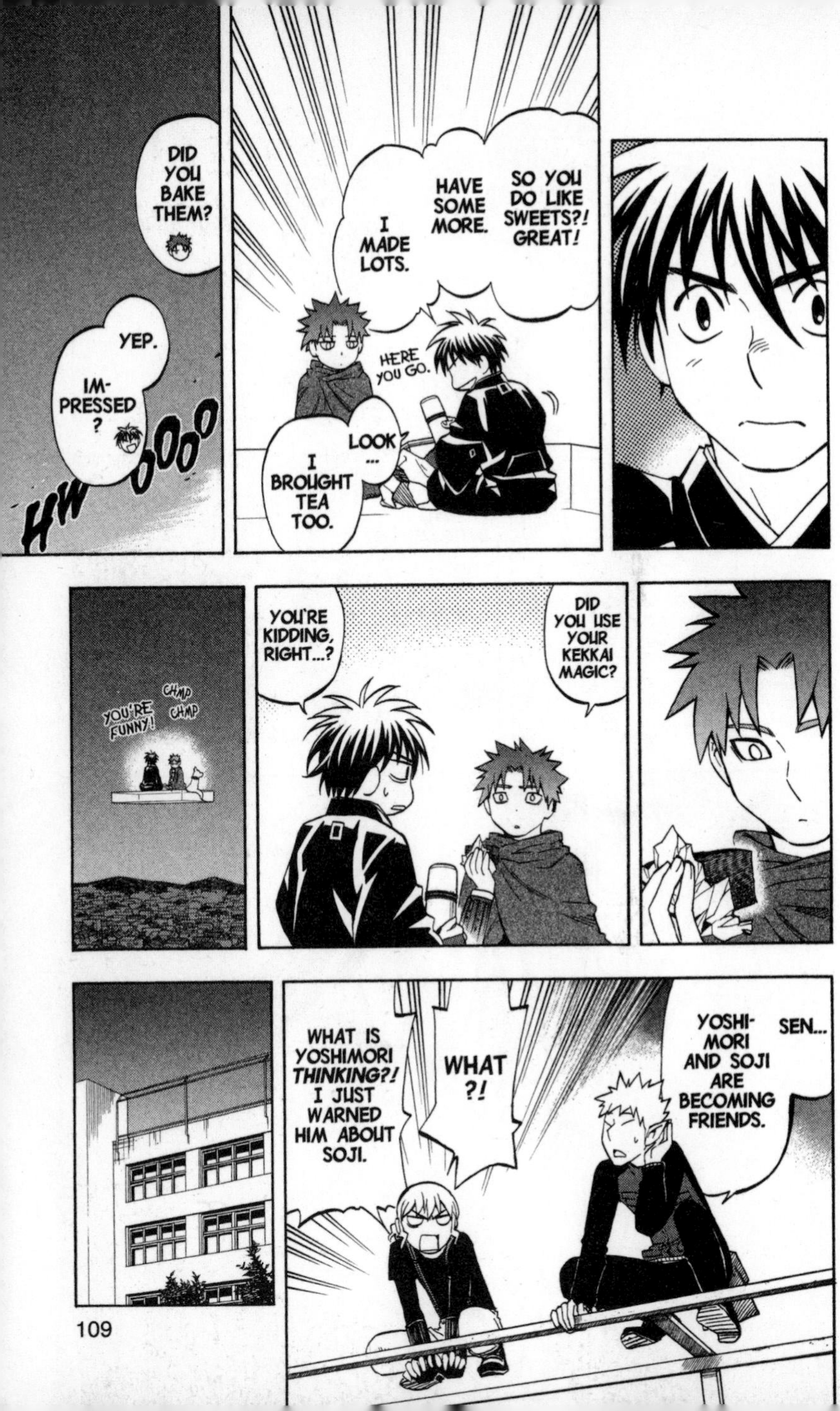
SO YOU DO LIKE SWEETS?! GREAT!
HAVE SOME MORE.
I MADE LOTS.
HERE YOU GO.
LOOK ... I BROUGHT TEA TOO.
DID YOU BAKE THEM?
YEP. IM-PRESSED?
HWOOOO
DID YOU USE YOUR KEKKAI MAGIC?
YOU'RE KIDDING, RIGHT...?
CHMP CHMP
YOU'RE FUNNY!
SEN...
YOSHI-MORI AND SOJI ARE BECOMING FRIENDS.
WHAT?!
WHAT IS YOSHIMORI THINKING?! I JUST WARNED HIM ABOUT SOJI.

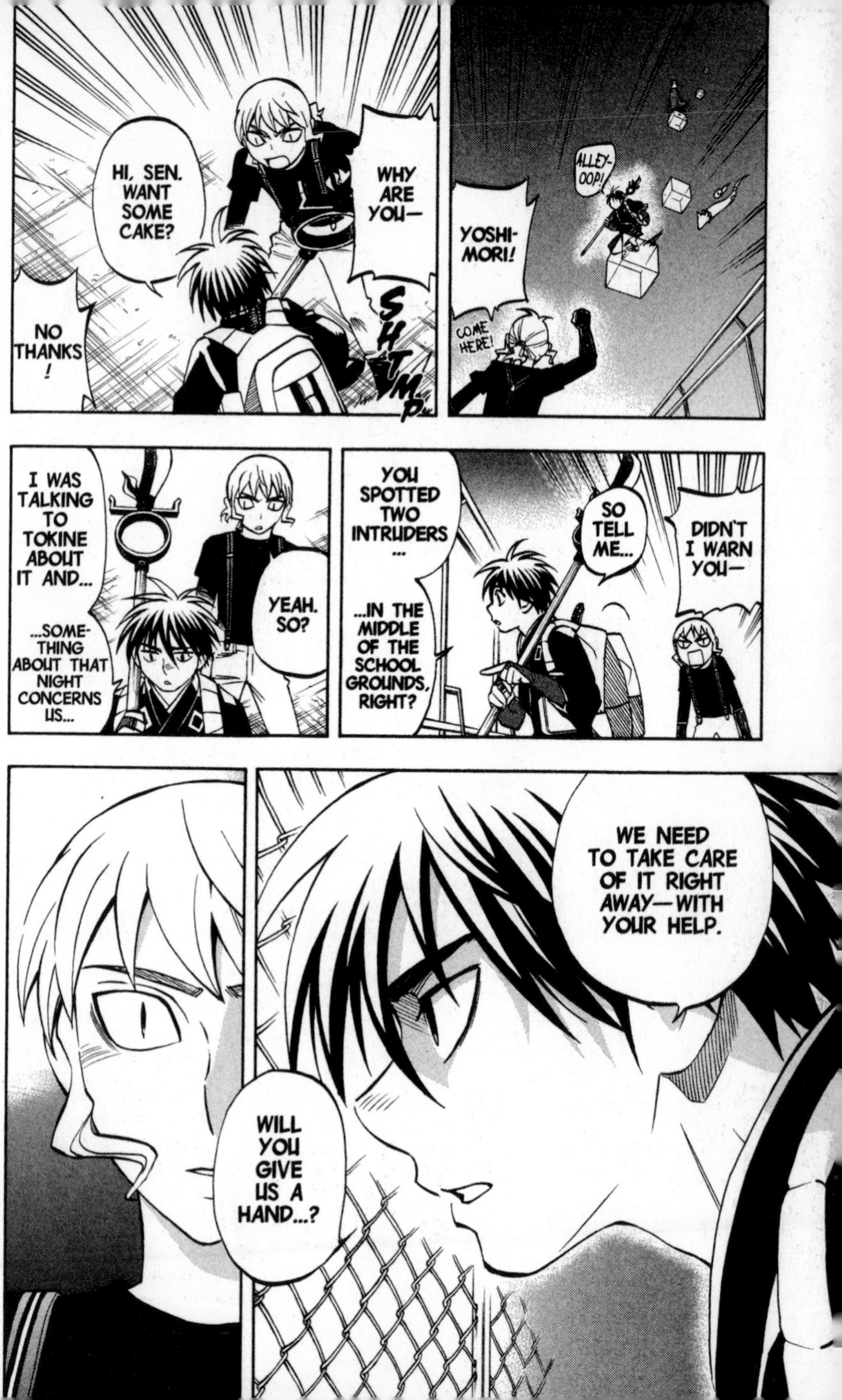
YOSHI-MORI!
ALLEY-OOP!
COME HERE!
WHY ARE YOU—
HI, SEN. WANT SOME CAKE?
SHTMP
NO THANKS!
DIDN'T I WARN YOU—
SO TELL ME...
YOU SPOTTED TWO INTRUDERS...
...IN THE MIDDLE OF THE SCHOOL GROUNDS, RIGHT?
YEAH. SO?
I WAS TALKING TO TOKINE ABOUT IT AND...
...SOME-THING ABOUT THAT NIGHT CONCERNS US...
WE NEED TO TAKE CARE OF IT RIGHT AWAY—WITH YOUR HELP.
WILL YOU GIVE US A HAND...?

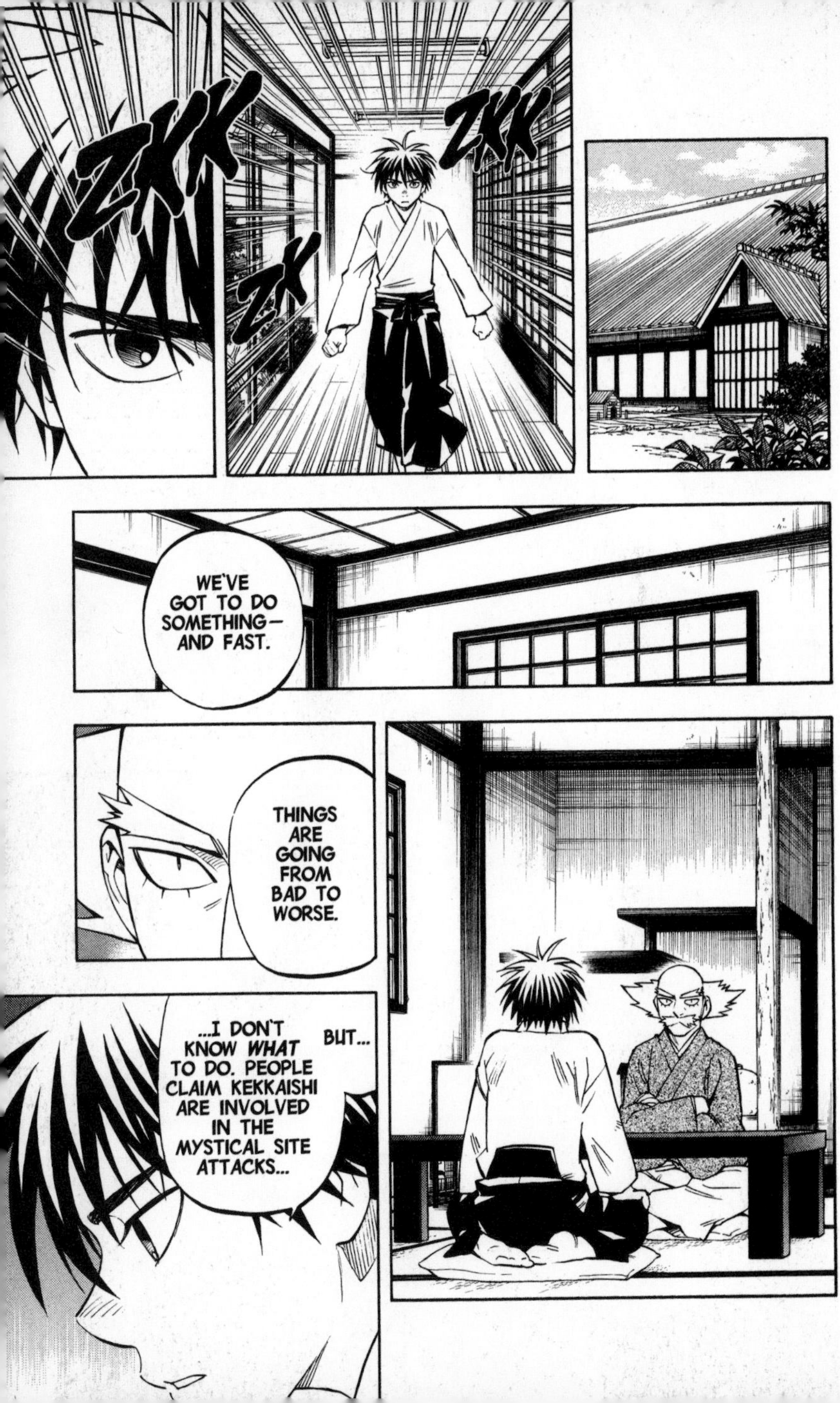
ZKK
ZK
ZKK
WE'VE GOT TO DO SOMETHING— AND FAST.
THINGS ARE GOING FROM BAD TO WORSE.
BUT...
...I DON'T KNOW *WHAT* TO DO. PEOPLE CLAIM KEKKAISHI ARE INVOLVED IN THE MYSTICAL SITE ATTACKS...

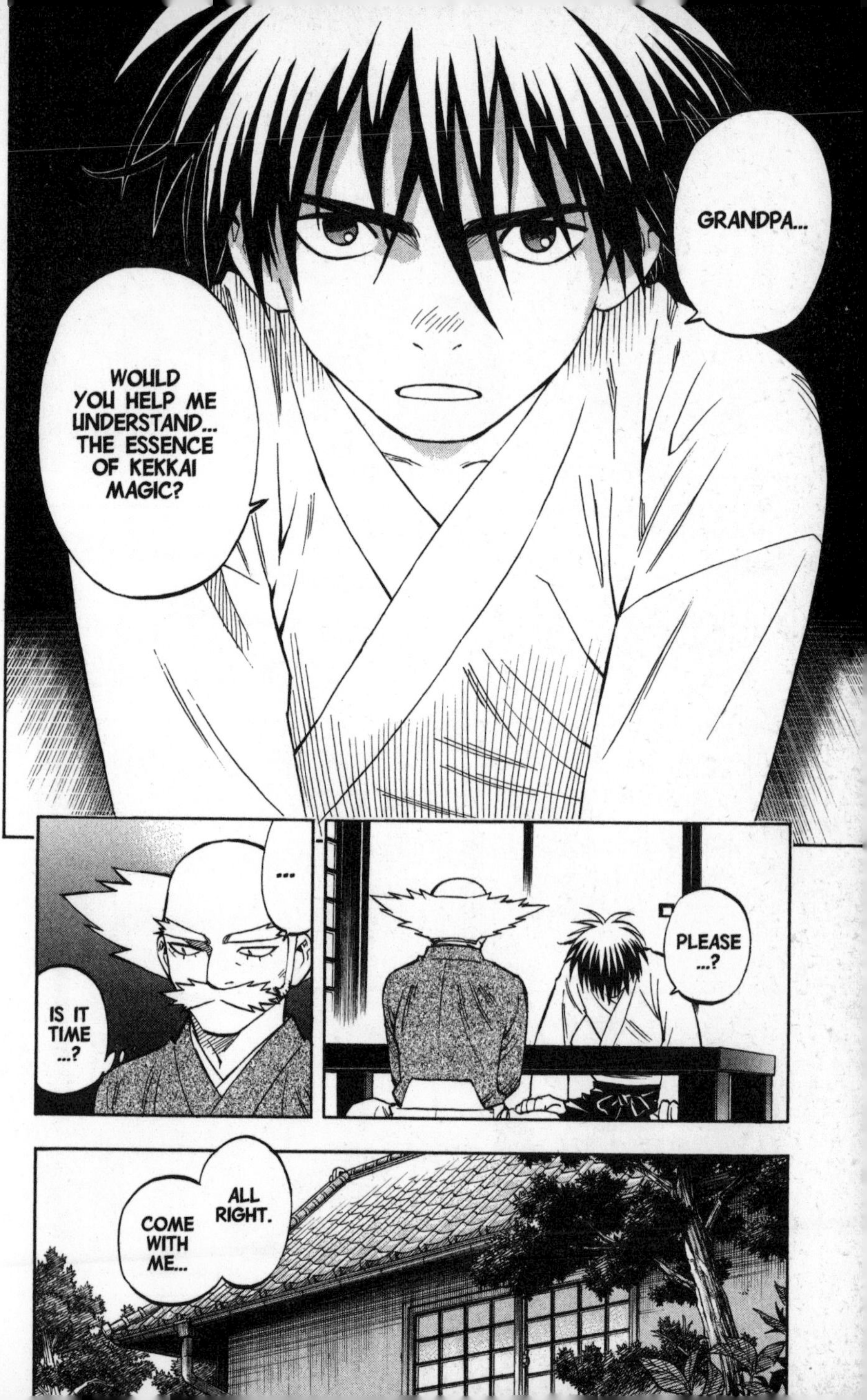
GRANDPA...
WOULD YOU HELP ME UNDERSTAND... THE ESSENCE OF KEKKAI MAGIC?
PLEASE ...?
...
IS IT TIME ...?
ALL RIGHT.
COME WITH ME...

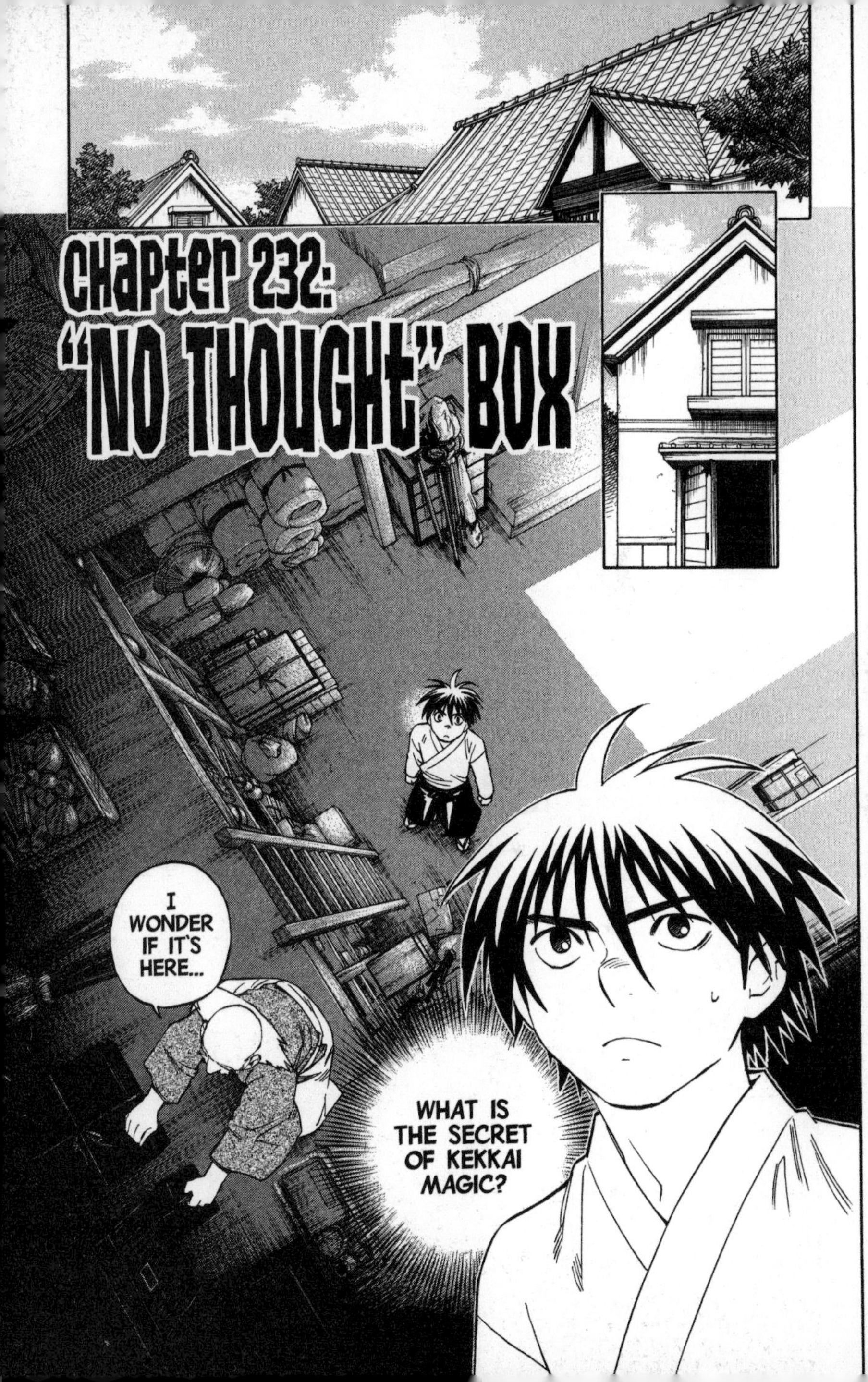
CHAPTER 232:
"NO THOUGHT" BOX
I WONDER IF IT'S HERE...
WHAT IS THE SECRET OF KEKKAI MAGIC?

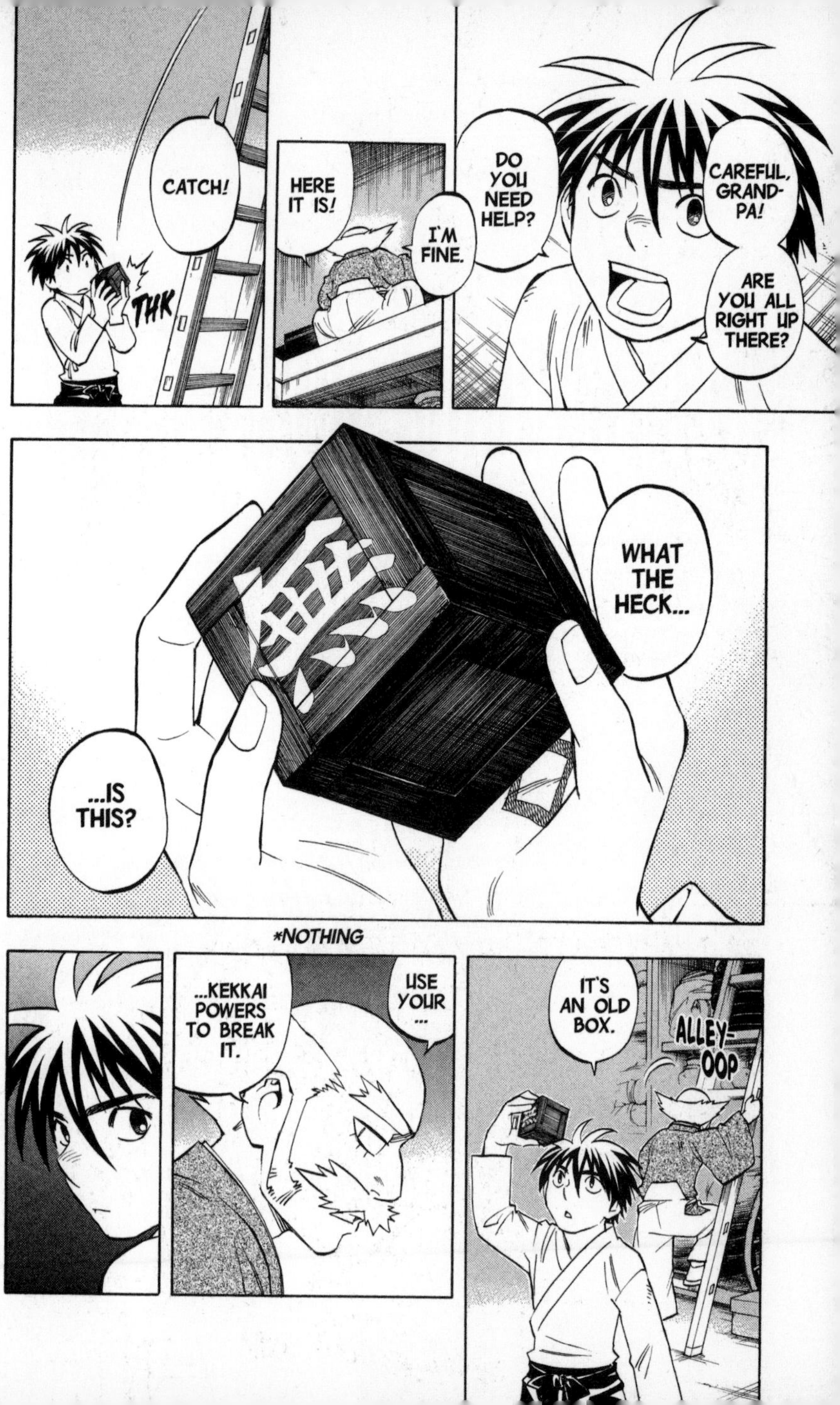
CAREFUL, GRANDPA!
ARE YOU ALL RIGHT UP THERE?
DO YOU NEED HELP?
I'M FINE.
HERE IT IS!
CATCH!
THK
WHAT THE HECK...
...IS THIS?
*NOTHING
IT'S AN OLD BOX.
ALLEY-OOP
USE YOUR ...
...KEKKAI POWERS TO BREAK IT.

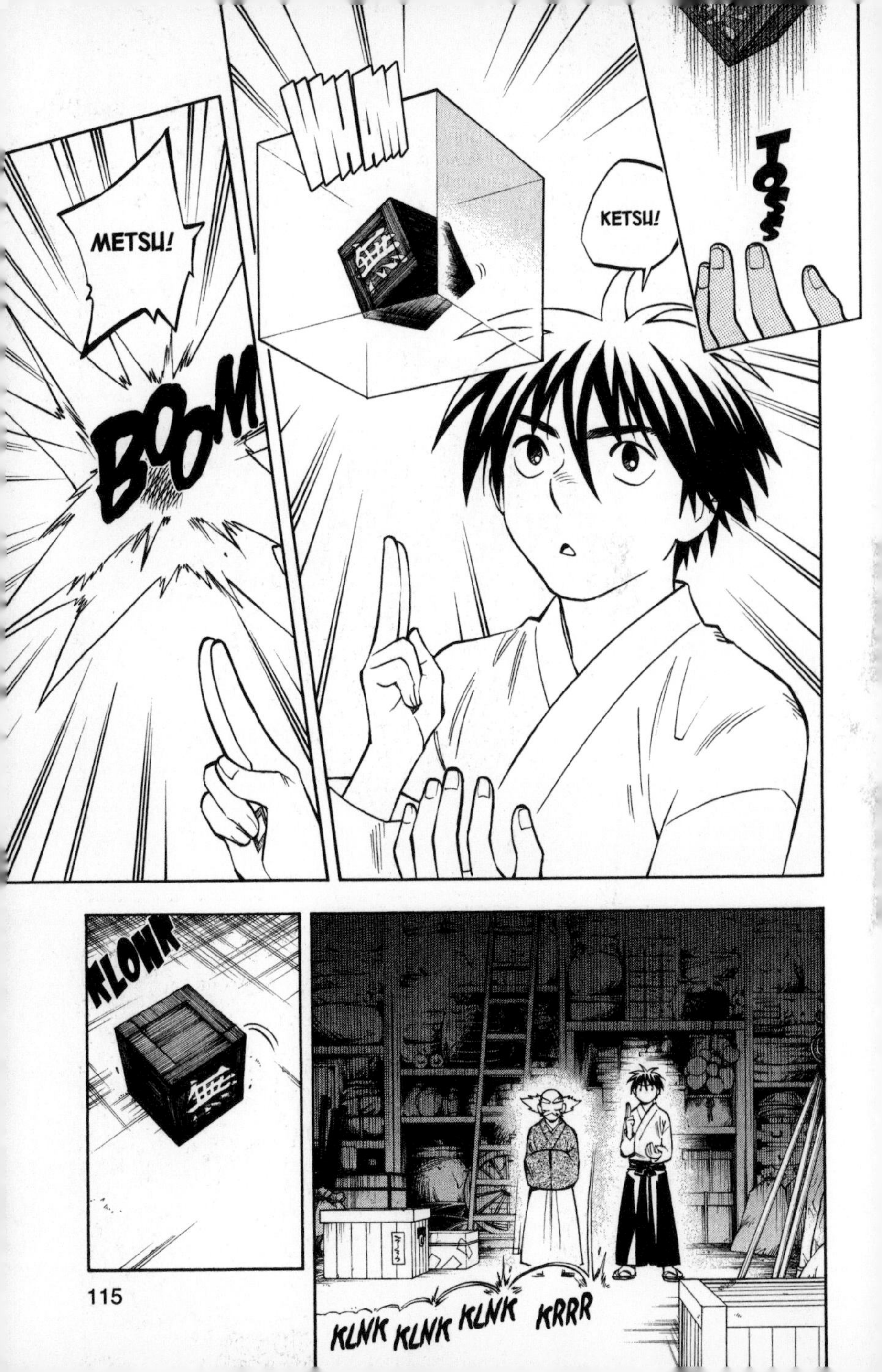
TOSS
KETSU!
WHAM
METSU!
BOOM
KLNK KLNK KLNK KRRR
KLONK

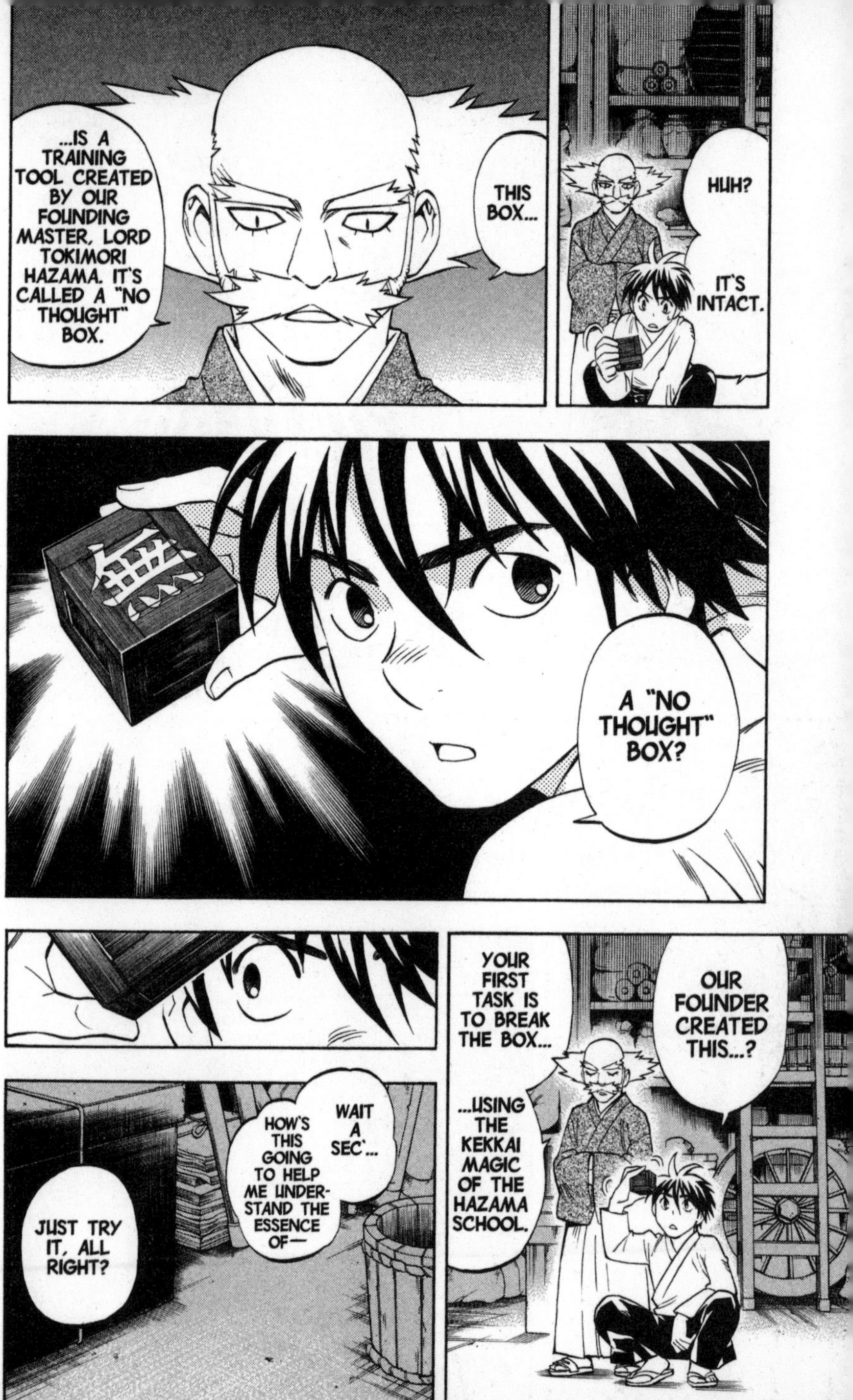
HUH?
IT'S INTACT.
THIS BOX...
...IS A TRAINING TOOL CREATED BY OUR FOUNDING MASTER, LORD TOKIMORI HAZAMA. IT'S CALLED A "NO THOUGHT" BOX.
A "NO THOUGHT" BOX?
OUR FOUNDER CREATED THIS...?
YOUR FIRST TASK IS TO BREAK THE BOX...
...USING THE KEKKAI MAGIC OF THE HAZAMA SCHOOL.
WAIT A SEC'...
HOW'S THIS GOING TO HELP ME UNDER-STAND THE ESSENCE OF—
JUST TRY IT, ALL RIGHT?

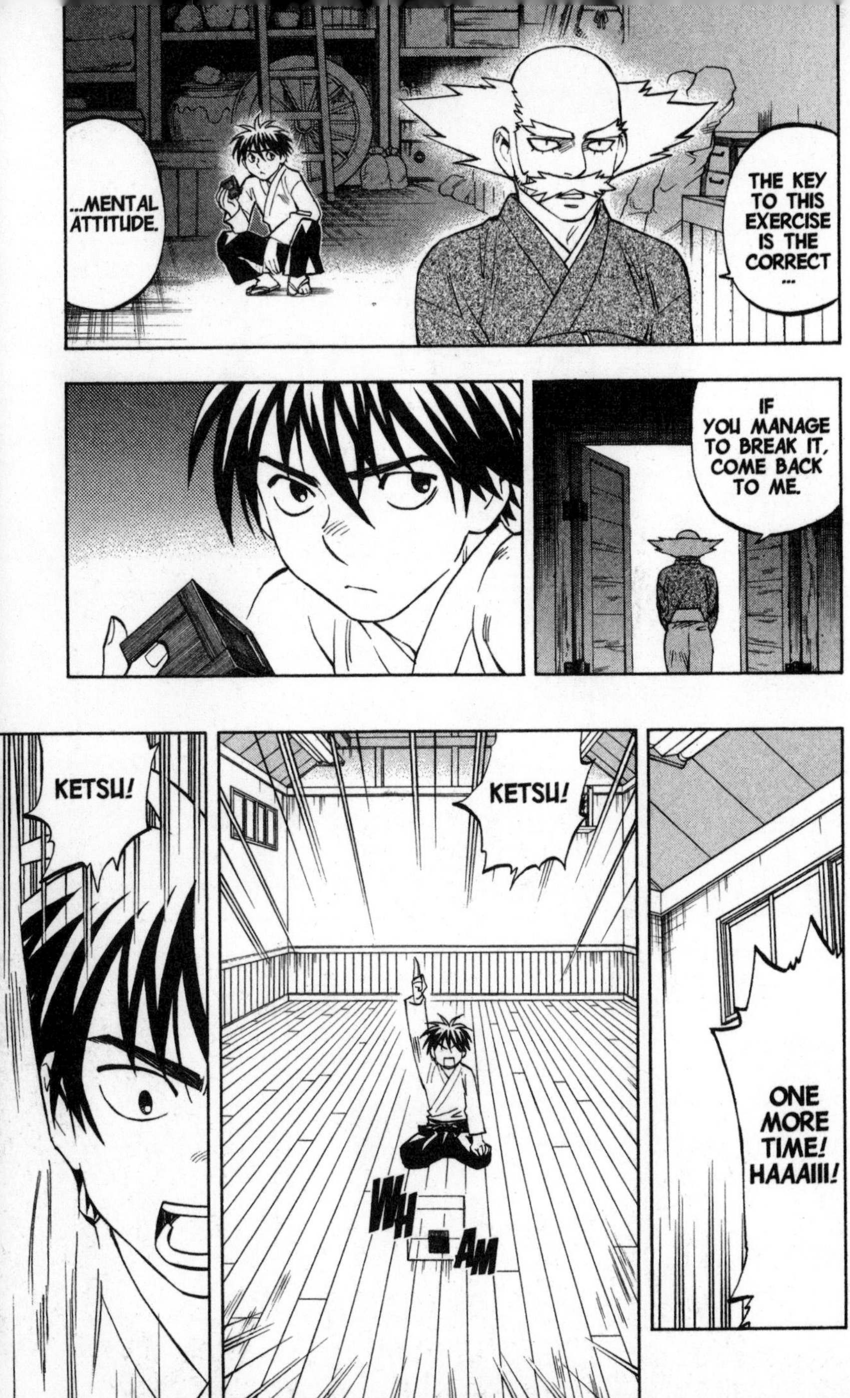
THE KEY TO THIS EXERCISE IS THE CORRECT ...
...MENTAL ATTITUDE.
IF YOU MANAGE TO BREAK IT, COME BACK TO ME.
ONE MORE TIME! HAAAIII!
KETSU!
WH-AM
KETSU!

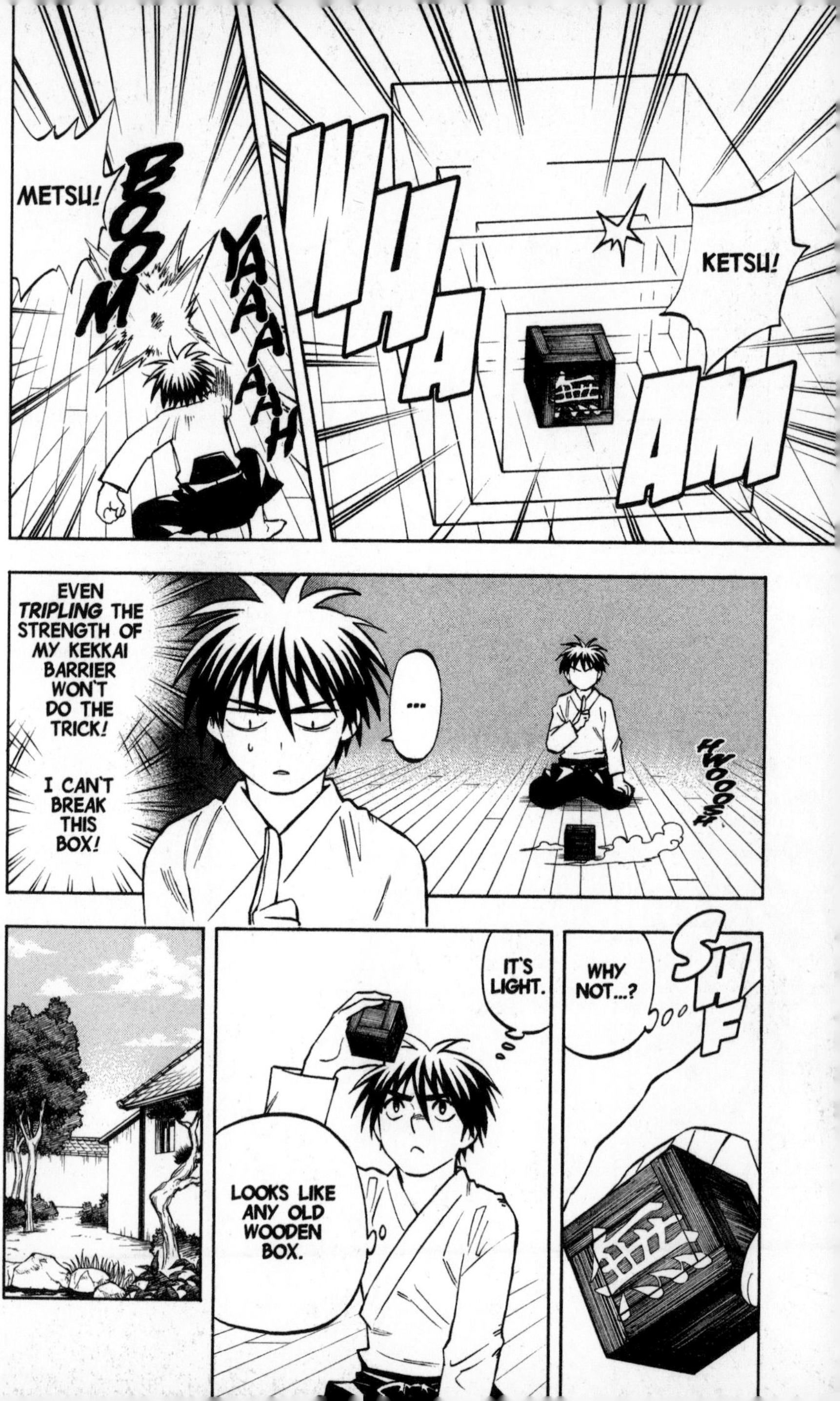
KETSU!
WHA
AM
METSU!
BOOM
YAAAAAH
...
HWOOOSH
EVEN *TRIPLING* THE STRENGTH OF MY KEKKAI BARRIER WON'T DO THE TRICK!
I CAN'T BREAK THIS BOX!
SHF
WHY NOT...?
IT'S LIGHT.
LOOKS LIKE ANY OLD WOODEN BOX.

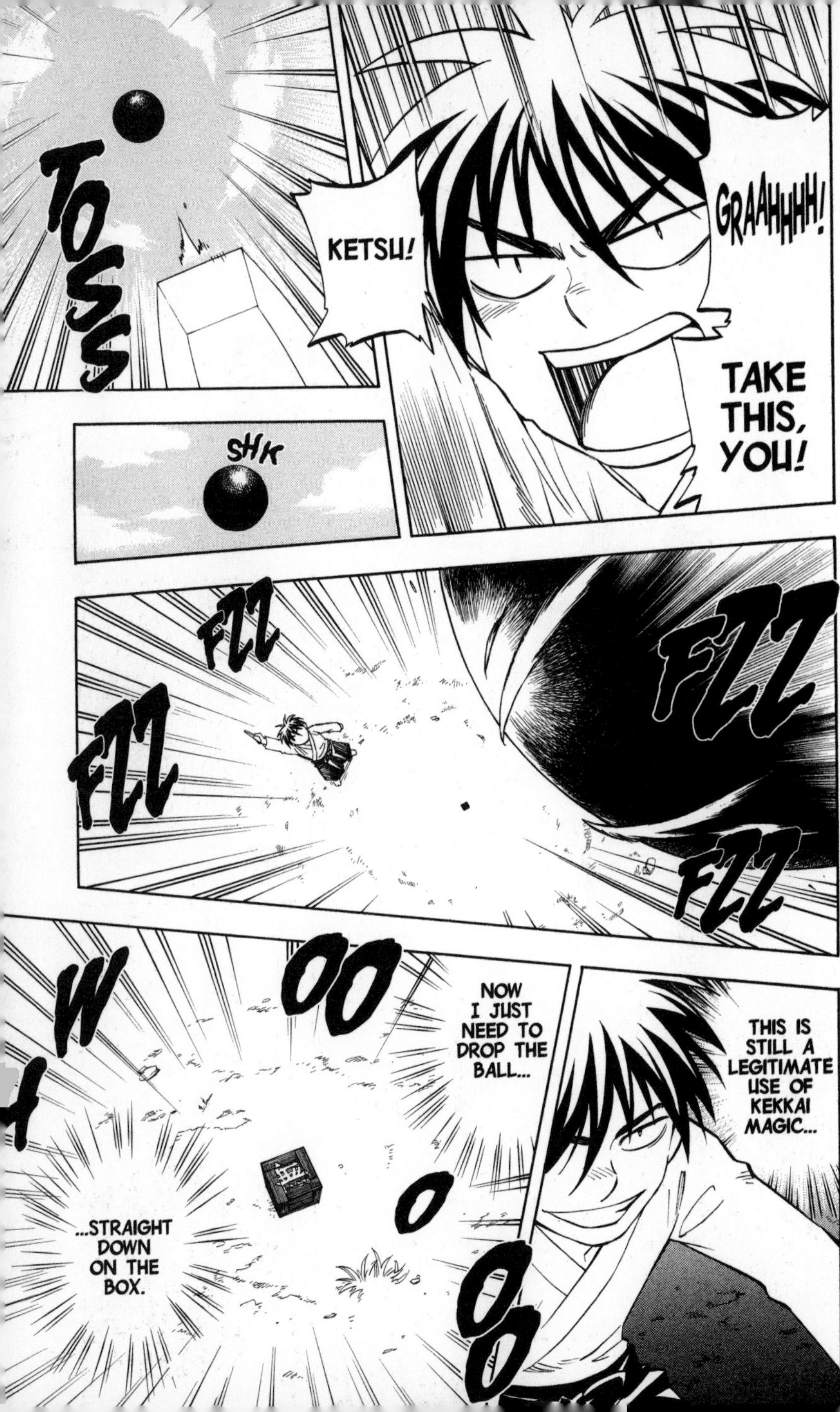
GRAAHHHH!
KETSU!
TAKE THIS, YOU!
TOSS
SHK
FZZ
FZZ
FZZ
FZZ
THIS IS STILL A LEGITIMATE USE OF KEKKAI MAGIC...
NOW I JUST NEED TO DROP THE BALL...
WHOOOOOO
...STRAIGHT DOWN ON THE BOX.

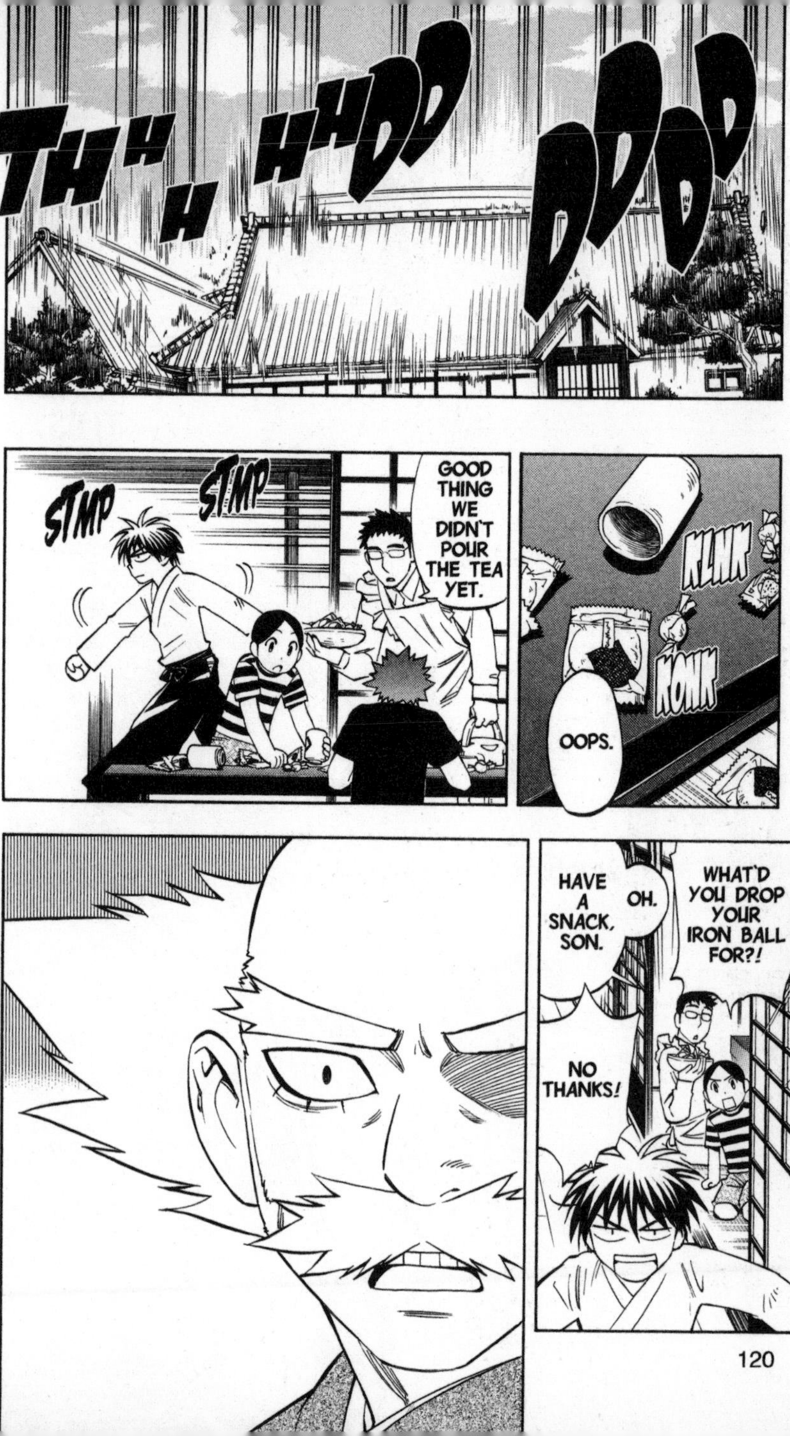
THHHHHDDDDDDD
KLNK
KONK
OOPS.
GOOD THING WE DIDN'T POUR THE TEA YET.
STMP
STMP
WHAT'D YOU DROP YOUR IRON BALL FOR?!
OH.
HAVE A SNACK, SON.
NO THANKS!

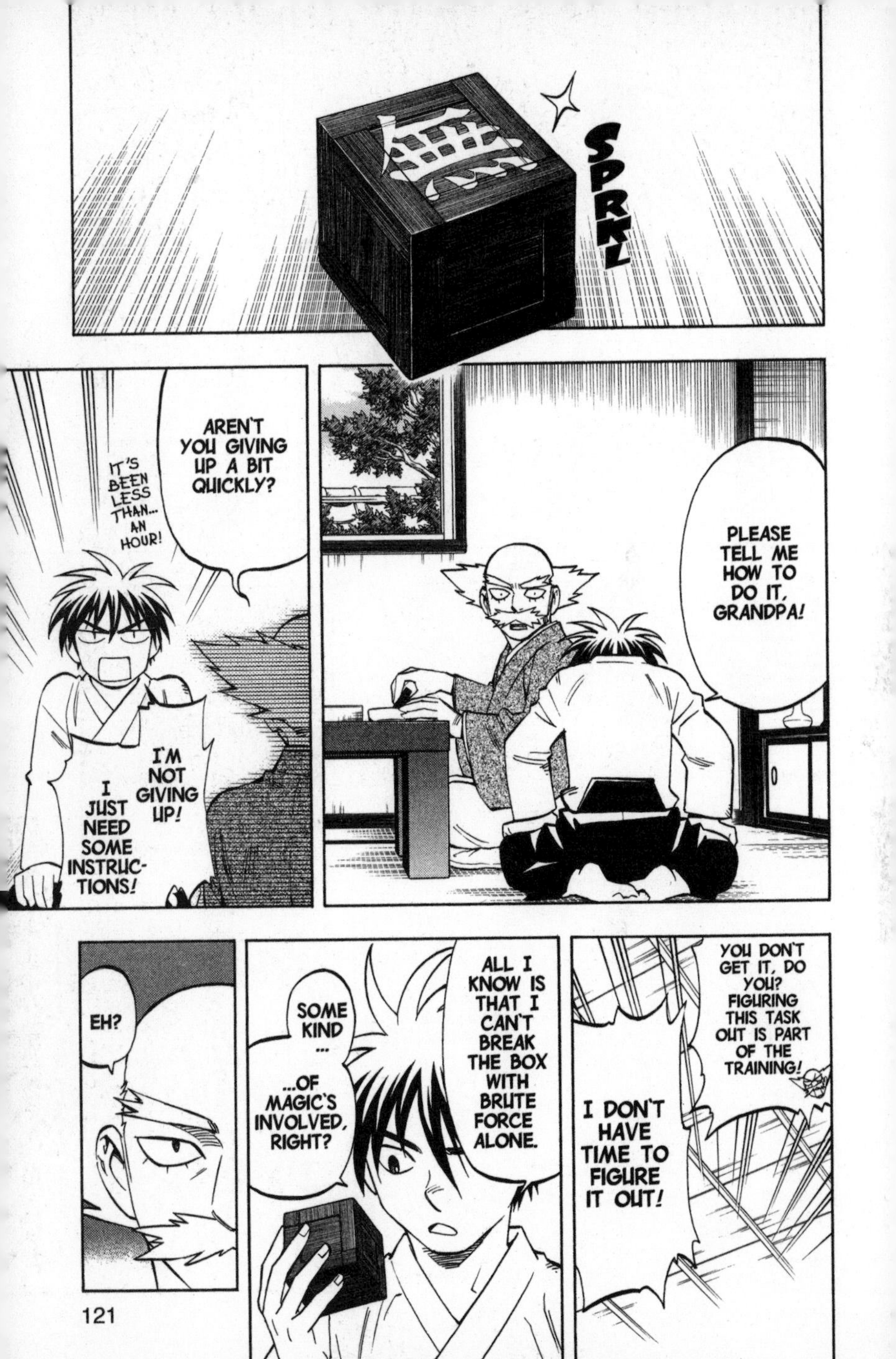
SPRKL
PLEASE TELL ME HOW TO DO IT, GRANDPA!
AREN'T YOU GIVING UP A BIT QUICKLY?
IT'S BEEN LESS THAN... AN HOUR!
I'M NOT GIVING UP!
I JUST NEED SOME INSTRUCTIONS!
YOU DON'T GET IT, DO YOU? FIGURING THIS TASK OUT IS PART OF THE TRAINING!
I DON'T HAVE TIME TO FIGURE IT OUT!
ALL I KNOW IS THAT I CAN'T BREAK THE BOX WITH BRUTE FORCE ALONE.
SOME KIND ...
...OF MAGIC'S INVOLVED, RIGHT?
EH?

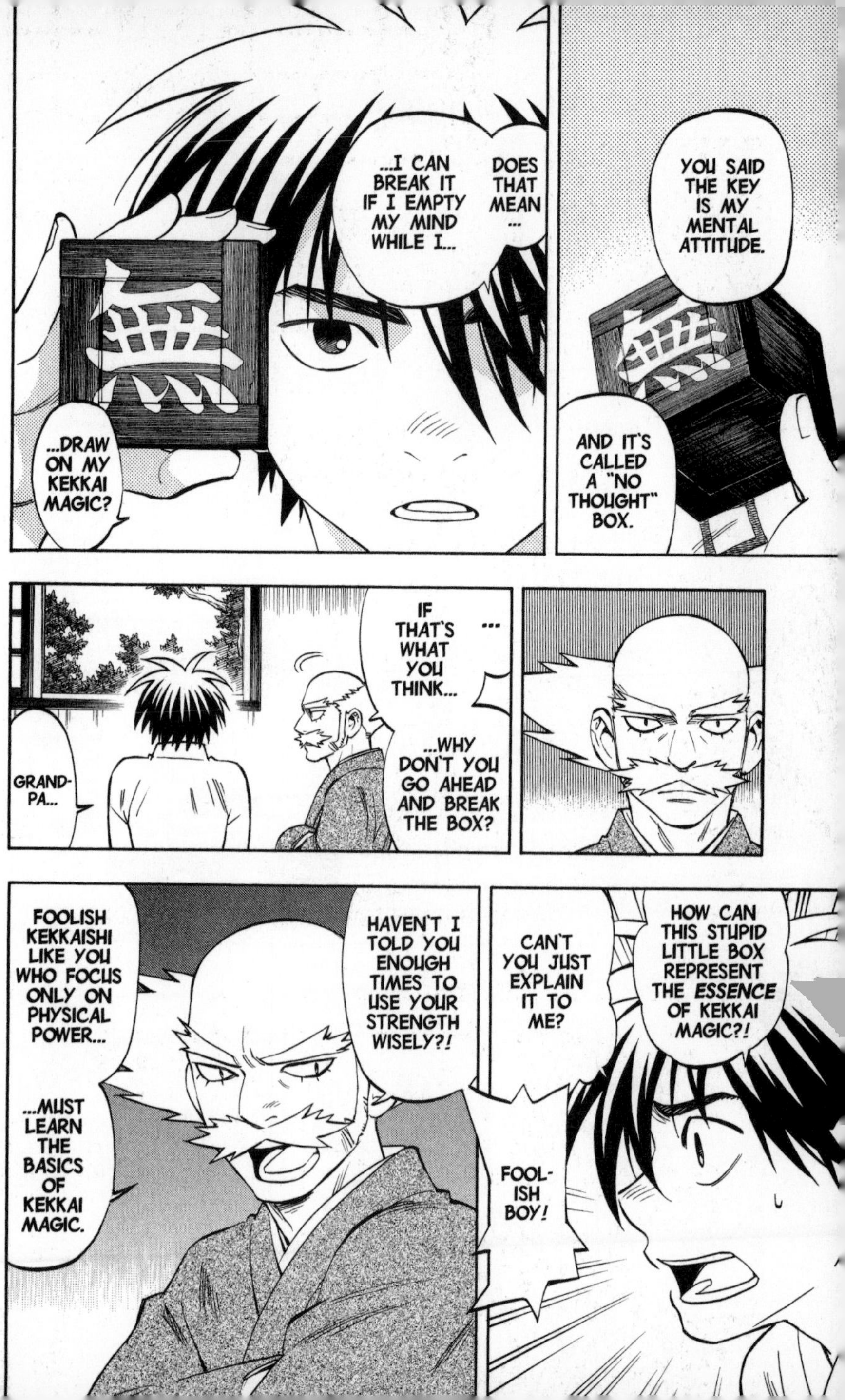
YOU SAID THE KEY IS MY MENTAL ATTITUDE.
AND IT'S CALLED A "NO THOUGHT" BOX.
DOES THAT MEAN...
...I CAN BREAK IT IF I EMPTY MY MIND WHILE I...
...DRAW ON MY KEKKAI MAGIC?
...
IF THAT'S WHAT YOU THINK...
...WHY DON'T YOU GO AHEAD AND BREAK THE BOX?
GRAND-PA...
HOW CAN THIS STUPID LITTLE BOX REPRESENT THE *ESSENCE* OF KEKKAI MAGIC?!
CAN'T YOU JUST EXPLAIN IT TO ME?
FOOL-ISH BOY!
HAVEN'T I TOLD YOU ENOUGH TIMES TO USE YOUR STRENGTH WISELY?!
FOOLISH KEKKAISHI LIKE YOU WHO FOCUS ONLY ON PHYSICAL POWER...
...MUST LEARN THE BASICS OF KEKKAI MAGIC.

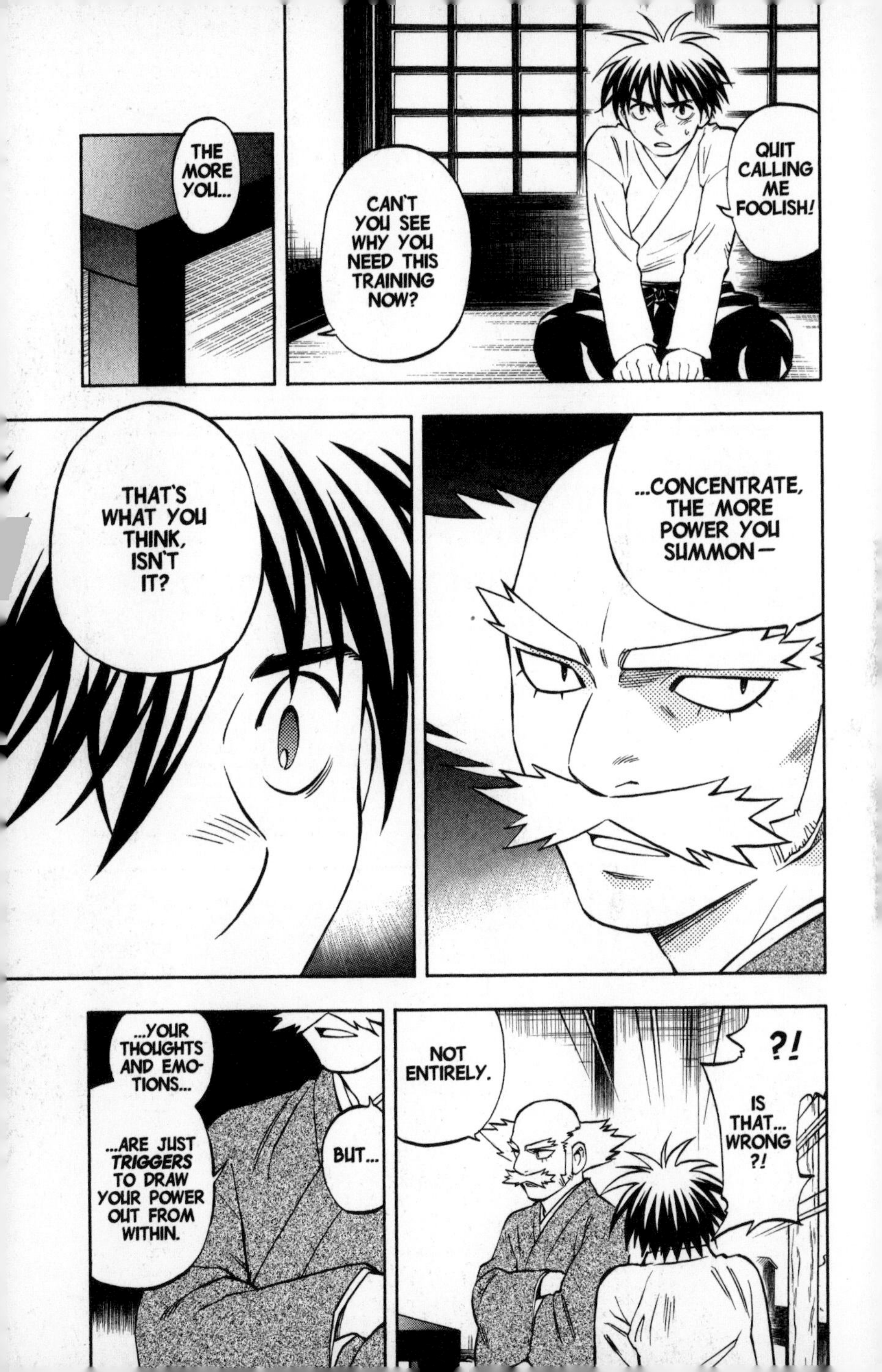
QUIT CALLING ME FOOLISH!
CAN'T YOU SEE WHY YOU NEED THIS TRAINING NOW?
THE MORE YOU...
...CONCENTRATE, THE MORE POWER YOU SUMMON—
THAT'S WHAT YOU THINK, ISN'T IT?
?!
IS THAT... WRONG?!
NOT ENTIRELY.
BUT...
...YOUR THOUGHTS AND EMOTIONS...
...ARE JUST *TRIGGERS* TO DRAW YOUR POWER OUT FROM WITHIN.

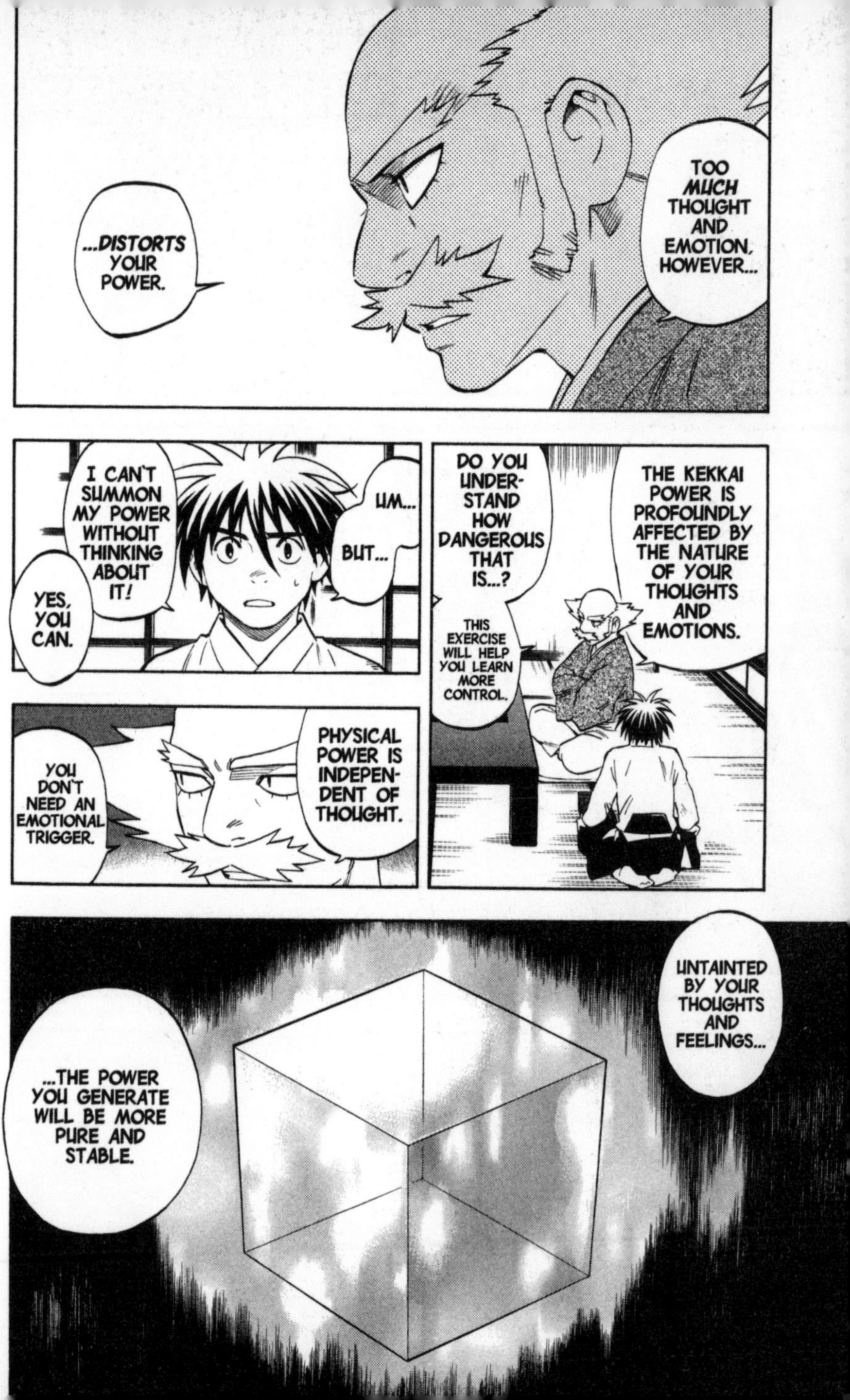
TOO MUCH THOUGHT AND EMOTION, HOWEVER...
...DISTORTS YOUR POWER.
THE KEKKAI POWER IS PROFOUNDLY AFFECTED BY THE NATURE OF YOUR THOUGHTS AND EMOTIONS.
DO YOU UNDER-STAND HOW DANGEROUS THAT IS...?
THIS EXERCISE WILL HELP YOU LEARN MORE CONTROL.
UM...
BUT...
I CAN'T SUMMON MY POWER WITHOUT THINKING ABOUT IT!
YES, YOU CAN.
PHYSICAL POWER IS INDEPEN-DENT OF THOUGHT.
YOU DON'T NEED AN EMOTIONAL TRIGGER.
UNTAINTED BY YOUR THOUGHTS AND FEELINGS...
...THE POWER YOU GENERATE WILL BE MORE PURE AND STABLE.

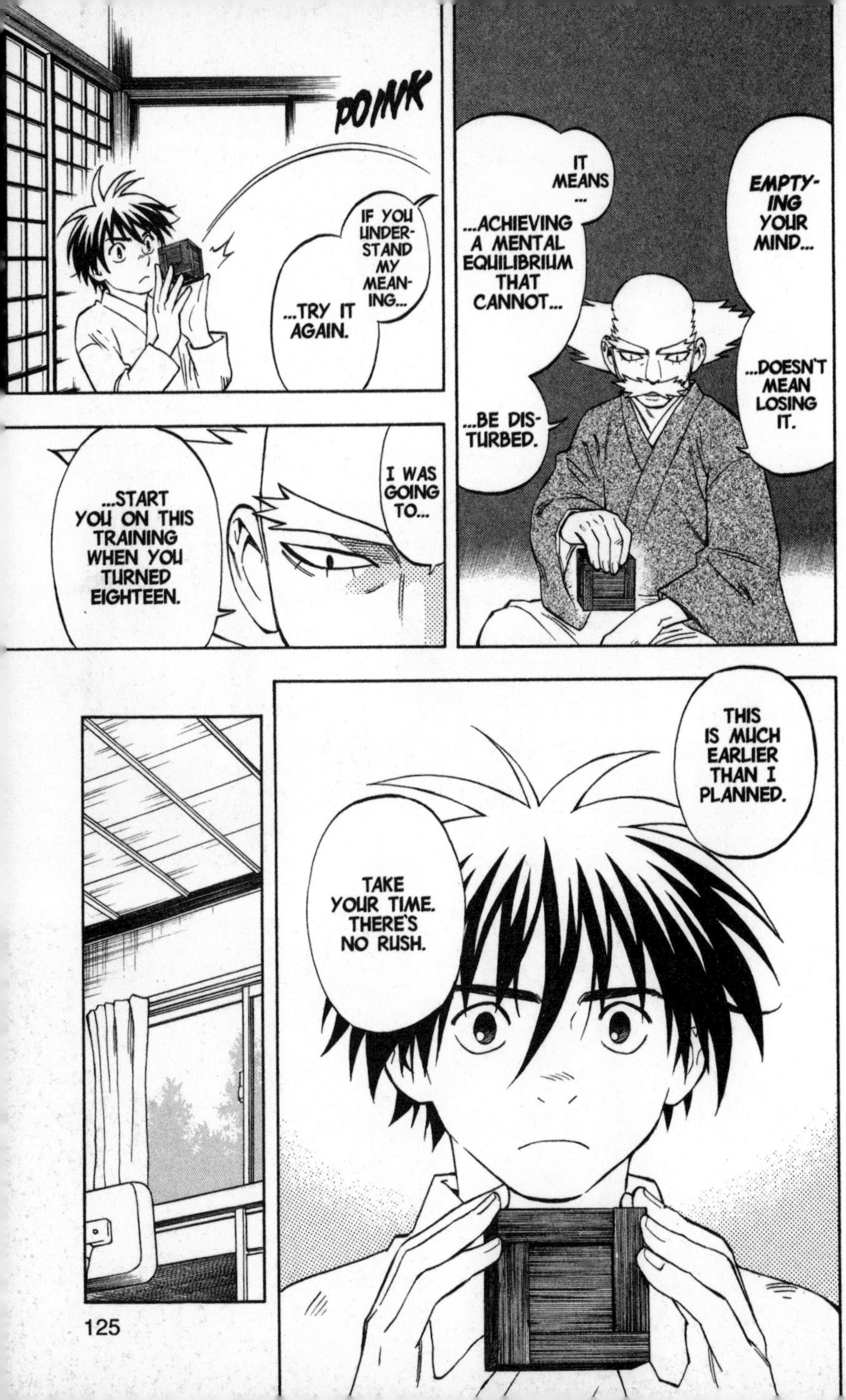
EMPTYING YOUR MIND...
...DOESN'T MEAN LOSING IT.
IT MEANS...
...ACHIEVING A MENTAL EQUILIBRIUM THAT CANNOT...
...BE DISTURBED.
POINK
IF YOU UNDERSTAND MY MEANING...
...TRY IT AGAIN.
I WAS GOING TO...
...START YOU ON THIS TRAINING WHEN YOU TURNED EIGHTEEN.
THIS IS MUCH EARLIER THAN I PLANNED.
TAKE YOUR TIME. THERE'S NO RUSH.

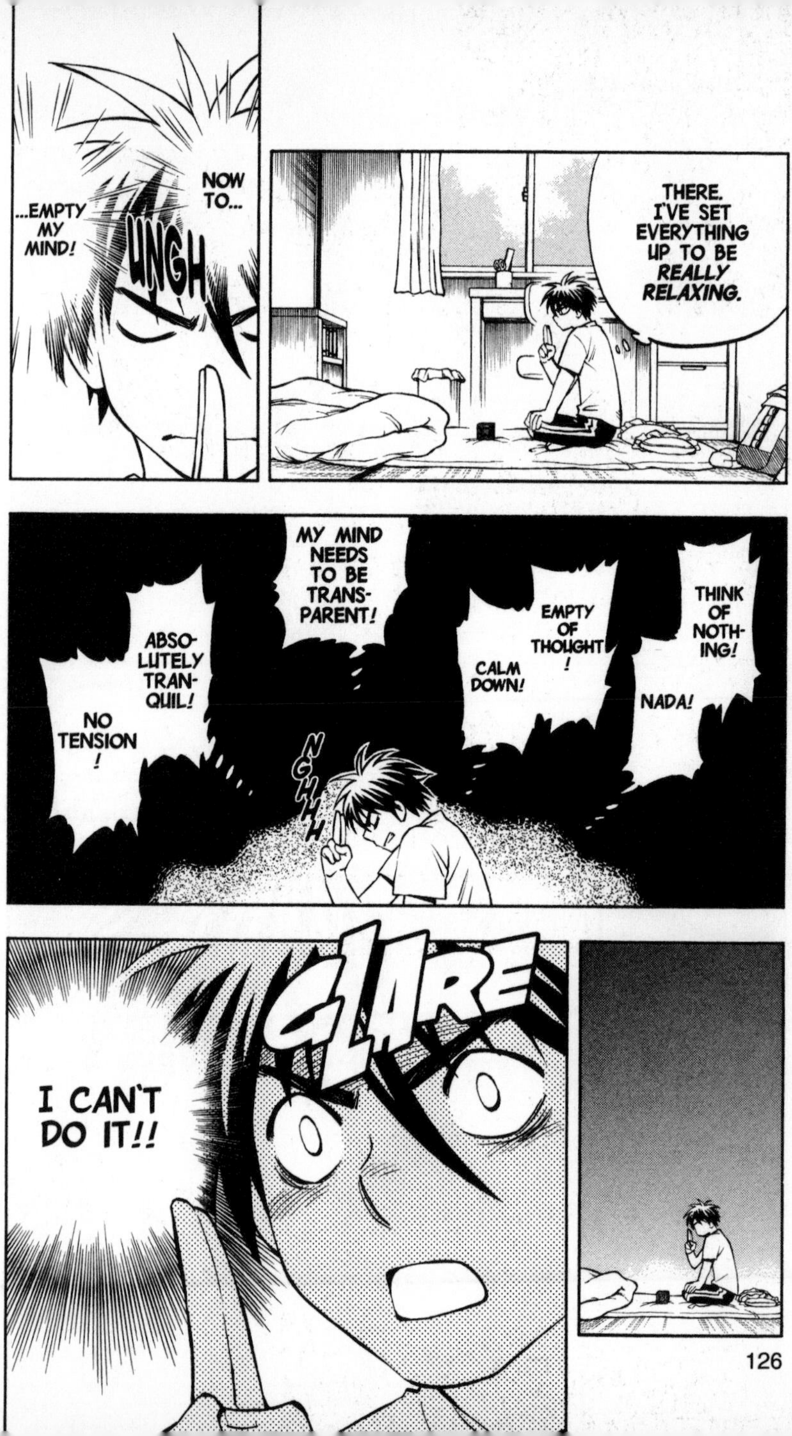
THERE. I'VE SET EVERYTHING UP TO BE *REALLY RELAXING.*
NOW TO...
...EMPTY MY MIND!
UNGH
THINK OF NOTHING!
NADA!
EMPTY OF THOUGHT!
CALM DOWN!
MY MIND NEEDS TO BE TRANSPARENT!
ABSOLUTELY TRANQUIL!
NO TENSION!
NGHHH
GLARE
I CAN'T DO IT!!

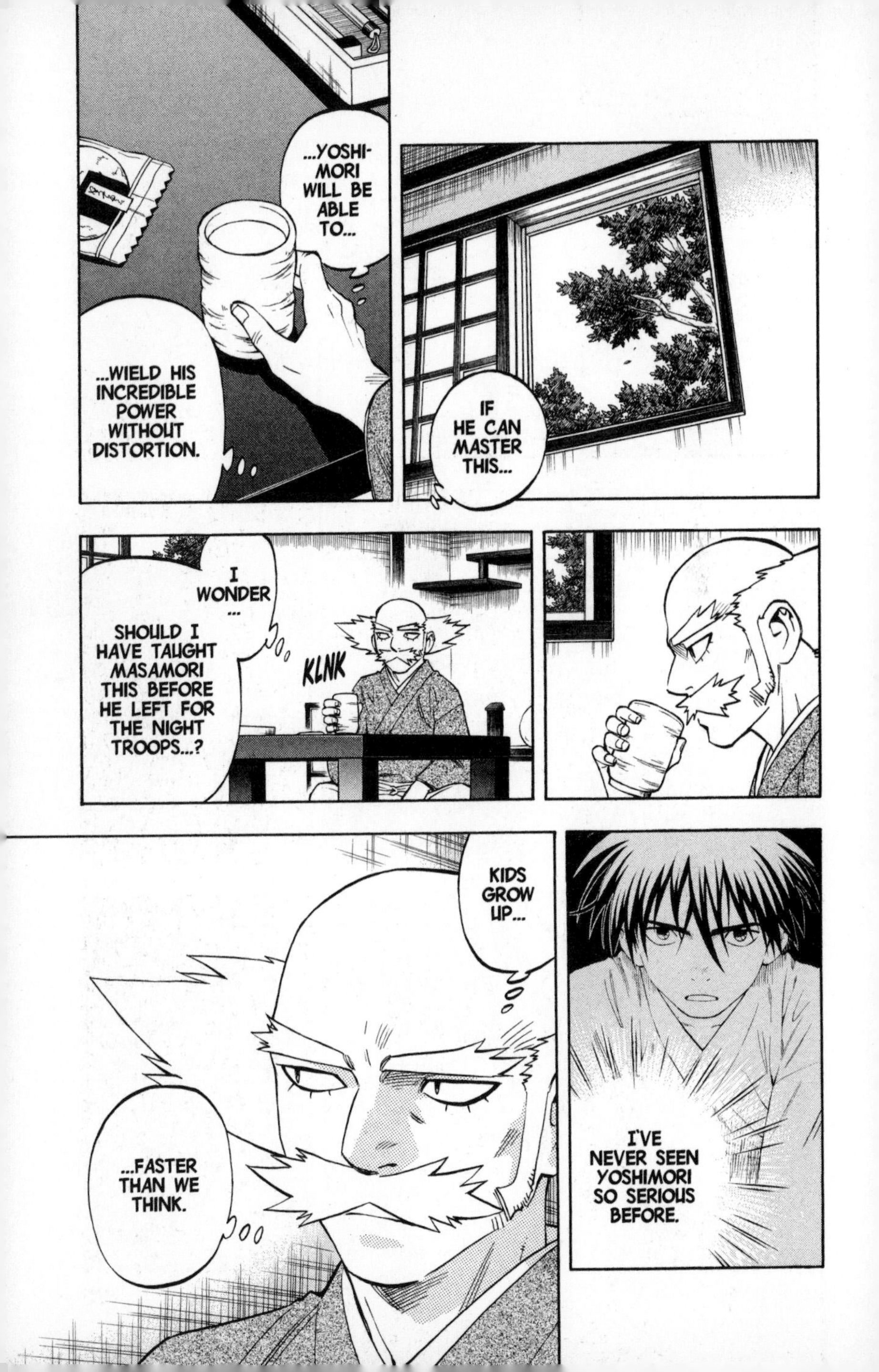
IF HE CAN MASTER THIS...
...YOSHIMORI WILL BE ABLE TO...
...WIELD HIS INCREDIBLE POWER WITHOUT DISTORTION.
I WONDER...
SHOULD I HAVE TAUGHT MASAMORI THIS BEFORE HE LEFT FOR THE NIGHT TROOPS...?
KLNK
I'VE NEVER SEEN YOSHIMORI SO SERIOUS BEFORE.
KIDS GROW UP...
...FASTER THAN WE THINK.

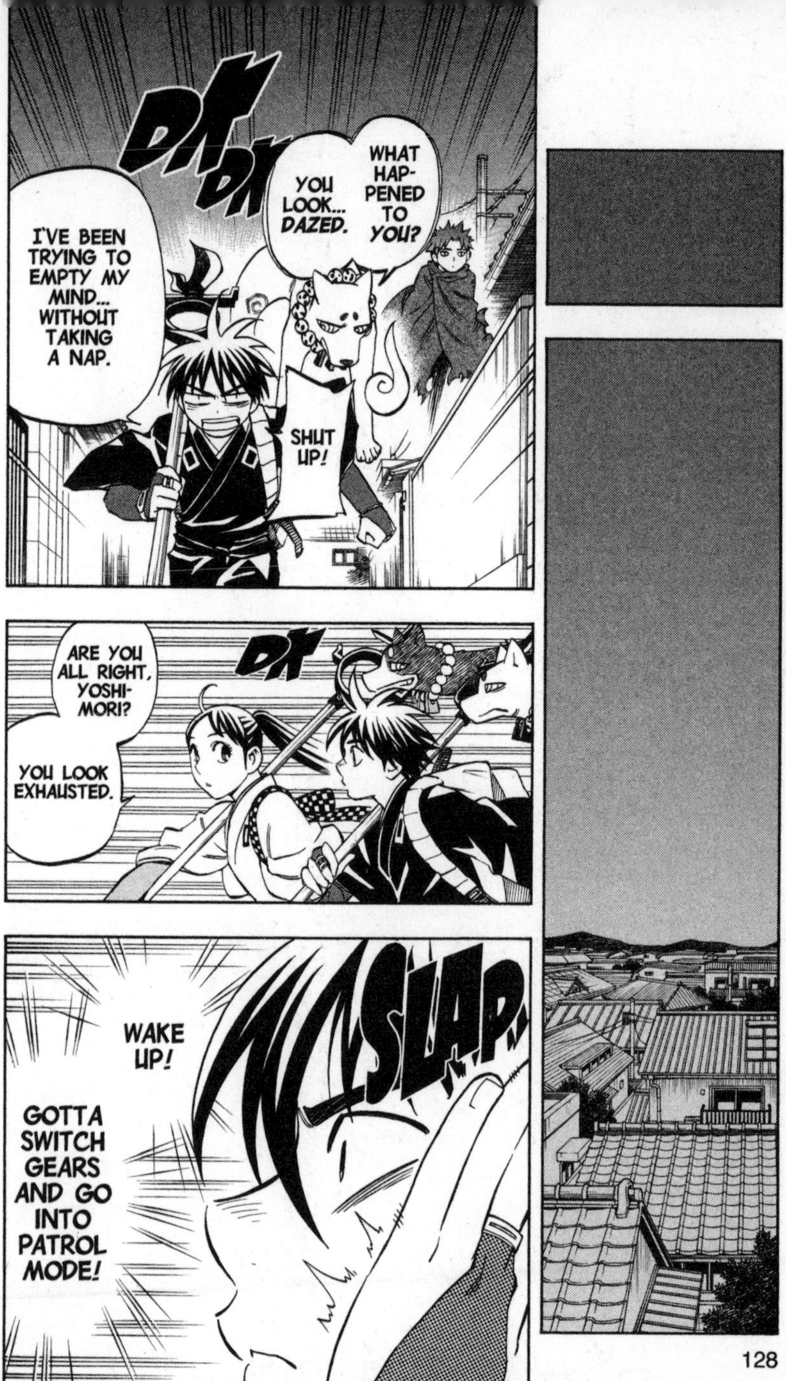
DADA
WHAT HAPPENED TO YOU?
YOU LOOK... DAZED.
I'VE BEEN TRYING TO EMPTY MY MIND... WITHOUT TAKING A NAP.
SHUT UP!
DA
ARE YOU ALL RIGHT, YOSHIMORI?
YOU LOOK EXHAUSTED.
SLAP
WAKE UP!
GOTTA SWITCH GEARS AND GO INTO PATROL MODE!

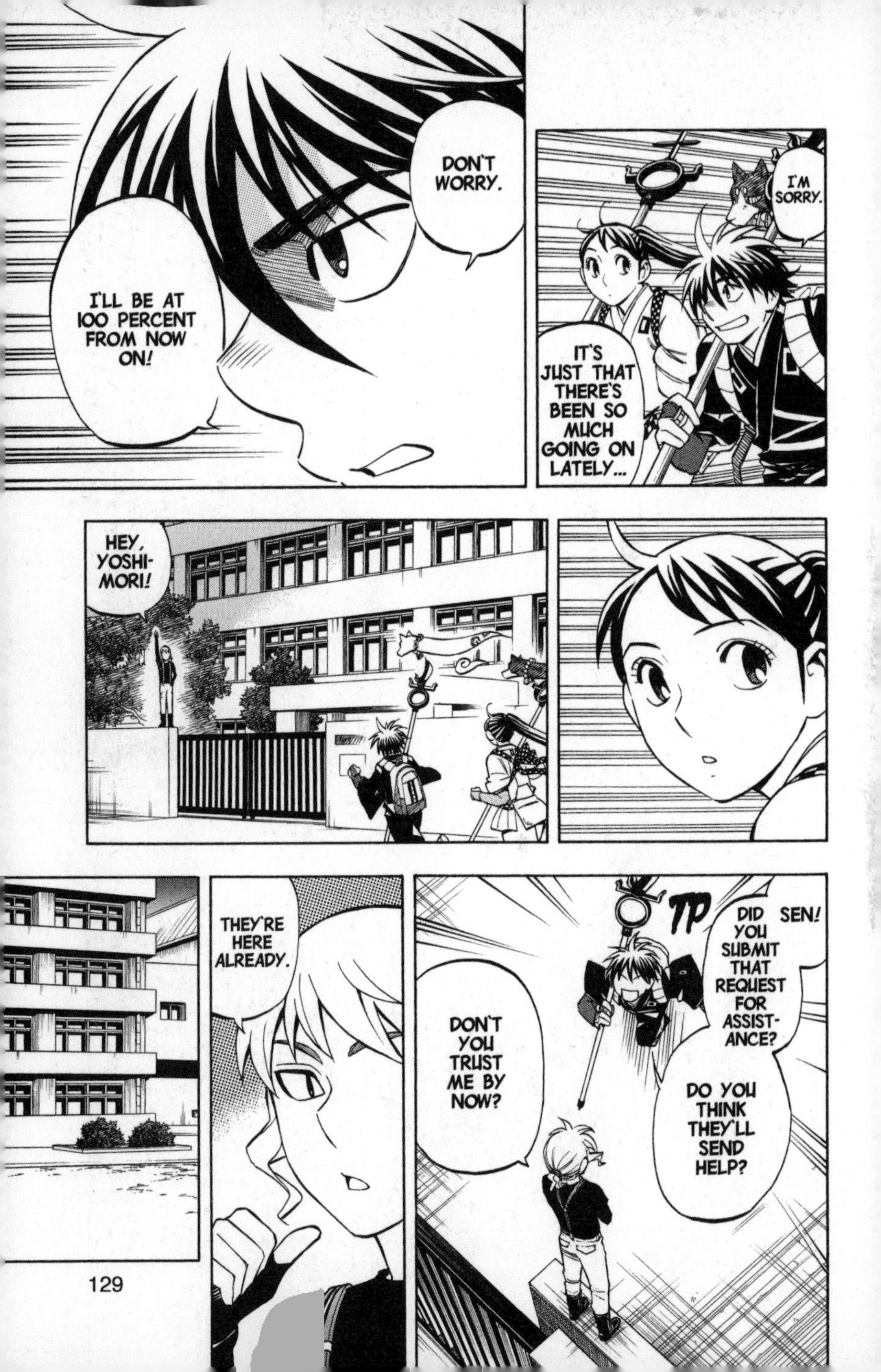
I'M SORRY.
IT'S JUST THAT THERE'S BEEN SO MUCH GOING ON LATELY...
DON'T WORRY.
I'LL BE AT 100 PERCENT FROM NOW ON!
HEY, YOSHI-MORI!
TP
SEN!
DID YOU SUBMIT THAT REQUEST FOR ASSIST-ANCE?
DO YOU THINK THEY'LL SEND HELP?
DON'T YOU TRUST ME BY NOW?
THEY'RE HERE ALREADY.

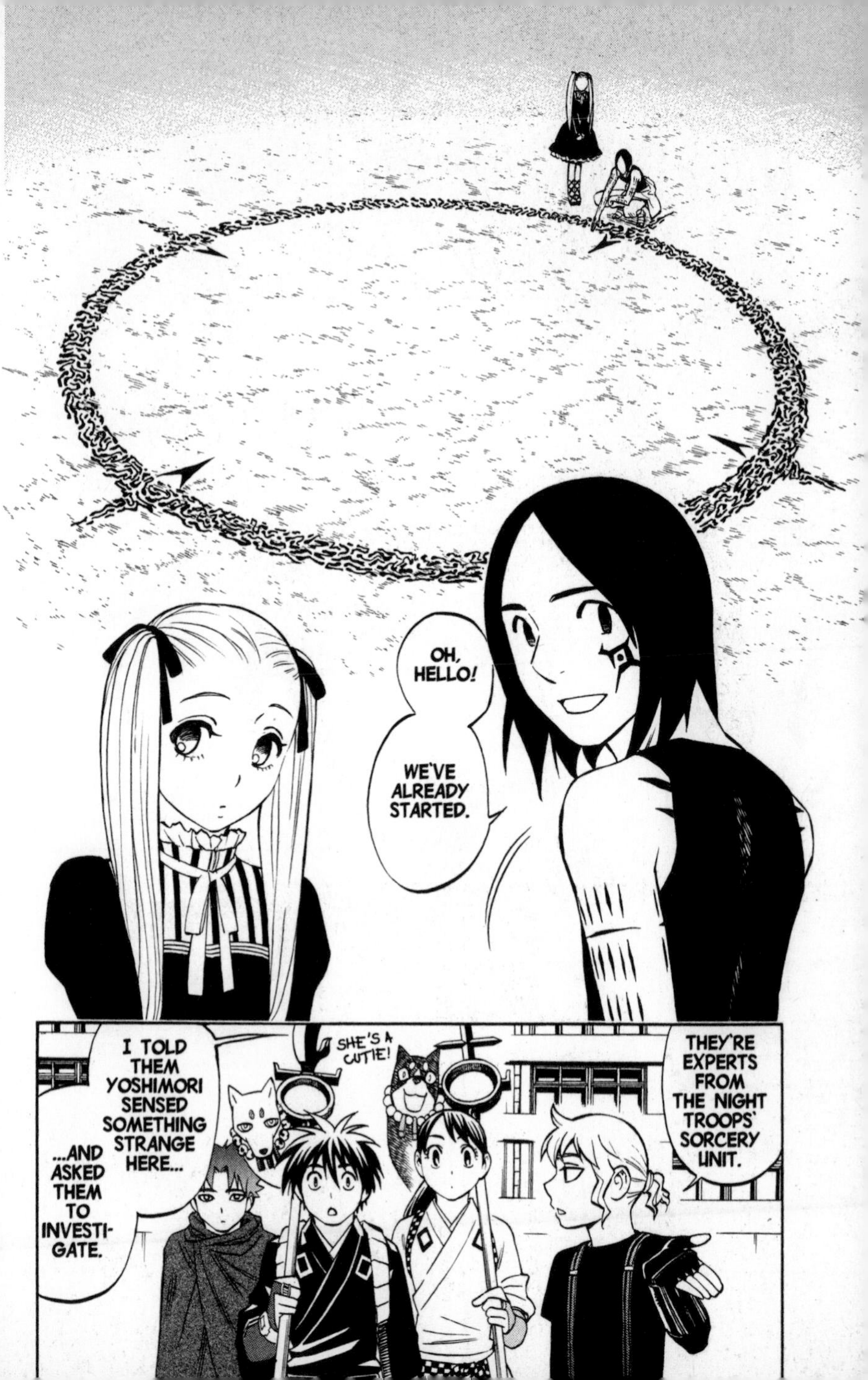
OH, HELLO!
WE'VE ALREADY STARTED.
THEY'RE EXPERTS FROM THE NIGHT TROOPS' SORCERY UNIT.
SHE'S A CUTIE!
I TOLD THEM YOSHIMORI SENSED SOMETHING STRANGE HERE...
...AND ASKED THEM TO INVESTI-GATE.

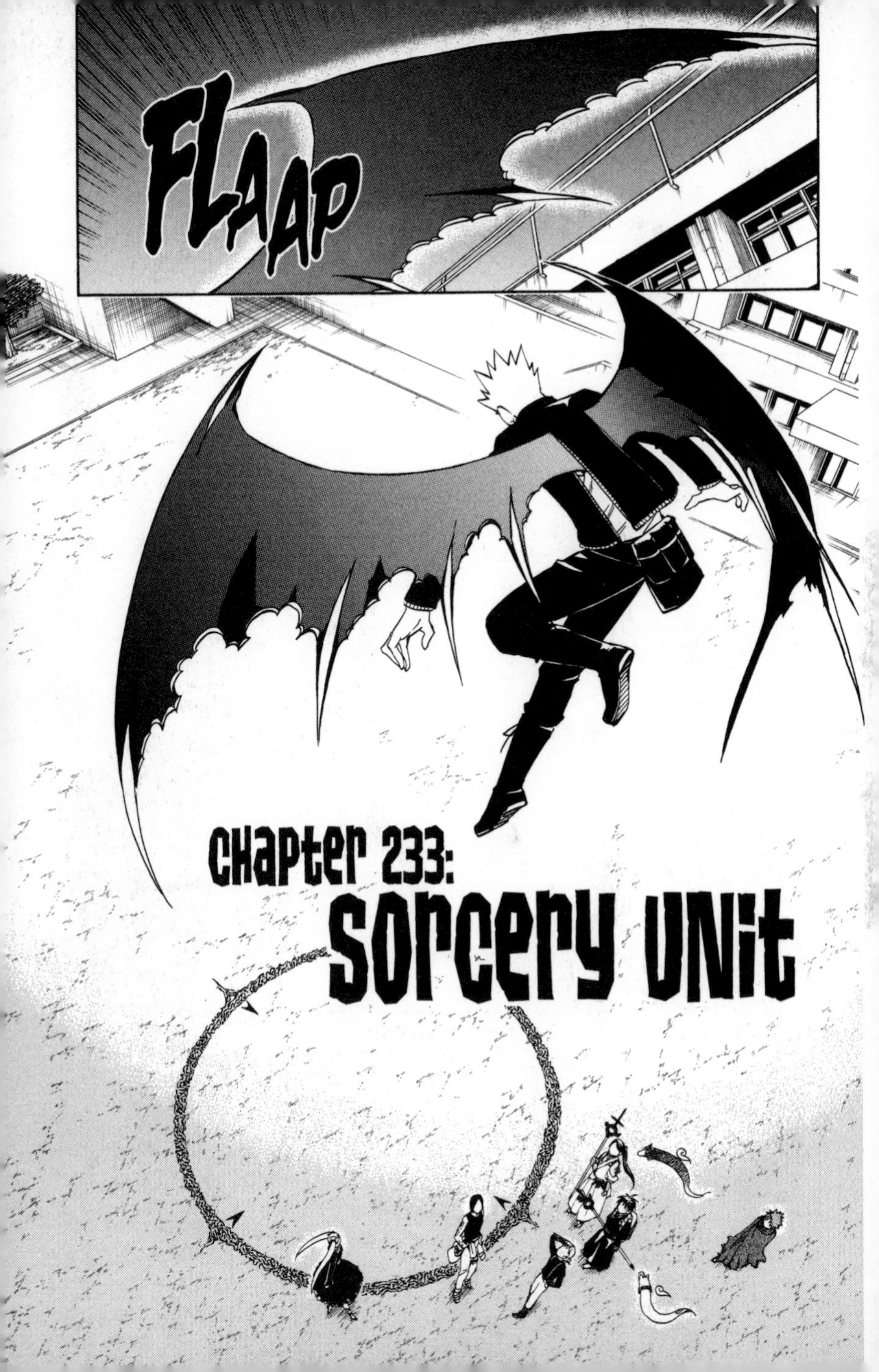
FLAAP
Chapter 233:
Sorcery Unit

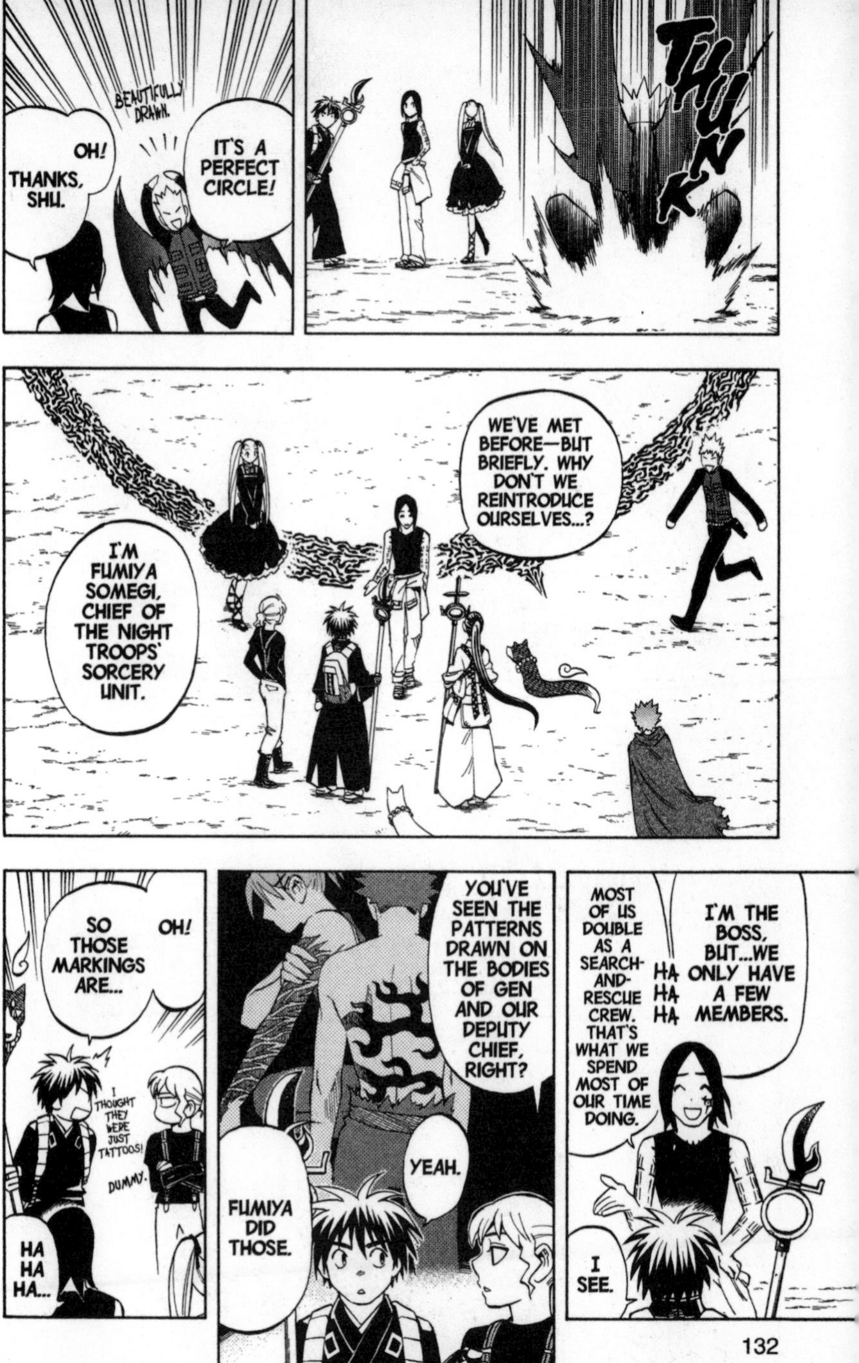
THUNK
IT'S A PERFECT CIRCLE!
BEAUTIFULLY DRAWN.
OH! THANKS, SHU.
WE'VE MET BEFORE—BUT BRIEFLY. WHY DON'T WE REINTRODUCE OURSELVES...?
I'M FUMIYA SOMEGI, CHIEF OF THE NIGHT TROOPS' SORCERY UNIT.
I'M THE BOSS, BUT...WE ONLY HAVE A FEW MEMBERS.
HA HA HA
MOST OF US DOUBLE AS A SEARCH-AND-RESCUE CREW. THAT'S WHAT WE SPEND MOST OF OUR TIME DOING.
I SEE.
YOU'VE SEEN THE PATTERNS DRAWN ON THE BODIES OF GEN AND OUR DEPUTY CHIEF, RIGHT?
YEAH.
FUMIYA DID THOSE.
OH!
SO THOSE MARKINGS ARE...
I THOUGHT THEY WERE JUST TATTOOS!
DUMMY.
HA HA HA...

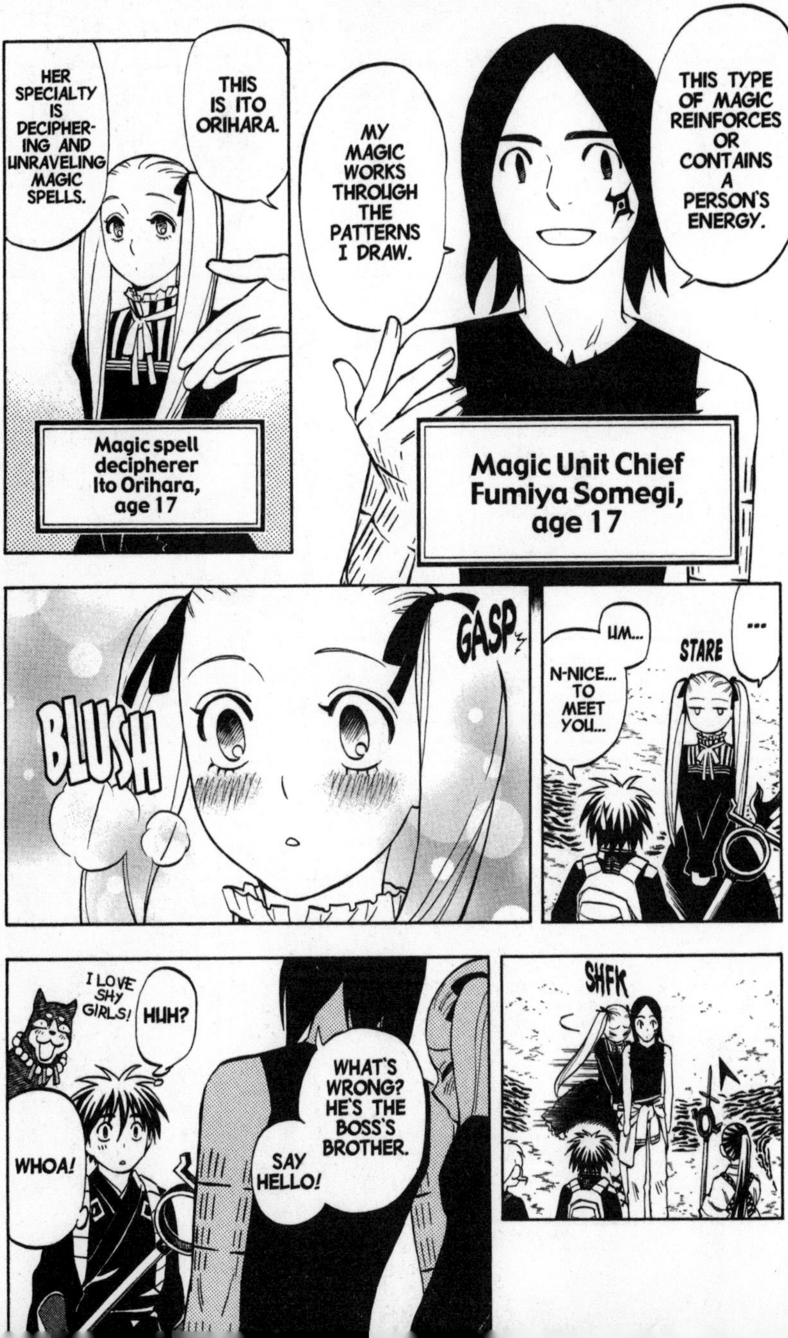
THIS TYPE OF MAGIC REINFORCES OR CONTAINS A PERSON'S ENERGY.
MY MAGIC WORKS THROUGH THE PATTERNS I DRAW.
Magic Unit Chief Fumiya Somegi, age 17
THIS IS ITO ORIHARA.
HER SPECIALTY IS DECIPHERING AND UNRAVELING MAGIC SPELLS.
Magic spell decipherer Ito Orihara, age 17
...
STARE
UM...
N-NICE... TO MEET YOU...
GASP
BLUSH
SHFK
WHAT'S WRONG? HE'S THE BOSS'S BROTHER.
SAY HELLO!
HUH?
I LOVE SHY GIRLS!
WHOA!

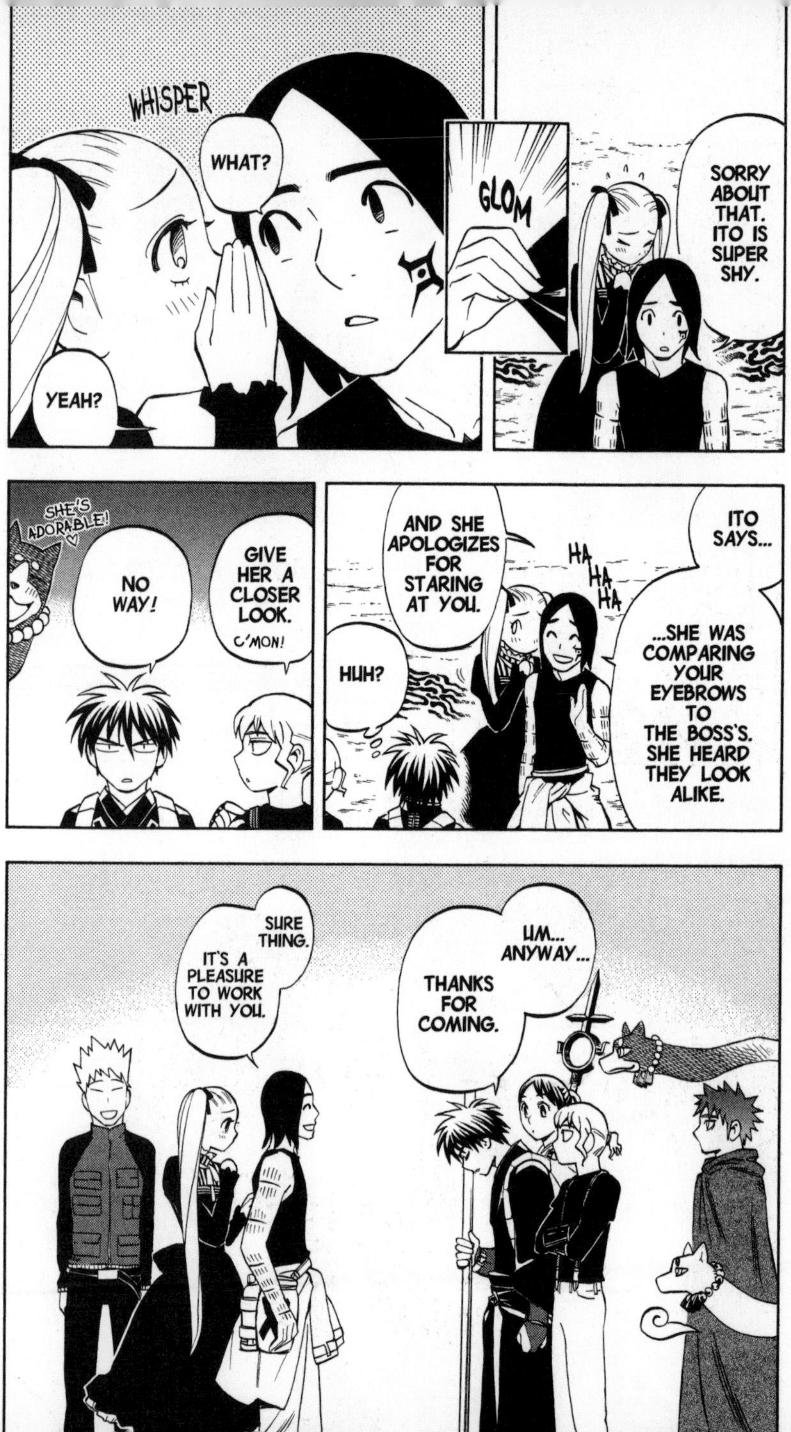

SORRY ABOUT THAT. ITO IS SUPER SHY.
GLOM
WHISPER
WHAT?
YEAH?
ITO SAYS...
...SHE WAS COMPARING YOUR EYEBROWS TO THE BOSS'S. SHE HEARD THEY LOOK ALIKE.
HA HA HA
AND SHE APOLOGIZES FOR STARING AT YOU.
HUH?
GIVE HER A CLOSER LOOK.
C'MON!
NO WAY!
SHE'S ADORABLE! ♡
UM... ANYWAY...
THANKS FOR COMING.
SURE THING.
IT'S A PLEASURE TO WORK WITH YOU.

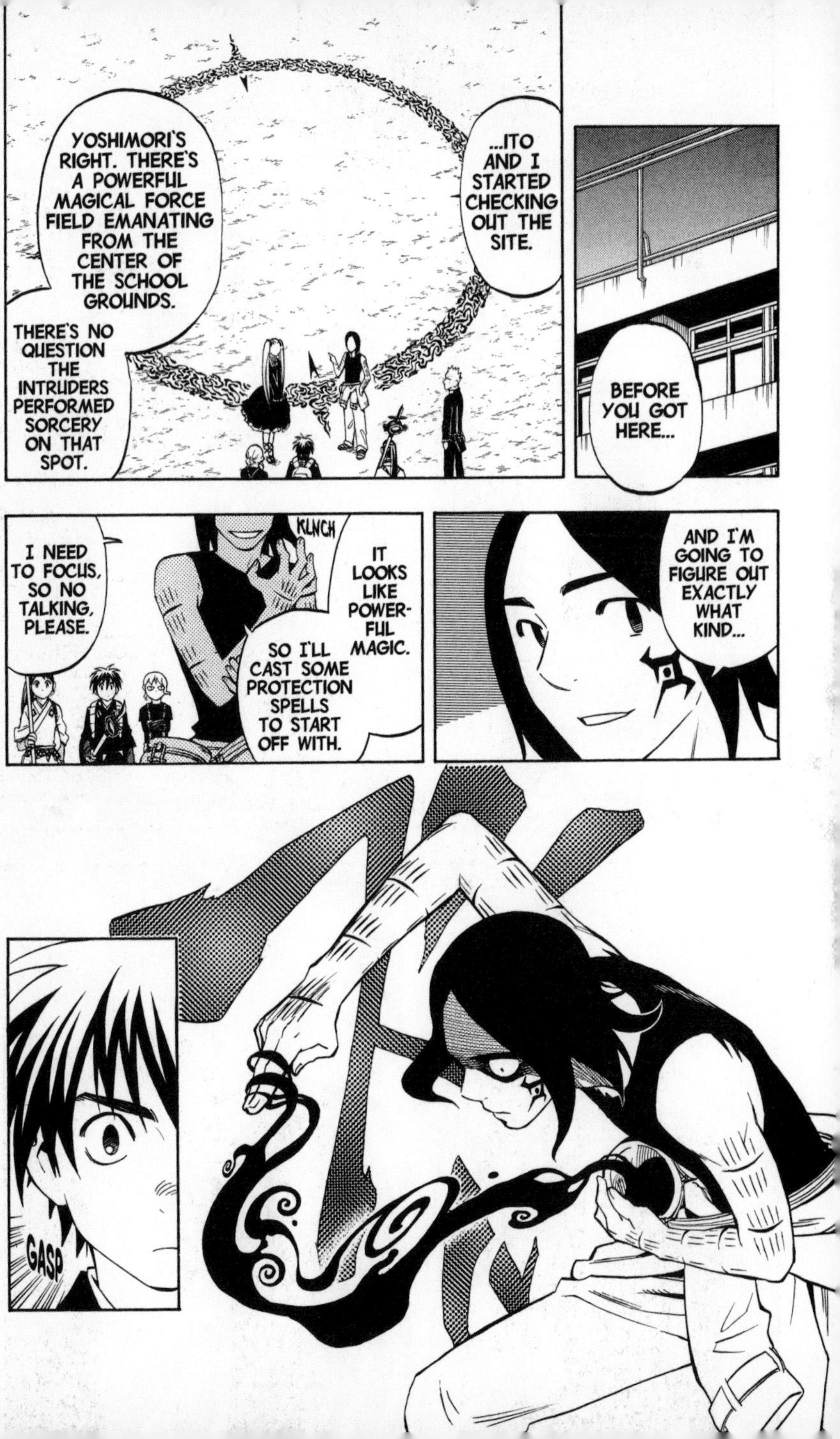
BEFORE YOU GOT HERE...
...ITO AND I STARTED CHECKING OUT THE SITE.
YOSHIMORI'S RIGHT. THERE'S A POWERFUL MAGICAL FORCE FIELD EMANATING FROM THE CENTER OF THE SCHOOL GROUNDS.
THERE'S NO QUESTION THE INTRUDERS PERFORMED SORCERY ON THAT SPOT.
AND I'M GOING TO FIGURE OUT EXACTLY WHAT KIND...
IT LOOKS LIKE POWER-FUL MAGIC.
KLNCH
SO I'LL CAST SOME PROTECTION SPELLS TO START OFF WITH.
I NEED TO FOCUS, SO NO TALKING, PLEASE.
GASP

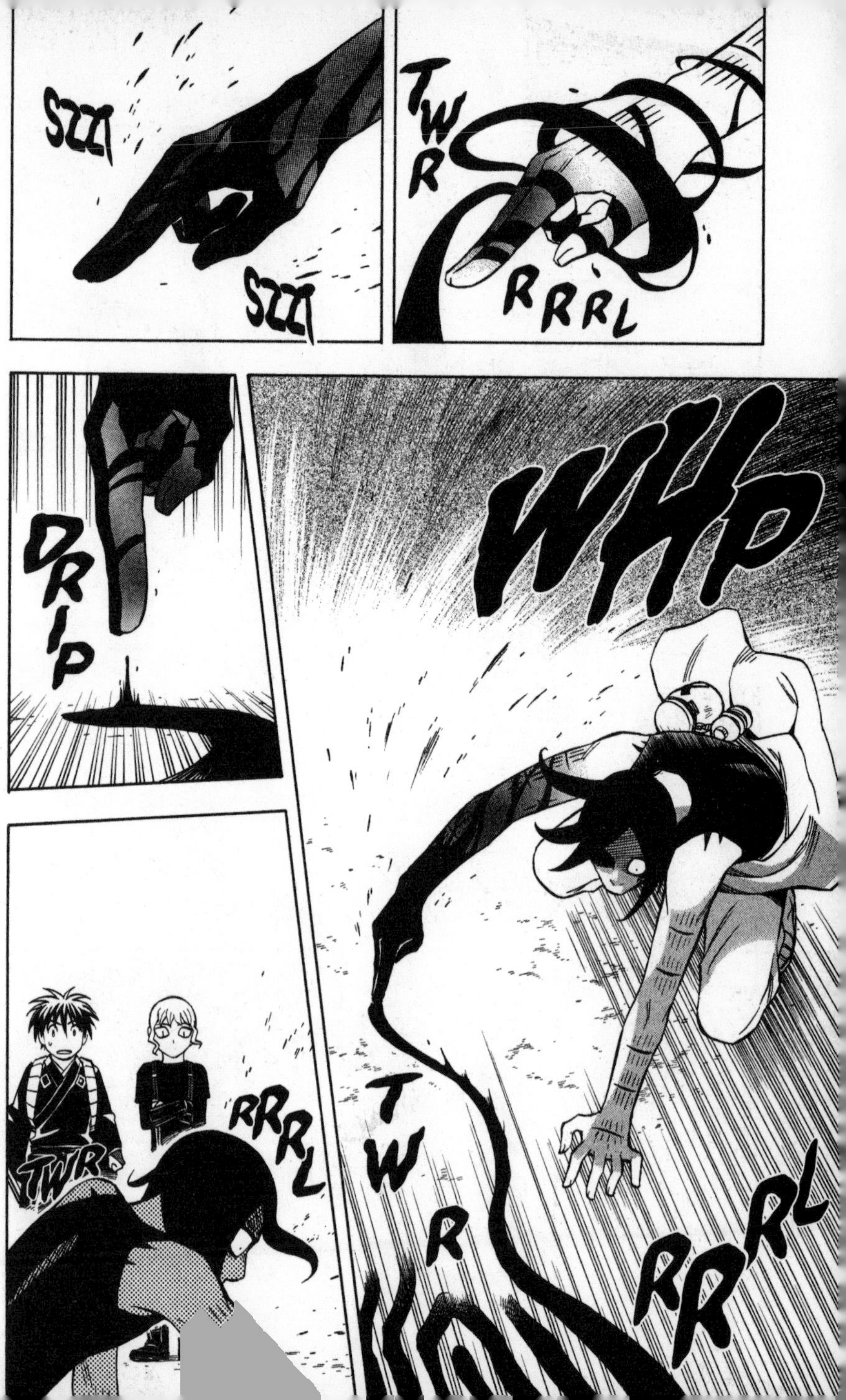
TWR
RRRL
SZZT
SZZT
WHIP
TWR
RRRL
DRIP
RRRL
TWR

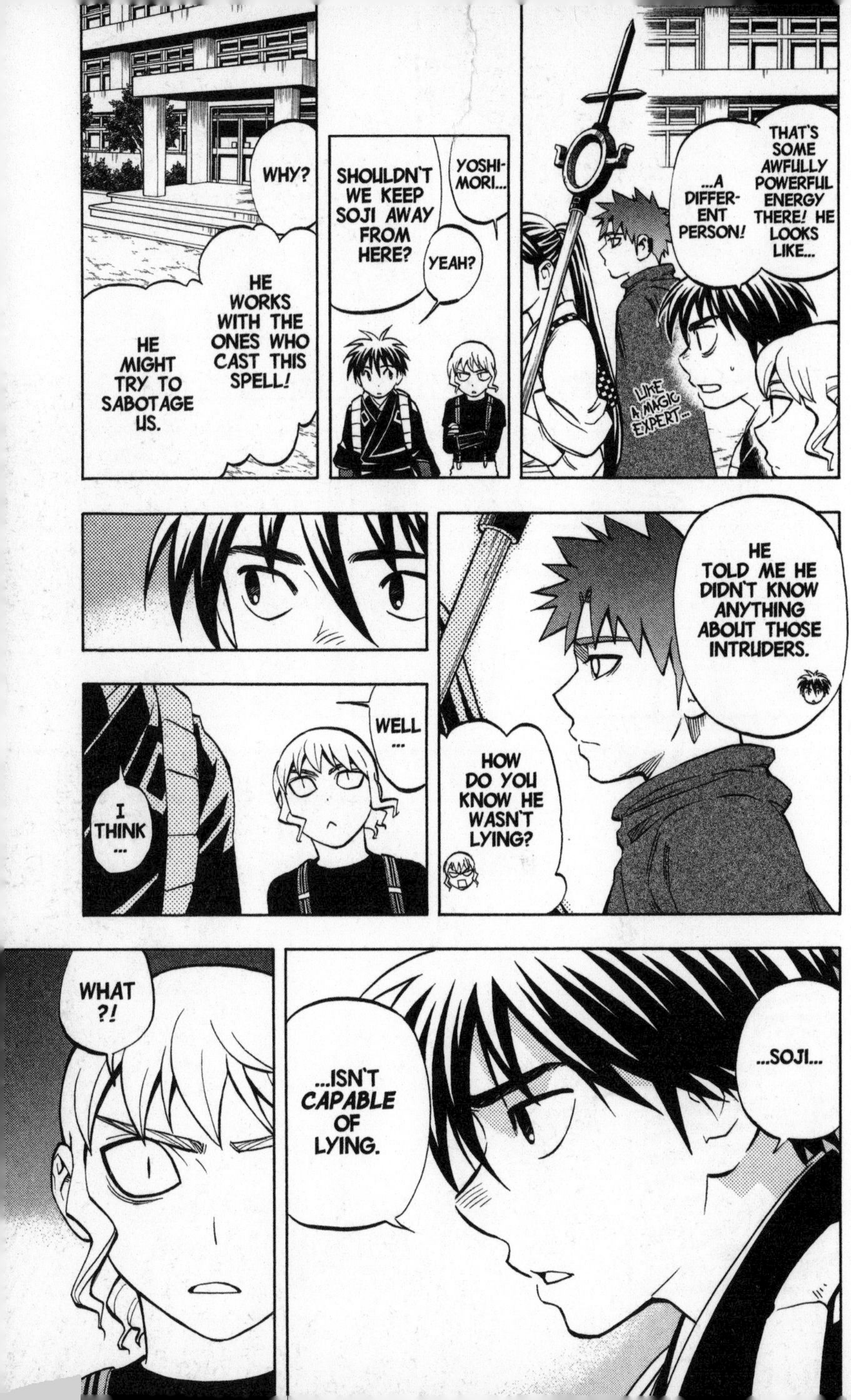
THAT'S SOME AWFULLY POWERFUL ENERGY THERE! HE LOOKS LIKE...
...A DIFFERENT PERSON!
LIKE A MAGIC EXPERT...
YOSHIMORI...
YEAH?
SHOULDN'T WE KEEP SOJI AWAY FROM HERE?
WHY?
HE WORKS WITH THE ONES WHO CAST THIS SPELL!
HE MIGHT TRY TO SABOTAGE US.
HE TOLD ME HE DIDN'T KNOW ANYTHING ABOUT THOSE INTRUDERS.
HOW DO YOU KNOW HE WASN'T LYING?
WELL ...
I THINK ...
...SOJI...
...ISN'T CAPABLE OF LYING.
WHAT?!

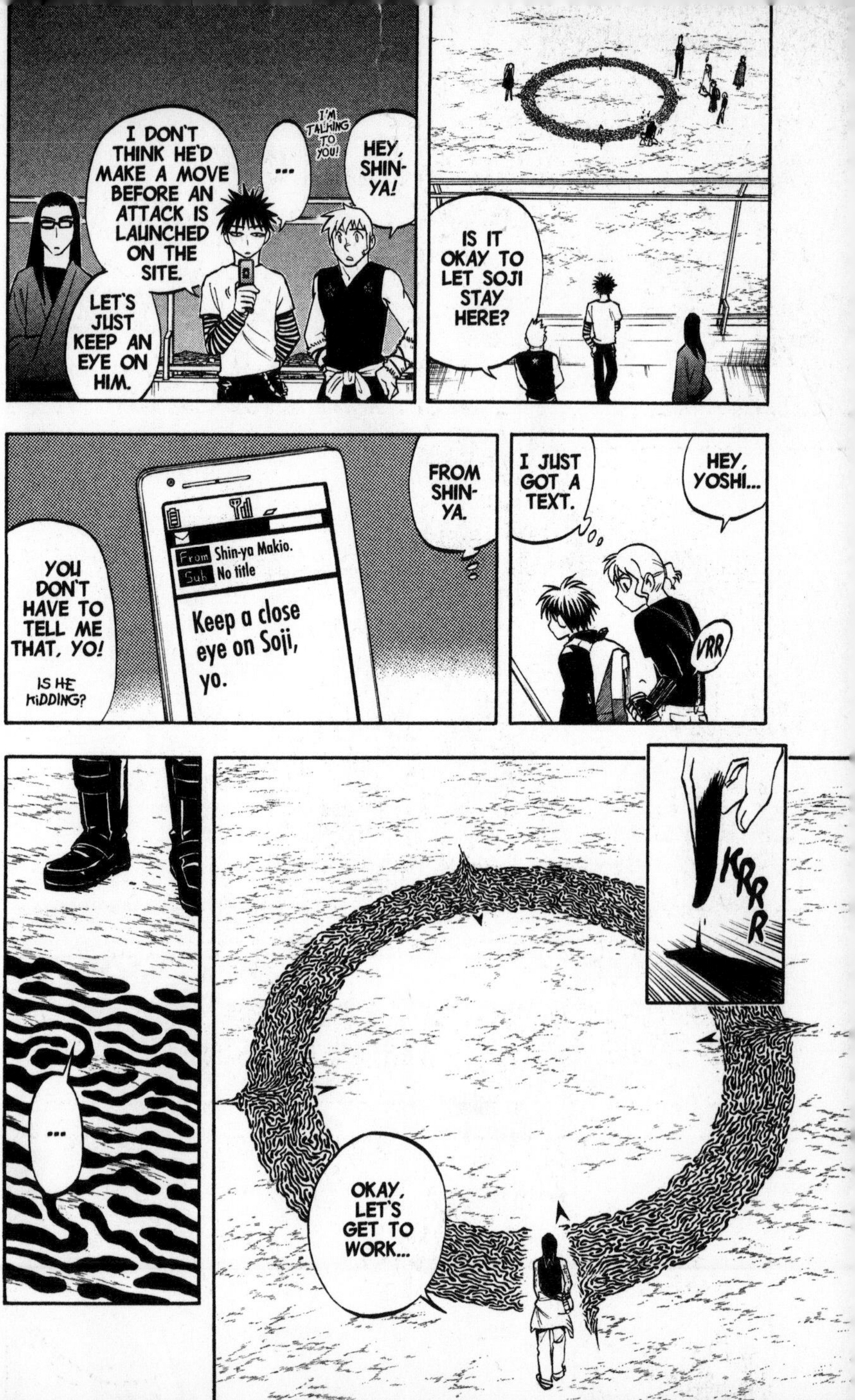
IS IT OKAY TO LET SOJI STAY HERE?
HEY, SHIN-YA!
I'M TALKING TO YOU!
...
I DON'T THINK HE'D MAKE A MOVE BEFORE AN ATTACK IS LAUNCHED ON THE SITE.
LET'S JUST KEEP AN EYE ON HIM.
HEY, YOSHI...
I JUST GOT A TEXT.
VRR
FROM SHIN-YA.
From Shin-ya Makio.
Sub No title
Keep a close eye on Soji, yo.
YOU DON'T HAVE TO TELL ME THAT, YO!
IS HE KIDDING?
KRRR
OKAY, LET'S GET TO WORK...
...

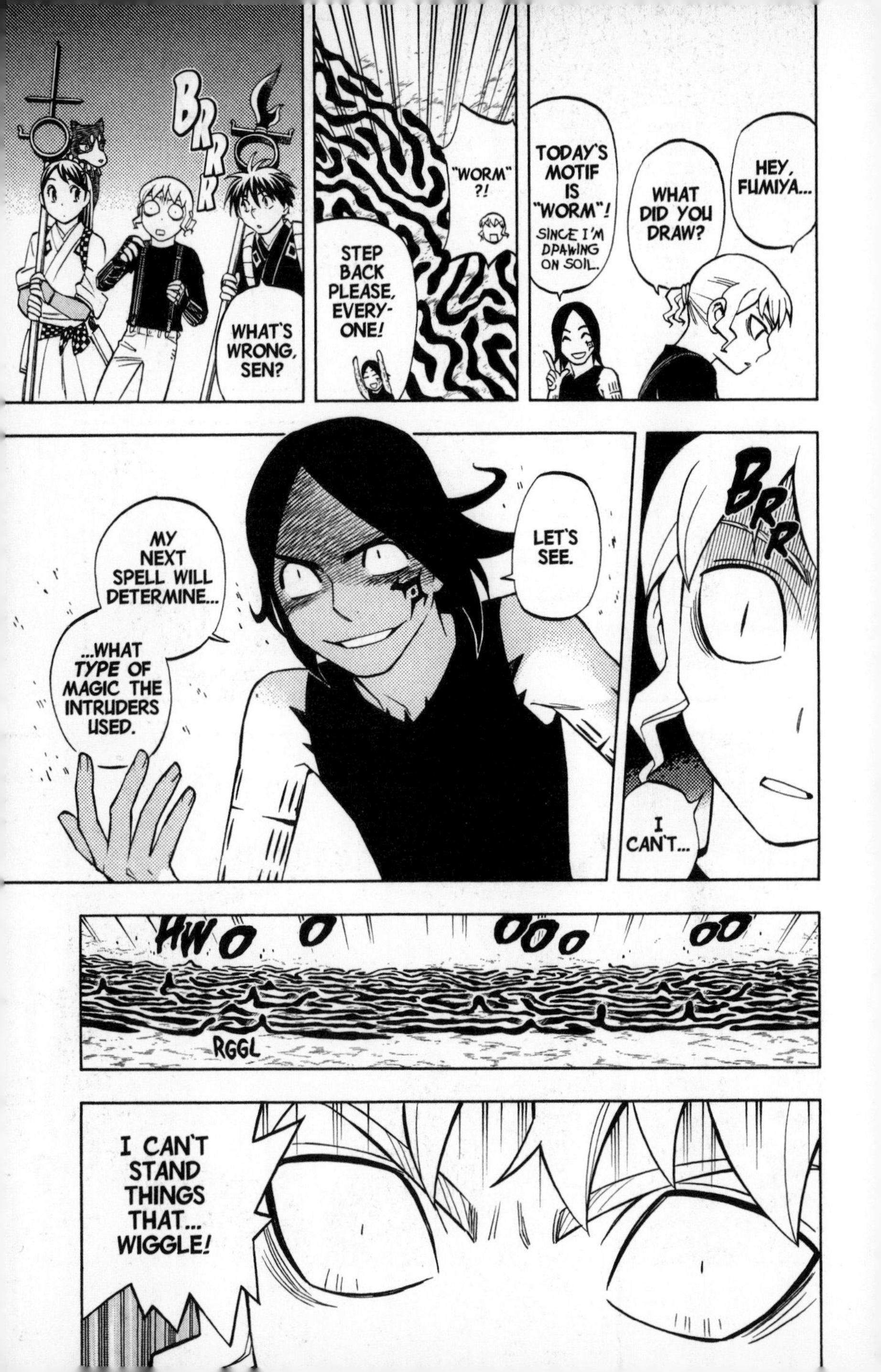
HEY, FUMIYA...
WHAT DID YOU DRAW?
TODAY'S MOTIF IS "WORM"! SINCE I'M DRAWING ON SOIL.
"WORM"?!
STEP BACK PLEASE, EVERY-ONE!
BRRR
WHAT'S WRONG, SEN?
BRR
I CAN'T...
LET'S SEE.
MY NEXT SPELL WILL DETERMINE...
...WHAT *TYPE* OF MAGIC THE INTRUDERS USED.
HWOOOOOOO
RGGL
I CAN'T STAND THINGS THAT... WIGGLE!

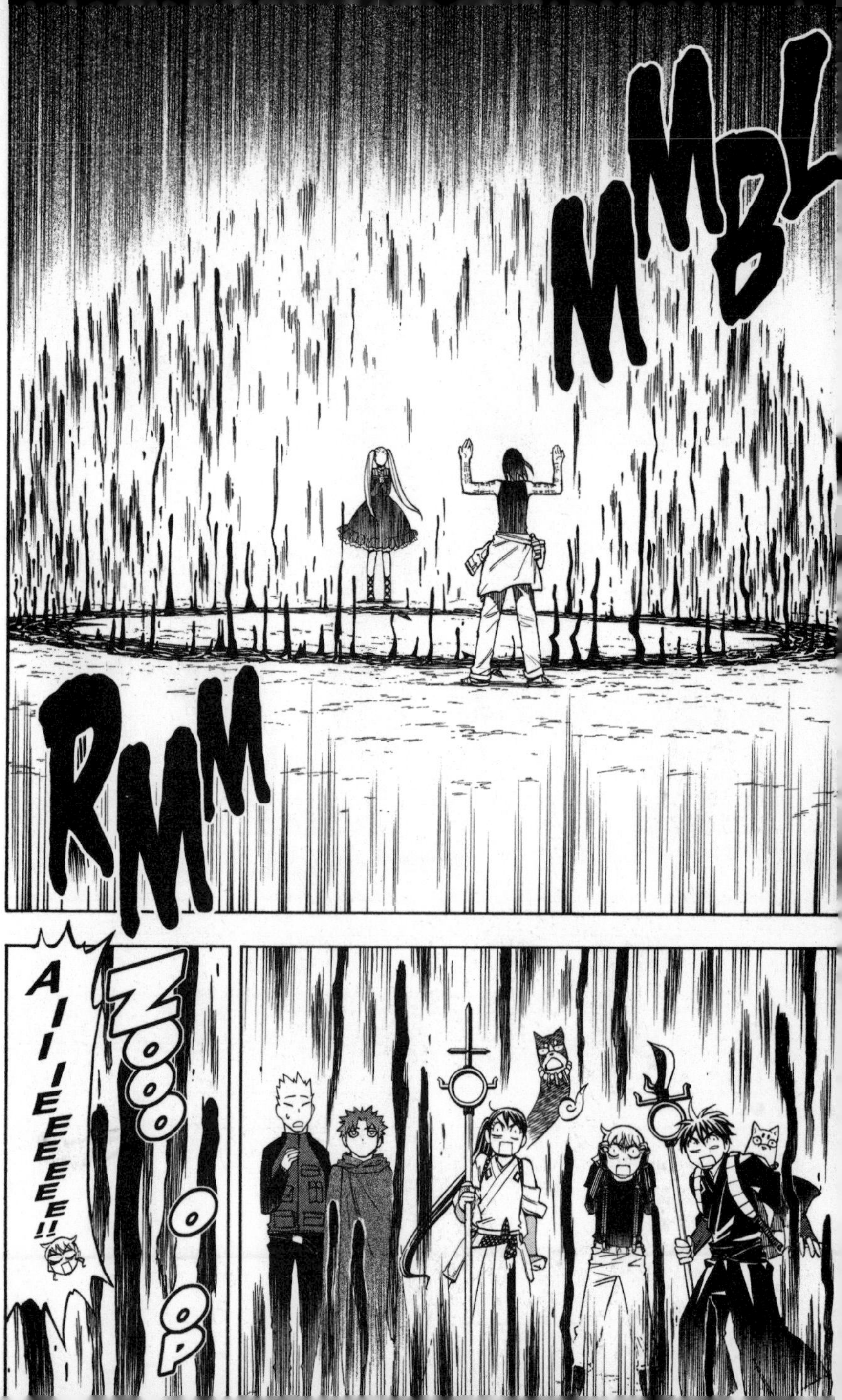
MMBL
RMM
ZOOOOOP
AIIIEEEEEE!!

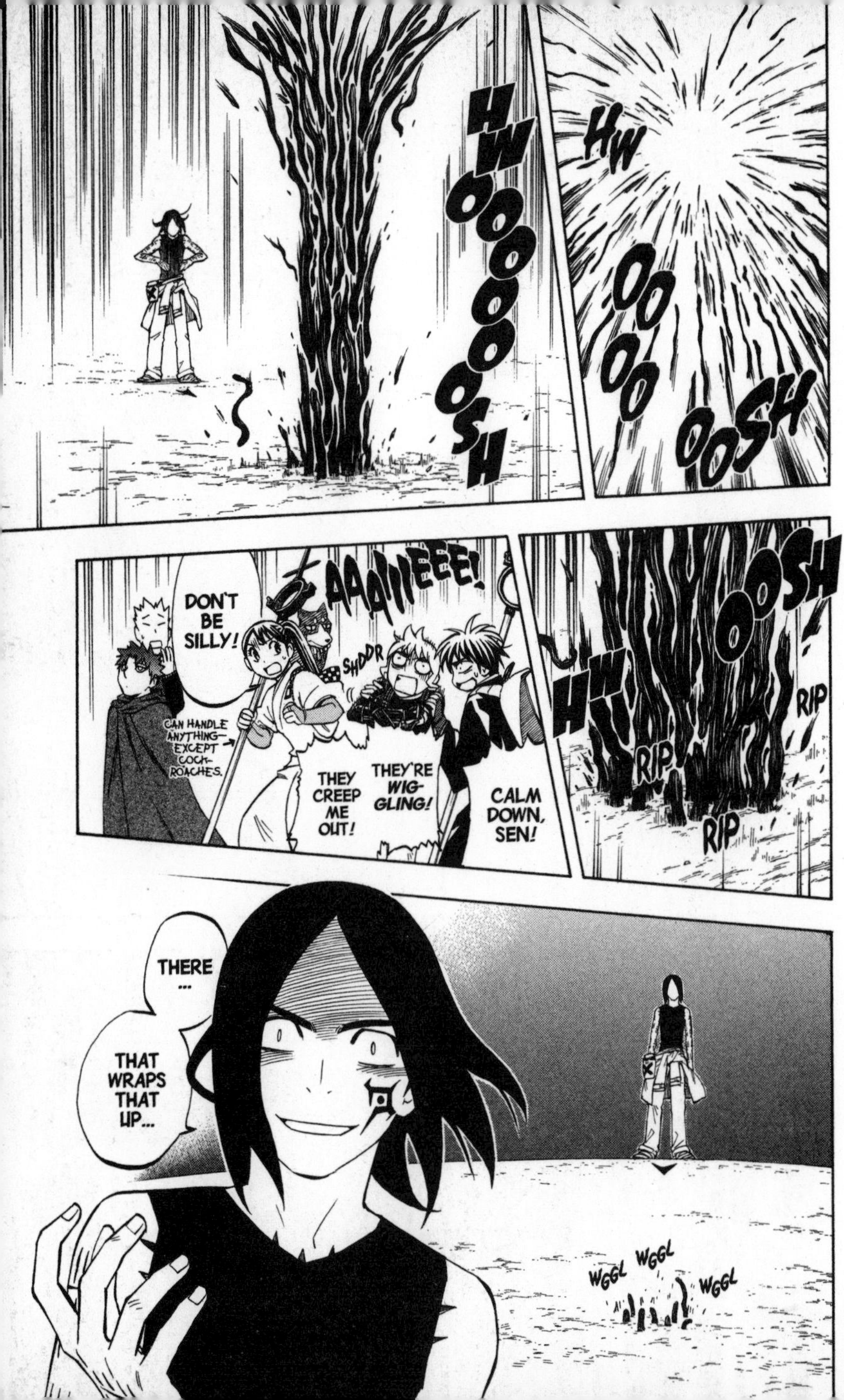
HWOOOOOOSH
HWOOOOOOOOSH
HWOOOSH!
RIP
RIP
RIP
AAAIIEEEE!
DON'T BE SILLY!
SHDDR
CALM DOWN, SEN!
THEY'RE WIG-GLING!
THEY CREEP ME OUT!
CAN HANDLE ANYTHING—EXCEPT COCK-ROACHES.
WGGL WGGL WGGL
THERE...
THAT WRAPS THAT UP...

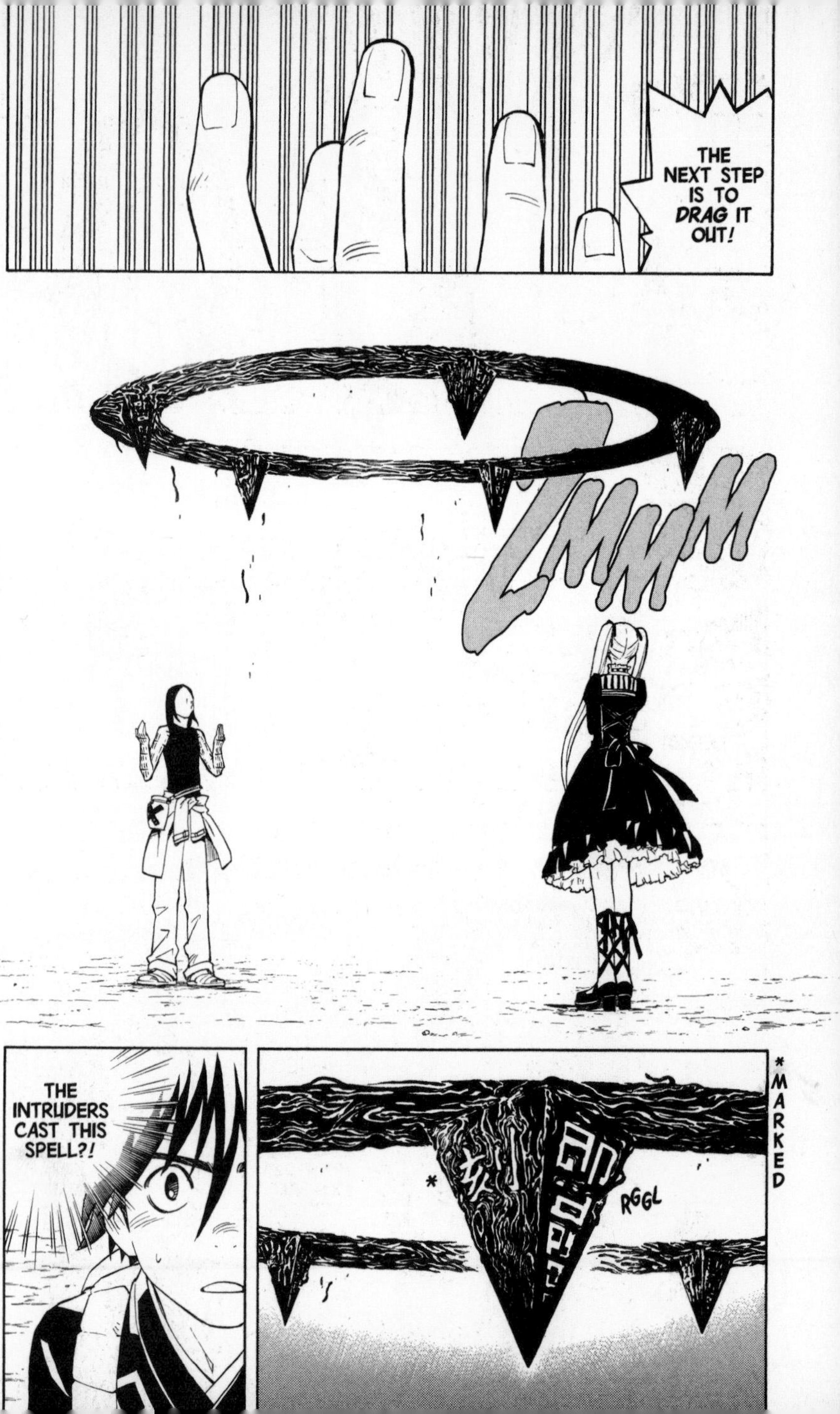
THE NEXT STEP IS TO DRAG IT OUT!
ZMMM
*MARKED
RGGL
THE INTRUDERS CAST THIS SPELL?!

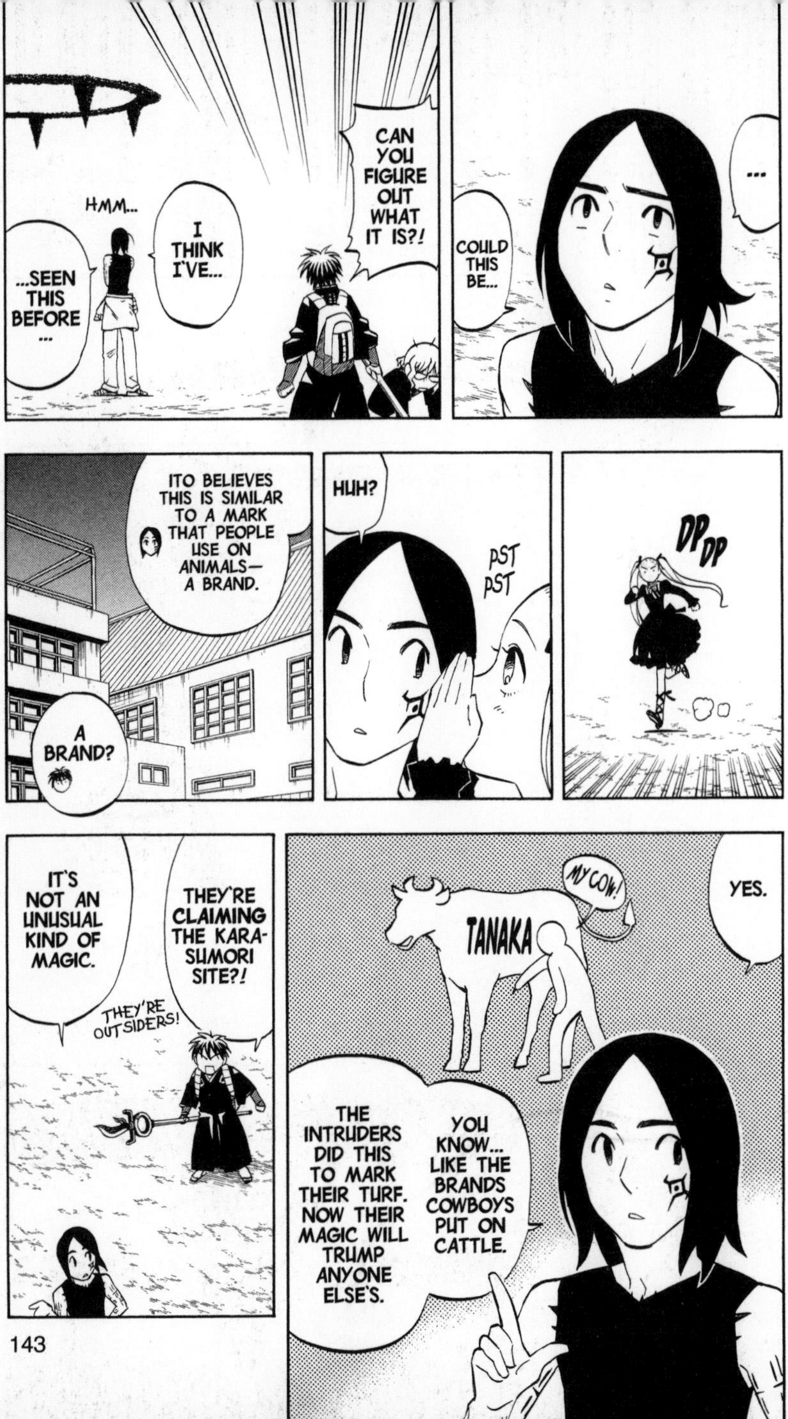

...
COULD THIS BE...
CAN YOU FIGURE OUT WHAT IT IS?!
I THINK I'VE...
HMM...
...SEEN THIS BEFORE ...
DP DP
PST PST
HUH?
ITO BELIEVES THIS IS SIMILAR TO A MARK THAT PEOPLE USE ON ANIMALS— A BRAND.
A BRAND?
YES.
MY COW!
TANAKA
YOU KNOW... LIKE THE BRANDS COWBOYS PUT ON CATTLE.
THE INTRUDERS DID THIS TO MARK THEIR TURF. NOW THEIR MAGIC WILL TRUMP ANYONE ELSE'S.
THEY'RE CLAIMING THE KARA-SUMORI SITE?!
IT'S NOT AN UNUSUAL KIND OF MAGIC.
THEY'RE OUTSIDERS!

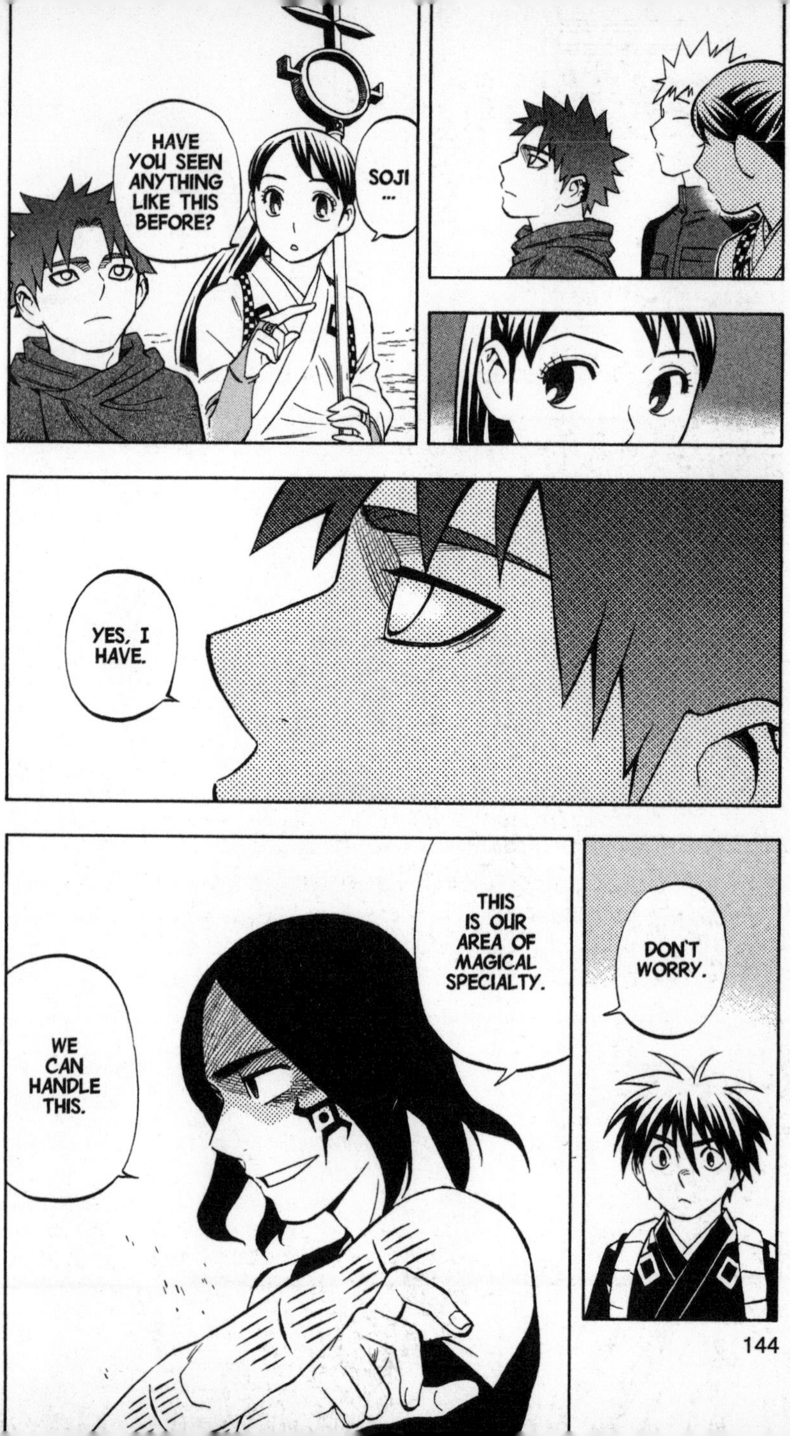
SOJI ...
HAVE YOU SEEN ANYTHING LIKE THIS BEFORE?
YES, I HAVE.
DON'T WORRY.
THIS IS OUR AREA OF MAGICAL SPECIALTY.
WE CAN HANDLE THIS.

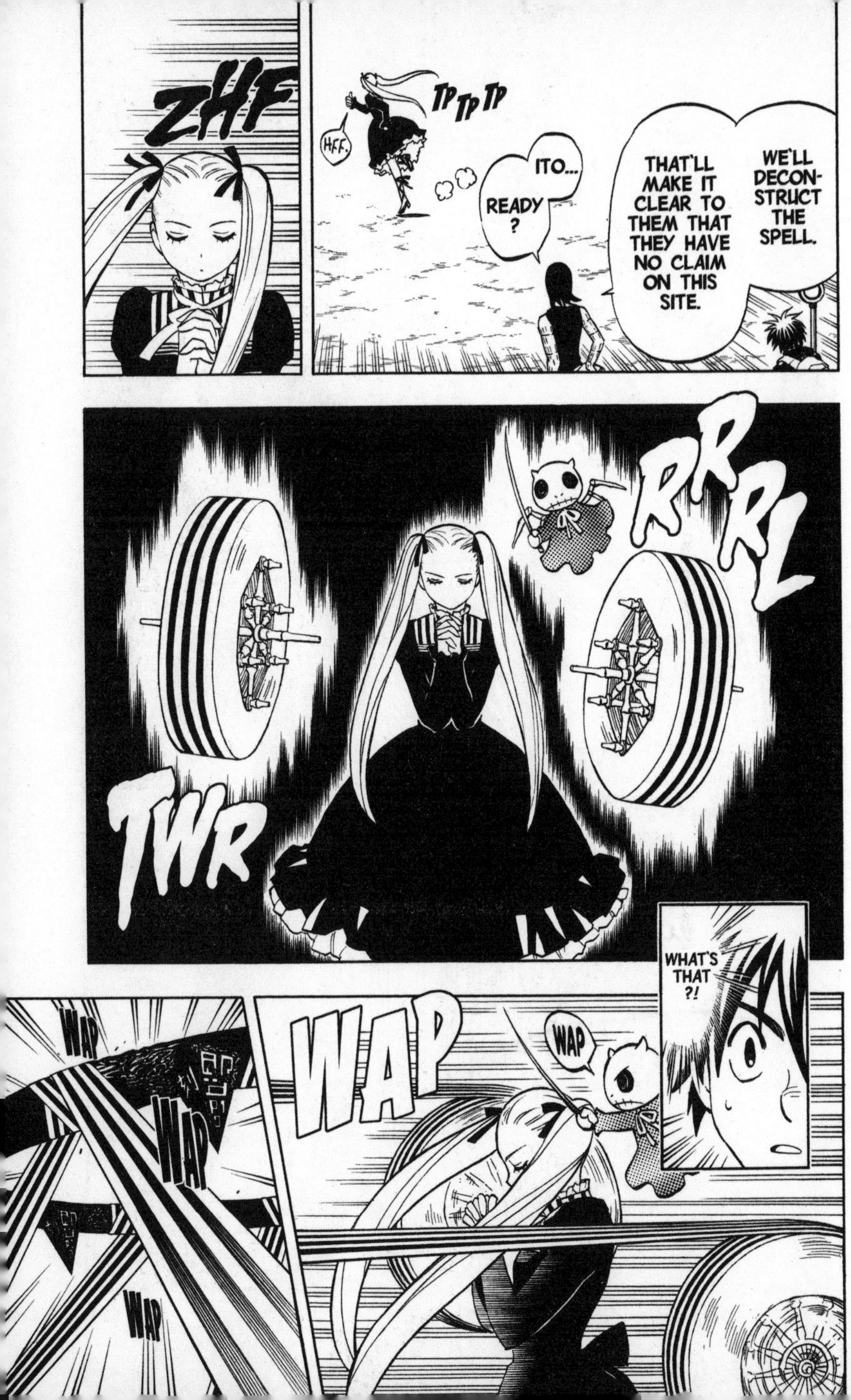
WE'LL DECONSTRUCT THE SPELL.
THAT'LL MAKE IT CLEAR TO THEM THAT THEY HAVE NO CLAIM ON THIS SITE.
ITO... READY?
TP TP TP
HFF.
ZHF
RRRL
TWR
WHAT'S THAT?!
WAP
WAP
WAP
WAP
WAP

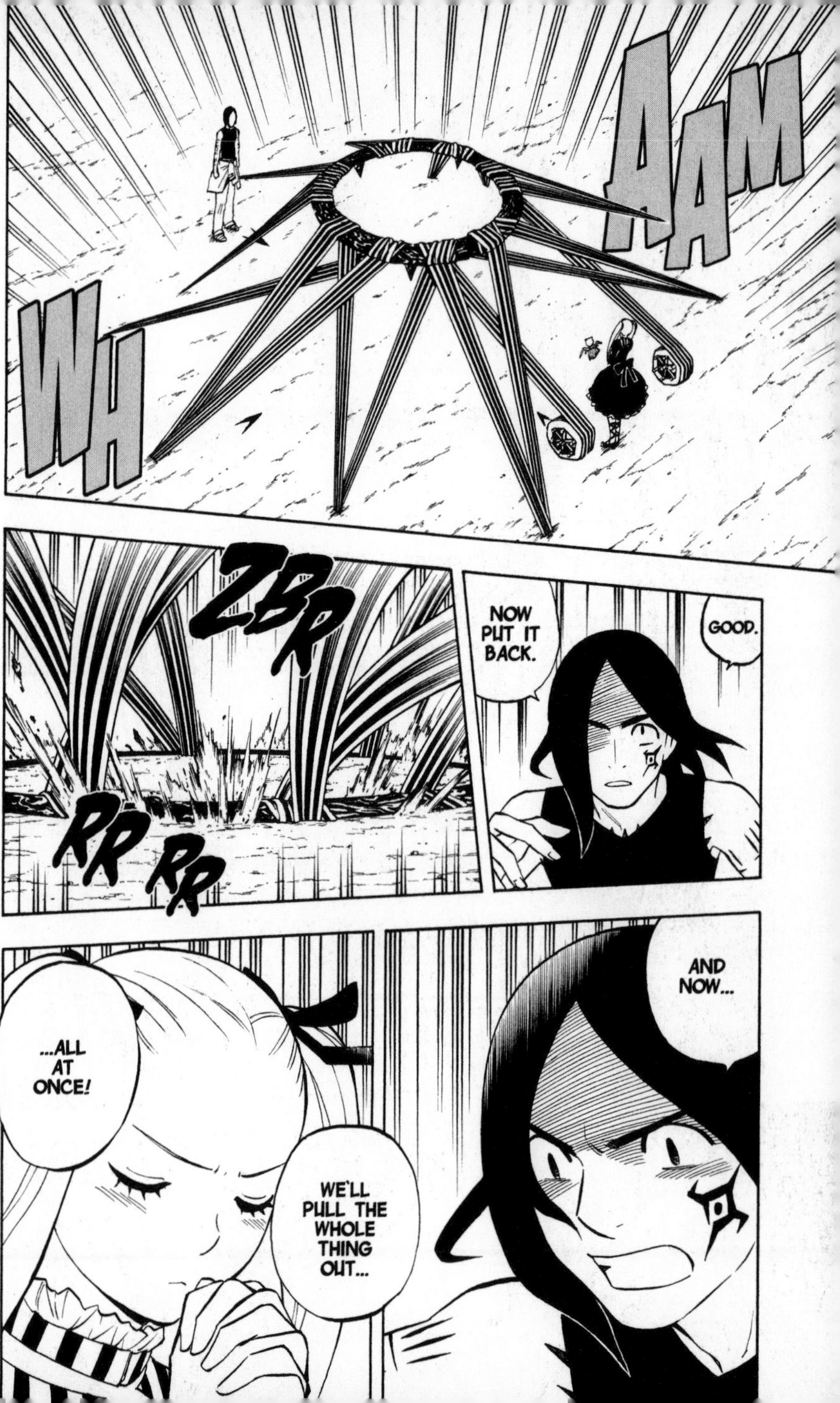
WHAAM
GOOD.
NOW PUT IT BACK.
ZBRRRRR
AND NOW...
WE'LL PULL THE WHOLE THING OUT...
...ALL AT ONCE!

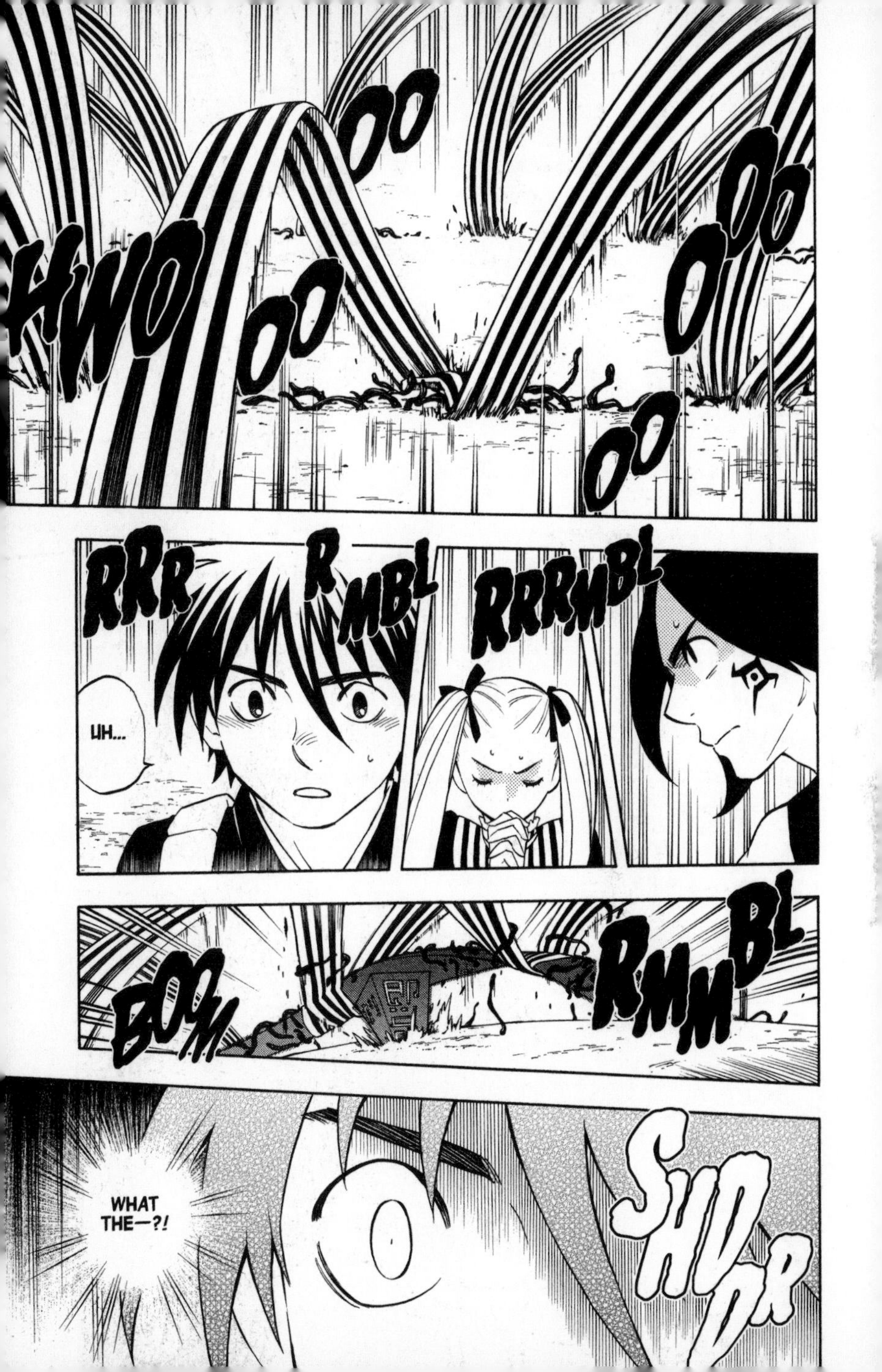
HWOOOOOOO
RRRRMBL
RRR RMBL
UH...
RMMBL
BOOM
SHDDR
WHAT THE—?!

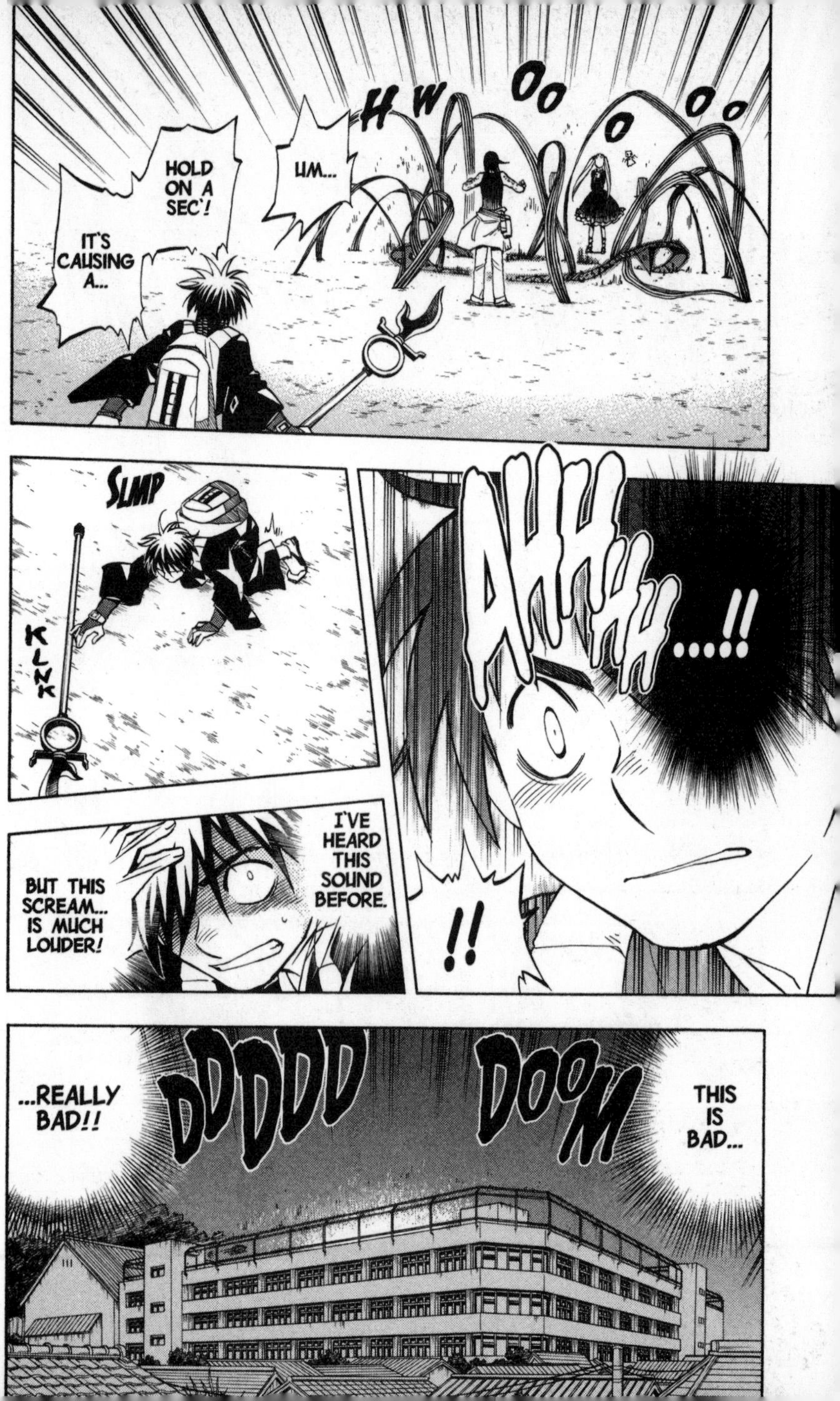
HWOOOOO
UM...
HOLD ON A SEC'!
IT'S CAUSING A...
AHHHH...!!
!!
SLMP
KLNK
I'VE HEARD THIS SOUND BEFORE.
BUT THIS SCREAM... IS MUCH LOUDER!
THIS IS BAD...
DDDDD DOOM
...REALLY BAD!!

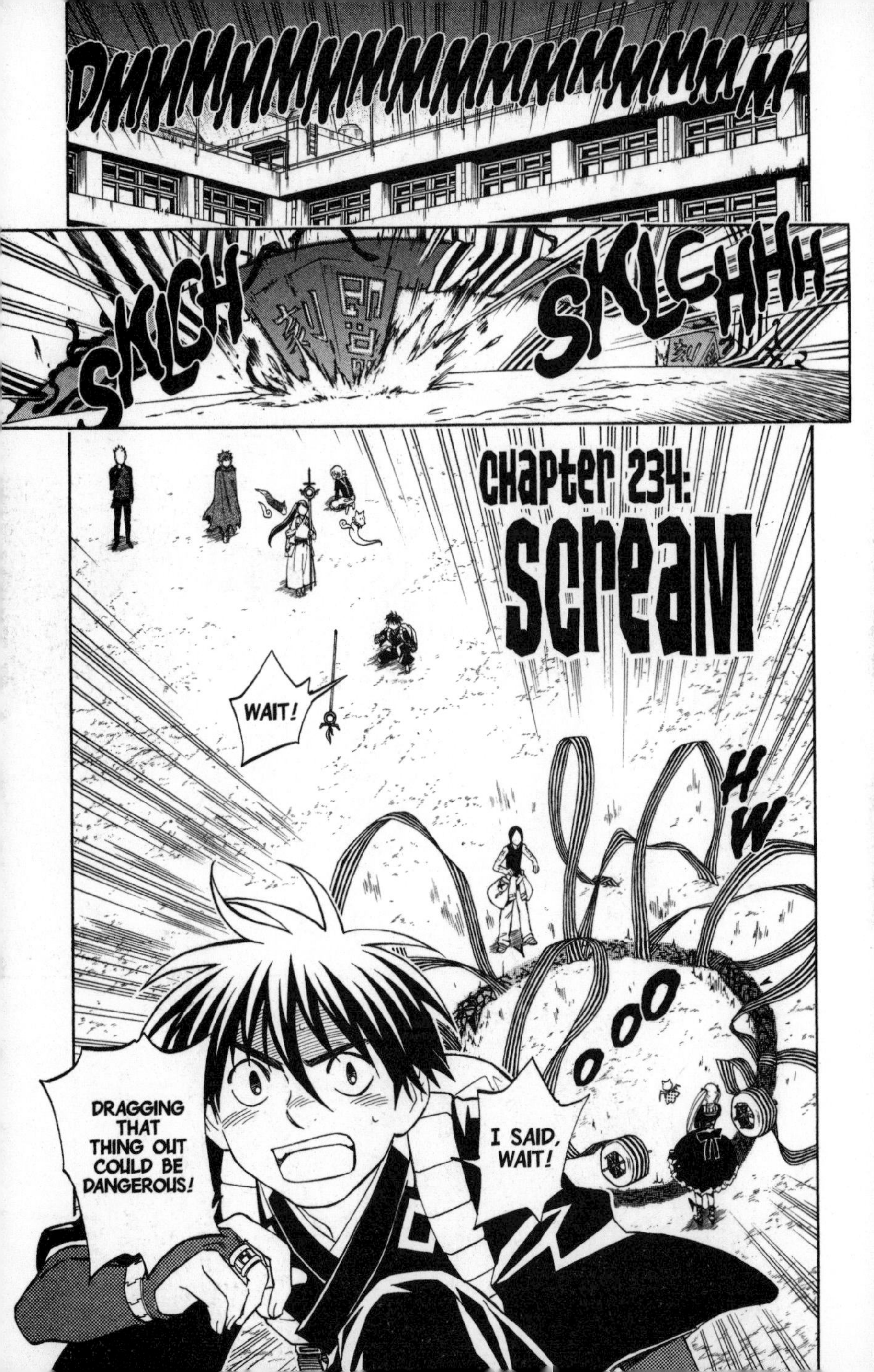
DMMMMMMMMMMMMMMMMMMMMM-
SKLCHHH
SKLCH
Chapter 234:
Scream
WAIT!
HW
OOO
I SAID, WAIT!
DRAGGING THAT THING OUT COULD BE DANGEROUS!

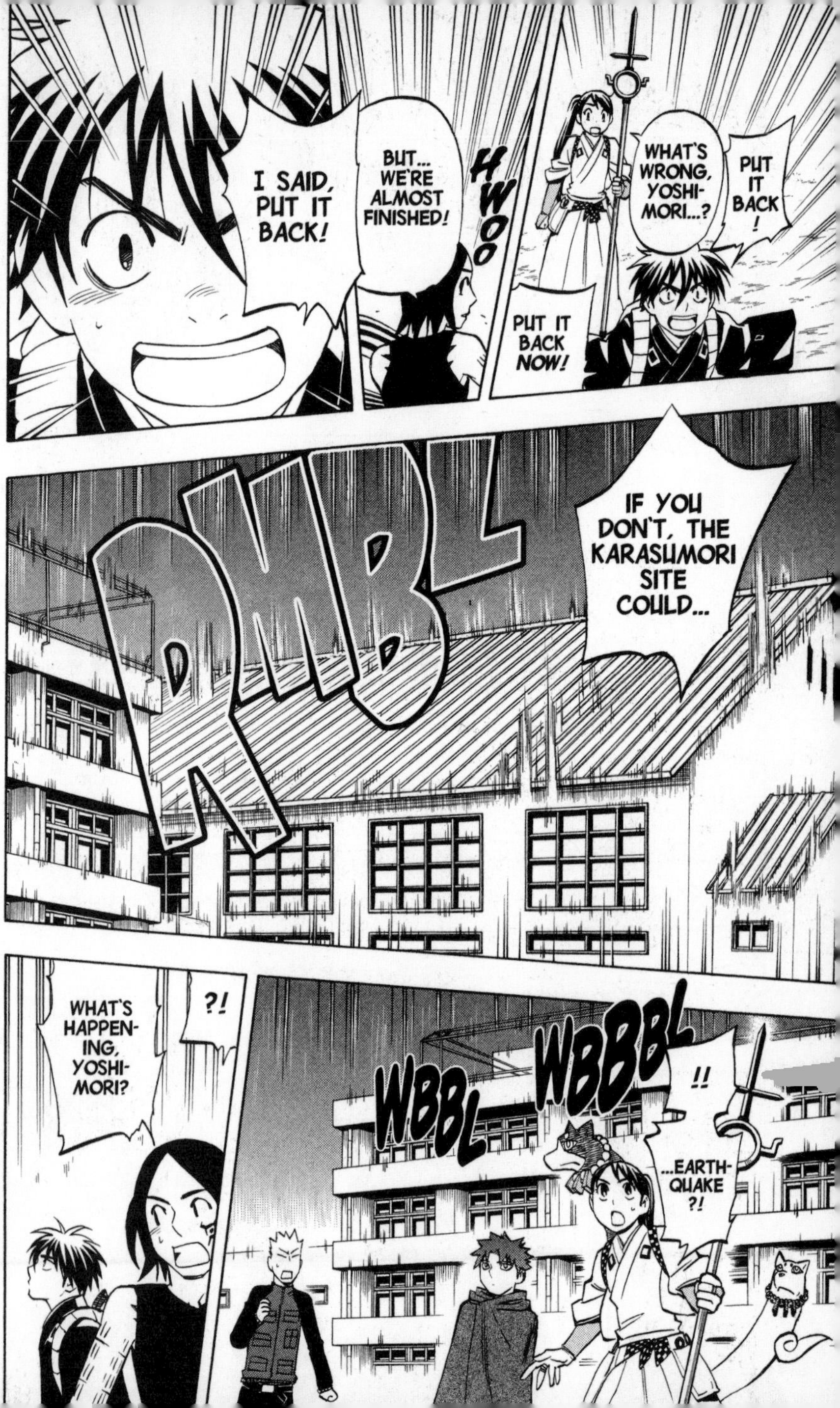
PUT IT BACK!
WHAT'S WRONG, YOSHIMORI...?
PUT IT BACK NOW!
HWOO
BUT... WE'RE ALMOST FINISHED!
I SAID, PUT IT BACK!
IF YOU DON'T, THE KARASUMORI SITE COULD...
RMBL
!!
...EARTHQUAKE?!
WBBBL
WBBL
?!
WHAT'S HAPPENING, YOSHIMORI?

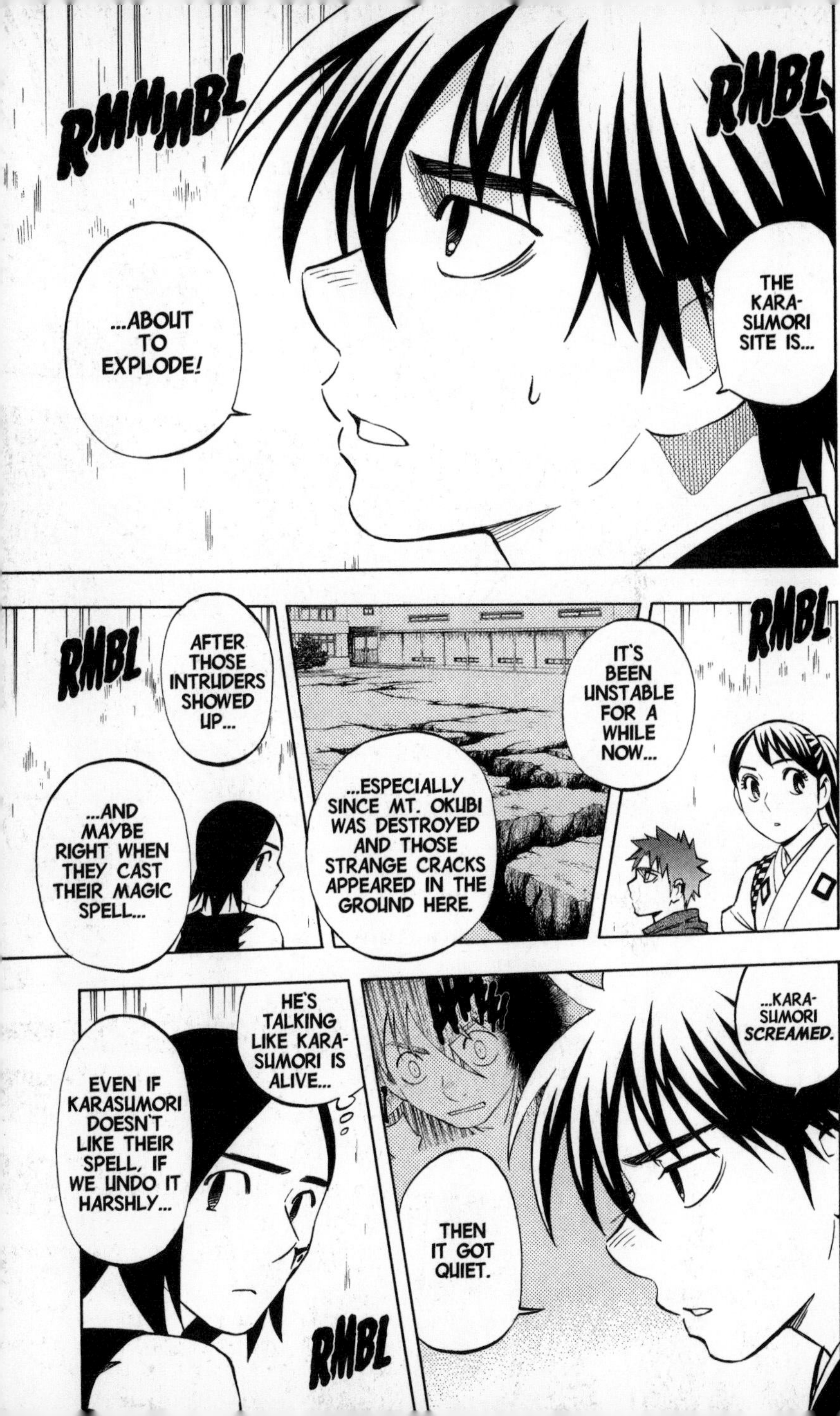
RMBL
RMMMBL
THE KARA-SUMORI SITE IS...
...ABOUT TO EXPLODE!
RMBL
IT'S BEEN UNSTABLE FOR A WHILE NOW...
...ESPECIALLY SINCE MT. OKUBI WAS DESTROYED AND THOSE STRANGE CRACKS APPEARED IN THE GROUND HERE.
RMBL
AFTER THOSE INTRUDERS SHOWED UP...
...AND MAYBE RIGHT WHEN THEY CAST THEIR MAGIC SPELL...
...KARA-SUMORI *SCREAMED.*
THEN IT GOT QUIET.
HE'S TALKING LIKE KARA-SUMORI IS ALIVE...
EVEN IF KARASUMORI DOESN'T LIKE THEIR SPELL, IF WE UNDO IT HARSHLY...
RMBL

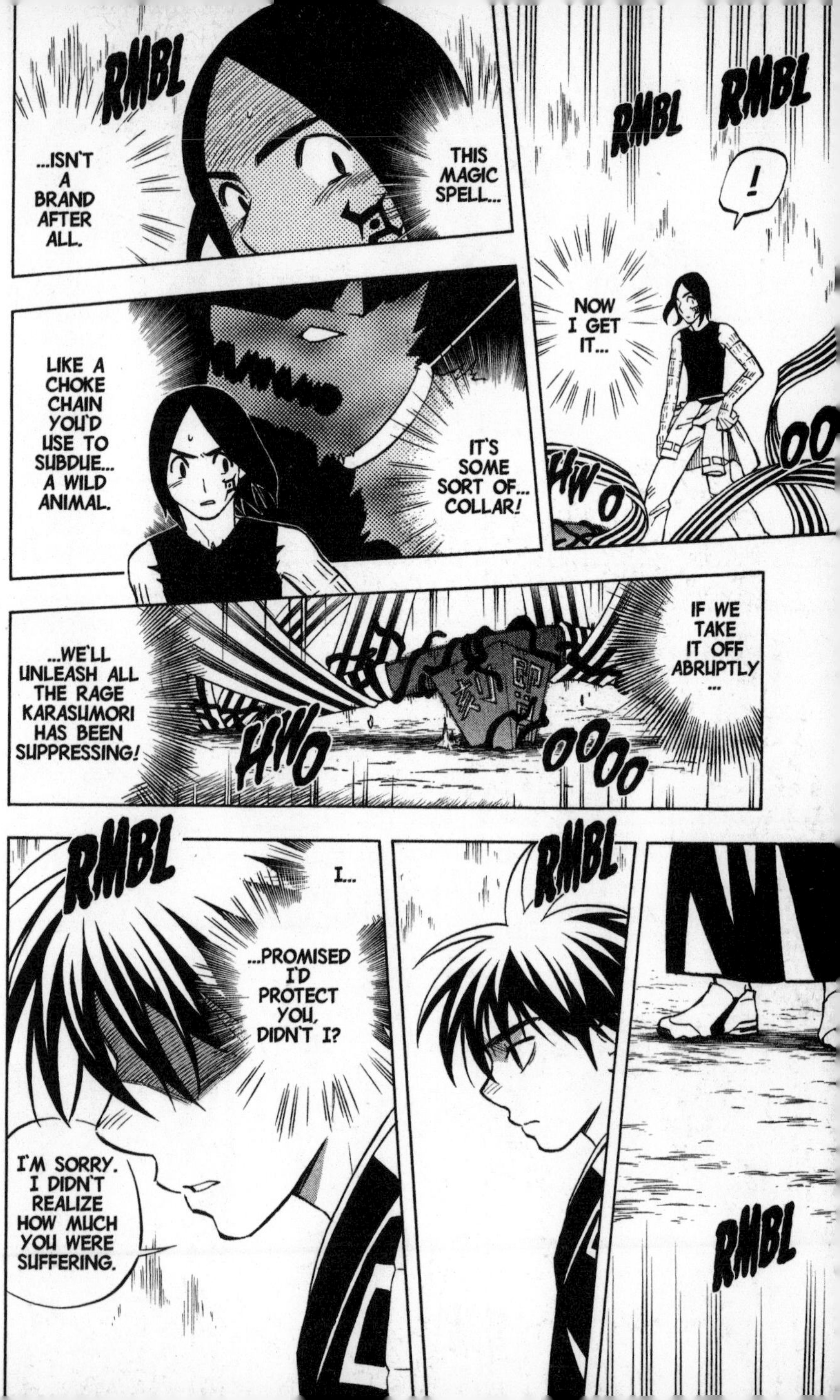
RMBL
RMBL
!
NOW I GET IT...
HWOOO
RMBL
THIS MAGIC SPELL...
...ISN'T A BRAND AFTER ALL.
IT'S SOME SORT OF... COLLAR!
LIKE A CHOKE CHAIN YOU'D USE TO SUBDUE... A WILD ANIMAL.
IF WE TAKE IT OFF ABRUPTLY...
...WE'LL UNLEASH ALL THE RAGE KARASUMORI HAS BEEN SUPPRESSING!
HWOOOOO
RMBL
RMBL
RMBL
I...
...PROMISED I'D PROTECT YOU, DIDN'T I?
I'M SORRY. I DIDN'T REALIZE HOW MUCH YOU WERE SUFFERING.

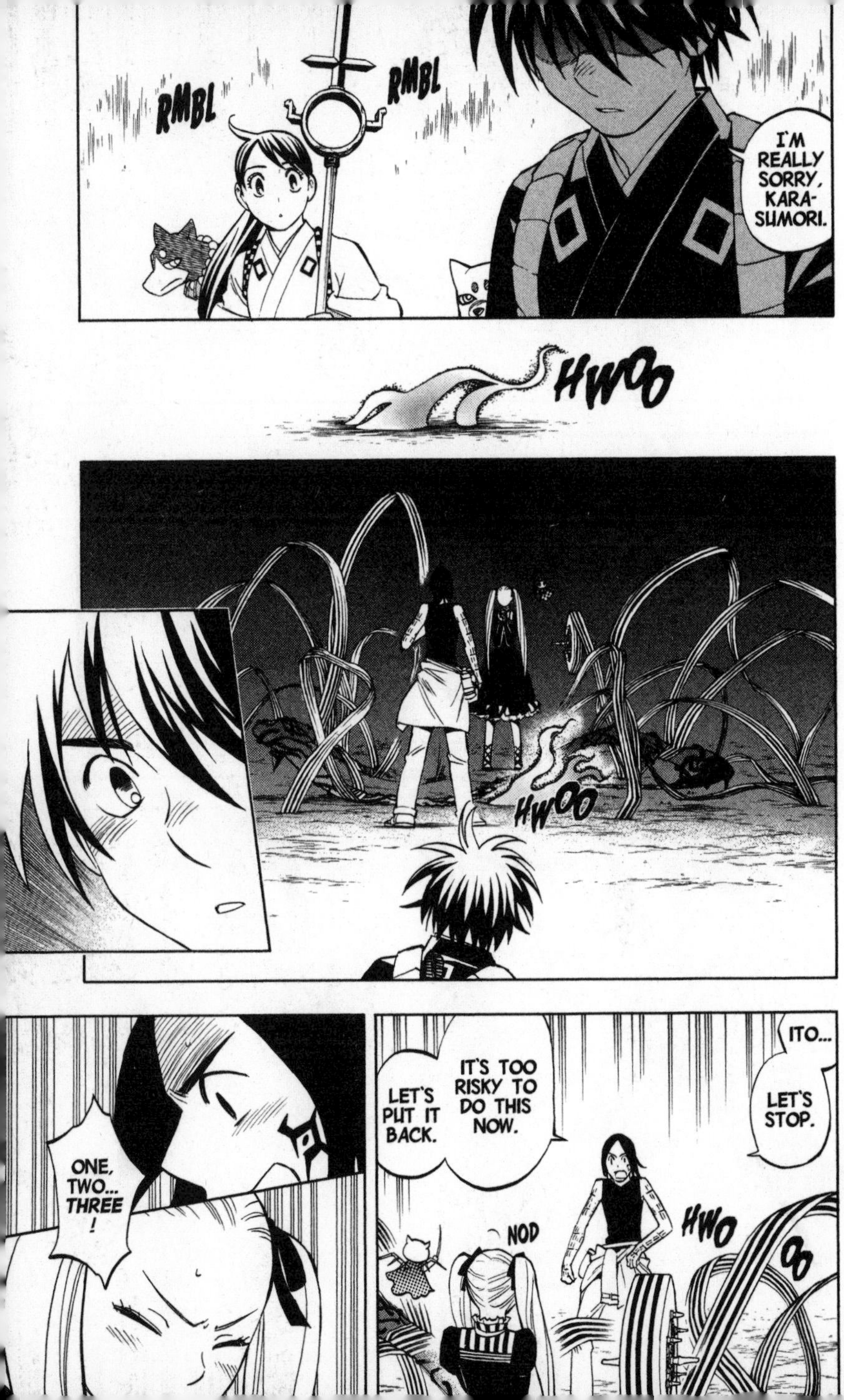
I'M REALLY SORRY, KARASUMORI.
RMBL
RMBL
HWOO
HWOO
ITO...
LET'S STOP.
IT'S TOO RISKY TO DO THIS NOW.
LET'S PUT IT BACK.
HWOOO
NOD
ONE, TWO... THREE!

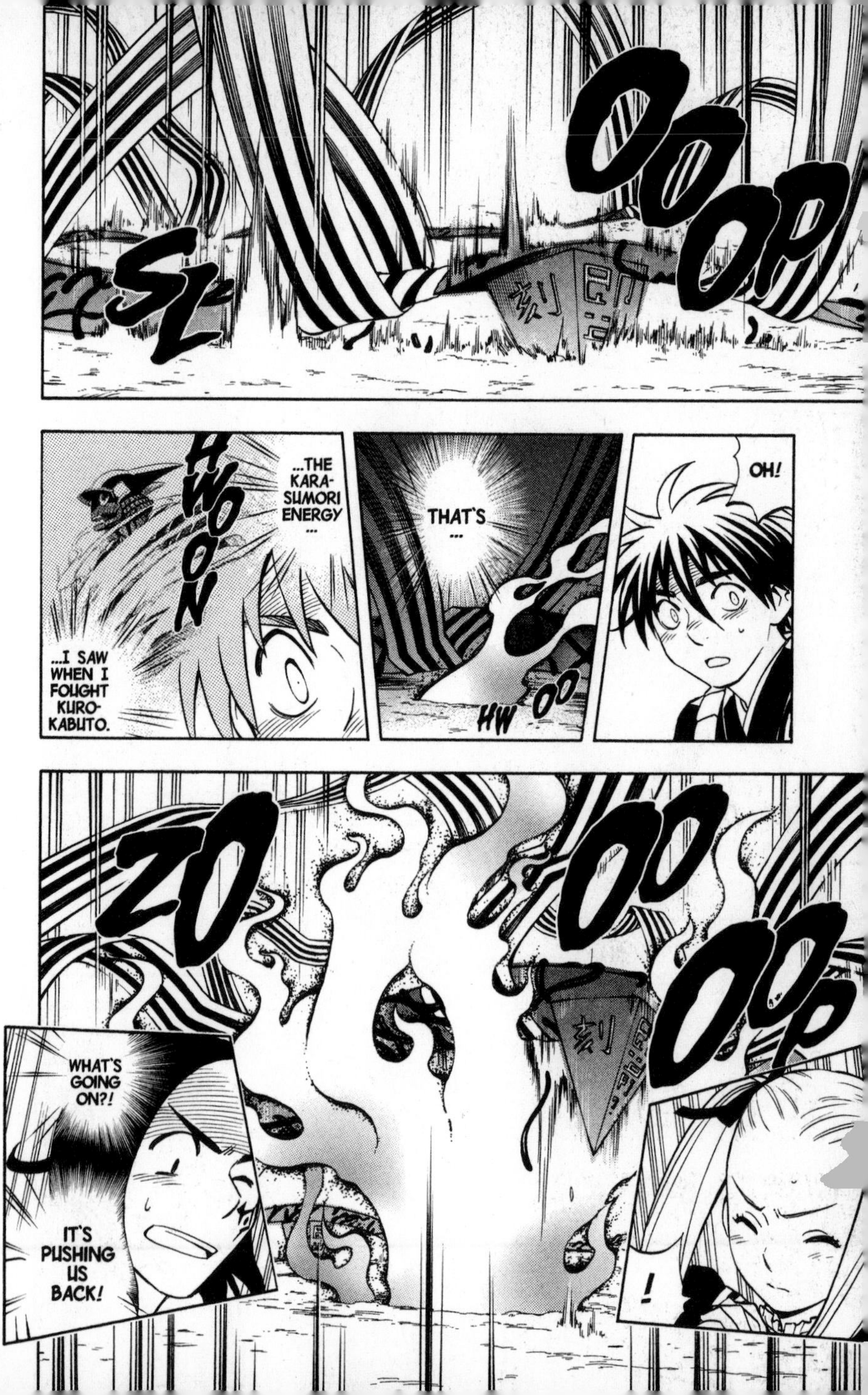
OOOOPP
OH!
THAT'S ...
HW OO
...THE KARA-SUMORI ENERGY ...
HWOOON
...I SAW WHEN I FOUGHT KURO-KABUTO.
ZO
OOOOOP
!
WHAT'S GOING ON?!
IT'S PUSHING US BACK!

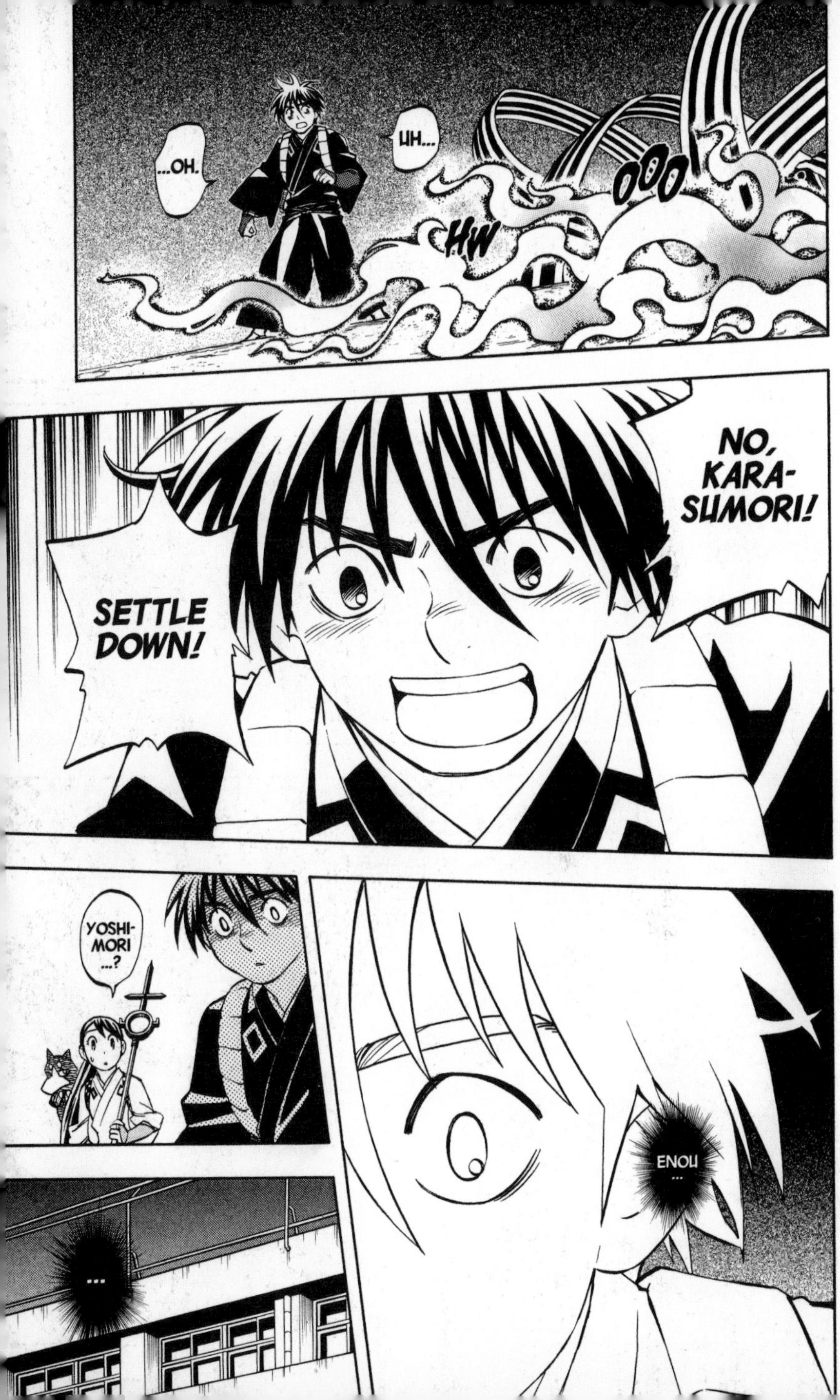
HW
OOOO
UH...
...OH.
NO, KARA-SUMORI!
SETTLE DOWN!
ENOU ...
YOSHI-MORI ...?
...

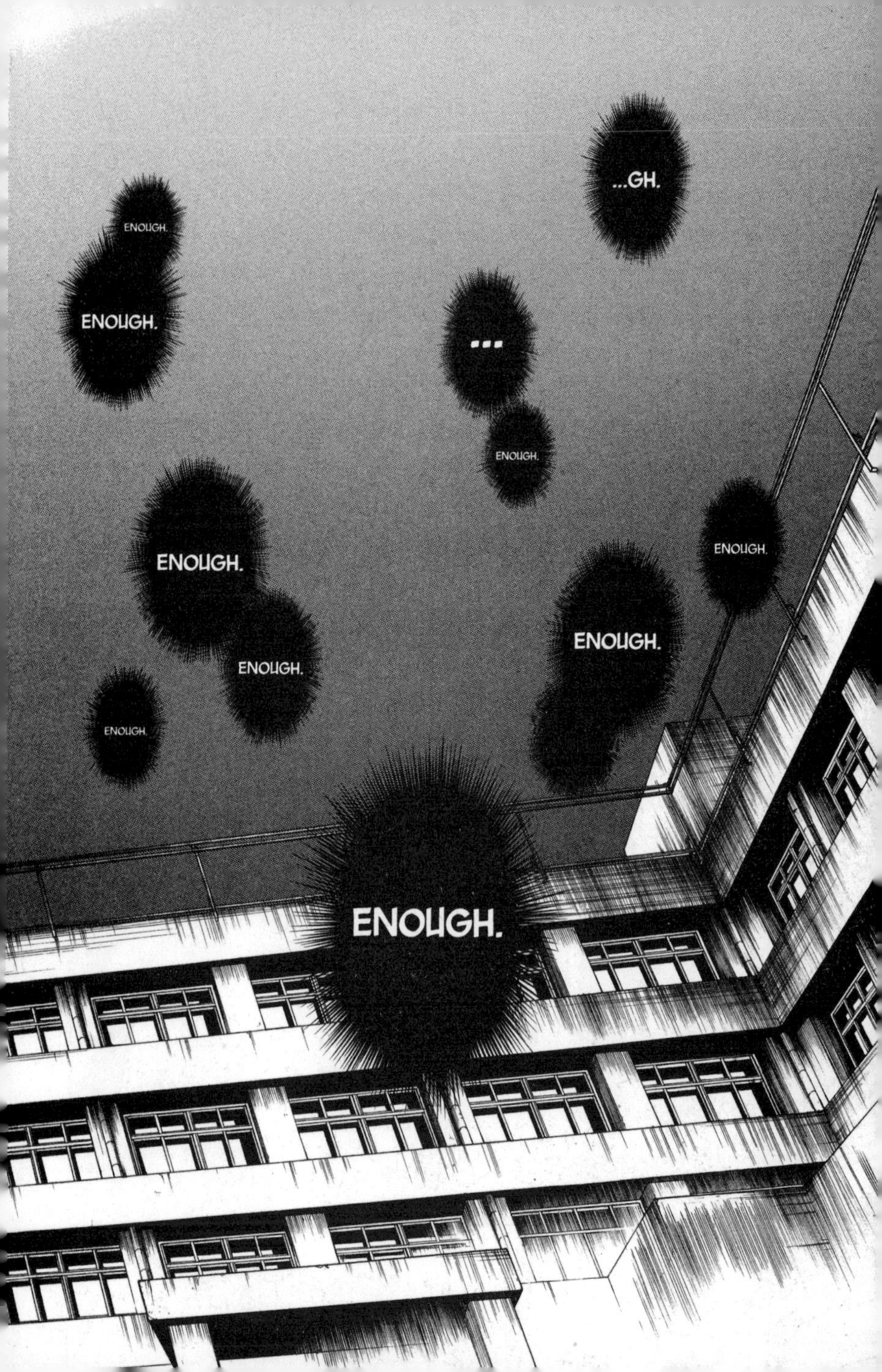
...GH.
...
ENOUGH.
ENOUGH.
ENOUGH.
ENOUGH.
ENOUGH.
ENOUGH.
ENOUGH.
ENOUGH.
ENOUGH.

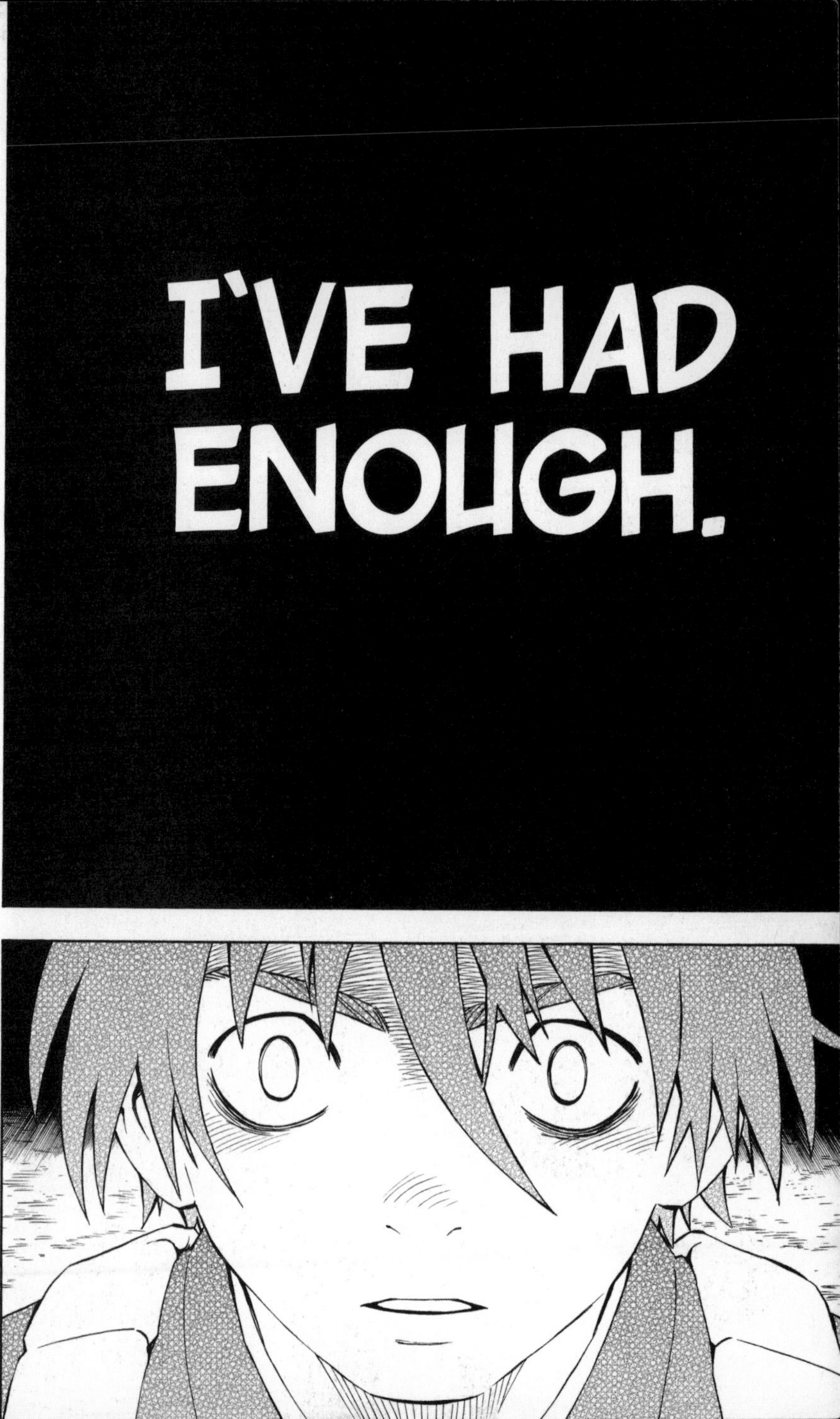
I'VE HAD ENOUGH.

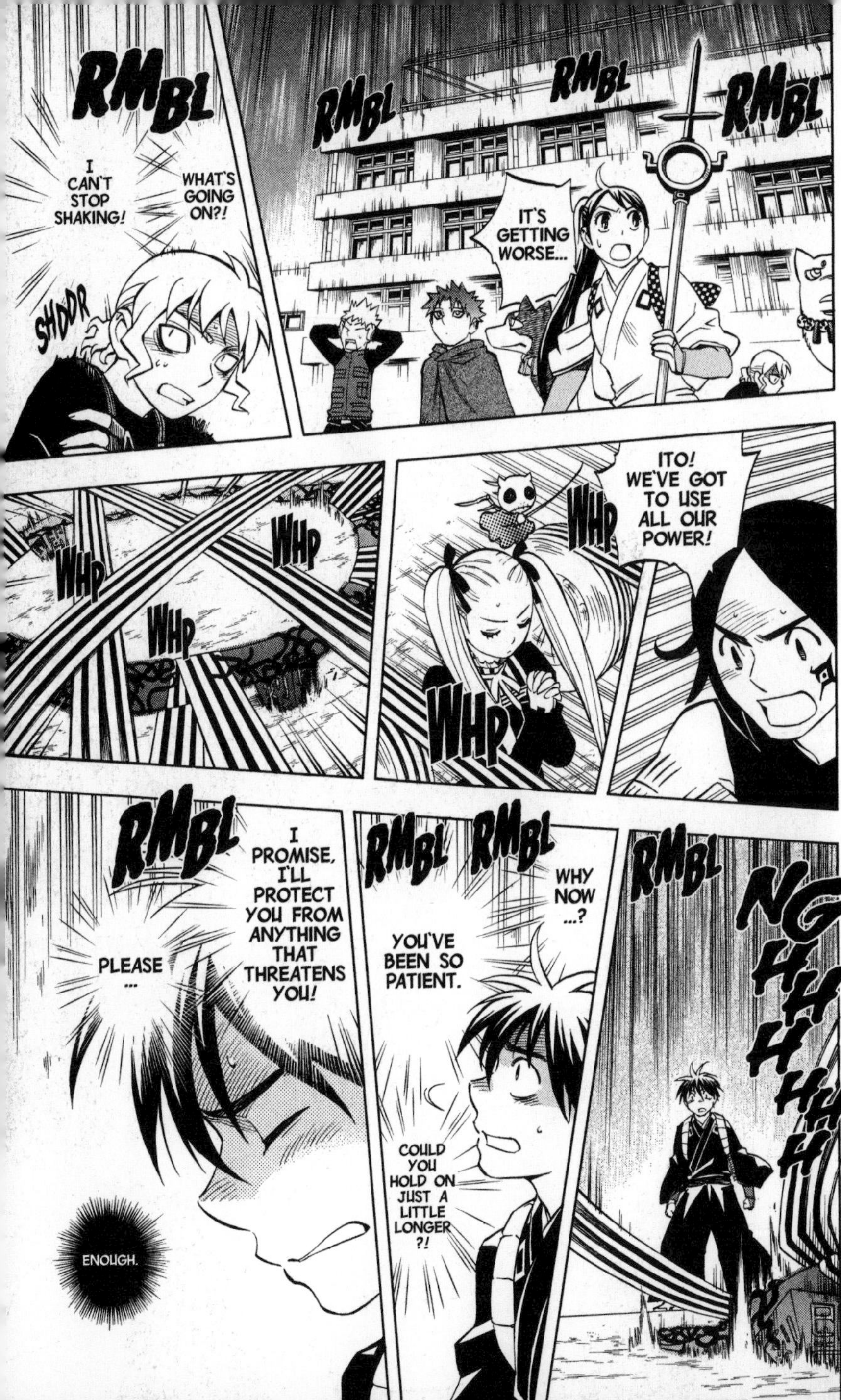
RMBL
RMBL
RMBL
IT'S GETTING WORSE...
RMBL
WHAT'S GOING ON?!
I CAN'T STOP SHAKING!
SHDDR
ITO! WE'VE GOT TO USE ALL OUR POWER!
WHP
WHP
WHP
WHP
WHP
RMBL
NGHHHHHHH
RMBL
RMBL
WHY NOW ...?
YOU'VE BEEN SO PATIENT.
COULD YOU HOLD ON JUST A LITTLE LONGER ?!
RMBL
I PROMISE, I'LL PROTECT YOU FROM ANYTHING THAT THREATENS YOU!
PLEASE ...
ENOUGH.

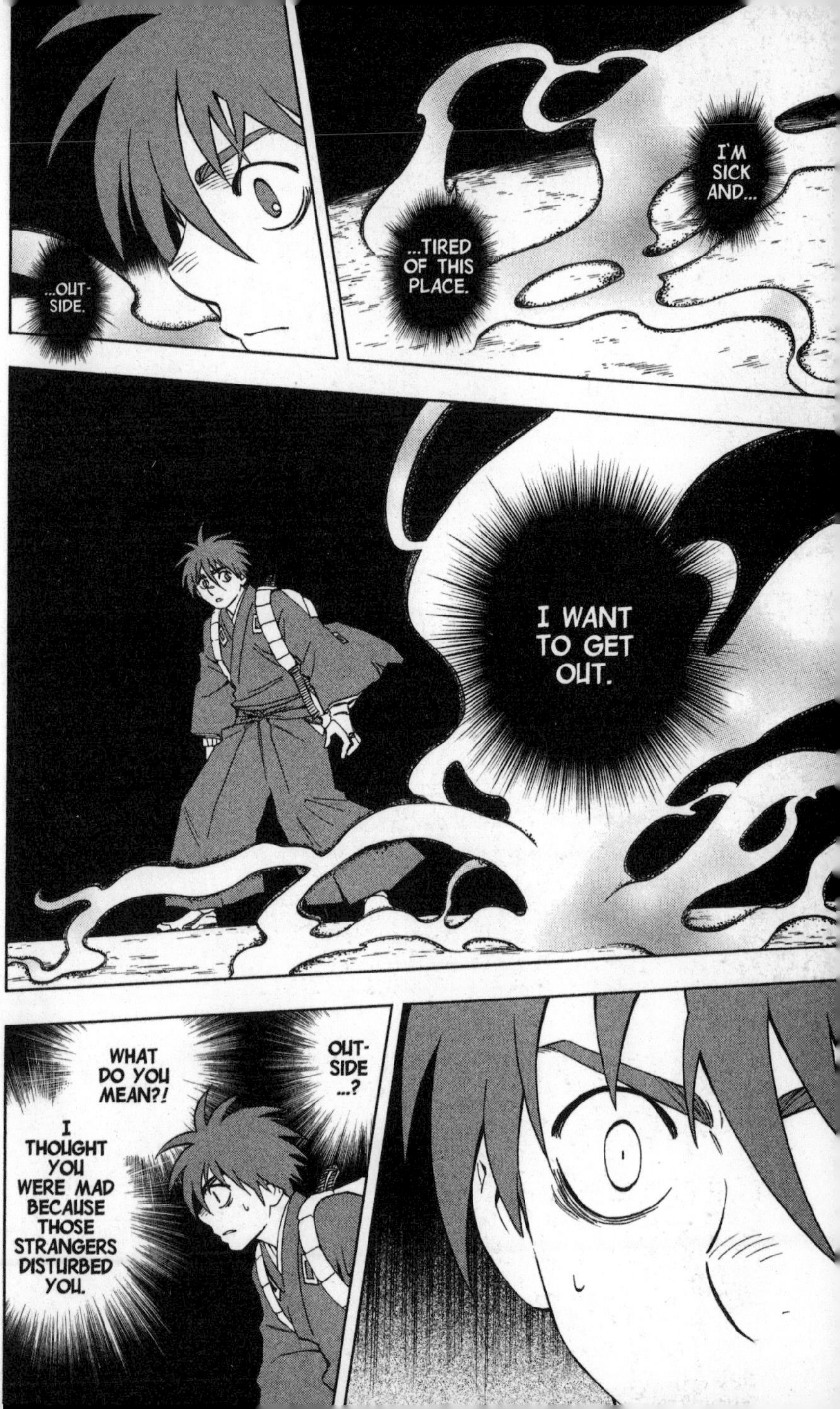
I'M SICK AND...
...TIRED OF THIS PLACE.
...OUT-SIDE.
I WANT TO GET OUT.
OUT-SIDE ...?
WHAT DO YOU MEAN?!
I THOUGHT YOU WERE MAD BECAUSE THOSE STRANGERS DISTURBED YOU.

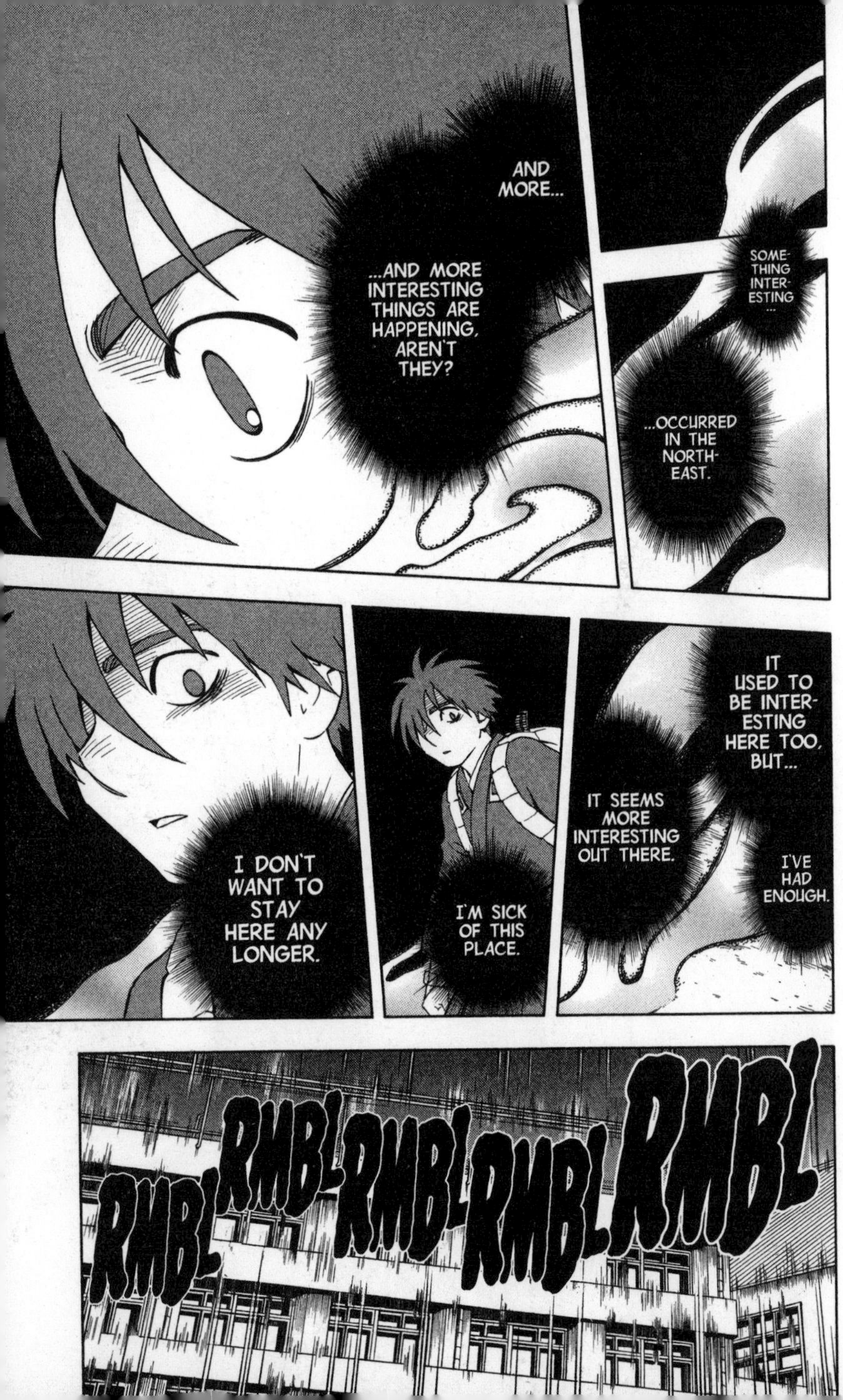
SOMETHING INTERESTING...
...OCCURRED IN THE NORTHEAST.
AND MORE...
...AND MORE INTERESTING THINGS ARE HAPPENING, AREN'T THEY?
IT USED TO BE INTERESTING HERE TOO, BUT...
IT SEEMS MORE INTERESTING OUT THERE.
I'VE HAD ENOUGH.
I'M SICK OF THIS PLACE.
I DON'T WANT TO STAY HERE ANY LONGER.
RMBL RMBL RMBL RMBL RMBL

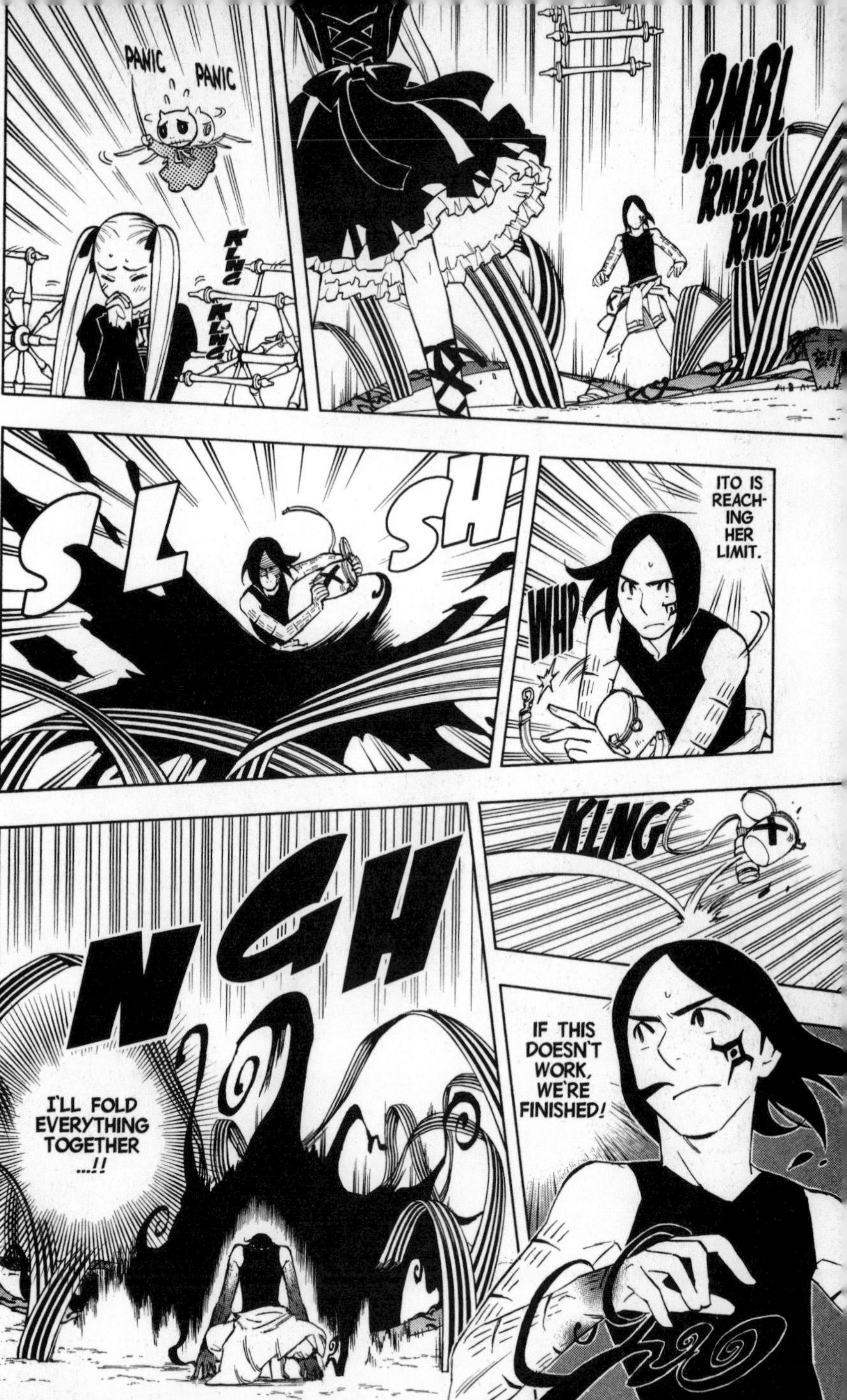
RMBL
RMBL
RMBL
PANIC
PANIC
KLNG
KLNG
ITO IS REACHING HER LIMIT.
WHP
SLSH
KLNG
IF THIS DOESN'T WORK, WE'RE FINISHED!
NGH
I'LL FOLD EVERYTHING TOGETHER ...!!

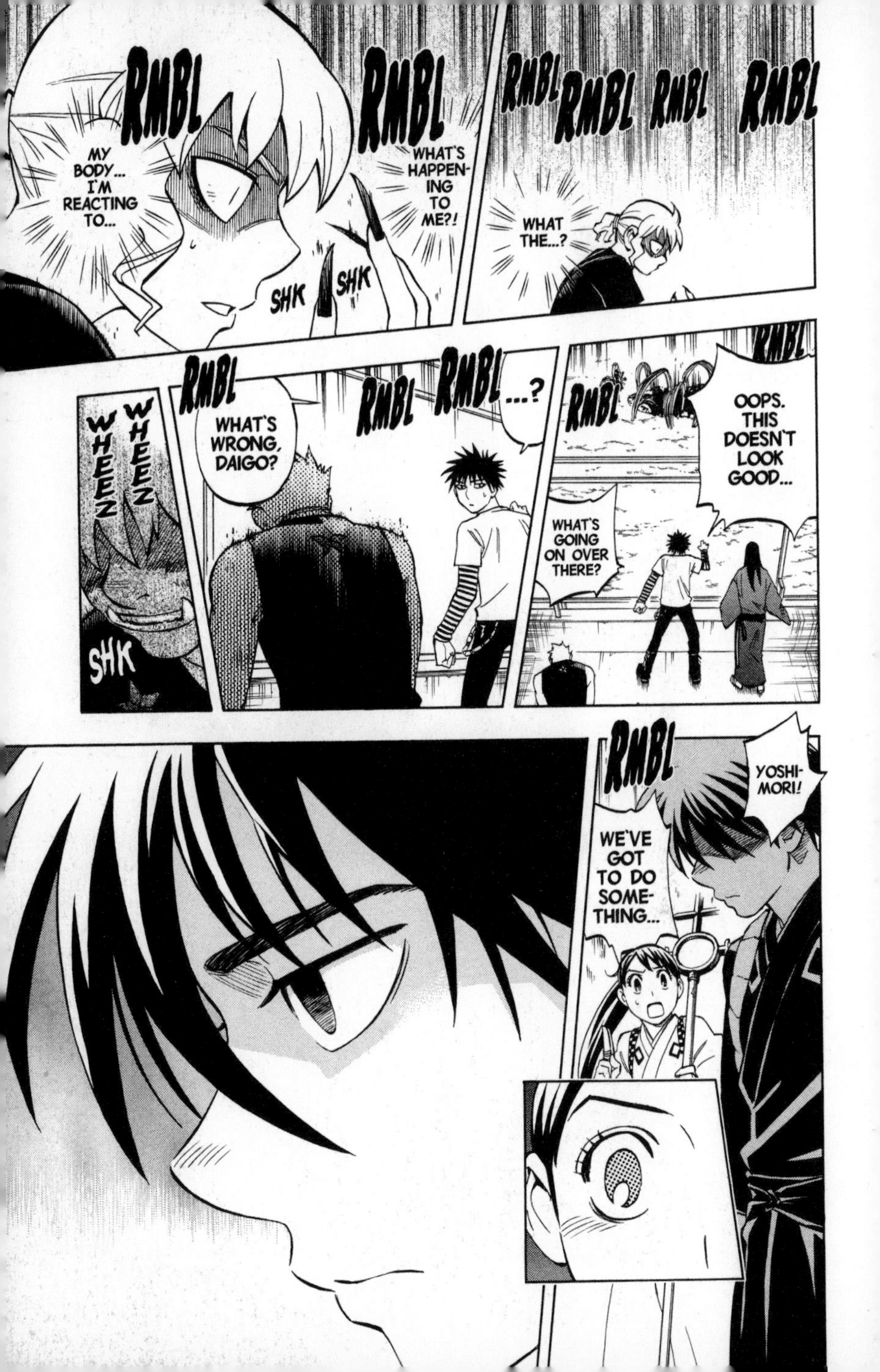
RMBL RMBL RMBL RMBL
WHAT THE...?
RMBL
RMBL
WHAT'S HAPPENING TO ME?!
MY BODY... I'M REACTING TO...
SHK SHK
RMBL
RMBL
OOPS. THIS DOESN'T LOOK GOOD...
WHAT'S GOING ON OVER THERE?
RMBL RMBL
...?
RMBL
WHAT'S WRONG, DAIGO?
WHEEZ WHEEZ
SHK
RMBL
YOSHI-MORI!
WE'VE GOT TO DO SOME-THING...

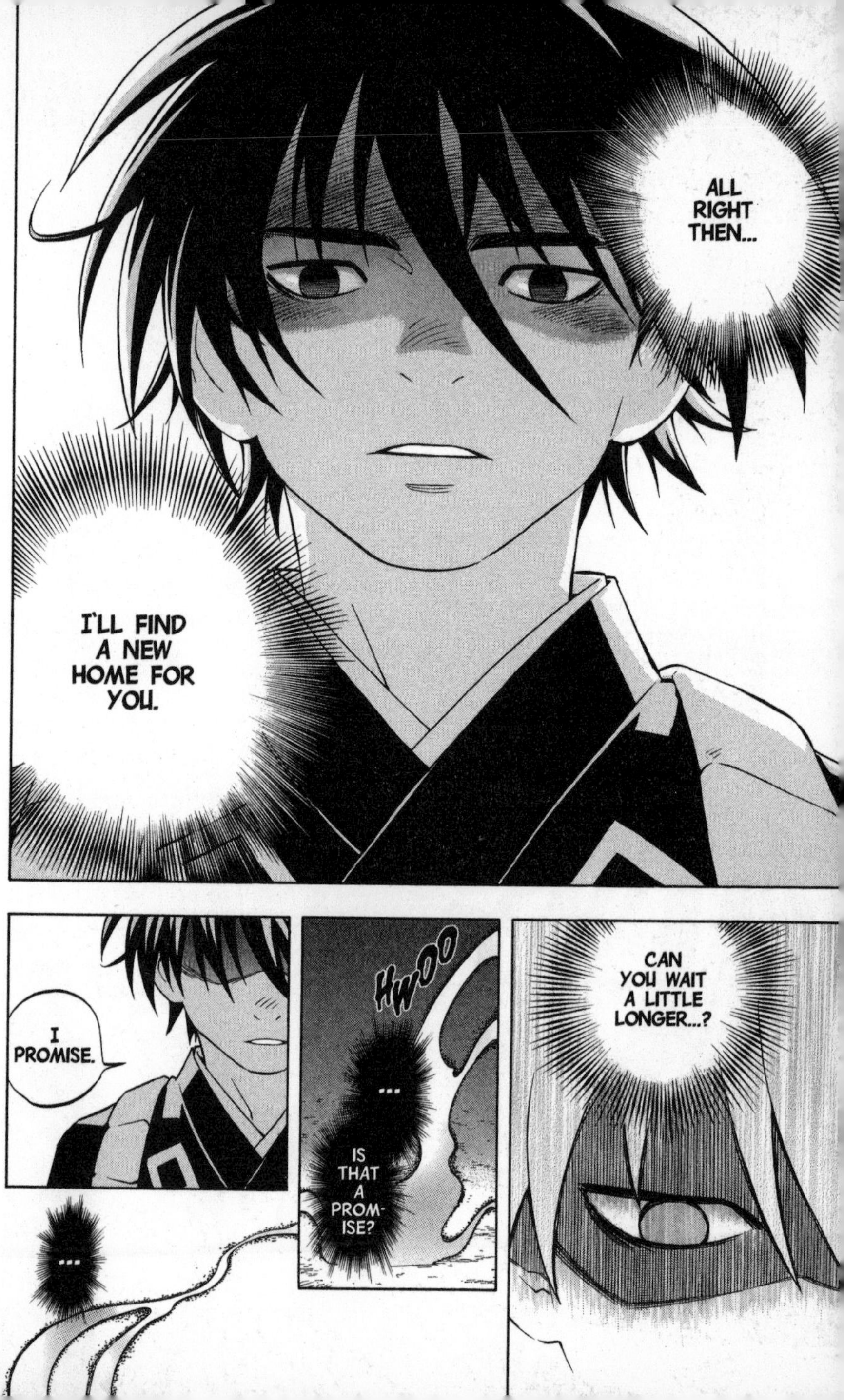
ALL RIGHT THEN...
I'LL FIND A NEW HOME FOR YOU.
CAN YOU WAIT A LITTLE LONGER...?
HWOO
...
IS THAT A PROM-ISE?
I PROMISE.
...

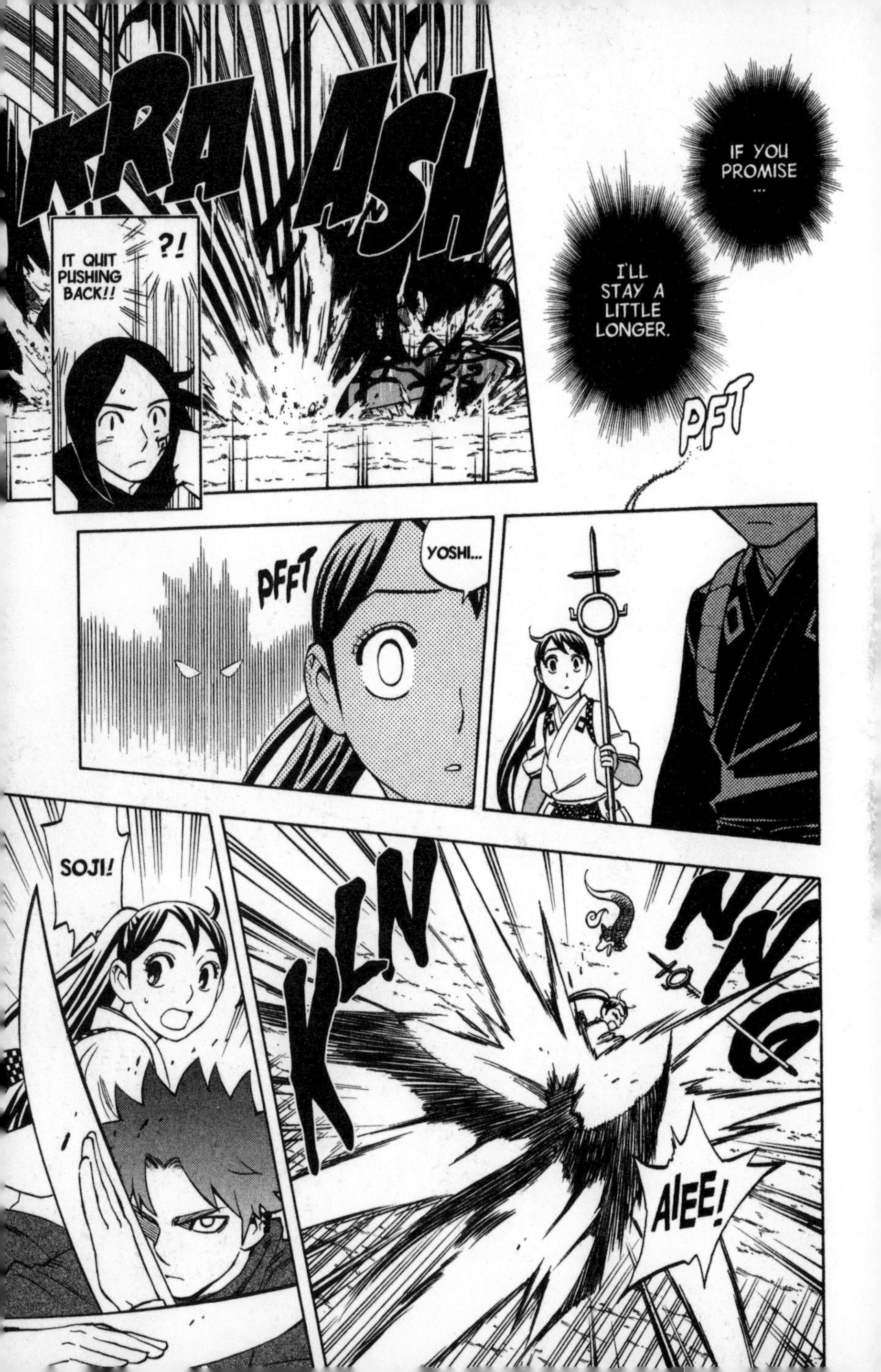
IF YOU PROMISE ...
I'LL STAY A LITTLE LONGER.
KRAASH
?!
IT QUIT PUSHING BACK!!
PFT
YOSHI...
PFFT
NNG
KLN
AIEE!
SOJI!

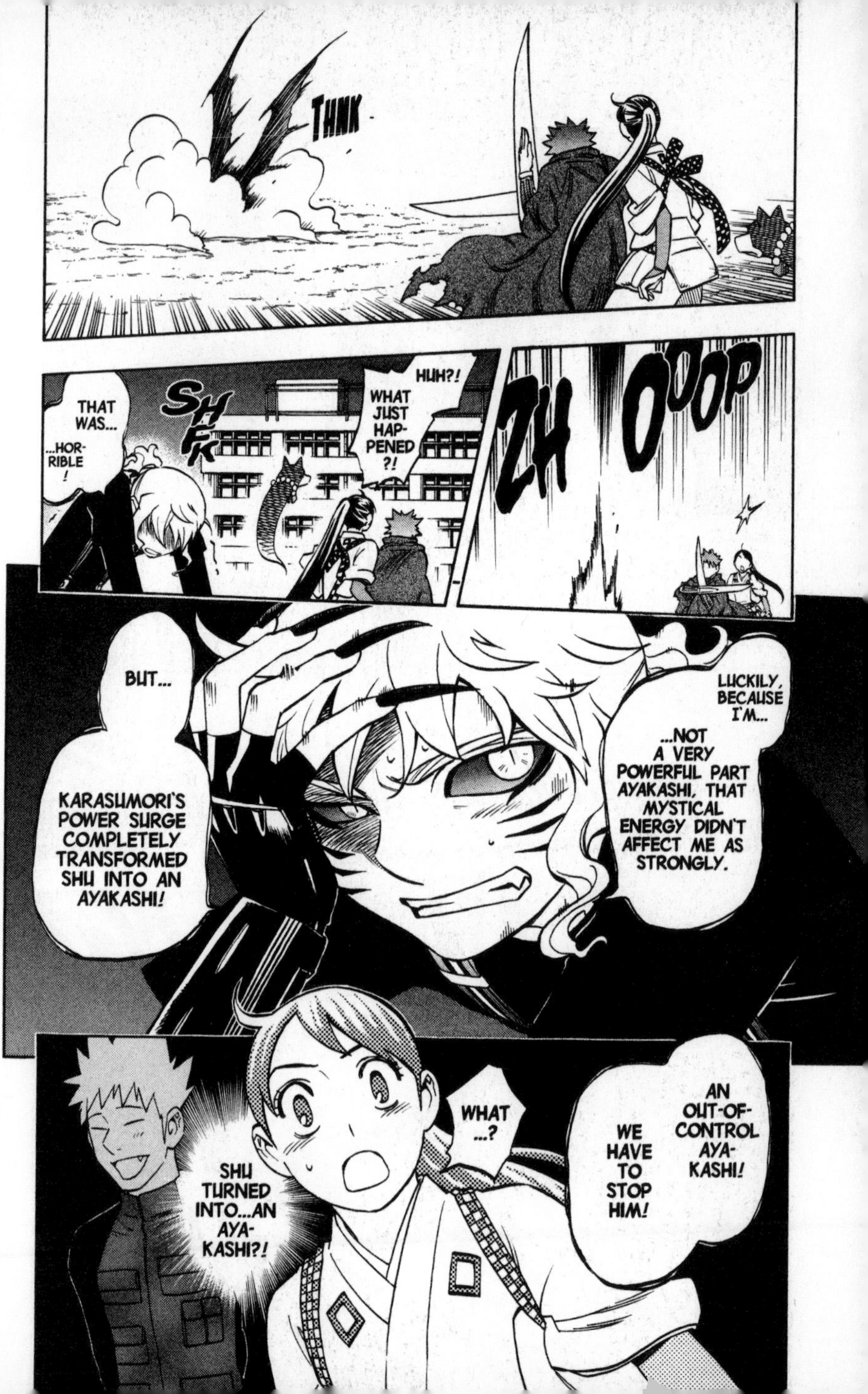
THNK
ZH OOOP
HUH?! WHAT JUST HAPPENED?!
SHFK
THAT WAS...
...HORRIBLE!
LUCKILY, BECAUSE I'M...
...NOT A VERY POWERFUL PART AYAKASHI, THAT MYSTICAL ENERGY DIDN'T AFFECT ME AS STRONGLY.
BUT...
KARASUMORI'S POWER SURGE COMPLETELY TRANSFORMED SHU INTO AN AYAKASHI!
AN OUT-OF-CONTROL AYAKASHI!
WE HAVE TO STOP HIM!
WHAT...?
SHU TURNED INTO...AN AYAKASHI?!

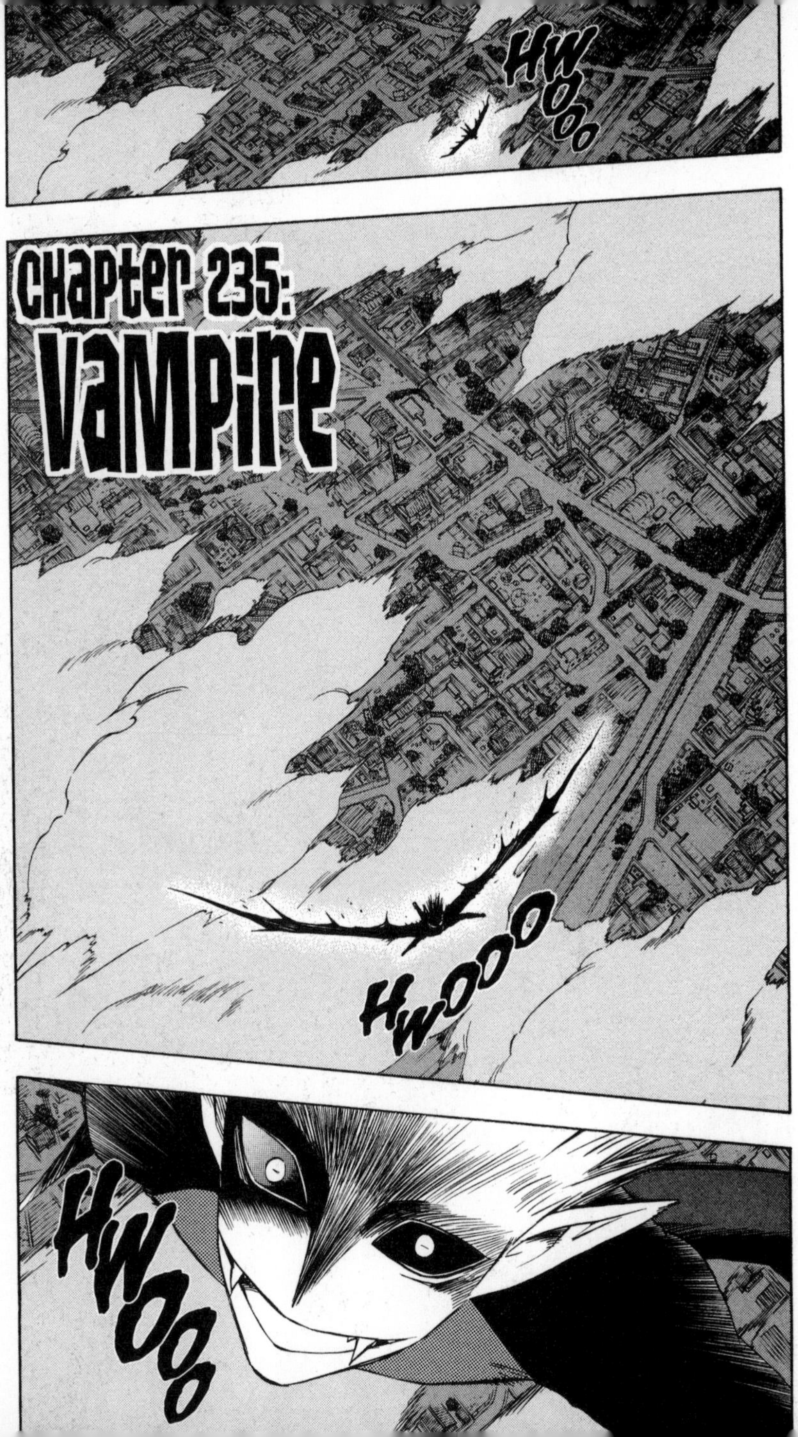
HWOOO
CHAPTER 235:
VAMPIRE
HWOOO
HWOOO

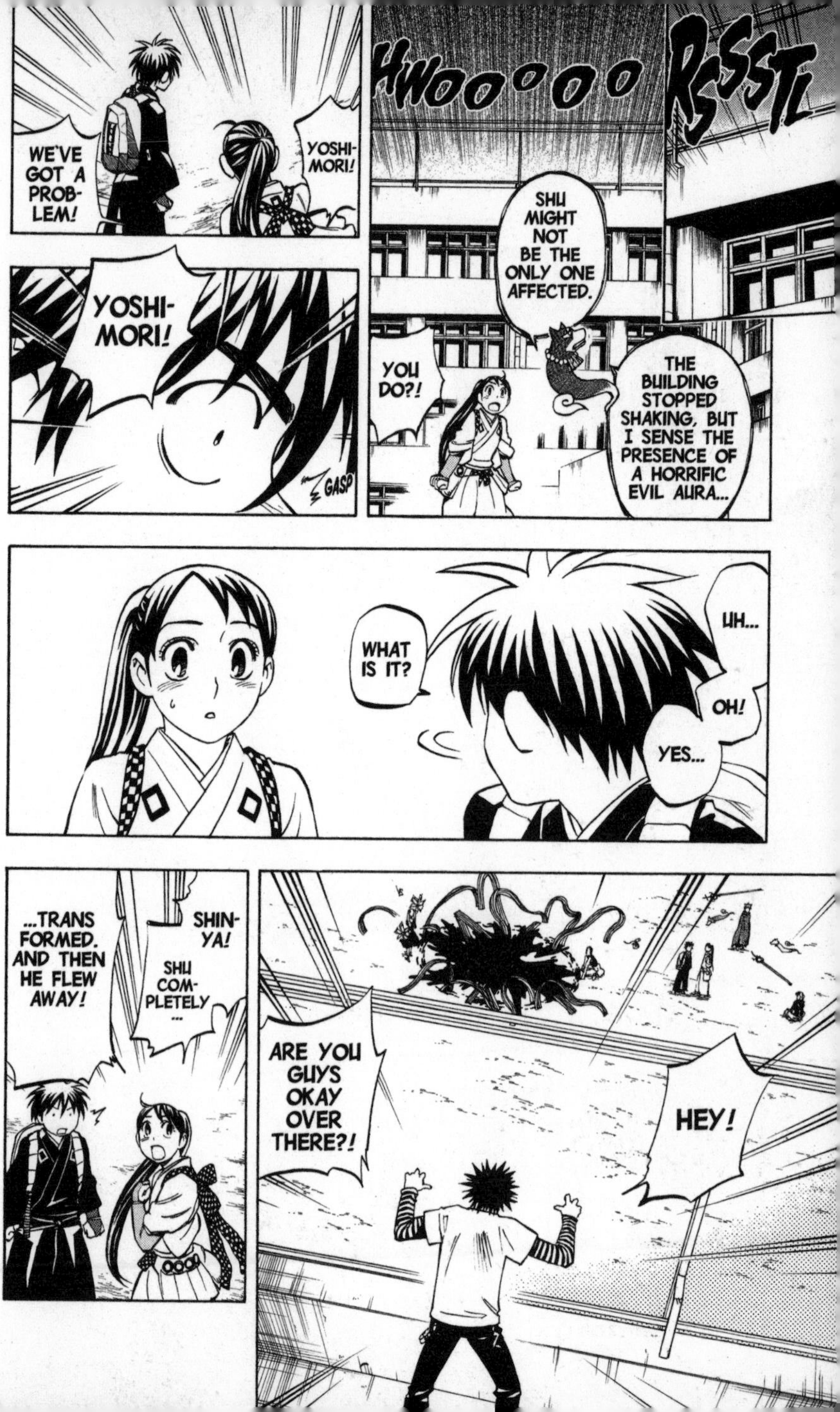
RSSSTL
HWOOOOOO
SHU MIGHT NOT BE THE ONLY ONE AFFECTED.
THE BUILDING STOPPED SHAKING, BUT I SENSE THE PRESENCE OF A HORRIFIC EVIL AURA...
YOU DO?!
YOSHI-MORI!
WE'VE GOT A PROB-LEM!
YOSHI-MORI!
GASP
UH...
OH!
YES...
WHAT IS IT?
HEY!
ARE YOU GUYS OKAY OVER THERE?!
SHIN-YA!
SHU COM-PLETELY...
...TRANS FORMED. AND THEN HE FLEW AWAY!

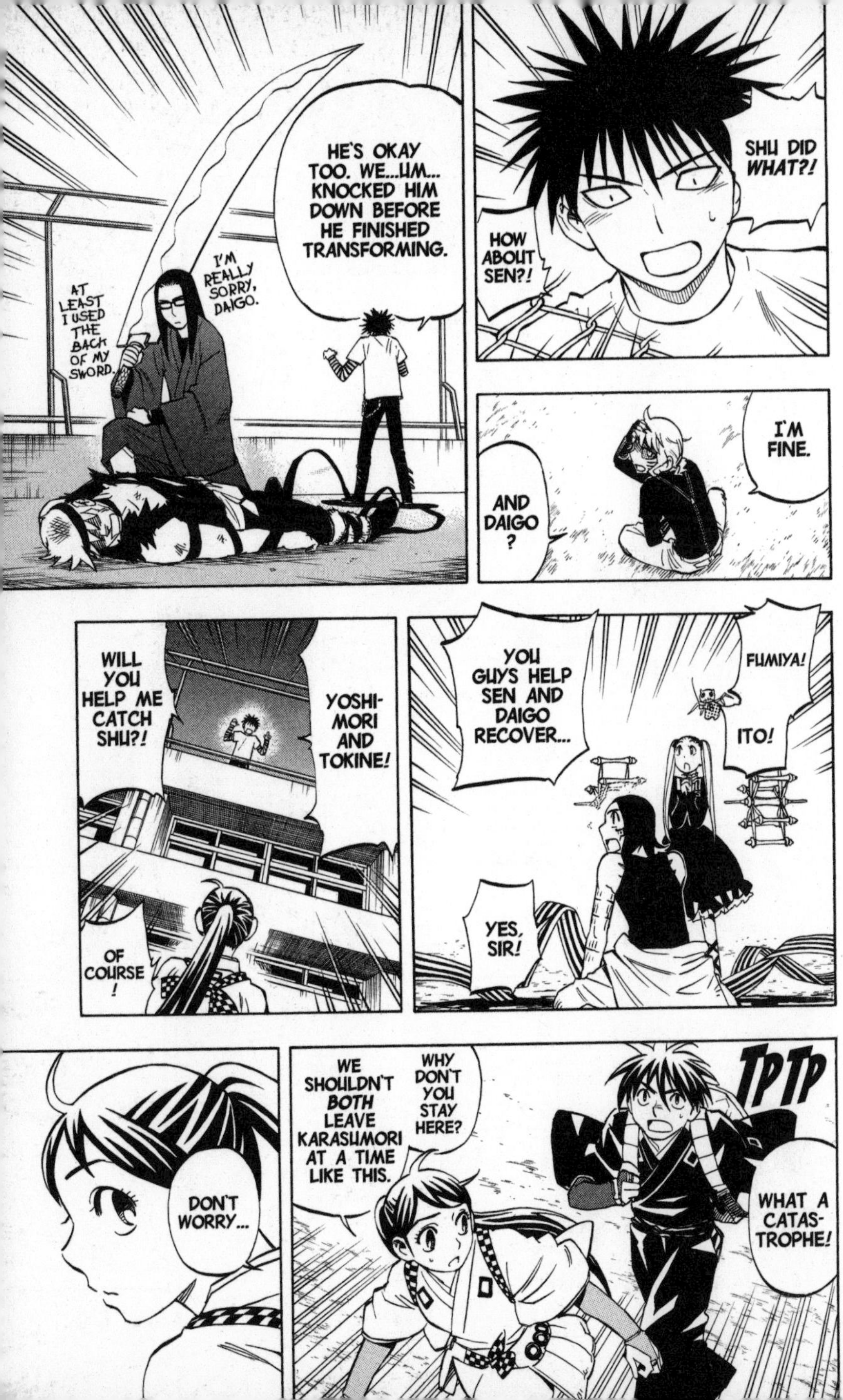
SHU DID *WHAT?!*
HOW ABOUT SEN?!
I'M FINE.
AND DAIGO?
HE'S OKAY TOO. WE...UM... KNOCKED HIM DOWN BEFORE HE FINISHED TRANSFORMING.
I'M REALLY SORRY, DAIGO.
AT LEAST I USED THE BACK OF MY SWORD.
FUMIYA!
ITO!
YOU GUYS HELP SEN AND DAIGO RECOVER...
YES, SIR!
YOSHIMORI AND TOKINE!
WILL YOU HELP ME CATCH SHU?!
OF COURSE!
TPTP
WHAT A CATASTROPHE!
WHY DON'T YOU STAY HERE?
WE SHOULDN'T *BOTH* LEAVE KARASUMORI AT A TIME LIKE THIS.
DON'T WORRY...

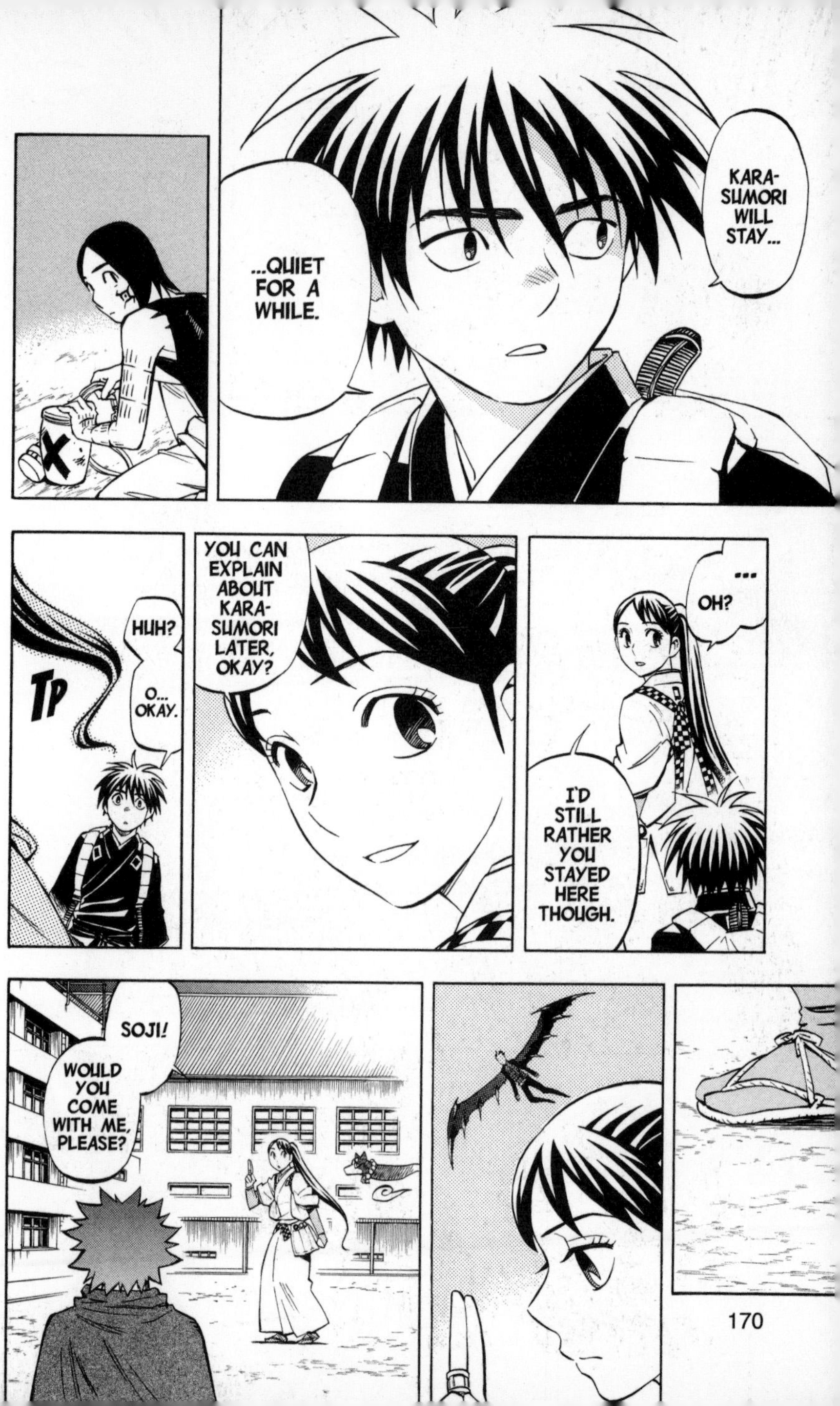
KARA-SUMORI WILL STAY...
...QUIET FOR A WHILE.
...
OH?
I'D STILL RATHER YOU STAYED HERE THOUGH.
YOU CAN EXPLAIN ABOUT KARA-SUMORI LATER, OKAY?
HUH?
TP
O... OKAY.
SOJI!
WOULD YOU COME WITH ME, PLEASE?

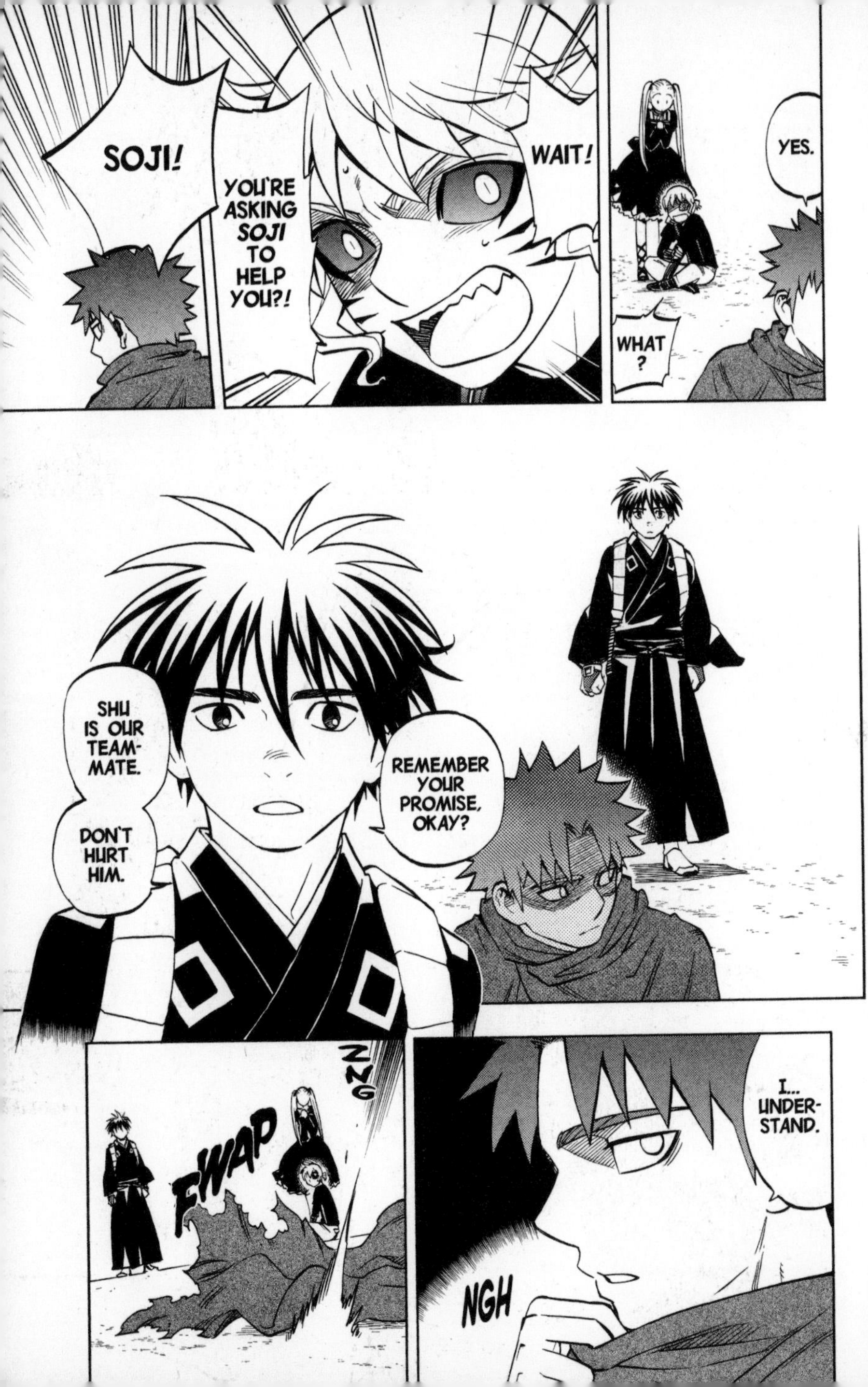
YES.
WHAT?
WAIT!
YOU'RE ASKING SOJI TO HELP YOU?!
SOJI!
REMEMBER YOUR PROMISE, OKAY?
SHU IS OUR TEAM-MATE.
DON'T HURT HIM.
I... UNDER-STAND.
NGH
ZNG
FWAP

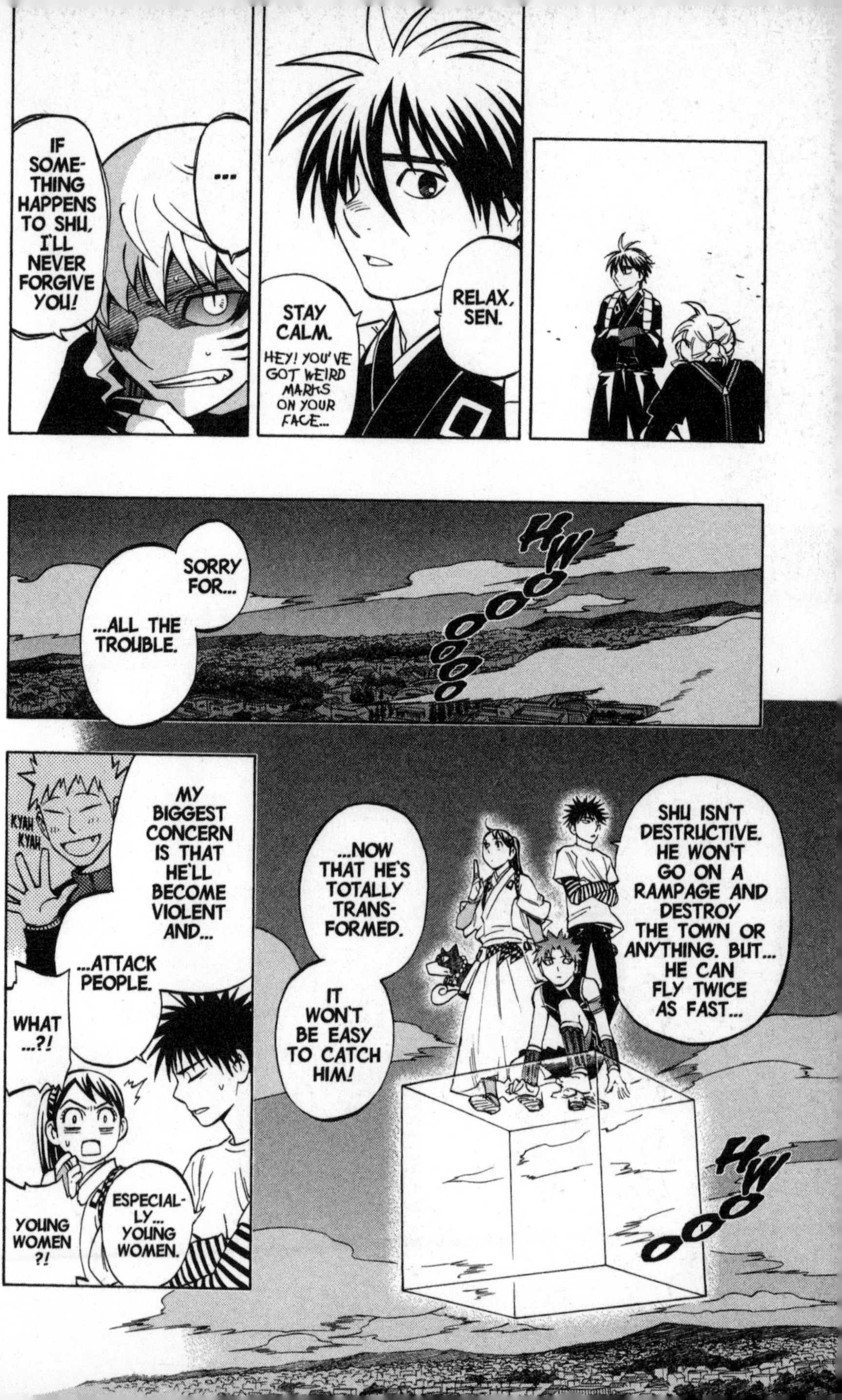
RELAX, SEN.
STAY CALM.
HEY! YOU'VE GOT WEIRD MARKS ON YOUR FACE...
...
IF SOMETHING HAPPENS TO SHU, I'LL NEVER FORGIVE YOU!
HWOOOOOOOO
SORRY FOR...
...ALL THE TROUBLE.
HWOOOO
SHU ISN'T DESTRUCTIVE. HE WON'T GO ON A RAMPAGE AND DESTROY THE TOWN OR ANYTHING. BUT... HE CAN FLY TWICE AS FAST...
...NOW THAT HE'S TOTALLY TRANSFORMED.
IT WON'T BE EASY TO CATCH HIM!
MY BIGGEST CONCERN IS THAT HE'LL BECOME VIOLENT AND...
KYAH KYAH
...ATTACK PEOPLE.
WHAT ...?!
ESPECIAL-LY... YOUNG WOMEN.
YOUNG WOMEN ?!

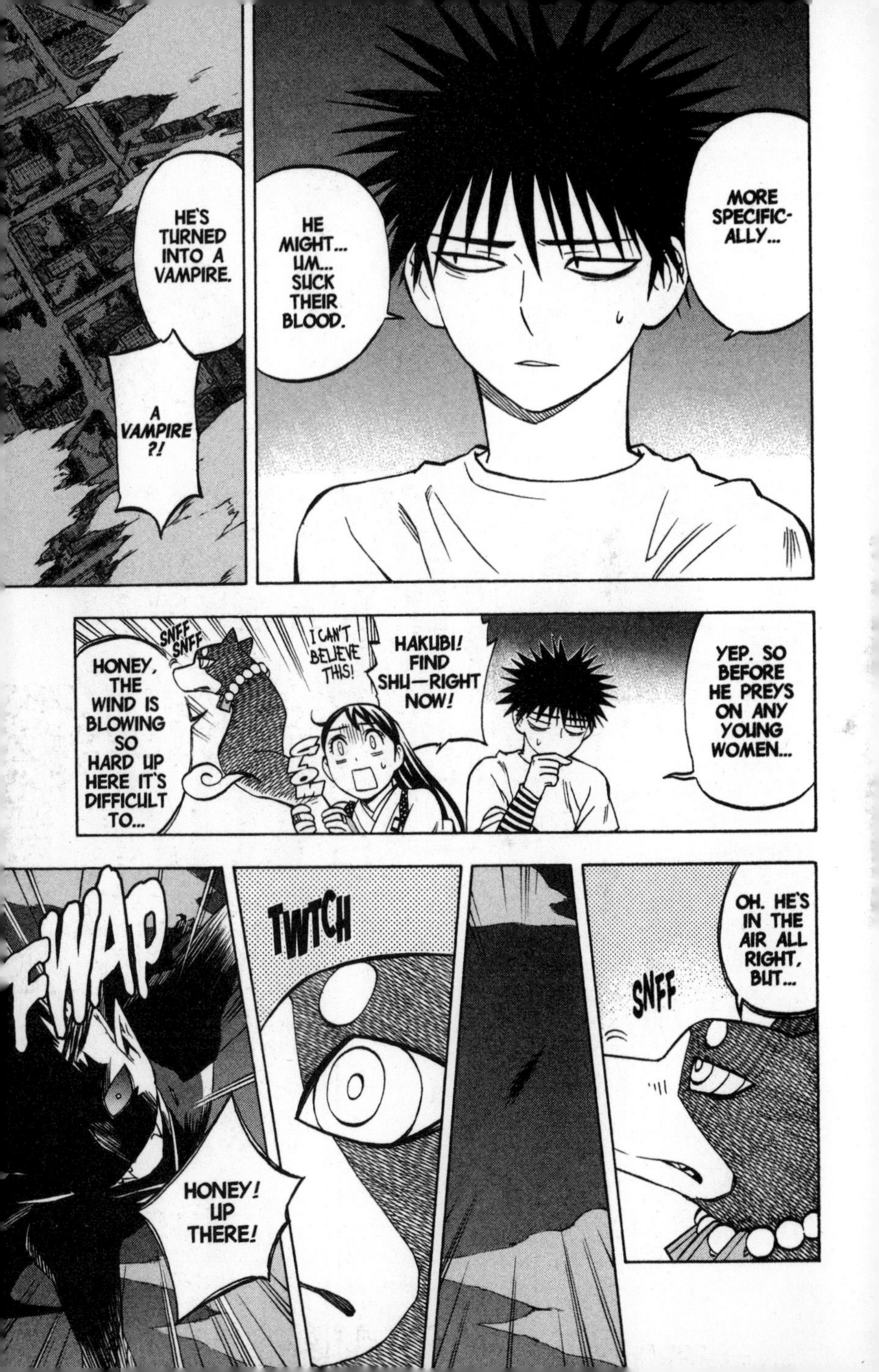
MORE SPECIFIC-ALLY...
HE MIGHT... UM... SUCK THEIR BLOOD.
HE'S TURNED INTO A VAMPIRE.
A VAMPIRE ?!
YEP. SO BEFORE HE PREYS ON ANY YOUNG WOMEN...
HAKUBI! FIND SHU—RIGHT NOW!
I CAN'T BELIEVE THIS!
SNFF SNFF
HONEY, THE WIND IS BLOWING SO HARD UP HERE IT'S DIFFICULT TO...
OH. HE'S IN THE AIR ALL RIGHT, BUT...
SNFF
TWITCH
HONEY! UP THERE!
FWAP

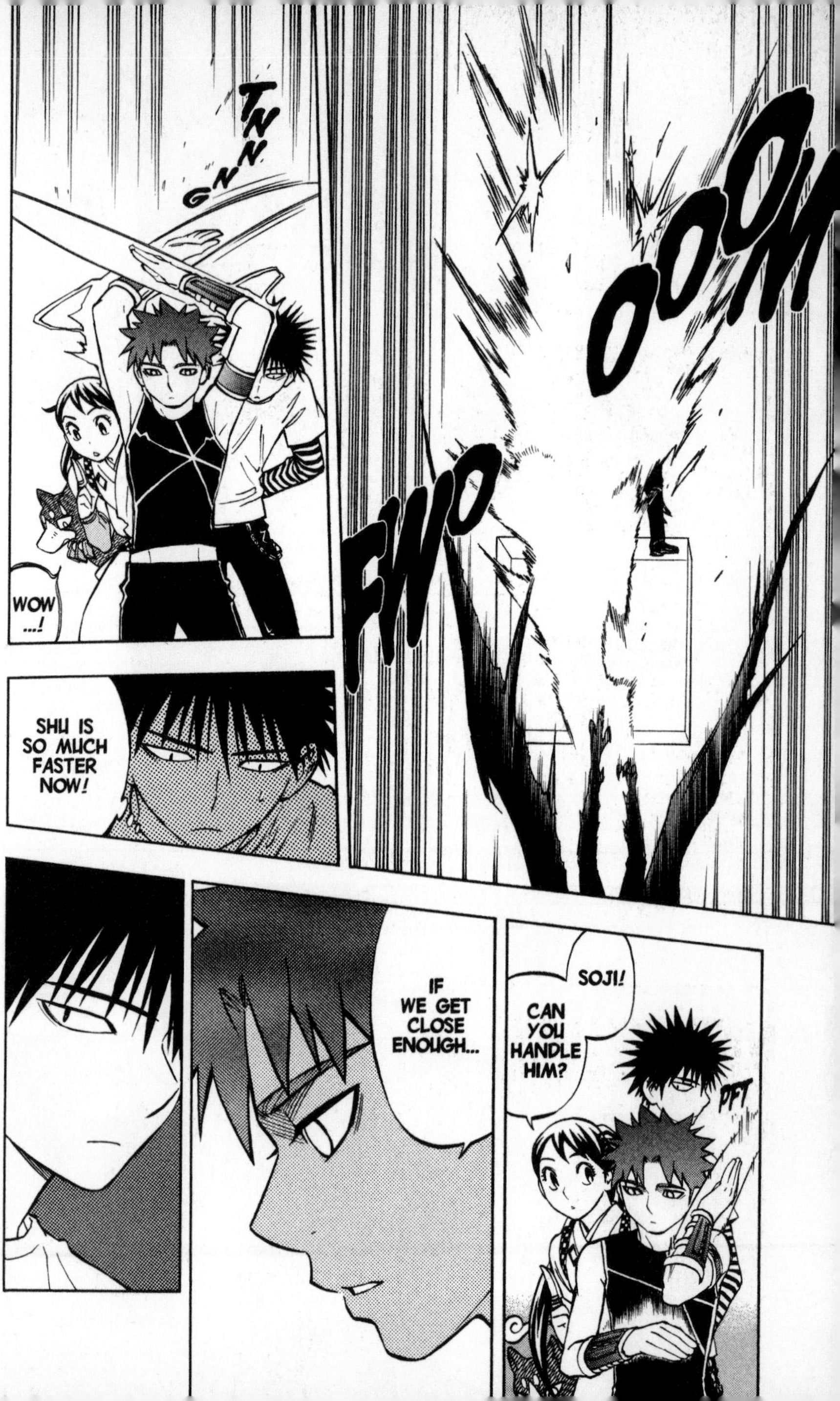
FWOOOM
TNNNG
WOW ...!
SHU IS SO MUCH FASTER NOW!
SOJI!
CAN YOU HANDLE HIM?
PFT
IF WE GET CLOSE ENOUGH...

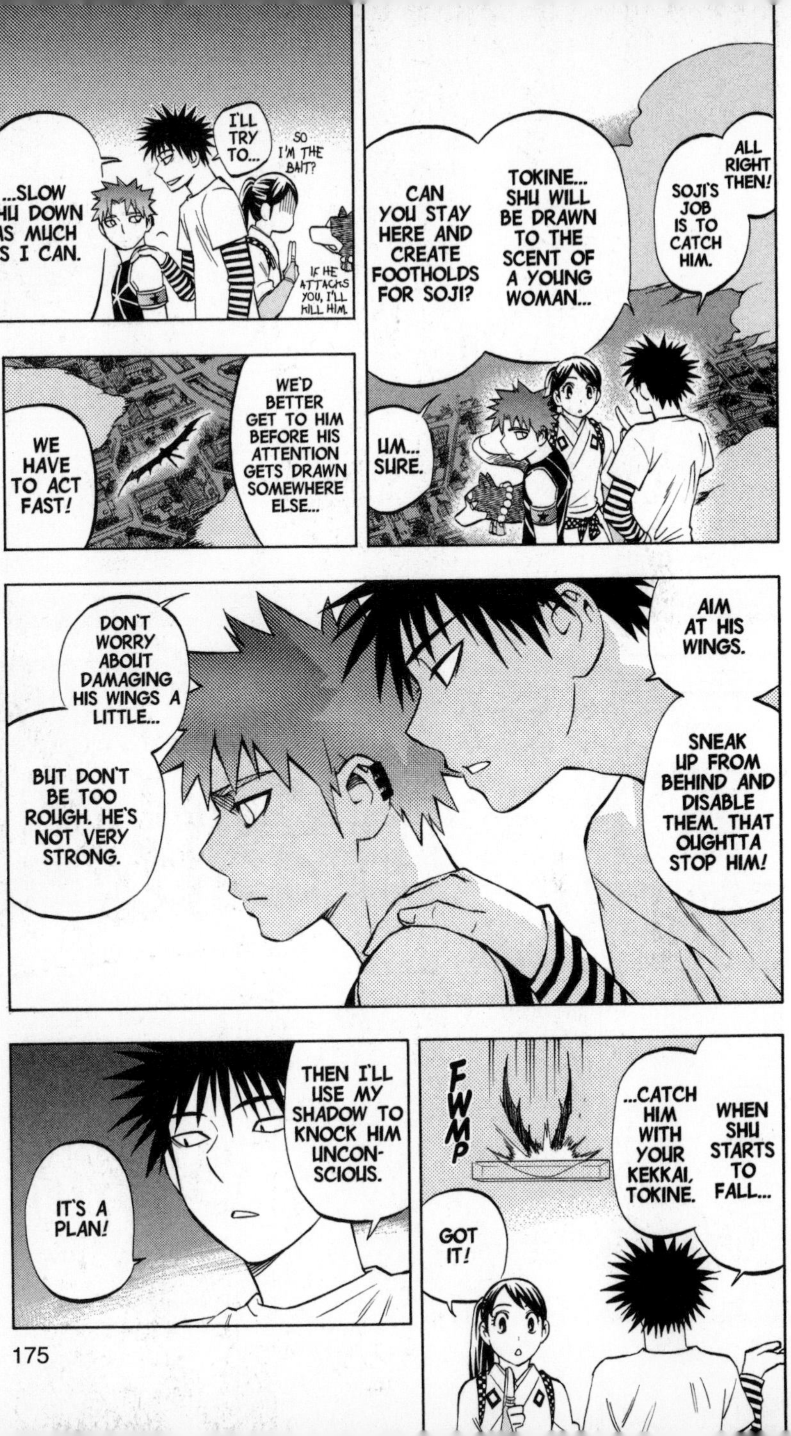
ALL RIGHT THEN!
SOJI'S JOB IS TO CATCH HIM.
TOKINE... SHU WILL BE DRAWN TO THE SCENT OF A YOUNG WOMAN...
CAN YOU STAY HERE AND CREATE FOOTHOLDS FOR SOJI?
UM... SURE.
SO I'M THE BAIT?
IF HE ATTACKS YOU, I'LL KILL HIM.
I'LL TRY TO...
...SLOW SHU DOWN AS MUCH AS I CAN.
WE'D BETTER GET TO HIM BEFORE HIS ATTENTION GETS DRAWN SOMEWHERE ELSE...
WE HAVE TO ACT FAST!
AIM AT HIS WINGS.
SNEAK UP FROM BEHIND AND DISABLE THEM. THAT OUGHTTA STOP HIM!
DON'T WORRY ABOUT DAMAGING HIS WINGS A LITTLE...
BUT DON'T BE TOO ROUGH. HE'S NOT VERY STRONG.
WHEN SHU STARTS TO FALL...
...CATCH HIM WITH YOUR KEKKAI, TOKINE.
FWMP
GOT IT!
THEN I'LL USE MY SHADOW TO KNOCK HIM UNCON-SCIOUS.
IT'S A PLAN!

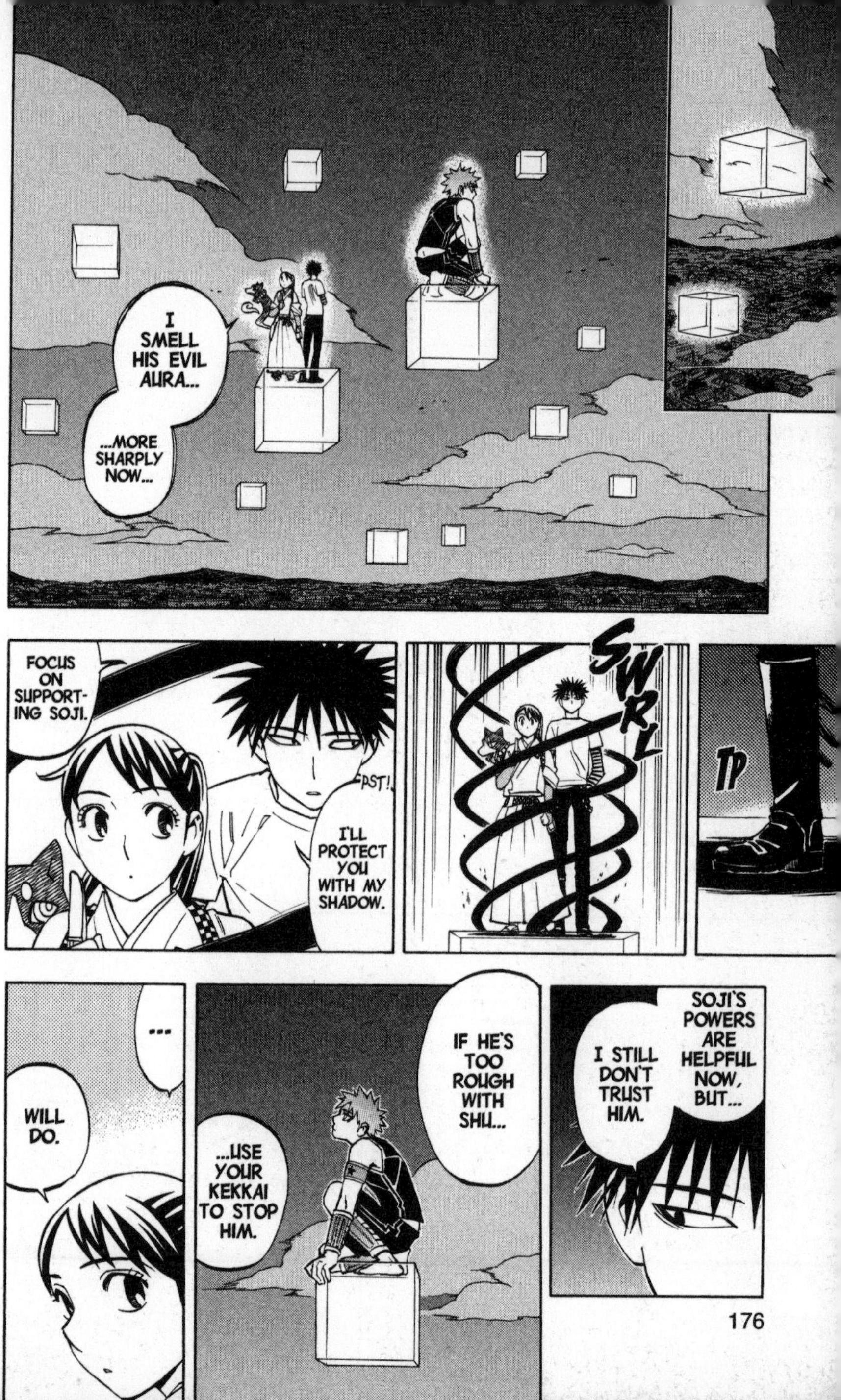
I SMELL HIS EVIL AURA...
...MORE SHARPLY NOW...
TP
SWRL
FOCUS ON SUPPORT-ING SOJI.
PST!
I'LL PROTECT YOU WITH MY SHADOW.
SOJI'S POWERS ARE HELPFUL NOW, BUT...
I STILL DON'T TRUST HIM.
IF HE'S TOO ROUGH WITH SHU...
...USE YOUR KEKKAI TO STOP HIM.
...
WILL DO.

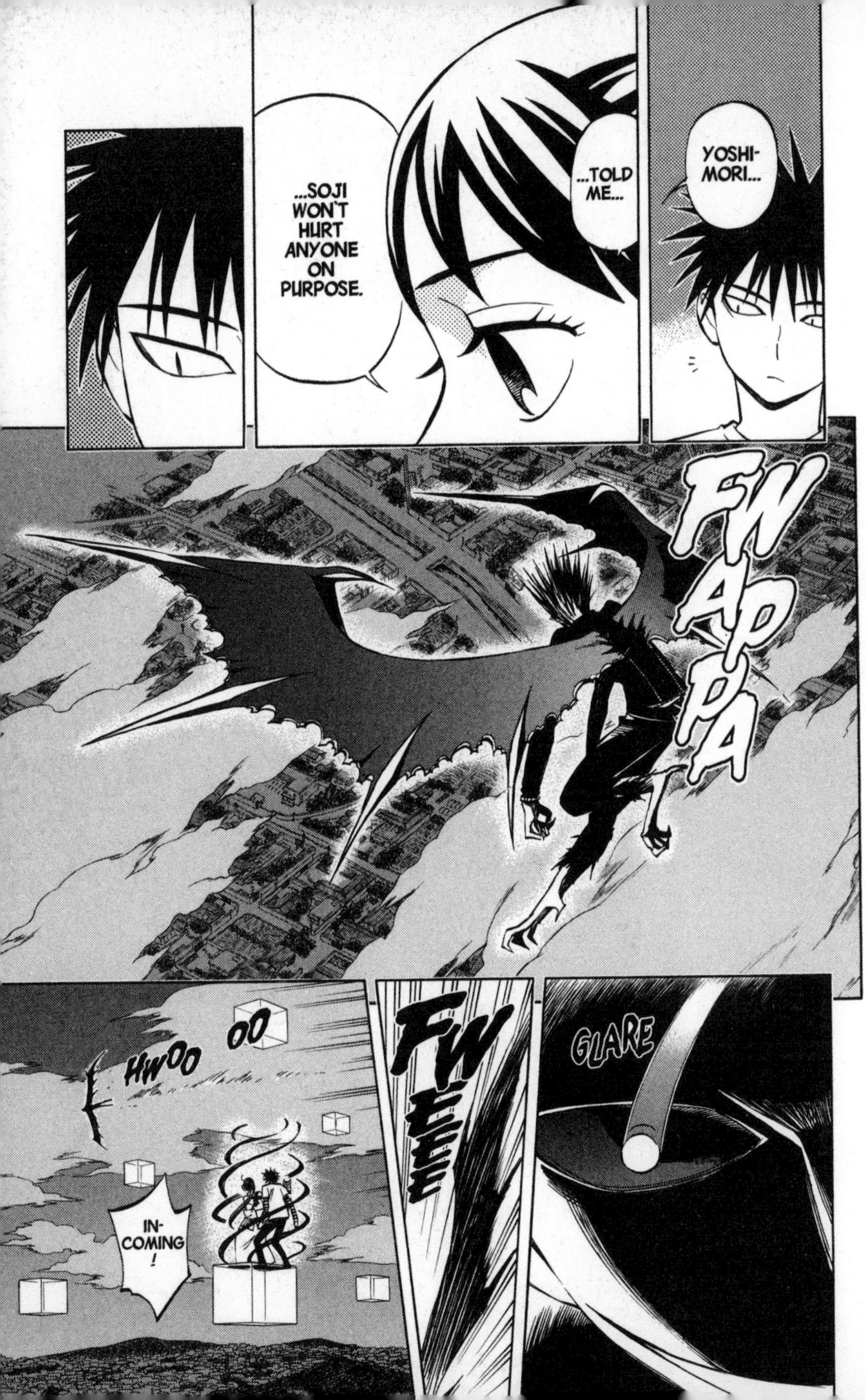
YOSHI-MORI...
...TOLD ME...
...SOJI WON'T HURT ANYONE ON PURPOSE.
FWAPAPA
GLARE
FWEEEE
HWOO OO
IN-COMING!

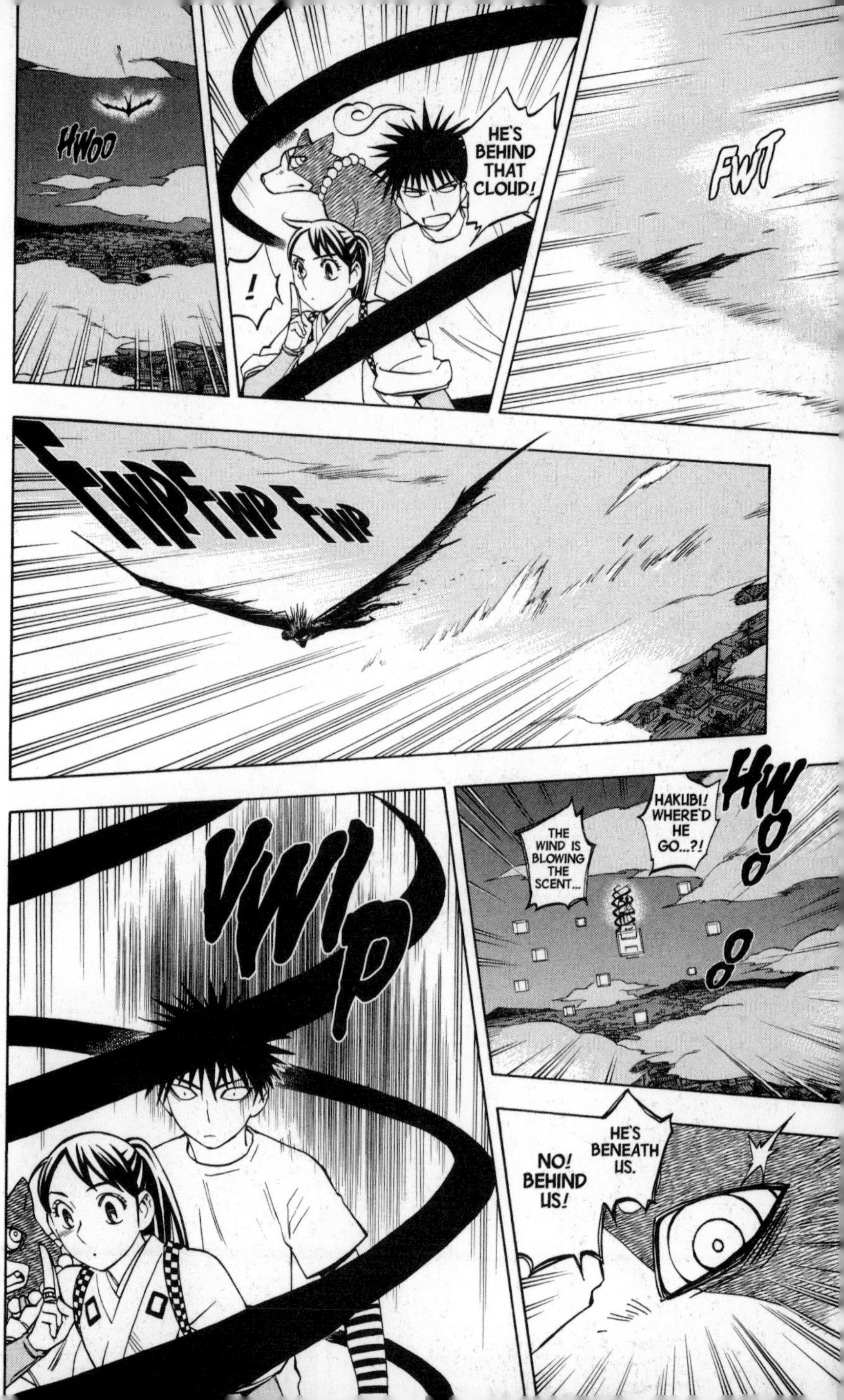
FWT
HE'S BEHIND THAT CLOUD!
!
HWOO
FWP FWP FWP
HAKUBI! WHERE'D HE GO...?!
THE WIND IS BLOWING THE SCENT...
HWOO
HE'S BENEATH US.
NO! BEHIND US!
VWIP

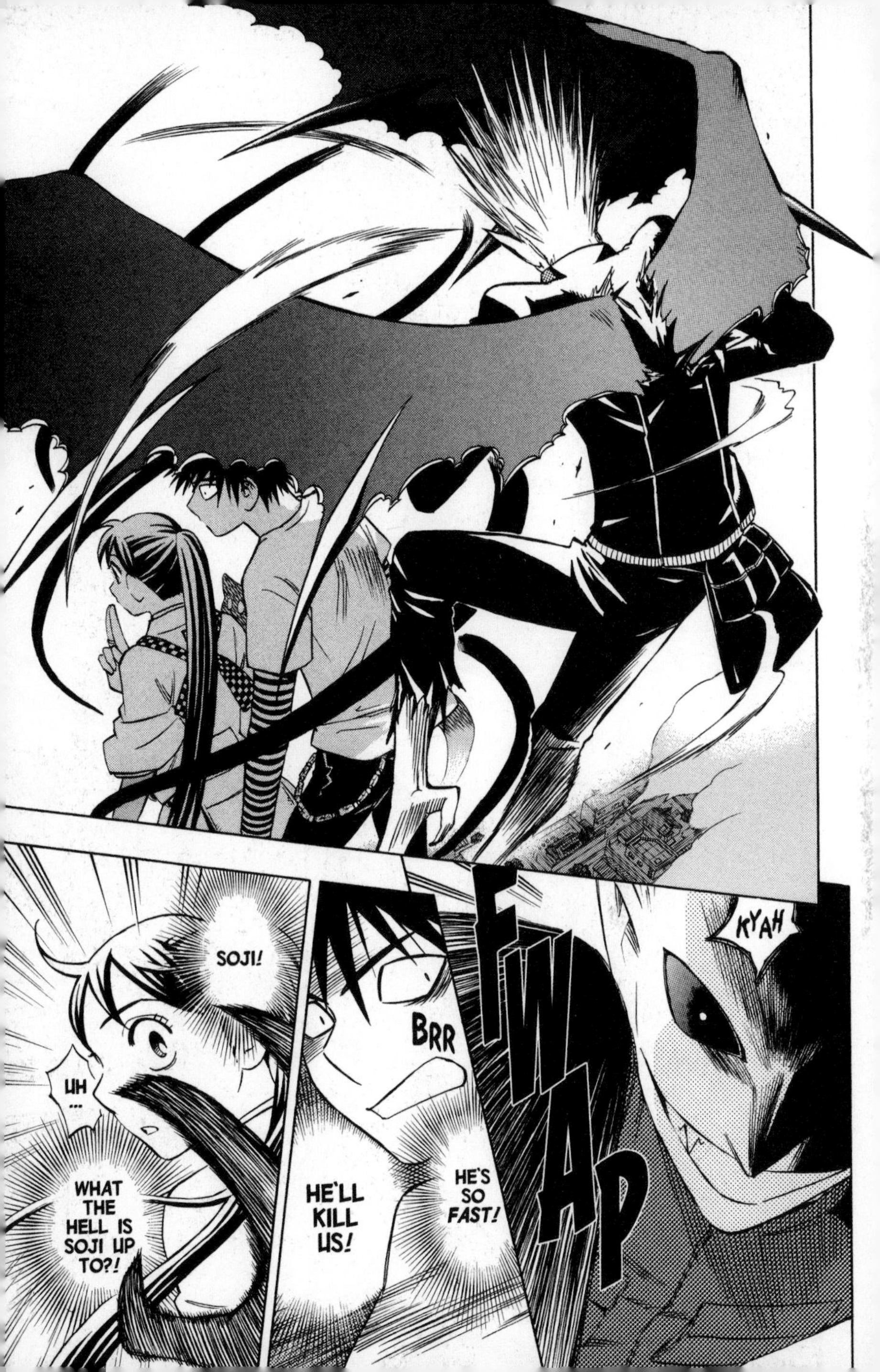
KYAH
FWAP
BRR
HE'S SO FAST!
HE'LL KILL US!
SOJI!
UH...
WHAT THE HELL IS SOJI UP TO?!

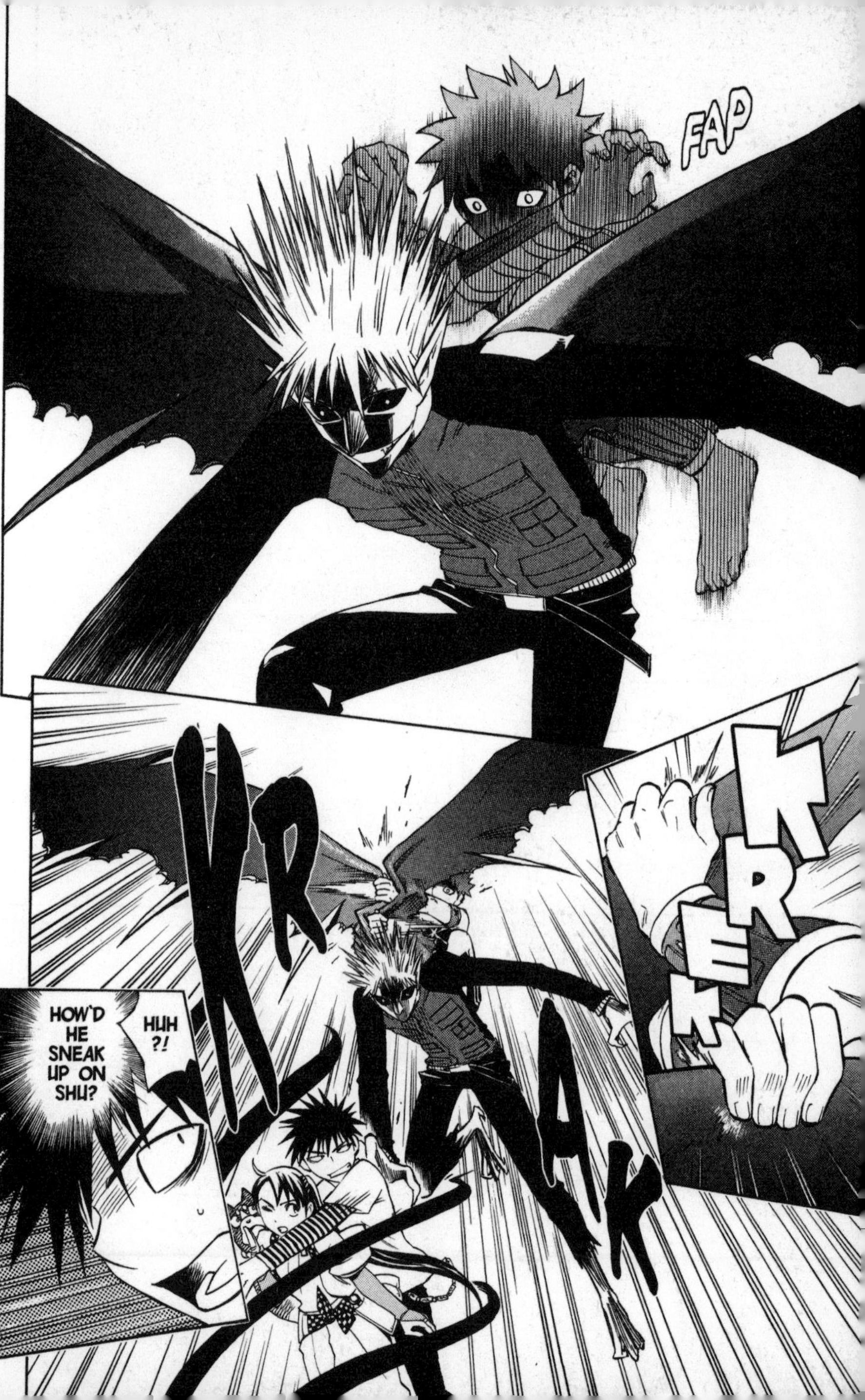
FAP
KREK
KRAK
HUH ?!
HOW'D HE SNEAK UP ON SHU?

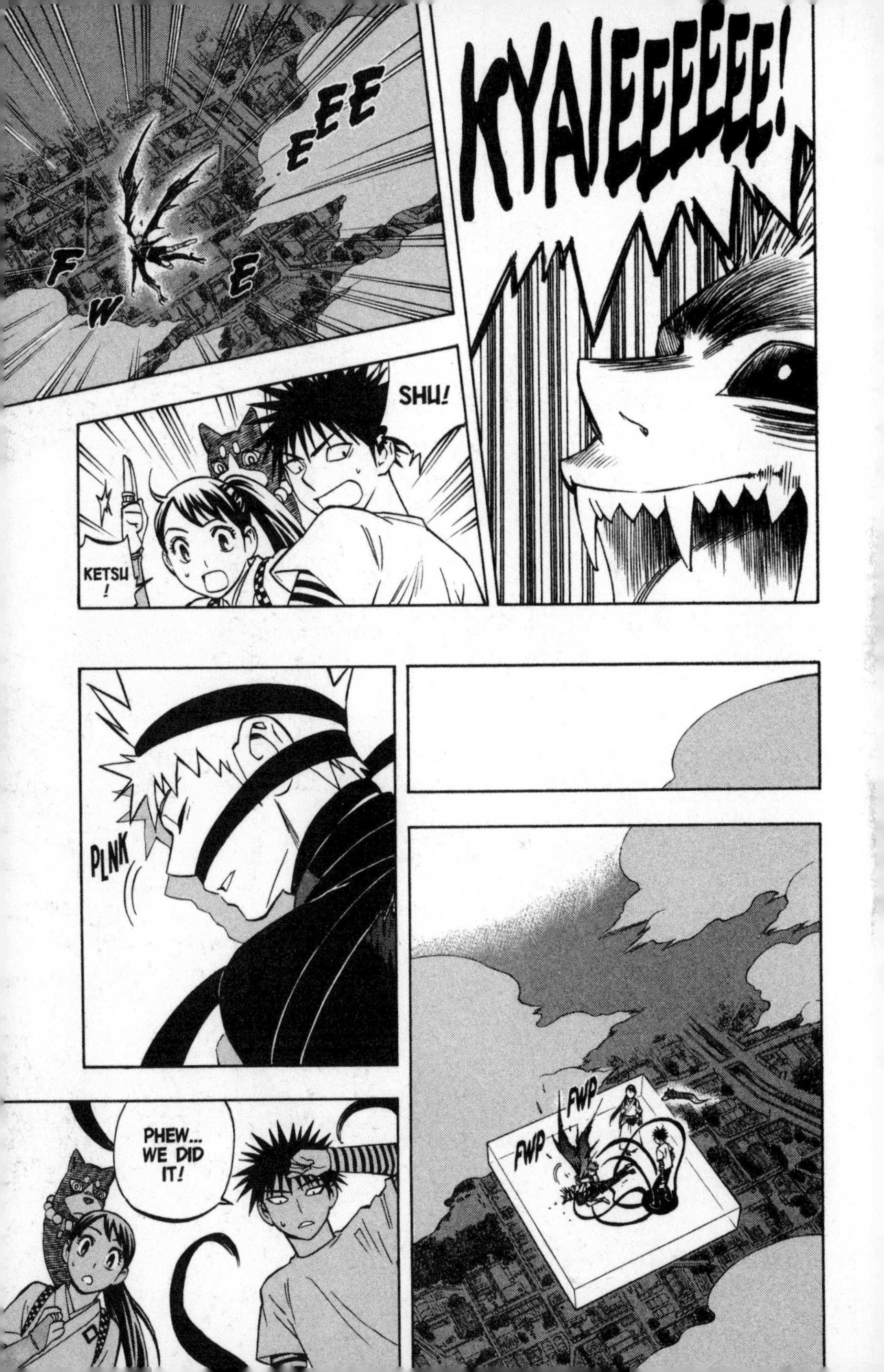
KYAJEEEEEE!
FWEEEE
SHU!
KETSU!
FWP
FWP
PLNK
PHEW... WE DID IT!

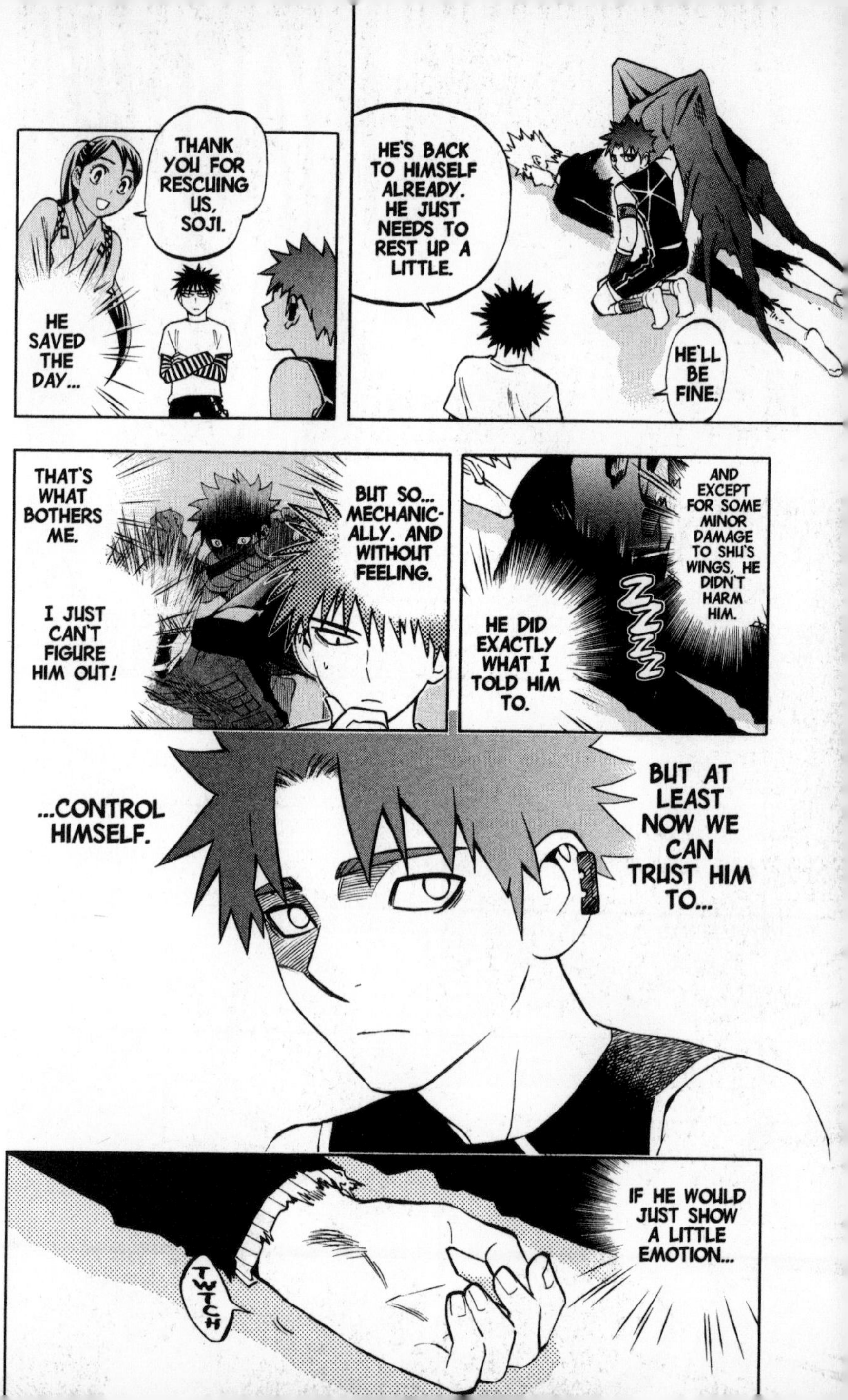
HE'S BACK TO HIMSELF ALREADY. HE JUST NEEDS TO REST UP A LITTLE.
HE'LL BE FINE.
THANK YOU FOR RESCUING US, SOJI.
HE SAVED THE DAY...
AND EXCEPT FOR SOME MINOR DAMAGE TO SHU'S WINGS, HE DIDN'T HARM HIM.
ZZZZ
HE DID EXACTLY WHAT I TOLD HIM TO.
BUT SO... MECHANIC-ALLY. AND WITHOUT FEELING.
THAT'S WHAT BOTHERS ME.
I JUST CAN'T FIGURE HIM OUT!
BUT AT LEAST NOW WE CAN TRUST HIM TO...
...CONTROL HIMSELF.
IF HE WOULD JUST SHOW A LITTLE EMOTION...
TWTCH

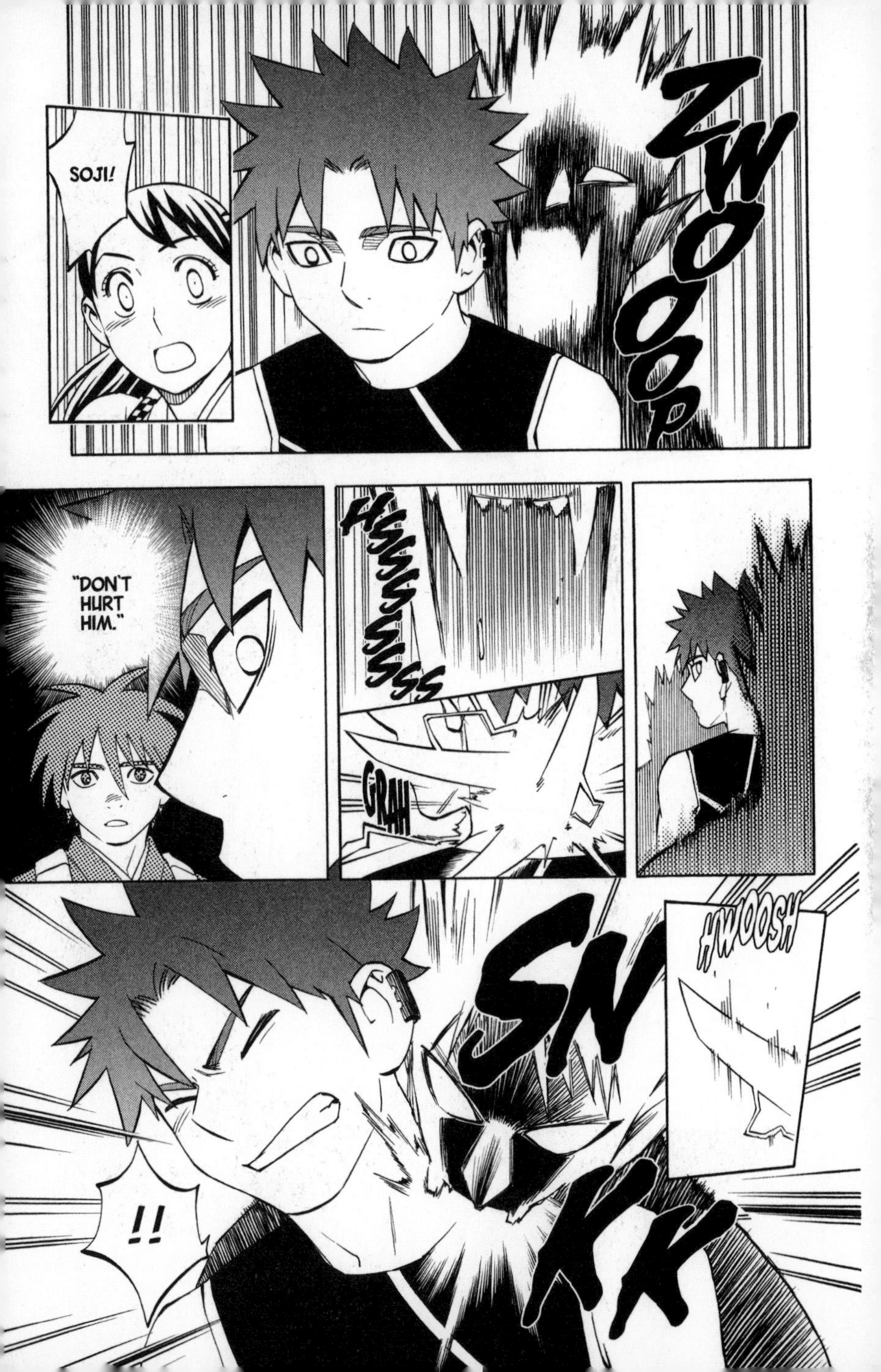
ZWOOOOP
SOJI!
HSSSSSSSSS
GRAH
"DON'T HURT HIM."
HWOOSH
SNKKT
!!

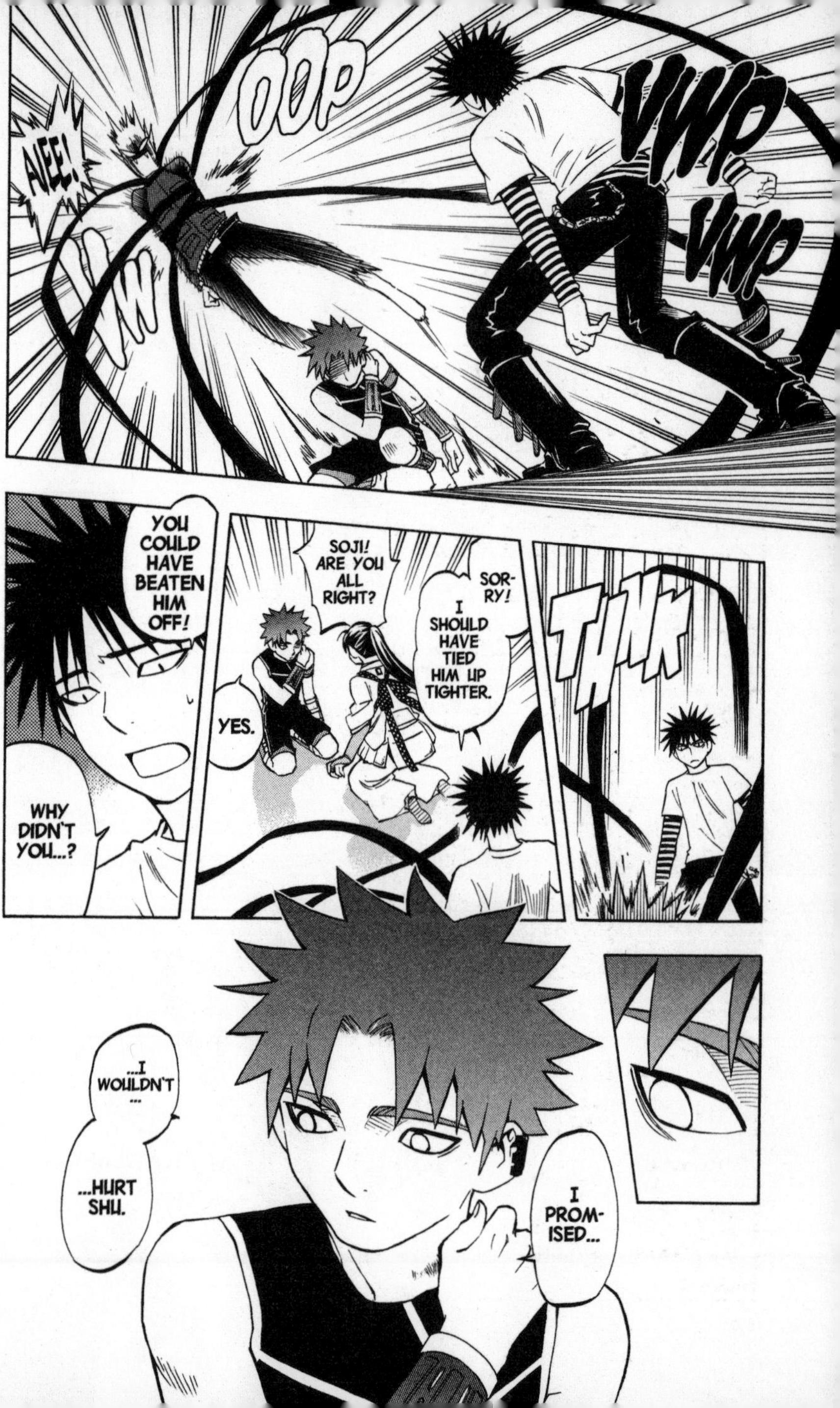
VWP
VWP
OOP
AIEE!
THNK
SOJI! ARE YOU ALL RIGHT?
SOR-RY! I SHOULD HAVE TIED HIM UP TIGHTER.
YES.
YOU COULD HAVE BEATEN HIM OFF!
WHY DIDN'T YOU...?
I PROM-ISED...
...I WOULDN'T ...
...HURT SHU.

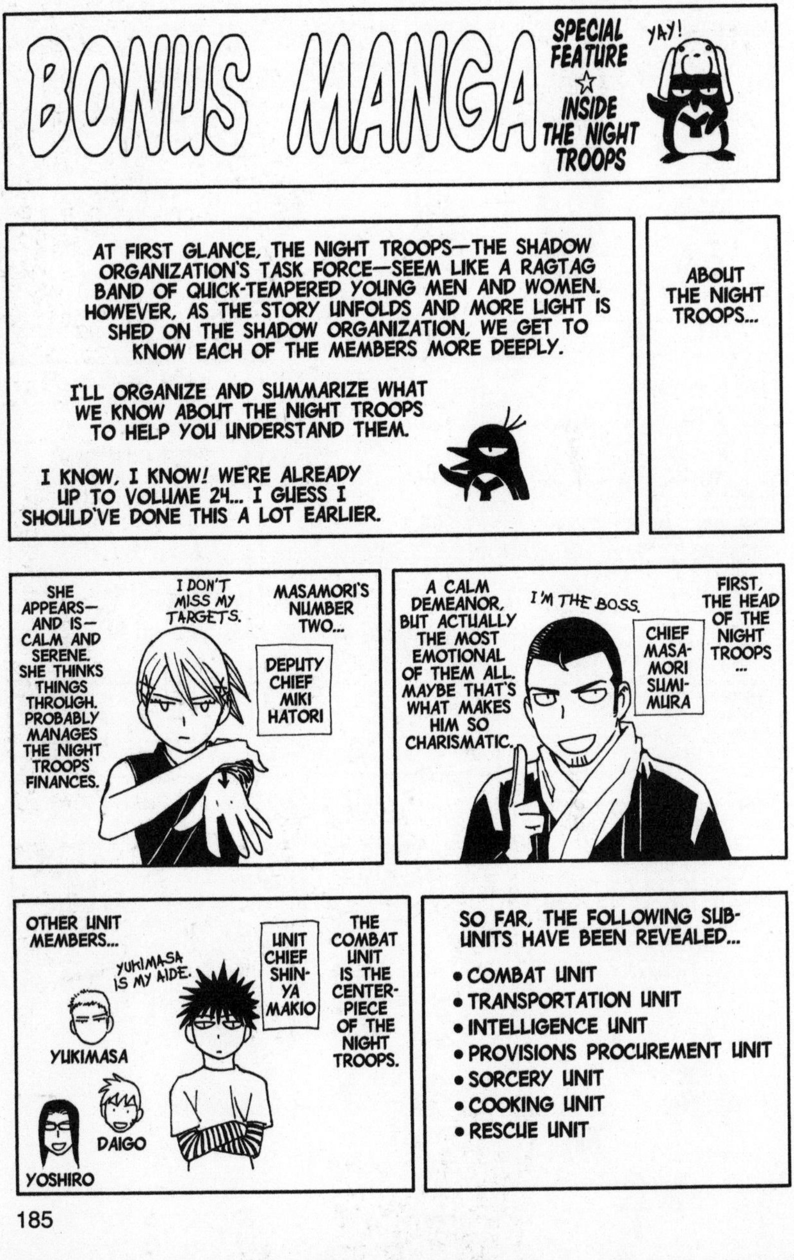
BONUS MANGA
SPECIAL FEATURE ☆ INSIDE THE NIGHT TROOPS
YAY!
ABOUT THE NIGHT TROOPS...
AT FIRST GLANCE, THE NIGHT TROOPS—THE SHADOW ORGANIZATION'S TASK FORCE—SEEM LIKE A RAGTAG BAND OF QUICK-TEMPERED YOUNG MEN AND WOMEN. HOWEVER, AS THE STORY UNFOLDS AND MORE LIGHT IS SHED ON THE SHADOW ORGANIZATION, WE GET TO KNOW EACH OF THE MEMBERS MORE DEEPLY.
I'LL ORGANIZE AND SUMMARIZE WHAT WE KNOW ABOUT THE NIGHT TROOPS TO HELP YOU UNDERSTAND THEM.
I KNOW, I KNOW! WE'RE ALREADY UP TO VOLUME 24... I GUESS I SHOULD'VE DONE THIS A LOT EARLIER.
FIRST, THE HEAD OF THE NIGHT TROOPS...
CHIEF MASAMORI SUMIMURA
I'M THE BOSS.
A CALM DEMEANOR, BUT ACTUALLY THE MOST EMOTIONAL OF THEM ALL. MAYBE THAT'S WHAT MAKES HIM SO CHARISMATIC.
MASAMORI'S NUMBER TWO...
DEPUTY CHIEF MIKI HATORI
I DON'T MISS MY TARGETS.
SHE APPEARS—AND IS—CALM AND SERENE. SHE THINKS THINGS THROUGH. PROBABLY MANAGES THE NIGHT TROOPS' FINANCES.
SO FAR, THE FOLLOWING SUB-UNITS HAVE BEEN REVEALED...
• COMBAT UNIT
• TRANSPORTATION UNIT
• INTELLIGENCE UNIT
• PROVISIONS PROCUREMENT UNIT
• SORCERY UNIT
• COOKING UNIT
• RESCUE UNIT
THE COMBAT UNIT IS THE CENTERPIECE OF THE NIGHT TROOPS.
UNIT CHIEF SHIN-YA MAKIO
YUKIMASA IS MY AIDE.
OTHER UNIT MEMBERS...
YUKIMASA
DAIGO
YOSHIRO

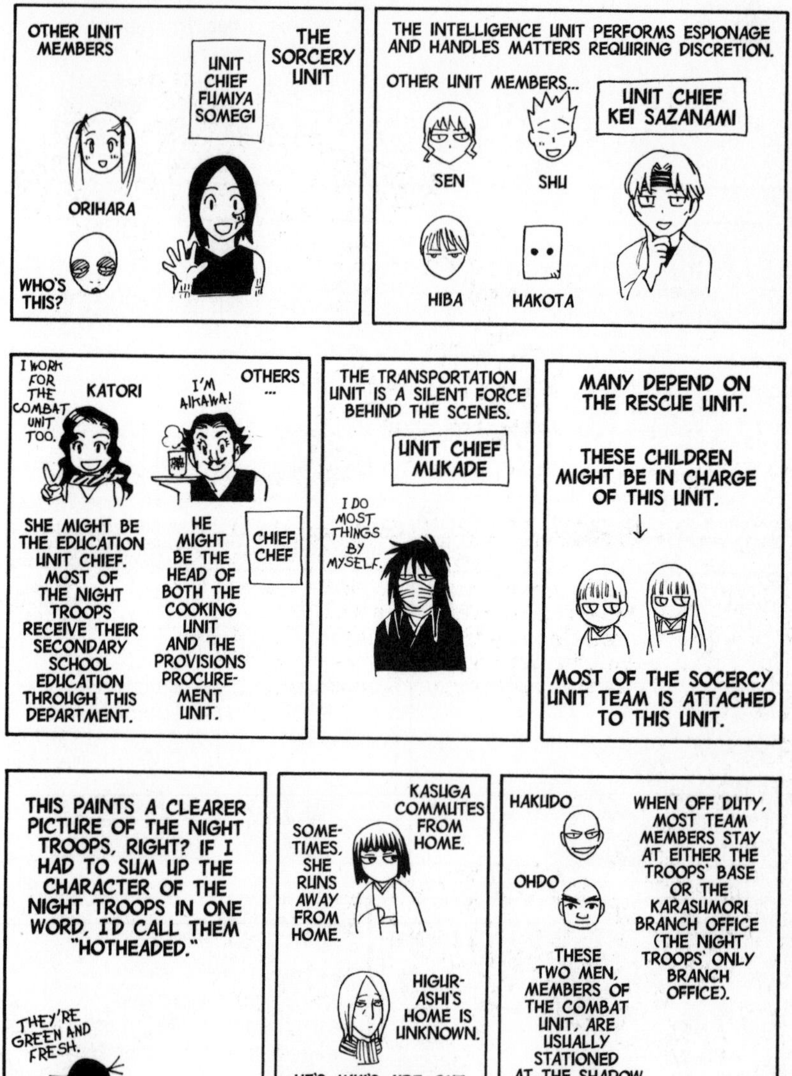
THE INTELLIGENCE UNIT PERFORMS ESPIONAGE AND HANDLES MATTERS REQUIRING DISCRETION.
UNIT CHIEF KEI SAZANAMI
OTHER UNIT MEMBERS...
SHU
SEN
HAKOTA
HIBA
THE SORCERY UNIT
UNIT CHIEF FUMIYA SOMEGI
OTHER UNIT MEMBERS
ORIHARA
WHO'S THIS?
MANY DEPEND ON THE RESCUE UNIT.
THESE CHILDREN MIGHT BE IN CHARGE OF THIS UNIT.
↓
MOST OF THE SOCERCY UNIT TEAM IS ATTACHED TO THIS UNIT.
THE TRANSPORTATION UNIT IS A SILENT FORCE BEHIND THE SCENES.
UNIT CHIEF MUKADE
I DO MOST THINGS BY MYSELF.
OTHERS ...
CHIEF CHEF
I'M AIKAWA!
HE MIGHT BE THE HEAD OF BOTH THE COOKING UNIT AND THE PROVISIONS PROCUREMENT UNIT.
KATORI
I WORK FOR THE COMBAT UNIT TOO.
SHE MIGHT BE THE EDUCATION UNIT CHIEF. MOST OF THE NIGHT TROOPS RECEIVE THEIR SECONDARY SCHOOL EDUCATION THROUGH THIS DEPARTMENT.
WHEN OFF DUTY, MOST TEAM MEMBERS STAY AT EITHER THE TROOPS' BASE OR THE KARASUMORI BRANCH OFFICE (THE NIGHT TROOPS' ONLY BRANCH OFFICE).
HAKUDO
OHDO
THESE TWO MEN, MEMBERS OF THE COMBAT UNIT, ARE USUALLY STATIONED AT THE SHADOW ORGANIZATION HEADQUARTERS.
KASUGA COMMUTES FROM HOME.
SOMETIMES, SHE RUNS AWAY FROM HOME.
HIGURASHI'S HOME IS UNKNOWN.
HE'S MIKI'S AIDE, BUT DOESN'T BELONG TO THE NIGHT TROOPS. HOWEVER, HE SOMETIMES HELPS THE TRANSPORTATION UNIT.
THIS PAINTS A CLEARER PICTURE OF THE NIGHT TROOPS, RIGHT? IF I HAD TO SUM UP THE CHARACTER OF THE NIGHT TROOPS IN ONE WORD, I'D CALL THEM "HOTHEADED."
THEY'RE GREEN AND FRESH.

TO BE CONTINUED...

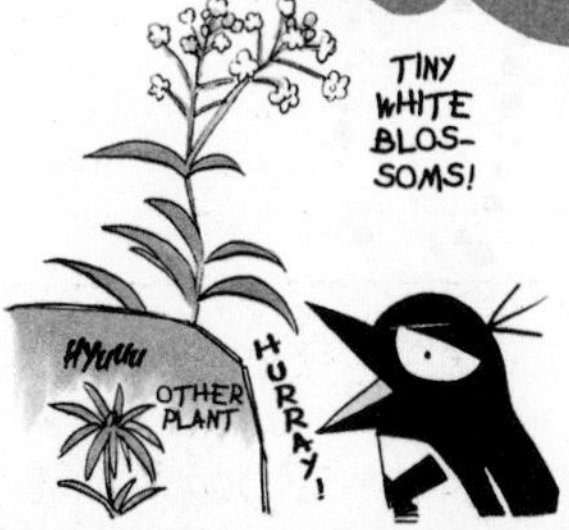
TINY WHITE BLOS-SOMS!
HURRAY!
HYUUU
OTHER PLANT

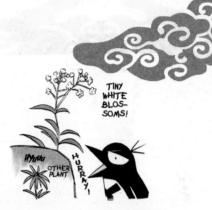

MESSAGE FROM YELLOW TANABE

Update on my garden kit: I finally have some flowers on my plants! They're really tiny but adorable. I'm growing two types of plants, but the other one isn't doing much of anything. Should I keep hoping it'll bloom or give up on it?

KEKKAISHI
VOLUME 24
SHONEN SUNDAY EDITION
STORY AND ART BY YELLOW TANABE

Original Japanese edition "KEKKAISHI" published by SHOGAKUKAN Inc.

Translation/Yuko Sawada
Touch-up Art & Lettering/Stephen Dutro
Cover Design & Graphic Layout/Julie Behn
Editor/Annette Roman

The rights of the author(s) of the work(s) in this publication to be so identified have been asserted in accordance with the Copyright, Designs and Patents Act 1988. A CIP catalogue record for this book is available from the British Library.

Printed in the U.S.A.

Published by VIZ Media, LLC
P.O. Box 77010
San Francisco, CA 94107

10 9 8 7 6 5 4 3 2 1
First printing, January 2011

www.viz.com

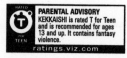

PARENTAL ADVISORY
KEKKAISHI is rated T for Teen and is recommended for ages 13 and up. It contains fantasy violence.
ratings.viz.com

WWW.SHONENSUNDAY.COM

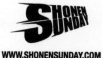

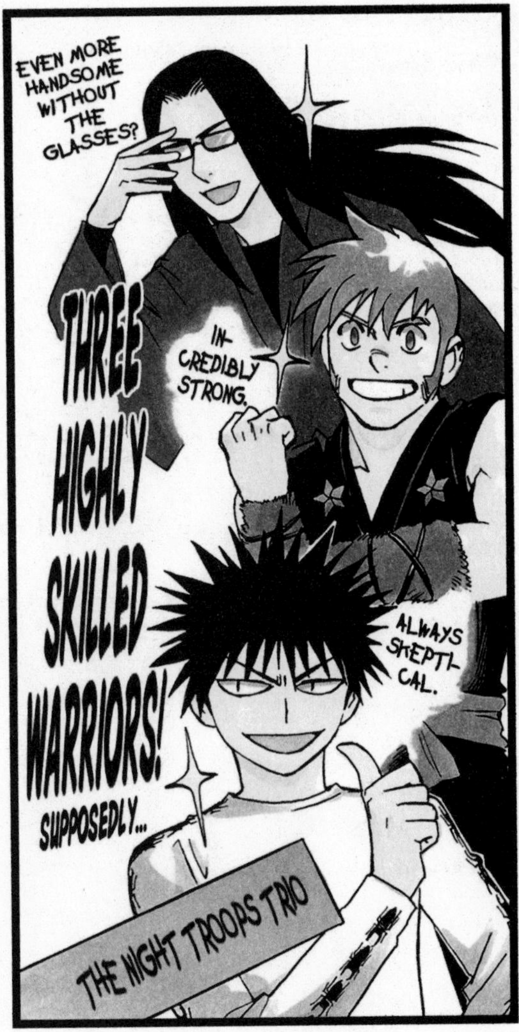
EVEN MORE HANDSOME WITHOUT THE GLASSES?
THREE HIGHLY SKILLED WARRIORS!
IN-CREDIBLY STRONG.
ALWAYS SKEPTI-CAL.
SUPPOSEDLY...
THE NIGHT TROOPS TRIO

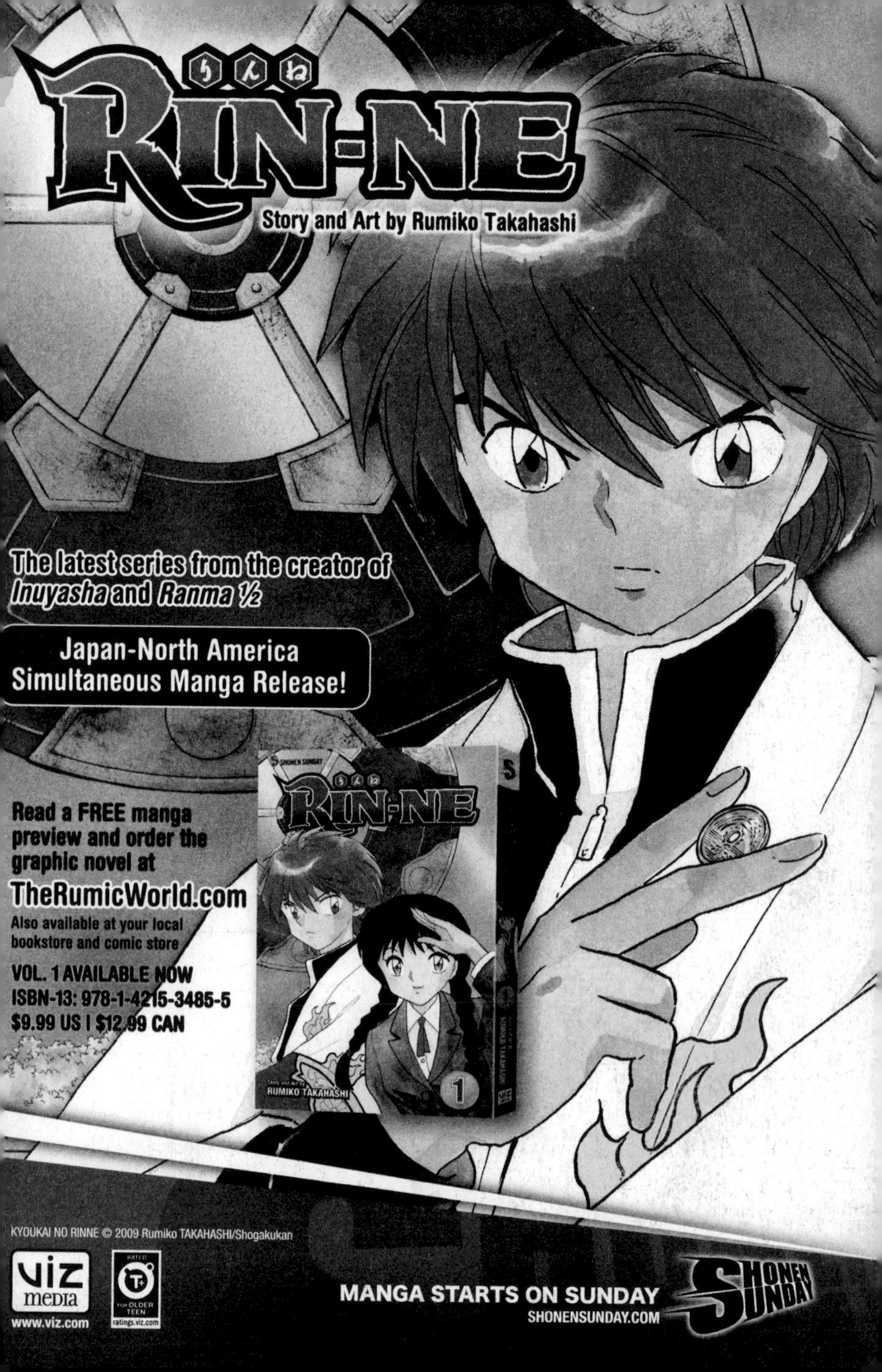

りんね
RIN-NE
Story and Art by Rumiko Takahashi
The latest series from the creator of
Inuyasha and Ranma ½
Japan-North America
Simultaneous Manga Release!
Read a FREE manga preview and order the graphic novel at
TheRumicWorld.com
Also available at your local bookstore and comic store
VOL. 1 AVAILABLE NOW
ISBN-13: 978-1-4215-3485-5
$9.99 US | $12.99 CAN
SHONEN SUNDAY
RIN-NE
Story and Art by
RUMIKO TAKAHASHI
1
KYOUKAI NO RINNE © 2009 Rumiko TAKAHASHI/Shogakukan
viz media
www.viz.com
RATED T+ FOR OLDER TEEN
ratings.viz.com
MANGA STARTS ON SUNDAY
SHONENSUNDAY.COM
SHONEN SUNDAY

LOVE ♥ MANGA?

Let us know what you think!

Our **MANGA SURVEY** is now available **ONLINE**.

Please visit: **VIZ.COM/MANGASURVEY**

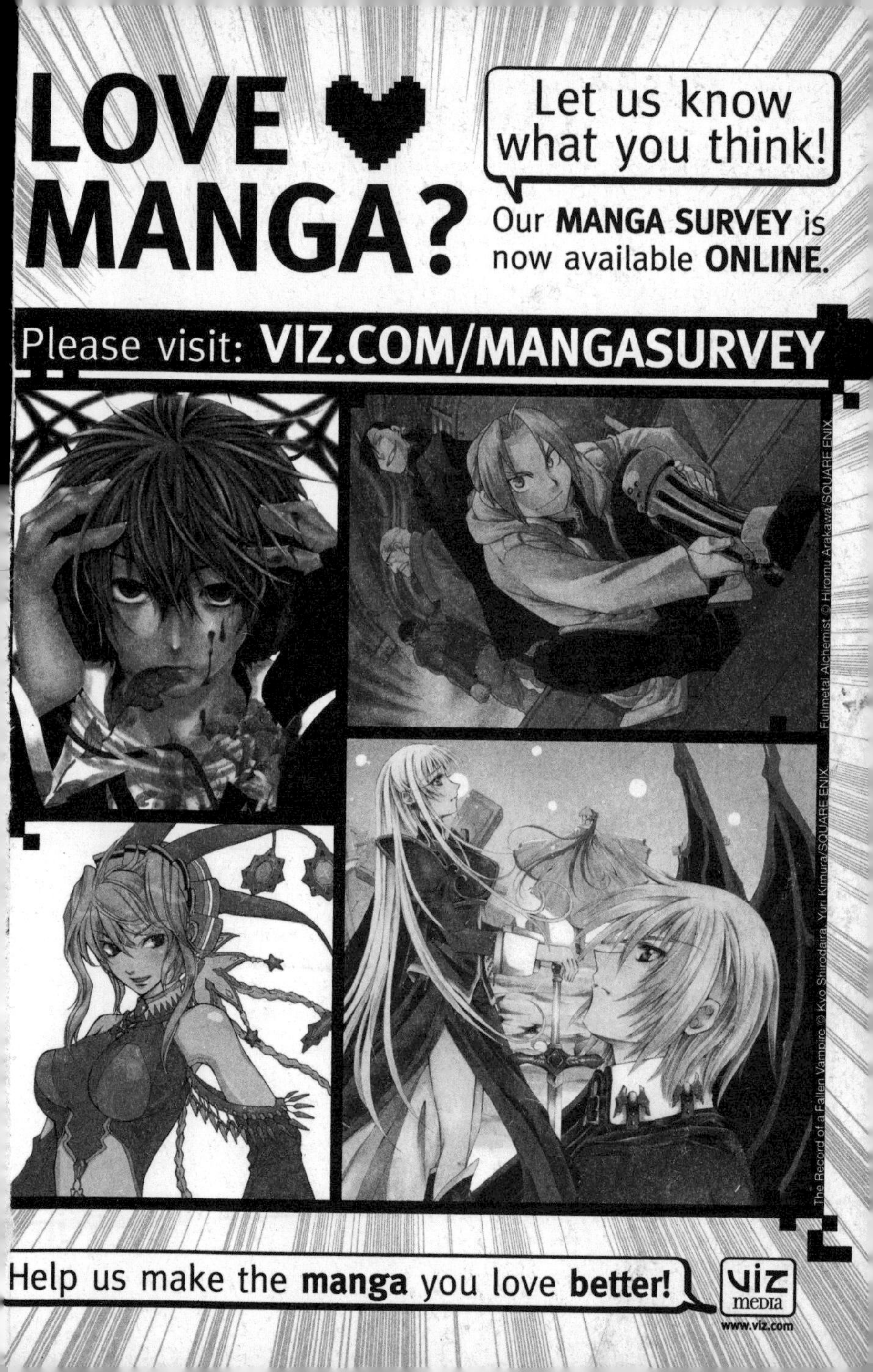

Help us make the **manga** you love **better!**

VIZ MEDIA
www.viz.com